SUN CIRCLES
and
HUMAN HANDS

THE SOUTHEASTERN INDIANS
ART AND INDUSTRIES

Edited by
Emma Lila Fundaburk
Mary Douglass Fundaburk Foreman
With a New Foreword by Vernon James Knight Jr.

THE UNIVERSITY OF ALABAMA PRESS
Tuscaloosa

Originally published in 1957 by Emma Lila Fundaburk

Paperback edition published by
The University of Alabama Press, 2001, 2008

The University of Alabama Press
Tuscaloosa, Alabama 35487-0380
Manufactured in the United States of America

∞
The paper on which this book is printed meets the minimum requirements of
American National Standard for Information Science–Permanence of Paper for
Printed Library Materials, ANSI Z39.48-1984.

Library of Congress Cataloging-in-Publication Data

Fundaburk, Emma Lila, 1922–
      Sun circles and human hands : the southeastern Indians art and industries /
edited by Emma Lila Fundaburk, Mary Douglass Fundaburk Foreman.
            p. cm.
      Originally published: 1957.
      Includes bibliographical references and index.
   ISBN-10: 0-8173-1077-0; ISBN-13: 978-0-8173-1077-6 (pbk. : alk. paper)
   ISBN-13: 978-0-8173-8368-8 (electronic)
      1. Indian art—Southern States. 2. Indians of North America—Material
culture—Southern States. 3. Indians of North America—Southern States—Antiquities. 4. Southern States—Antiquities. I. Foreman, Mary Douglass Fundaburk,
1925– II. Title.

E78.S55 F8 2001
975'.01—dc21   00-049103

FOREWORD

Vernon James Knight, Jr.

Sun Circles and Human Hands is arguably the most widely read book on southeastern archaeology ever published. Having undergone twelve printings to date, it has been almost continually in print since its initial imprint in 1957. Generations of readers interested in the art and artifacts of the southeastern Indians, lay people and professional scholars alike, have used this book as a staple source on the prehistoric Indians of the southern states. Professors on occasion have employed *Sun Circles* as a textbook in their courses. For many, it has been their initiation into a fascinating, vanished world.

What accounts for this book's long-term popularity? At first glance, this would seem difficult to explain. *Sun Circles* is the product of two sisters hailing from Luverne, a tiny town in Crenshaw County, south central Alabama, neither of whom were archaeologists, neither of whom were collectors of Native American artifacts, and neither of whom were prominent in the Alabama Archaeological Society. For many years the book was privately published and distributed by the authors themselves rather than by a scholarly press. So what is it that elevates this work above the various illustrated works emanating from amateur enthusiasts on this topic that have come and gone in the last four decades?

Part of the answer surely lies in the fact that the book met an extraordinarily high standard for thoroughness of coverage, both in the text and in the art chosen for illustration. And lying behind that thoroughness is the character of the authors, Emma Lila Fundaburk and Mary Douglass Fundaburk Foreman, for these were not merely uncredentialed amateurs. One was an accomplished professional scholar, the other an educator with an advanced degree in art education.

The original jacket copy of *Sun Circles and Human Hands* opens with the line, "This is a book of pictures. . . ." That it certainly is, with 160 plates covering a large range of artifacts, but the accompanying text is a quite sophisticated and carefully researched production too. The author of that text, Dr. Emma Lila Fundaburk, was an economist, holding a Ph.D. in economics from Ohio State University, an M.A. in economics from Northwestern University, and a B.A. in economics from George Washington University.

She is the author of ten books, bearing such titles as *History of Economic Thought and Analysis: A Selective International Bibliography* (1973), *Art in Public Places in the United States* (1974, co-authored with T. H. Davenport), and *Business Corporations in Alabama in the Nineteenth Century* (1982). At the time *Sun Circles* was published, she was professor of economics at Bowling Green State University, having also taught at Ohio State University, the University of Hawaii, Huntingdon College, and the University of Alabama Center, Montgomery.

Sun Circles was, however, Dr. Fundaburk's first book. Her motivation for writing it, she has said, was her dissatisfaction with the summaries of southeastern archaeology available at that time. While working on the manuscript for *Parade of Alabama: An Epic of Southern History* (1959), Dr. Fundaburk was dismayed by the lack of published information available on the southeastern Indians, which did not seem to do justice to the remarkable southeastern Indian artistry in museums and private collections with which she was familiar. She was so dissatisfied that she suspended research on *Parade* and devoted her full attention to the work that became *Sun Circles*. During the research she also amassed hundreds of illustrations of Indians and their daily life, which she subsequently published in *Southeastern Indians: Life Portraits, A Catalogue of Pictures 1564–1860* (1958). Having completed her work on the art of the southeastern Indians and remedied the problem she herself had identified, she then returned to *Parade*, which was eventually published in 1959.

In *Sun Circles*, Dr. Fundaburk shows her acquaintance with a large corpus of technical works in archaeology and ethnohistory. There are some 487 published references, demonstrating an impressive command of the literature by any standard. She also made use of unpublished source material gleaned from archives and microfilmed collections regarding the southeastern Indians. Dr. Fundaburk spent much time at Moundville Archaeological Park making copies of the elaborate engraved art on pottery there, which until recently remained the only published documentation of this art. Her list of correspondents in preparing the volume is a who's who of North American professional archaeologists of the late 1950s. The text is, by consequence, in no sense the casually researched effort of an avocational enthusiast, but rather is a first-rate summary of southeastern prehistory for its day. Many of the details have, of course, been superseded by new field discoveries in the years since publication, but that does not detract from her work. Behind this popular synthesis, we still see the work of a professional scholar.

And what of the pictures? The design and layout were the work of Mary Douglass Fundaburk Foreman. Foreman attended Huntingdon College, Columbia University, George Washington University, and the University of South Alabama. She received a B.A. in Fine Art from Ohio State University and an M.S. in Art Education from Troy State University. In the layout of artifact illustrations and text, we see an artistic and graphic sensibility that was state-of-the-art for its time. The artifacts themselves are a mix of professionally photographed museum specimens and artifacts photographed from private collections.

The most remarkable thing about *Sun Circles and Human Hands* is its continued utility decades after it was published. The photographs are numerous and excellent. Packaged together in this manner, they still inspire wonder about the artistic productions of ten thousand years of Native American culture. Beyond the book's educational value as a popular summary, it is a source of many illustrated objects that can be found in no other published place. This gives the book an additional research value, as it continues to be consulted by serious students of southeastern archaeology at all levels. It is thus in many ways a unique resource, and the University of Alabama Press is pleased, with this reprinting, to keep it in the hands of people with an interest in native southeastern North America.

CONTENTS

Chapter	Plate		Page

Chapter 1

FOUR CULTURES

Thousands of Indian artifacts have been discovered in the Southeastern United States. Projectile points, tools, ceremonial objects, and ornaments mark the remains of village sites, burial grounds, and native camps. These are found along rivers and creeks, in plowed fields, at springs, salt licks, rock shelters, caves, shell mounds, earth mounds, and valley passes. Archeological evidence indicates that Indians in varying numbers inhabited parts of the Southeast as early as eight to fifteen thousand years ago and possibly earlier. These were the descendants of the many waves of migrants, who came from Asia into extreme northwestern North America at successive times during pre-Christian centuries; the migration is thought to have begun some twenty to thirty thousand years B. C.[1]

Successive Indian cultures in the Southeast are often classified into four general culture periods: Paleo-Indian, Archaic, Woodland, and Mississippi.[2] Calendrical or time-dating has been difficult to establish and is subject to change as more advance is made in archeological methods; however, the chronological succession of cultures has been established by several procedures. Stratigraphic archeological excavation has resulted in the skillful removal of soil and debris; layer after layer has been carefully examined to recover every evidence of human occupation. Many sites have yielded proof of long habitation.

Closely associated with stratigraphic excavation has been the careful observation and study of the relationship between the archeological and geological remains; it is significant, for instance, that fluted projectile points have been found with the bones of animals now extinct, and near stream beds, far from existing river courses.

The presence or absence of European trade goods at various Mississippi Period sites has aided in time-dating. Two other methods of projecting calendrical dates are by dendrochronology or tree-ring dating and by radiocarbon dating.[3]

Archeological discoveries indicate that the various culture traits did not change abruptly from one general culture period to the other. There were many centuries of transition between each of the four major stages of cultural development; when, simultaneous with the introduction of new methods and artifacts, there was continued use of certain of the old articles. The gradual modification of types and practices frequently developed at different rates, even among contemporary, near sites. However, there were basic changes in craftsmanship and circumstances of living which were shared to some extent, by most of the southeastern sites at some time in their progression of cultures.

Since all of the artifacts pictured in this book were not contemporary productions, it is necessary to call attention to some of the chief characteristics, developments, and changes in craftsmanship during the four general culture periods. A calendrical chart is included herein; such dates are subject to fluctuation as

[1] Georg K. Neumann, "Archeology and Race in the American Indian,"ARCHEOLOGY OF EASTERN UNITED STATES, edited by James B. Griffin, 1952, pp. 13-34.
[2] In "Culture Periods in Eastern United States Archeology," Ibid., James B. Griffin lists five culture periods; he separates the Woodland into Early, Middle, and Late; discusses the first two separately, and links the Late Woodland with the Mississippi; pp. 352-364. In ARCHEOLOGY OF EASTERN UNITED STATES there are articles by many eminent archeologists which give a detailed discussion of the culture periods in some 22 regions of the Eastern United States. One of the first comprehensive articles discussing general culture periods in the Southeast was published in THE AMERICAN ANTHROPOLOGIST by J. A. Ford and G. R. Willey in 1941. Publications by the Bureau of American Ethnology have discussed culture periods. A story-type account of the culture characteristics is given by Lewis and Kneberg, 1954. Most archeological literature appearing during the last twenty years refers to the general chronological succession of culture periods.
[3] The work of Dr. A. E. Douglass in tree-ring dating in the Southwest is well known. For a brief discussion regarding Eastern United States, see, R. E. Bell, in Griffin, 1952, pp. 345-51. For comments on carbon dating see James B. Griffin, 1952, pp. 365-370. The radiocarbon dating method resulted from work of the Institute of Nuclear Studies at the University of Chicago.

more evidence is found and more reliable dating projected. The chart is placed herein to show in a very general way, the tentative calendrical as well as the chronological progression of general culture periods.

? 8000	5000	4000	3000	2000	1000	BC-AD	400	800	1200	1600
PALEO	Transition	ARCHAIC		Transition		WOODLAND	Transition		MISSISSIPPI	

PALEO-INDIAN CULTURE PERIOD

The first inhabitants of the Southeast came in gradual influx over a long period of centuries; as new waves of migrants entered extreme northwestern North America, pushing down into the western plains, the older inhabitants were gradually pressed outward toward the then uninhabited areas of the continent. The first immigrants traveled in small bands probably one or a few families; they rarely came in contact with other natives, and inbred for centuries. Paleo-Indians lived a nomadic life; ate the meat of large animals they collectively killed; and supplemented their diet with berries, bark, nuts, and fruits in season. They sought convenient and natural habitation sites, as caves or over-hanging rocks; in the Tennessee Valley area, their habitation sites included small knolls near springs, lakes, or streams, and sites at pass approaches to a valley or on slopes near.[4]

No human skeletal remains have been found at Paleo-Indian camp sites; there is also an absence of bone tools, which were probably used. The lithic material which remains, indicates that Paleo-Indians produced a variety of tools, including points, scrapers, gravers, knives, and choppers; these were made from lamellar flakes, struck from cores of flint or similar materials. Many of the projectile points show remarkable craftsmanship; they are expertly chipped or flaked into shape; they sometimes have concave bases; ground basal edges, to prevent cutting the thongs used in hafting; and central fluting, for blood-letting or ease in hafting. Since men were the hunters, they were doubtless responsible for the excellent craftsmanship displayed on the points. Their weapons included spears, stones, and clubs, and the Late Paleo-Indian probably used the throwing-stick.

Knowledge and use of fire for light, warmth, and the crudest culinary purposes, is believed to have been brought into North America by early migrants from Asia. The Paleo-Indian doubtless had to struggle constantly against the elements of his environment; he probably seldom gathered anything to store, and wandered frequently in search of food.

ARCHAIC CULTURE PERIOD

As centuries passed and primitives gained more knowledge of their surroundings, a slow progression of changes in their economic habits and habitation sites resulted. To supplement the food supply, they learned to gather mussels from the river shoals and bivalves from the flats of bays and coastal areas. These shells were discarded in gradually mounting heaps along the banks of rivers, bays, and coasts.[5] Upon the rising heaps of shells natives built temporary huts of poles, hide, and brush; they dug fire pits, lined them with large river pebbles, dumped in bivalves, and broiled them over the hot stones and coals; they probably heated stones and dropped them into stone, wooden, or leather containers to heat food. The many broken river pebbles found at Archaic sites may have resulted from such practices. In outdoor kitchens or temporary huts Archaic people probably stored small quantities of roots, bark, berries, nuts, and dried meat.

A distinctive feature of the Archaic Period was the occurrence of "flint workshops" in the shell middens.[6] At many sites in the Tennessee Valley area, these occurred during the Middle Archaic Period; below that level, there was only a limited amount of chipped flint in the midden. The flint workshops were covered

---

[4] E. C. Mahan, 1954; Frank J. Soday, 1954.

[5] Though many of the well-known Archaic sites are found at such shell mounds, there are probably hundreds of other Archaic sites located elsewhere, which have never been explored. (correspondence, James B. Griffin).

[6] W. S. Webb and David L. DeJarnette (1942) refer to such flint workshops: "This was a concentrated layer of flint chips and cores which covered an elliptical area 8 feet long and 5 feet broad in the central cut. It extended into the unexcavated profile to an undetermined distance. It was (discovered) at a depth of 7.5 feet below the surface (of a shell mound). . . . The flint chips were made by percussion fracture and were large and crude. There were found in the layer with the chips, many cores, three flint points, and one hammerstone which showed usage." (p. 135). Also. "After the north profile (shell mound) was cleared, a compact layer of flint chips some 6 inches thick was observed extending the full length of the profile at about the 9-foot level . . . These dark-blue flint chips were evidently struck off by percussion fracture, from larger blocks of flint in the manufacture of rather large and crude blanks. The chips showed no evidence of secondary chipping by pressure. The flint layer was quite compact and the individual chips were reasonably uniform in size and color. Here, then, was definite observable stratification indicative of a change in the habits of the dwellers in the shell mound. The depth of the shell midden, at this point, was approximately 18 feet." (p. 247) Pickwick Basin, Alabama.

with chips, spalls, cores, broken points, and rejects. Hammerstones and evidence of percussion chipping were found. In addition to chipped points, the Archaic natives developed a variety of other chipped tools, including drills, scrapers, knives, and celts.

PECKED, GROUND, POLISHED, AND DRILLED STONES. The first stone artifacts of this type are found at Archaic sites. These include throwing-stick weights or charms, beads, bar gorgets, axes, and tubular pipes. Other stone artifacts of the Archaic Period were stone bowls, bell-shaped pestles, mortars, grinding stones, and pitted or nutting stones.

Bone and antler tools and ornaments frequently occur at Archaic sites. These include awls, bodkins, needles, drifts, flakers, projectile points, fishhooks, prickers (used by basket makers), shaft straighteners, animal jaw scrapers, pins, and combs; the Archaic craftsmen decorated some of these with carved geometric designs. Occasionally the remains of a worked human bone is found, as in the case of the bowl made of a human skull found in the Pickwick Basin, Alabama.[7] Animal teeth were notched or drilled for ornaments and tools.

During the Archaic Period, natives began using plant fibers (vines, canes, rushes, and barks) for baskets. The bivalves may have been gathered by means of nets, for stone net sinkers are found at some Archaic sites. Fiber baskets and wooden vessels were forerunners of stone bowls. Wood was also used for hafting points and tools, building huts and frames, and for making canoes.

BURIALS. Many of the Archaic people buried their dead in circular graves near their hut; they often flexed the bodies, and sometime placed them in a sitting position; some bodies were wrapped in skins, placed in baskets, or covered with bark; skull burials, interment of disarticulated bones, and cremation were practiced also. At Archaic sites dog burials are occasionally found beside the human burials. It is significant that a few material possessions as stone pipes, bowls, or ornaments were purposely placed with some of the Late Archaic burials. Though such articles did not accompany all burials, they do point to the possible beginning of a burial-ceremonial complex. Some of the artifacts in graves appear to have been purposely broken, or ceremonially "killed;" it is speculated that this might have been done in order to allow the spirit of the ornament or tool to escape and be of further service to the deceased.

LONG-DISTANCE TRADE. One of the significant developments of the Archaic Period was the beginning of long-distance trade. At some Late Archaic sites are found drilled shell beads, made from the columella and whorl of marine univalves, traded inland from the Atlantic and Gulf coasts. Rolled copper beads have been found in limited quantities; the raw material possibly originated as far away as Lake Superior. Steatite, flint, mica, sandstone, and ochre were other articles of Archaic exchange.

The primary weapon of the Archaic Period was the throwing-stick; a discovery which is thought to have been introduced from Asia by Paleo-Indians. It is believed to have been used throughout the Archaic Period and well into the Woodland centuries. The throwing-stick was designed to add leverage to a man's arm; it enabled the hunter to hurl a missile a greater distance.

The increased number and variety of weapons, tools, and ornaments produced during the Archiac Period, indicates that rudimentary specialization in craftsmanship was developing; it was natural for some natives to be more skilled than others as hunters, flint workers, basket makers, wood carvers, stone quarriers, or stone drillers; with the development of special skills was doubtless also the beginning of simple barter, whereby one native could exchange his surplus fishhooks, baskets, or flints for another's surplus bowls, beads, or pipes. The appearance of new types of artifacts indicated a growing list of wants and needs and an attempt to supply them. They were probably more conscious of their personal appearance or more ceremonial in activities, as is implied by their practice of depositing red ochre and ornaments with burials.

The most revolutionary craft to appear in the top layers of some shell mound sites, amid predominantly Archaic material, was pottery. From the Late Archaic site, Poverty Point, La., Ford and Webb (1956) report pottery vessel sherds, several small figurines, tubular pipe fragments, and unusual ball and cylindrical shapes (some effigy forms), which they regarded as substitutes for "cooking stones." (See Plate 129). Though fiber-tempered and even granular-tempered pot sherds occur at transitional Archaic-Woodland levels, the development of pottery is generally considered a Woodland characteristic.

---

[7] Ibid., Plate 298.

WOODLAND CULTURE PERIOD

Population continued to grow and to spread from the largest streams to the smaller creeks and quiet sloughs. This spread of the more numerous Woodland population probably accelerated as the bow and arrow gradually displaced the throwing-stick.[8] Near these secluded village sites, the Woodland people constructed burial mounds to hold their dead. These relatively small mounds, often conical in shape, were sometimes near a river; frequently there were two or more such mounds together. The number of burials in a mound varied from one to several dozen; some were single interments, others were multiple burials on the same or different prepared surfaces. Some of the burial mounds were constructed over a period of time, and built up in several layers; occasionally shells, clay, logs, or stone slabs separated the layers or were placed around the individual or mass graves. A prominent feature of this specialized burial custom was the placement of ornaments and tools with the bodies. The tools and ornaments of the Woodland people were similar to those of the Archaic cultures, but they were more varied and often showed finer workmanship. Their tools included chipped drills, knives, celts, scrapers, axes, and a variety of smaller projectile points. A new addition to the tool assemblage was the large chipped greenstone, limestone, or flint spade; the presence of the spade may have indicated a rudimentary agricultural development; however, it was probably used for digging graves, scooping soil for burial mound fills, and excavating post holes for house framing. These spades are sometimes found in the graves under the skull of the skeleton or in the fill of the mound. Specialized pecked, ground, and polished stone articles found with Woodland remains were poled celts; plummets—net sinkers or ornaments; pipes—elbow, platform, and occasional zoomorphic forms; medicine tubes; boatstones; expanding center gorgets; and a few ornamental or ceremonial effigies. Many Archaic-introduced tools, as stone axes, continued to be used.

Copper artifacts increased in number and variety; they included reel-shaped objects, chisels, celts, bicymbal ear spools, drilled beads, bracelets, rolled-sheet beads (tubes), a few copper plated objects (over stone or wood), including ear spools; and gorgets. Galena, mica, hematite, tar, red ochre, and asphalt have also been found in Woodland graves. Bone and antler tools, as skeletal remains, are much rarer than at Archaic sites; such tools were probably extensively used, but have decayed.

Shells other than mussel were more numerous at Woodland than at Archaic sites. Marginella and olivella shells are numerous at some sites. Pearl beads and turtle carapaces have also been found. In addition to conch shell beads, conch dippers are a significant burial deposit. Shell tools have also occurred at some Woodland sites. The Woodland people doubtless made extensive use of wood also; fragments and impressions of mats, baskets, and house frames are frequently found.

POTTERY. The presence of pottery vessels and pottery sherds at Woodland Period sites give evidence of a revolutionary change in culinary equipment. Since women did the storing and cooking of food, they doubtless were responsible for most of the domestic pottery. Pottery vessels increased the ease and effectiveness of preparing food; enabled women to cook in pots over the fire; and provided a way to transport and store liquids easily. In addition the making of vessels gave women an outlet for creative abilities, which allowed more freedom of design than did basketry.

The first pottery in the Southeast was molded and modeled, fiber-tempered pottery; it is believed to have been indigenous, though the idea may have come from outside the area; there is no proof. This was soon replaced by coil pottery made from clay tempered with a variety of granular materials. Over the long span of centuries of the Woodland Culture Period, the potter experimented with temper, firing, form, and application of design. Much of the pottery was plain; however, on some of it, the maker attempted to imitate the chisel marks on stone bowls and the designs of basket-weaves; in order to produce these likenesses, the maker developed a variety of stamping and impressing methods; she used reed and brush marks; cord and fabric marking; and stamped designs with carved wooden paddles. When these were impressed on the plastic clay, they left a variety of check stamps, parallel lines, textile-weaves, and complicated geometric designs. The potter also experimented with simple incising; and with impressions made with the crinkled edge of a scalloped shell. At some transitional Woodland-Mississippi Period sites, the remains of clay-plaster—wattle-and-

---

[8] Though the throwing-stick had probably generally been displaced by the bow and arrow by the Late Woodland Period, there were still some tribes using it even in the Mississippi Culture Period. Cushing (1896) found the throwing-stick rather than the bow and arrow in the Key Marco remains. The Eskimo fisherman used the throwing-stick as late as historic times; it was easier to use from a boat.

daub—from fallen house walls has been found. That, however, is generally a Mississippi Period characteristic. Woodland people often lined their fire pits, and sometimes their graves, with puddled clay, but rarely plastered their houses with it.

COPENA CULTURE FOCUS. In the Tennessee Valley and other parts of Alabama and near area, the Middle Woodland Culture has been termed "Copena," because of the frequent presence of copper and galena burial offerings. [9]   At these sites the initial burials beneath the mounds were often placed into clay-lined pits; the clay for the pits was brought in for that purpose; some graves appear to have prepared head and foot rests made of clay. Carefully placed burial offerings were arranged near the body, which in some cases had been wrapped in a mat or hide; occasionally, bark or logs were placed over the body and offerings, before the grave was finally sealed with clay. The items they buried with their dead were distinctive and well-made. They included[10] highly polished, pointed-pole, greenstone celts; stone elbow and occasional zoomorphic pipes; large schist spades; finely chipped, ovate, flint knives; stone gorgets — flat with expanding center; conch shell dippers and large disk beads made from marine univalve shells; distinctive, stemless, shield-shaped projectile points, and a variety of copper articles, including, reel-shaped objects, celts, beads (drilled and rolled), large ear spools, and flat-bar bracelets; also galena in the shape of cones, balls, or fragments. In the graves, ornaments are often found near the skeleton in their natural wearing position.

Though pottery sherds have occasionally been found in the Copena mound fills, the pottery vessel was not a characteristic burial tribute of this focus as it was at a few other Woodland sites. Some of the Copena artifacts found in burials appear to have been ceremonially broken and the parts deposited together. In this and other respects, the copper-galena complex seems to be related to the advanced Hopewell culture of the Upper Mississippi, Illinois, and Ohio Valley areas. The grave offerings of copper, galena, and conch shell indicated that north-south trade had increased.

MISSISSIPPI CULTURE PERIOD

During the Mississippi Period cultural changes appear to have been telescoped into a relatively few centuries. Among the sites well known for their distinctive ceremonial objects are Spiro, Oklahoma; Moundville, Alabama; and Etowah, Georgia. Certain elements of their cultures seem to represent a relatively abrupt change from Southeastern Woodland Culture traits; however, other of their methods and designs express a continuity with the past and near sites, as the practice of stamp-impressing some of the pottery at Etowah. It is debatable as to whether or not the influence of Indian traders and the influx of "foreign" native trade goods alone could have brought about all the changes and expansion in Southeastern designs, methods of craftsmanship, and ceremonial activities which were represented in the Middle Mississippi Culture. The Mississippi Period climaxed in the highest type Indian culture known to have existed in the Southeast; it is thought to have reached a peak probably between 1300 and 1600 A. D.

MOUNDS. The custom of building truncated, platform mounds was widespread in the Mississippi Period. Many show a profile of successive layers, built gradually over many years of occupation. The large flattened-top rectangular structures of earth were used as foundations for important buildings—temples, council houses, and dwellings of tribal leaders. At a few sites, burial and domiciliary mounds are found in the same village plan. More frequently however, there are no burial type mounds with the truncated earth pyramids. Occasionally what has appeared to be a substructure mound has had in it one or more large burial pits or crypts, with single or mass burials, which were probably those of tribal leaders. However, most of the large truncated mounds were primarily used as a base for buildings which, in some cases, appeared to have been a mortuary temple or "bone-houses;" many archeological excavations have revealed post-mold patterns and the impressions of fallen timber defining the dimensions of public buildings and houses which were built on the truncated mounds.

A few of the substructure mounds reached the height of 50 to 75 feet and the ground dimensions of 300 to 600 feet; often they were more rectangular than square. However, the majority of hundreds of such earth structures scattered throughout the Southeast have been reported to be from 5 to 30 feet high and from 50

---

[9] W. S. Webb and D. L. DeJarnette (1942) describe several "Copena" sites in BAE, Bulletin 129—Pickwick Basin. On pp. 301-306 they summarize in detail the culture traits of the Copena culture. D. L. DeJarnette (In J. B. Griffin, 1952, pp. 278-279), briefly discusses this culture focus. [10] W. S. Webb (1939, p. 201), discusses Copena sites in the Wheeler Basin and lists outstanding traits.

to 250 feet in ground dimensions, usually tapering toward the flattened top. At a few of the larger Mississippi Period sites, as Moundville, Alabama, the natives constructed 30 to 40 mounds of varying sizes; at most sites the number varied from 1 to 10. That doubtless depended upon the population of the site, its importance to the surrounding area, and the total length of time the site was occupied. The truncated, domiciliary pyramid and its accompanying distinctive Mississippi Period Culture spread through the Southeast and far into the Upper Mississippi Valley area.

Where there was more than one mound at a site, their placement and gradation in size appear to have been part of a total village plan. The temple mound was presumably the tallest and elevated toward the sun. The council house was sometimes on an opposite mound, and a public square between. Smaller mounds graded away from these. Ramps or steps were provided for easy access to the top;[11] the steps were often reinforced with packed clay or carefully placed logs. Caches of finely-finished artifacts, as blades, celts, points, etc., are occasionally found in the mound fills, in isolation, and may have had a ceremonial significance, as in Central America.

The mounds were surrounded by the village area and cornfields. They were often built on a bluff by a river near arable land. Frequently the earth for building the mounds was secured from holes, dug in the near area, which holes, possibly served later as fish ponds. Some sites had a canal or moat surrounding exposed sides; such ditches probably furnished soil for the mounds, protection for the site, and were used for bringing canoes and fish nearer the village. Many sites had earth walls surrounding their unprotected side. Construction of the colossal earth structures doubtless required the expenditure of millions of man-hours; the natives had to dig the earth, transport it (probably in baskets), shape and spread the dirt, and pack it into place. The erection of earth mounds was doubtless a major community undertaking.

AGRICULTURAL VILLAGES. Location of hundreds of such mound sites near arable land, the frequent occurrence of charred remains of corn cobs, and the remaining impressions of field rows in excavated areas, indicate that agriculture was an important part of the Mississippi Period economic life.[12] Flourishing agricultural villages were found in the Southeast when the first European explorers arrived in the sixteenth century. Early colonial writers and painters picture villages surrounded by corn fields.

With a more secure means of making a living, natives could settle longer at one site and build permanent-type houses. The post molds of many Middle Mississipppi houses were rectangular to square; the vertical poles of the side walls were often placed into trenches, rather than set into individual holes, as was more frequent at Woodland sites. The poles were set from six inches to several feet apart and interlaced with branches or cane, and plastered with clay; others were covered with substantial mats. The hut roof was often thatched; in some areas, as the Norris Basin, Tennessee,[13] the roof was also covered with earth, as was the "earth-lodge" type structure found in the Macon Plateau Culture, Ocmulgee, Georgia. Clay was used not only for plastering the wattle, but also for making house floors, fire basins, and raised bench-or-step-like seats in council houses and dwellings.

BURIAL CUSTOMS. A diagnostic characteristic of the Mississippi Period was the burial of pottery and other artifacts with the deceased. Many such objects represent the finest of native craftsmanship. The abundance of grave associations indicates the existence of a complicated burial-ceremonial complex. Some of the vessels and other artifacts appear to have been purposely broken or "killed," and many of the "grave goods" of the Middle Mississippi people were decorated with "cult" or ceremonial symbols, as the hand, eye, bones, skull, and others. In addition to objects of native craftsmanship, Indian graves of the Late Mississippi Period contained many European trade goods. The burial associations appear to have been placed there for a combination of reasons. Many were apparently special tributes; others personal possessions of the deceased; still others, containers for food; the latter was probably thought to be of assistance to the deceased in his journey to another world.

Fragments of matting and skin found in some of the burials indicate that the bodies were often placed

[11] In the Lamar Complex, Ocmulgee, Macon, Georgia, a mound was built with a spiral ramp. At Battery's Landing in the Keys, Cushing, (1896, p. 343), describes an oval mound 58' high and 375' x 150 base, "built up of sand and thin strata of sea shells alternately. A graded way wound around it spirally from the southern base to the summit, which was comparatively narrow, but long and level like the tops of the shell mounds on the keys . . . . Potsherds of fine quality, chalky remains of human bones, broken shell ladles—their bottoms significantly punctured—all demonstrated the fact that this mound, which obviously had been used as the foundation of a temple structure, had also served as a place of burial."
[12] A. R. Kelly, 1938, describes and pictures rows of a prehistoric cornfield discovered in the mound-site excavations at Ocmulgee, Macon, Georgia. [13] W. S. Webb, 1938.

on these materials or wrapped in them. Fragments of these have survived because of their nearness to copper objects and impressions of them have been left in the puddled clay which lined many graves. The burial practices of Mississippi Period people were varied and numerous. A water color by John White, 1587, depicts the mortuary temple or "bone-house" of a North Carolina coastal tribe; other colonial writers describe temples in which bodies were placed for preservation of the skelton. Archeological excavations give evidence of the remains of burials in mounds which may have been similar. Stretched and flexed burials frequently occur; burial of disarticulated bones and cremated remains in urns, and skull burials also have been found. It is evident that many local customs accompanied burial of the dead; however, the general practice of placing offerings into the grave indicates a similar ceremonial custom throughout the Southeast.

POTTERY. In addition to making pottery for domestic purposes, Mississippi Period natives also made pottery for ceremonial and mortuary purposes, as mentioned above. The black ware of Moundville, decorated with engraved cult designs was special purpose pottery deposited with burials and possibly used in other ceremonials. Burial urns of the Alabama River were another type of mortuary pottery. The many bowls with effigy handles, the painted bottles, and the modeled bottles and bowls were probably primarily used in ceremonies and deposited with burials.

A variety of sizes of "pots, bowls, and bottles" are found throughout the Southeast; among the eccentric forms are vertical and horizontal compounds, stirrup-neck vessels, gourd shapes, and modeled effigies. Various types of long-neck bottles are a diagnostic trait of the Mississippi Period. Shell-tempered pottery has been found at most Middle Mississippi sites. However, at a few such sites, the tempering appears to include other granular substances, as found at Early and Late Mississippi sites. A small percent of the pottery at most Middle Mississippi sites was completely coated with a wash or slip, was decorated by direct or negative painting, or treated with a combination of these. At a few sites, as Nodena, Arkansas, painted pottery constituted a larger part of the total.

Other features of Mississippi Period pottery included applique or fillet bands and nodes; strap and loop handles; and arches or arcades around the neck of the vessel. Some of the modeled effigy vessel handles were hollow and were filled with pebbles for rattles. Many vessels were probably used interchangeably for domestic, ceremonial, and mortuary ware; the most elaborate in form and decoration were preserved in burials. Though pottery was primarily used in making vessels, it also was fashioned into pipes, spindle whorls, trowels, game disks, and a few ornaments. Several colonial writers refer to the use of pottery vessels for drums; skin was stretched over the opening.

TOOLS, ORNAMENTS, AND CEREMONIAL OBJECTS. Mississippi Period people used many pecked, ground, polished, and drilled stone objects. Among them were axes, celts, adzes, chisels, and pestles. Articles of more interesting shapes were the numerous and varied stone pipes which ranged from the massive flat-base platform pipes of the Middle Mississippi Culture to the slender, highly polished pipes of the historic era. Other polished stone objects included, game stones, monolithic axes, spatulate forms, paint palettes, stone images, ear spools, beads, and pendants.

Chipped flint was used for projectile points, drills, reamers, scrapers, and knives. Small triangular projectile points were found at many Middle Mississippi sites. Chipped flint maces, batons, and ceremonial knives of outstanding size and workmanship have been found at leading Middle Mississippi Period sites, and are depicted in native designs of the same period.

Outstanding craftsmanship was also achieved in the production of copper artifacts which were embossed and excised. The metal was hammered into thin sheets and fashioned into breastplates, hairpins, beads, batons, maces, celts, ear spools, and plaques. Repousse decoration was frequently applied to these. The thin copper was used to plate wood, stone, bone, and shell for ear spools and pendants.

INDIAN ART. Native art achieved remarkable symmetry and rhythm as a result of the craftsman's understanding of materials and technical skill. Ornaments and other artifacts were well-proportioned and carefully finished. They were usually horizontally, rather than vertically symmetrical.

Examples of inverted symmetry occur occasionally. The rhythm and often copied formal balance of design reflected the craftsman's patient skill and his unhurried, orderly, custom-controlled life. A few talented artists probably produced the outstanding objects, and they were models for the less skilled. Though designs were usually applied free-hand, they imitated traditional styles. Stone objects, especially, often reflect regional styles, while pottery decoration characteristically displays site stylization.

Southeastern Indian art often expressed simplicity, singleness, and directness of representation. It was functional—domestic and ceremonial. Though preoccupied with cult symbolism, Middle Mississippi artists exhibited individuality in realistic designs. On some objects, native artists added lines to represent texture. Geometric designs occur more frequently than any other. This tendancy might have developed from the craftsman's skill in working movements—spiral and plane; the ease with which many geometric designs can be made; and the native's long experience with such, beginning with Archaic basket decorations. There were few nature designs, as leaves, trees, and flowers; occasionally a pottery vessel was modeled or painted in imitation of a gourd. The sun, an object of worship, was frequently represented; stars and the moon were depicted infrequently. Humans, birds, and animals inspired realistic and conventional designs. At Spiro the human figure was pictured more frequently than at any other site. Though the head was usually shown in profile, while the body was in either a profile or a forward position, Spiro produced a number of face-front rather than profile heads.[14]

Although Southeastern Indian artists created few large objects, they produced many remarkable small artifacts on which the minuteness of design, form, or drill required technical skill. Free-flowing, well-proportioned designs in form and line are characteristic. Southeastern Indian art is distinctive because of its frequent harmony of materials, form, method of design, and decorative motif.

CEREMONIALS. Symbolism was an important element of the art of the Mississippi people. The designs found on art objects from the major Southeastern sites included the hand, eye, bone, skull, equal-arm cross, sun, star, triskel, step, arrow, human, bird, serpent, and spider. These doubtless had a special meaning for the natives who produced and used them. They were part of the burial-ceremonial complex of a people who deified the sun, named their clans for animals, and had a complicated primitive social structure.

It is believed that many of the customs of Middle Mississippi, prehistoric people, were reflected to some extent in the activities of historic tribes, as the Natchez and Creek Indians. The divisions of authority within the tribe—chief, medicine men, priests, warriors, council men, war and peace villages, and clans; the confederation of the Creeks; their annual harvest festival; the cross-placed logs used in their ceremonial fire; the careful arrangement of council house seating; the black drink; the custom of placing tributes and possessions with the dead, probably reflected much of the ritual of the life of Middle Mississippi people.

LATE MISSISSIPPI OR HISTORIC CULTURE PERIOD

Archeological investigations and historic writings indicate that the Middle Mississippi complex probably reached its height shortly before the exploration of the Southeast, and was possibly already declining when the sixteenth century explorers traversed the Southeast. Early descriptions of North America, as Le Moyne's description of Florida, 1564-65, and Hariot's description of the North Carolina coast, 1585, refer to the restlessness, frequent hostilities, and open war among the tribes. This may account for their decline in culture.

During the sixteenth, seventeenth, and eighteenth centuries as France, England, and Spain fought for a foothold in the "New World," they took advantage of the restlessness of the natives and provoked them to frequent war and intrigue. European trade goods, colonial rum, treachery, disabling epidemics of disease, and rapid depletion of wild game caused the Indians to become increasingly dependent upon trade with Europeans and Colonials. Iron pots, brass kettles, guns and ammunition, glass beads, bells, mirrors, cloth, vermilion, iron axes, knives, glass bottles, and other foreign trade goods caught the fancy of the natives. Objects of native craftsmanship rapidly declined in number and in quality. They degenerated in form and design, and those remaining often became a combination of the old and the new—tiny glass beads, rather than fur, quills, or fiber, were used for ornamenting cloth and leather; reworked metal—brass, copper, silver, iron, and gold—was fashioned into ornaments and tools; even projectile points were sometimes made from broken glass or iron. Though metal tools had many advantages over stone tools, the natives never again captured the remarkable designs and craftsmanship of the prehistoric cultures.

---

[14] Hamilton, 1952, Figs. 86, 87, 91B, 106, 119B, 125A, B, and 139A. For an excellent description of North American Indian art, see Vaillant, 1939; for a scholarly description of primitive art, see Boaz, 1951.

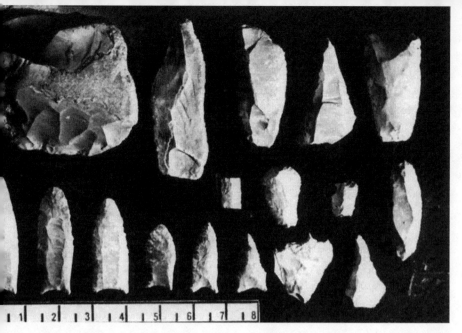

PALEO-INDIAN PERIOD

Plates 1 and 2

Lewis and Kneberg (1954, pp. 124-127) describe Paleo points:

"The Clovis, Folsom, Eden and other early points exhibit a degree of excellence rarely equalled . . . . The Folsom points represent a technical advance over the earlier Clovis form in workmanship. They are smaller in size, being only about two inches long on the average . . . quite thin . . . have a deeply incurved base . . . (an) extension of the longitudinal fluting almost to the tip of each face . . . (and) edges near the base usually show evidence of grinding . . . . Channels . . . would increase . . . the ability to penetrate . . . ."

ABOVE. Typical Paleo-Indian tool assemblage. Upper row. Left. Chopper or hand axe, probably used for cutting meat, bones, and hide. Second. A typical knife with a thick patina; the elements have almost converted the original flint to a chalky substance. Third and Fourth. Combination tools; some 24 types of such tools have been found at this site. Upper. Right. A gouge of the type found by Cyrus Ray in Pleistocene gravels at Clear Fork, Brazos River, Texas. Middle Row. A channel flake which was removed in the fluting process; some two dozen of these rare flakes have been found at the Quad site. Next. Two end-scrapers and a side-scraper; they are found in large numbers; and were probably used in working hides and shafts of wood. Lower Row. Four fluted points; the third has a thick patina; first and fourth are made from flinty materials imported into the area; fifth point is the unfluted type; sixth point was reworked by natives of a later culture, probably Archaic. Next. A graver with several typical sharp points which may have been used for engraving bone or wood, body tattooing, or other pricking. Lower Row. Right. A borer; found infrequently. Tools were made from lamellar flakes struck from flint cores. The tool assemblage above is from the Quad site, near Decatur, Morgan County, Alabama, Tennessee River Valley. The site was discovered by Dr. Frank J. Soday in 1951. The Alabama Archaeological Society is carefully collecting, studying, and indexing artifacts from this and other Paleo sites in that area, and will publish a summary of the information (Courtesy, Dr. Frank J. Soday; photograph by Jack D. Ray).

Lewis and Kneberg (1954, pp. 124-127) picture and describe several early projectile point forms, including fluted—Clovis and Folsom—and unfluted—Eva, Plainview, Eden, and Scottsbluff—points:

"In addition to finding (in a gravel pit near Clovis, New Mexico) more of the typical Folsom points, they (professional archaeologists) have discovered at lower depths a number of somewhat different forms which have shorter flutings and are larger in size. . . . Similar large, partly fluted forms have been found over much of the eastern United States; . . . . In Tennessee many have been found especially in and near Maury County. . . . The edges near the base of a Clovis point nearly always show evidence of grinding to remove the sharp edges. . . ." (Quoted by permission from Dr. T. M. N. Lewis).

ABOVE. LEFT. Fluted and unfluted Paleo-Indian projectile points; the smallest point is fluted on the reverse side; the larger point is about 3½" long. Tennessee Valley, Alabama (Courtesy, Huntsville Public Library). RIGHT. Three fluted points from Tennessee, 4½", 3½", and 2¾" long (Courtesy, D. B. Long; photograph by Tom-Clare Studio). Paleo projectile point types usually have been named for the site at which they were first discovered; most of them are named for western sites.

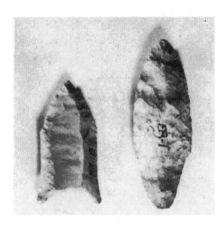

ABOVE. Two Paleo-Indian projectile points—Left. A short point with a long flute. Right. Leaf-shaped "Sandia" type, 2⅞" long. Franklin County, Alabama (Courtesy, H. K. Kleine).

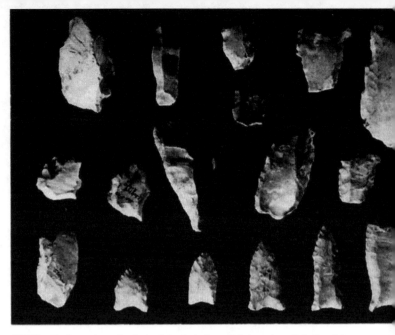

ABOVE. Tools and projectile points, including fluted and unfluted points, flake knives, gravers, side-scrapers, and end-scrapers. Longest object pictured is 3½". Madison and Jackson Counties, Alabama (Courtesy, Madison County Chapter, Alabama Archaeological Society). Lewis and Kneberg (1954, p. 125) state:

"The fluting of the Folsom and Clovis points raises a problem as to the technique by which it was accomplished. At the famous Lindenmeier site in Colorado a spall was found that fitted into part of the fluting on a Folsom point. Because the spall was chipped on one face only, it was concluded that the point had been finished before the spall was removed. While such a feat might have been accomplished by an exceptionally skilled workman, it seems unlikely that the procedure was commonly used. A powerful blow, applied either directly or indirectly, is required to produce the fluting. Our tests with small finished blades have been quite unsuccessful."

BELOW. Tools. Upper Row. Side scrapers and knives. Center. End-scrapers and side-scrapers. Bottom. Gravers and a spokeshave. Several of these are combination tools. The longest is about 3½". Limestone County, Alabama (Courtesy, J. W. Cambron; photograph by Ray. For a complete list of photographers and collections photographed see Acknowledgements).

ABOVE. Four fluted points; base and basal sides are ground; the longest is about 3⅜"; the shortest is about 2". Maury County, Tennessee (Courtesy, Judge H. L. Webster; photograph courtesy, University of Tennessee, Department of Anthropology; Lewis and Kneberg, 1954, Pl. IV, p. 135).

ABOVE. LEFT. Mural showing a native using a throwing-stick and dart. The throwing-stick has a hook-like projection at one end; it was often made of antler, horn, or carved wood. This fitted into a nock at the end of the dart, and held the dart secure until released in flight. The dart-thrower was probably introduced into the Southeast during the late Paleo-Indian Period; it was the primary weapon of the Archaic native; and continued in general use until well into the Woodland Period. In certain parts of the Southeast, as in the Florida Keys, the throwing-stick was used in the Mississippi Period. See Cushing, 1897 (Courtesy, National Park Service, Ocmulgee National Monument). RIGHT. Archaic artifacts. Upper Row. Left. Side view of a greenstone, shuttle-shaped, drilled bannerstone (throwing-stick weight or charm). Right. Side view of a quartzite, bell-shaped pestle. Middle Row. Left. Flint flaker made from a leg bone of a deer; tubular stone pipe; drilled greenstone pendant. Lower Row. Left to Right. Chipped knife-scraper; two stemmed projectile points and a drill made from local nodular flint; pecked and ground, grooved, greenstone axe. Lower. Right. Problematical stone—boatstone, unfinished gorget or weight? Limestone County, Alabama (Courtesy, Dr. F. J. Soday). See James B. Griffin, 1952, for illustrations of Archaic traits at various Southeastern sites.

ARCHAIC PERIOD

Plates 3 and 4

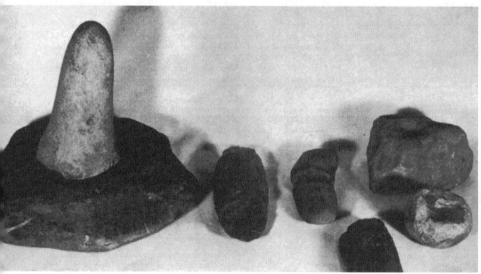

ABOVE. Quartzite bell-shaped pestle and mortar; flint celt; full-grooved, greenstone, pecked and ground axe; pitted or nutting stone; flint hammerstone or abrader. Limestone County, Alabama (Courtesy, J. W. Cambron).

RIGHT. Chipped flint celt, 8" long. Cullman County, Alabama (Courtesy, Mrs. J. B. Hay, Sr.).

Bone and shell traits of the "nonpottery dwellers on shell mounds in Pickwick Basin," Tennessee River, northern Alabama, are listed by Webb and DeJarnette (1942, p. 312):

"Bone traits: Bone bodkins; deer ulna awls; cannon-bone awls, deer; splinter bone awls; tibiotarsal awls of turkey; artifacts made from human bone; antler drifts; antler shaft straighteners; atlatl hooks; bone propectile points, one heavy end; antler spear points; fishhooks from deer toe or other bone; perforated canine teeth; hairpins, bone; needles, cylindrical, from deer bone. Shell traits: shell pendants, small, triangular; shell-composite atatl weight; long cylindrical columella beads; flat disk beads; anculosa beads." (Quotation from Bureau of American Ethnology, Bulletin 129, 1942).

Webb and DeJarnette (1942, pp. 306-319) discuss shell-mound site characteristics, and compare those found along the Tennessee River, northern Alabama, with those of the Green River area, Kentucky. See also: Webb, 1938, 1939; Webb and DeJarnette, 1948.

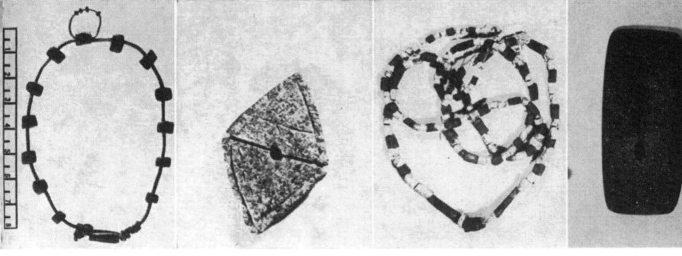

ABOVE. LEFT. Rolled copper beads made from strips of hammered native copper; longest about ⅝" diameter. Restrung on buckskin thong by owner. The beads were found with fragments of the original string inside; the yarn had been prepared by twisting thirteen filaments (probably bast fibers from wild nettle or flax). The yarn was preserved inside the beads by the action of copper salts. It is interesting to note that this string of beads containing preserved prehistoric strands of yarn was found within sight of the Chemstrand synthetic fiber plant, Decatur, Alabama, where fibers are now made from natural gas and air. Limestone County, Alabama (Courtesy, Dr. F. J. Soday and J. Carr). SECOND. Pecked steatite gorget; symmetrical design with rudimentary carving; 2⅝" long. Limestone County, Alabama (Courtesy, J. W. Cambron). THIRD. Rolled copper beads and bone beads in a necklace; longest about on inch. Limestone County, Alabama (Courtesy, J. W. Cambron). RIGHT. Two-hole bar gorget; pecked and ground steatite; about 3" long. North Alabama (Courtesy, D. C. Hulse).

BELOW. LEFT. Cupped, pitted, or nutting stone with 6 pits on photographed side; it is similarly marked on reverse side; maximum diameter about 10". Morgan County, Alabama (Courtesy, J. B. Ratliff). CENTER. Tubular clay-stone pipe, 2-¾" long, showing indentations around stem and carved parallel notches at bowl opening; typical flint awl or drill, which may have been used in working the stone. Morgan County, Alabama (Courtesy, Jack D. Ray. This and other photographs on these two plates were made by Jack D. Ray, who was the photographer for most of the pictures from private collections). RIGHT. Large, restored, steatite vessel showing chisel marks; approximately 15½" rim diameter; bottom worn thin and burned through. Limestone County, Alabama (Courtesy, J. Carr).

BELOW. LEFT. Large full-grooved limestone axe found with Archaic artifacts; 9¼" long. Such axes were usually hafted, and used to quarry rock, cut wood, drive stakes, chop meat, dress hides, and to break bones to obtain the marrow. This was found at a shell mound on the Tennessee River, Limestone County, Alabama (Courtesy, Dr. F. J. Soday). CENTER. Turkey bone needle, 4½" long; deer bone awl. Many worked bone and antler tools were left by the Archaic people; these include fishhooks, flakers, fleshers, hammers, hafts, projectile points, awls, needles, and expanding-stem pins with well executed, carved, geometric designs; bone prickers were important tools of the Archaic basket maker, as they were for all succeeding cultures. Lauderdale County, Alabama (Courtesy, Mr. and Mrs. C. G. Summers). RIGHT. Weight or charm for a throwing-stick or atlatl; highly polished mud-stone; about 4" long. From a cave in Jackson County, Alabama (Courtesy, Madison County Chapter, Alabama Archaeological Society).

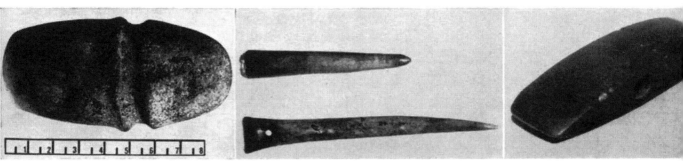

WOODLAND PERIOD

Plates 5 and 6

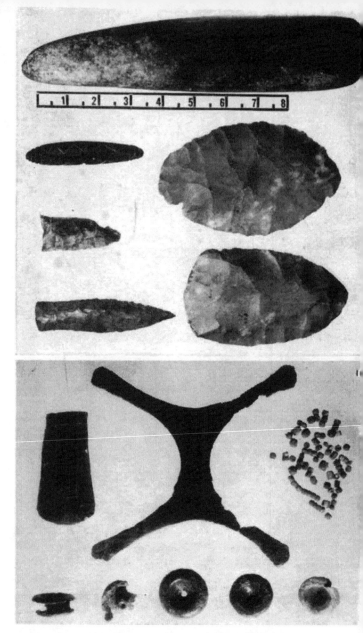

RIGHT. UPPER. Copena artifacts. Long greenstone poled celt; two projectile points; one shuttle-shaped stone with center groove and carved decoration; two knives or blanks. Madison County, Alabama (Courtesy, Madison County Chapter, Alabama Archaeological Society).

LEFT. The bow and arrow displaced the throwing-stick at many Southeastern sites during the Woodland Period. The bow shown here is of modern origin; it was made by a Cherokee, Guy King, who lived in the Tennessee Valley, Alabama. He would never sell it, but willed it to Dr. H. E. Wheeler, the present owner. It is 75" long, made of cedar, and is an example of careful workmanship (Courtesy, Indian Springs School).

BELOW. Digging or agricultural implements. Long chipped chert spade, 10½"; chipped limestone spade, 8" long; pecked and ground sandstone hoe, 4½". Used for excavating postholes, digging graves, and scooping dirt for building conical burial mounds; often found in mound fills. Limestone County, Alabama (Courtesy, Dr. F. J. Soday).

ABOVE. Copper artifacts from the Copena Focus, often found in burial mounds in the Tennessee Valley area. Typical reel-shaped object, 6½" x 7" of hammered copper; it is about 1/10" thick, and "the tip ends of each arm have been beaten to give them a broad, spatulate form." Copper celt, 1-8/10" wide and 2/10" thick; probably once hafted; pole end was formed by folding over the sheet copper for a distance of one-half inch. Some 75 beads in one string were made by drilling small nuggets of copper. Five circular ear spools, 1.3" to 2" diameter, made of thin sheet copper were constructed of two concave disks, riveted together at the center by a small cylinder of copper. "Each disk was made of a double sheet of copper and several contained remnants of string wound around the central rivet." String has been found in a similar position on such ear spools at other sites, and was presumably wrapped around the loosely fastened central cylinder to keep the spools spread apart. Two copper breastplates, not shown, were found at this site; they were size 7.5" x 4"; they had almost completely turned to copper salts, and leather and matting fragments ("flat fibers of bark about 1 inch wide, woven both warp and weft, 'under one and over four.'") had adhered to and been preserved by the copper salts. Lauderdale County, Alabama (Courtesy, Alabama Museum of Natural History; BAE, Bulletin 129, Pl. 184-1 and description by Webb and DeJarnette, p. 157). For an excellent depiction of Copena characteristics see: J. B. Griffin, 1952, Fig. 150.

ABOVE. A conical burial mound which has been cleared and staked for excavation. Copena Focus; 22 burials were found in this mound in individual pits. Lauderdale County, Alabama (Courtesy, Alabama Museum of Natural History; BAE, Bulletin 129, Pl. 129-2).

RIGHT. Stamped pottery vessel, partially restored, bottom broken, rounded to slightly conical originally about 8" high. Clark County, Alabama (Courtesy Alabama Museum of Natural History).

ABOVE. LEFT. Restored straight-base, platform pipe, 2-¾" high; 4½" long. Found in a cave; it was broken and the pieces were scattered over an area some 16 feet in diameter (Courtesy, Lt. T. F. Moebes). CENTER. Drawing of a restored, broken, pottery vessel, decorated with a zoomorphic form—incised lines surrounded by zoned stamping. This typical bird or serpent design was often repeated on opposite sides of a vessel. Rudimentary use of animal and human forms in Southeastern design generally began in the Woodland Period. (Ford and Webb, 1957, recently found more realistic bird and animal forms carved on two fragments of stone bowls, at Poverty Point, La., with Late Archaic remains). The Bynum Mounds, Mississippi. (After Cotter and Corbett, 1951, National Park Service). RIGHT. Marginella shells are often found in quantities with Woodland remains. The snail was probably eaten, as well as the shell used for ornamentation; ⅜" to ½" long. Morgan County, Alabama (Courtesy, J. W. Cambron).

BELOW. LEFT. Two boatstones. Large slate, excavated, 4" wide. Dallas County. Smaller, red hematite. Autauga County, Alabama (Courtesy, T. L. DeJarnette). SECOND. Hematite plummet, 3" long; grooved for attachment; it may have been used as an ornament or weight. Baldwin County, Alabama (Courtesy, Mrs. J. E. Jones). THIRD. Hematite cone; base 2" diameter; typical Copena artifact and burial association; similar cones were made of galena and steatite. Central Alabama (Courtesy, T. L. DeJarnette). RIGHT. Expanding-center, bar gorget, 4½" long. Originally it probably had only two drilled holes; the third was possibly added by the maker or another Indian at a later time. It is dark red stone—highly polished. Morgan County, Alabama (Courtesy, J. B. Ratliff).

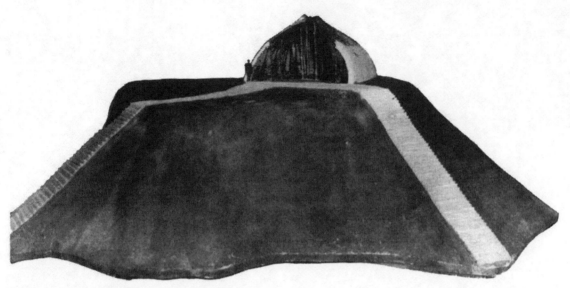

ABOVE. Model of truncated earth mound with public building on top; building construction—"wattle-and-daub," consisting of upright logs placed at intervals along side walls, connected by intertwined branches or canes, and plastered on outside; thatched roof (Courtesy, Alabama Museum of National History).

MISSISSIPPI PERIOD

Plates 7 and 8

BELOW. Skeleton with some 63 burial associations. "At the head was a large conch-shell cup, 9.5" x 4.5"—ceremonially 'killed' by having a large hole drilled through it. On each side of the skull were copper ear disk ornaments with bone pins, stained by copper. These were made by covering circular disks of wood (cedar) with very thin sheet copper; they were embossed with two concentric circles. Under the chin was a string of 958 shell columella beads and another copper ear ornament.

"Over the left arm and side were the following artifacts: one ungrooved greenstone celt, 7" x 2.8"; one dog-effigy pipe of shell-tempered pottery—light gray, 3.5" x 5.5" which had a 'cult' design at the eye—forked eye; one greenstone or amphibole schist spatulate, ceremonial form, 7.8" long x 6.3" maximum diameter, with conical hole, reamed from both sides; one beaver incisor; two perforated bear teeth; eight marine columella shell beads over left hand, largest 1" diameter, were covered by 14 bird sterna, which were cut out and drilled as pendants.

"On the left side and covering the left foot were 10 well-made needle awls, covered by fragments of bird-sternum pendants. The right foot was partially covered with seven bird-sternum pendants and a fragment of weathered hematite. On the right side and covering the right arm were the following: one greenstone celt, 7.3" x 2.4", and as the other celt with this burial, was highly polished and undamaged by use; one finely chipped flint knife, slightly non-symmetrical, 8" x 1.9"; two copper covered wood-disk ear ornaments;

covering the right hand were seven columella shell beads under seven sterna.

"Below the right hand, opposite the right thigh, there was a large marine shell cup, ceremonially 'killed,' and in it 4 needle awls; under the cup was a red sandstone disk, 6.3" diameter and 0.55" thick, flat and smooth on both sides, with 12 crude notches cut on convex margin and a conical hole near the rim, probably for suspension. Between the legs almost on top of left femur, were 8 copper pendants and a small copper pin; the pendants had eye and cross designs. About the pelvic girdle were 75 shell columella beads and a subcubical galena ball, 1.2" diameter, with corners abraded. In this grave was a fragmentary, small pot, 6.5" maximum diameter and 4.25" mouth diameter,

with one strap handle mounted on a collar incised with vertical parallel lines." Lauderdale County, Alabama. Description by Webb and DeJarnette, 1942, BAE Bulletin 129, pp. 219 and 227-228, Pl. 242-2. (Photograph, Courtesy, Alabama Museum of Natural History).

RIGHT. Burial with three shell-tempered pottery vessels in association; one is a long-neck bottle. North Alabama (Courtesy, The National Archives).

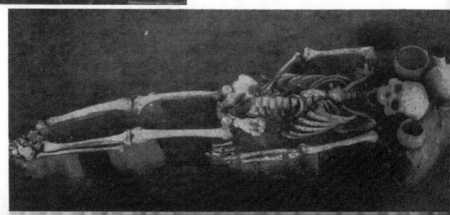

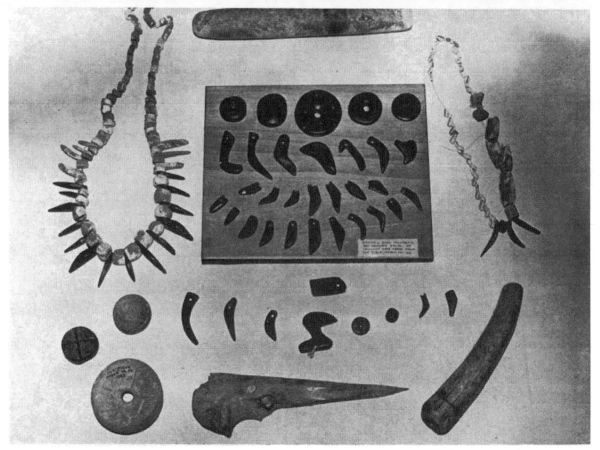

ABOVE. Upper Center. A round limestone ceremonial pick, 10-⅛" long with a discoloration from haft. Right. Necklace of 105 beads—marginella, conch, and three imitation bear teeth made from cannel coal. Center. Cannel coal disks, effigies, and ornaments, most are drilled for suspension and several are engraved. Left. Necklace of conch shell beads and imitation animal teeth made from shell and cannel coal. Lower Left. Discoidals. Center. Bone awl, 9" long. Right. Antler handle. Fort Ancient Culture Aspect. Mason County, Kentucky (Courtesy, Russ Thompson). For a careful illustration of Fort Anicent traits, see J. B. Griffin, 1952, Fig. 35.

BELOW. LEFT. Shell-tempered, dog effigy, painted, long-neck bottle—negative painting, dark brown, almost black paint outlines the design on the light cream pottery base. The dark paint is powdery; much has scaled off and left only a stain. This is a remarkably fine specimen, 9½" high. Sun circles design on side. Davidson County, Tennessee (Courtesy, Vanderbilt University, Thruston collection. All Vanderbilt photographs pictured herein were made by Peggy Wrenne). CENTER and RIGHT. Front and back views of a solid pottery image, 8⅛" high; shell-tempered and painted. It is a very excellent and unusual object. A similar image is found in the collection of the Peabody Museum, Harvard University. The object below is basically light cream pottery. Traces of brown paint remain on left shoulder, back; there are traces of red paint on the back of the head; most of the paint has worn off, and much of the surface is covered with a rough encrustation resulting from burial. The figure appears to be wearing a wide head-band and breechclout; the hair is plaited and ornamented. Holes at the top and bottom of the arms were probably for suspension. It was found in what appeared to be a child's grave. Davidson County, Tennessee (Courtesy, Vanderbilt University).

MISSISSIPPI PERIOD

Plates 9 and 10

LEFT. Mississippi Period Artifacts. Upper to Lower. Left. Inside view of shell-tempered pottery vessel; small greenstone celt or chisel, 3" long; small triangular projectile point and end scraper made from flint nodules; disk shell bead. Second Row. Stone discoidal of cream quartzite; conch shell gorget with equal-arm cross design—this was found under a small shell-tempered vessel at the head of a skeleton. Third Row. Three shell-tempered pottery objects—gaming disk, spindle whorl, and trowel. Right. Row. Shell spoon with carved handle; deer leg bone awl, 5½" long. Limestone County, Alabama (Courtesy, Dr. F. J. Soday).

ABOVE. LEFT. Copper-covered wooden disks; maximum diameter, about 2". The wood has been preserved by the action of copper salts. These were probably parts of ear spools or ceremonial ornaments. Found with a stone slab burial. Marion County, Alabama (Courtesy, Mr. and Mrs. H. R. Steeves, Jr.). RIGHT. Stone disk probably used as a paint palette, 10¼" diameter. Hale County, Alabama (Courtesy, Museum of the American Indian, Heye, Foundation, 17-1474).

RIGHT. Mississippi Period artifacts. Upper Row. Shell pendant; oliva shell; mussel shell spoon; shell gorget with incised world-quarters cross. Second Row. Copper ear spools; bone fishhooks from sections of long bones; limestone discoidal. Lower Row. Shark tooth pendants; shell beads. Lauderdale County, Alabama (Courtesy, Alabama Museum of National History, Museum Paper 25, Figure 15a).

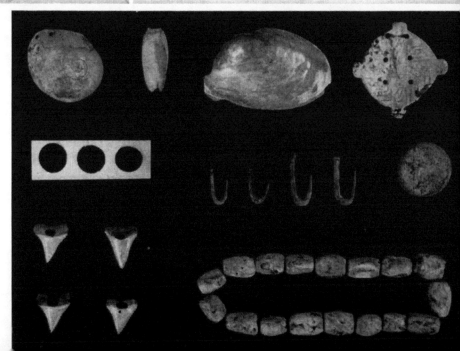

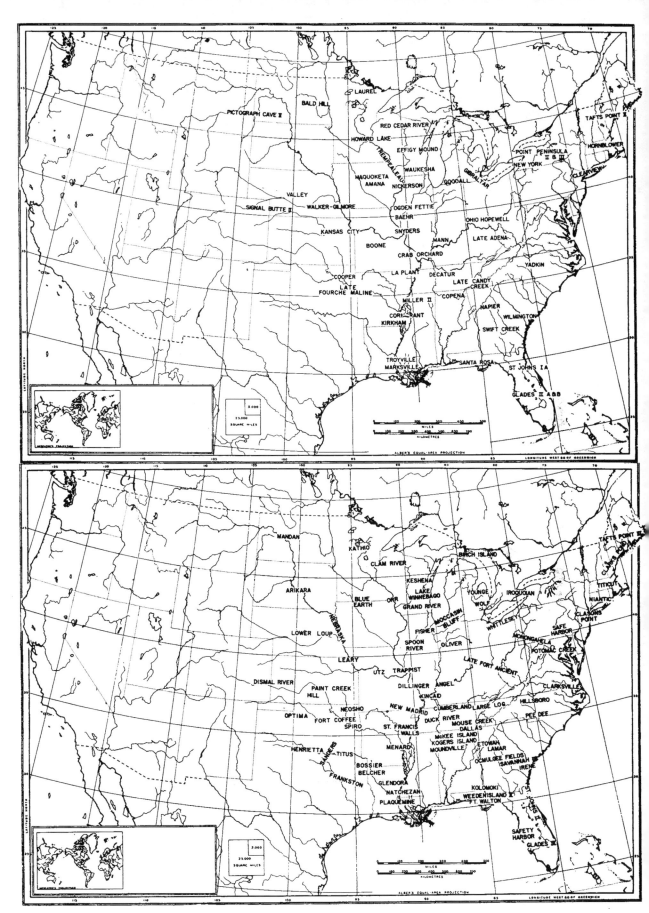

ABOVE. UPPER. "Distribution of sites and culture units during the Middle Woodland (Hopewellian) period." LOWER. "Distribution of sites and culture units during the climax and decline of the Mississippi period. Identified groups on the northern and northeastern periphery still maintained their basic Woodland tradition during this period." Reproduced by permission from John Wiley & Sons, Inc., and the University of Chicago Press. "Hall's Outline Maps and Graphs," published by John Wiley & Sons, Inc., New York; copyright, 1935, by Robert B. Hall. From ARCHEOLOGY IN EASTERN UNITED STATES, edited by James B. Griffin, University of Chicago Press, copyright 1952, Figures 202 and 204. Six similar maps in that publication give the distribution of sites and culture units by periods—Paleo-Indian and Early Archaic; Late Archaic; Early Woodland; Middle Woodland; Early Mississippi; and Middle Mississippi.

BELOW. Watchman in a cornfield, Indian town of Secotan (present North Carolina). Detail from an engraving by De Bry based on a water color by John White, 1587. Picture in the British Museum. (Photograph, courtesy, Smithsonian Institution, BAE, 41-468). "Bartram in describing agriculture in the Creek nation stated, 'While the corn was in the ground the young people, under the supervision of some of their elders, were stationed in the fields, where small shelters were often built for them, and drove away any animals or birds coming to disturb it.' The boys were armed with bows and arrows, and had acquired such skill with these that Bartram says they loaded themselves with squirrels, birds, and other small game in the course of the day. (Bartram, 1791, p. 192). According to the same writer the men took turns patrolling the fields at night, 'to protect their provisions from the depredations of night rovers, as bears, raccoons, and deer, the two former being immoderately fond of young corn, when the grain is filled with a rich milk, as sweet and nourishing as cream and the deer are as fond of the Potatoe vines.' " (Ibid., p. 510; Swanton, 1928, p. 444).

RIGHT. Wife of a Florida chief. After a De Bry engraving after John White. (Courtesy, Smithsonian Institution, BAE, 30-737-B).

HISTORIC PERIOD

Plates 11 and 12

"Du Pratz tells us that the Natchez prepared their fields for planting by means of a curved mattock made of hickory, but shoulder blades of the bison were observed among the neighboring Bayogoula. . . ." (Swanton, 1946, p. 310).

"In the first clearing of their plantations, they only bark the large timber, cut down the saplings and underwood, and burn them in heaps; as the suckers shoot up, they chop them off close to the stump, of which they make fires to deaden the roots, till in time they decay." (James Adair, 1775, 405-406).

BELOW. "Mode of tilling and planting." From an engraving by De Bry, after a drawing by Le Moyne, who visited Florida in 1564-65. Timucua Tribe, (BAE, 1186-B-1). "For Timucua agricultural methods, we have two parallel narratives, . . . Rene de Laudonniere: 'They sow their maize twice a year — to wit in March and in June—and all in one and the same soil. The said maize, from the time that it is sowed until the time that it be ready to be gathered, is but three months on the ground; . . . when they sow they set weeds on fire . . . and burn them all. They dig their ground with an instrument of wood, which is fashioned like a broad mattock . . . . they put two grains of maize together . . . . At the time when the maize is gathered, it is all carried into a common house, where it is distributed to every man, according to his quality. They sow no more but that which they think will serve their turn for six months . . . . (Laudonniere, 1856, pp. 11-12; Swanton, 1922, p. 359). Le Moyne: 'The Indians cultivate the earth diligently; and the men know how to make a kind of hoe from fish bones, which they fit to wooden handles, and with these they prepare the land well enough, as the soil is light. When the ground is sufficiently broken up and levelled, the women come with beans and millet, or maize. Some go first with a stick, and make holes, in which the others place the beans, or grains of maize. After planting they leave the fields alone, as the winter in that country . . . is pretty cold for about three months . . . ; and during that time, as they go naked, they shelter themselves in the woods. When the winter is over, they return to their homes to wait for the crops to ripen. After gathering in their harvest, they store the whole of it for the year's use, not employing any part of it in trade, unless, perhaps some barter is made for some little household article.' " (Le Moyne, 1875, p. 9, illus.; Swanton, 1922, p. 359 and 1946, pp. 308-390). Agriculture provided a relatively secure livelihood and leisure time for craftsmanship.

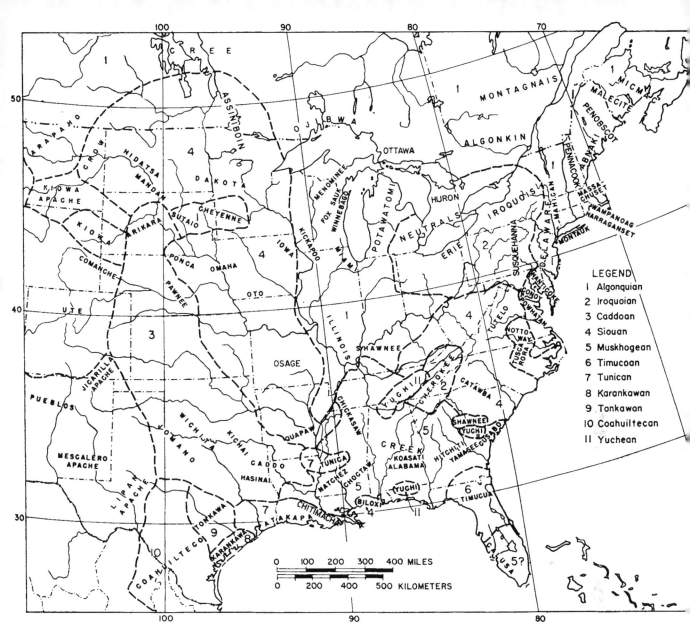

ABOVE. "Tribes and linguistic stocks in the eastern United States ca A. D. 1700 (after Swanton)." This map is Figure 10 in ARCH-EOLOGY OF EASTERN UNITED STATES, edited by James B. Griffin, published by the University of Chicago Press, Chicago, 1952. It is reproduced here by permission from the University of Chicago Press; copyright 1952, The University of Chicago.

In THE INDIANS OF THE SOUTHEASTERN UNITED STATES, John R. Swanton (1946, pp. 11-21) discusses the Indian population of the Southeast. In the summary he refers to Mooney's (1928) estimates of Indian population which he gives as follows:

Muskhogean (incl. Natchez and Taensa)	66,600	Caddo	8,500
Iroquoian	30,200	Tunican (Tunica 2,000; Chitimacha 4,000)	6,000
Siouan	24,000	South Florida tribes	4,000
Algonquian	16,500	Uchean	3,100
Timucua	13,000		

"Dividing the population between the coast and the interior, we get the following results, a proportion of about 4½ to 1. Interior, 141,500. Coast, 30,400.

"I believe it to be rather too high than too low for the years to which it is supposed to apply, 1600-1650. At an earlier period, however, there are evidences of a great expansion of population. My own independent estimates for part of the region yield substantially the same results as Mooney reached except that I should be inclined to reduce the figures for the Creeks and Chickasaw somewhat. The figures for Florida I should also be inclined to scale down and most of those for the Siouan tribes of the east. Nevertheless, the relative strength of the tribes enumerated, I think, would be altered little if we had absolutely trustworthy figures, and those we have will give us a very good idea of the distribution of population."

On Map 3 Swanton (1946) gives his population estimates of various tribes:

Cherokee (Iroquoian)	22,000	Chickasaw (Muskhogean)	5,000	Quapaw (Siouan)	2,500
Choctaw (Muskhogean)	15,000	Catawba (Siouan)	5,000	Yuchi	2,000
Creeks (Muskhogean)	12,000	Natchez (Muskhogean)	4,000	Yamasee	2,000
Timucua	10,000	Calusa	3,000	Gaule	2,000
Powhatan (Algonquian)	9,000	Chitimacha	2,700	Cusabo	1,200

Wars, land cessions, and migrations caused continual shifting of tribal relationships, areas, and population during the Colonial Period. For further information on this subject see: Swanton (1911, 1922, 1942, 1946, and 1953); Mooney (1928); Bushnell (1922); Griffin (1952). Each of these sources has a bibliography of other sources.

ABOVE. UPPER. Reproduction of a Creek Council House and Square of the historic period. Diorama (Courtesy, Peaboby Museum, Harvard University, 98193). LOWER. Diorama showing two of the four beds or arbors of a Creek Square; it depicts the new fire ceremony (Courtesy, National Park Service, Ocmulgee National Monument). BELOW. LEFT. Arrangements of a Creek Square showing the four arbors with benches in front and the hothouse located to the side; the ball ground was also located near the "Big House." (After Hewitt, 1939, Fig. 13).

Swanton states, "there were four arbors or beds, usually laid out toward the four points of the compass. The names given to these beds vary. Sometimes one name was applied to the entire bed, sometimes to a section, while the names themselves were somewhat different in the different towns. Nevertheless in each town there was usually a bed upon which the term chiefs' bed (mikalgi or mikagi intupa) may properly be bestowed, one which may be called the warriors' bed (tastanagalgi intupa), and one the boys' bed (tcibanagalgi), the last for youths busking for the first time and sometimes, at a later period, allowed to women and children except during the fast. The fourth bed is ofen called the 'peace bed,' or the henihas' bed (henihalgi intupa) and was known to the traders as the 'second man's' cabin. The henihalgi always acted as companions, seconds, or lieutenants of the chiefs, and during the busk each principal official must be accompanied by a heniha. . . ." (p. 191-192).

"The characteristic positions for these beds were, west for that of the chiefs, north for that of the warriors, south for the henihas, and east for the youths. However, the warriors' bed was often south or east, the henihas' east or north, and the youths' south. When the chiefs' bed was shifted out of the west it was almost always to the north. There is practically no native explanation for the different positions which the beds occupy in different towns." (p. 200).

" . . . . when the chief was selected from a certain clan that clan moved over in a body into the Chief's bed. . . . Turning to the nine first clans, which are representative of the leading Creek phratries (wind, bear, bird, beaver, alligator, deer, panther, raccoon, Aktayatci), we find that the White clans are found oftenest in the Chief's bed, and next in frequency in the bed of the Henihas, while comparatively seldom are they seated in the beds of the Warriors or Youths. It is to be observed that both the Chiefs' bed and that of the Henihas are frequently spoken of as 'White beds,' but the former is occupied by White clans more often than the latter. The Warriors' bed, too does not appear to have been occupied anciently by clans as such, except perhaps in the rear rows. In front were the tastanagalgi and imalalgi, who originally owed their positions to exploits in war and were drawn from various clans. (Swanton, 1928, p. 237).

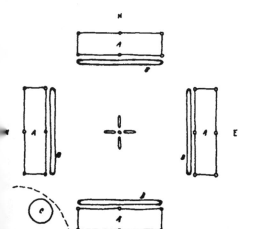

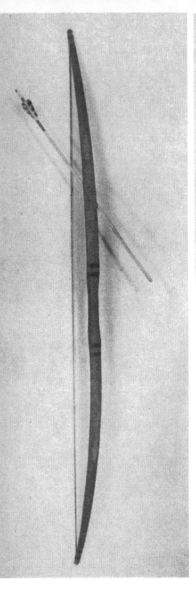

ABOVE. Powder horn; 16½" maximum length; 3¼" maximum diameter. Powder ladle or scoop, above horn is 3-5/16" long. The figures were carefully cut into this horn in thin outline, and the lines appear to have been filled with pine tar or pitch. The thirty two figures of the total design carved around the entire surface are shown below. They include such typical Indian designs as the snake, fish, turkey, crane, other birds, and deer. They also include new designs, as the log cabin, pig, horse, soldier, and peacock. This horn is carefully made, and was doubtless finished with wooden and metal parts in a gun shop with a lathe. The designs appear to be free-hand and applied to the horn before the wooden and metal parts were added. There is a stationary wooden bottom in the large end, and a wooden screw in the small end. It is from southwestern Alabama and thought by the owner to have been Choctaw (Courtesy, L. P. Goodwin).

HISTORIC PERIOD

Plates 13 and 14

ABOVE. Bow and arrow made by the late Chief Standingdeer, Cherokee, North Carolina. He described the manufacture of his bows and arrows: "I split up a maple log about 36" long, and the pieces must be about ½" in diameter. After it is worked down with a block plane, I round the arrow shaft and then use sandpaper with plenty of elbow grease, which makes it round. I feather the arrows by using water proof glue to make them stick." The bow above is made of osage wood or mock orange and is 66" long with painted symbols on it. The arrow is 26" long, and is sharpened wood, though metal was often used on the tip (Courtesy, Mrs. Gertrude Ruskin; photograph by Satterwhite). Bowwood, flint, and cane were frequent items of native trade. Though guns rapidly replaced bows and arrows, the latter continued in use even into the 19th century. The bow and arrow was used by hostile natives in the Creek war of 1813-1814.

Chapter 2

NATIVE TRADE

Quotation from William E. Myer, "Indian Trails of the Southeast," FORTY-SECOND ANNUAL REPORT, BUREAU OF AMERICAN ETHNOLOGY, 1924-1925, pp. 735-746. Quoted courtesy Smithsonian Institution, Bureau of American Ethnology.

"More or less well-established trails made by wild animals in search of food or drink existed upon the earth for long ages before the appearance of man, changing very slowly as local conditions were altered by erosion, climatic shifts, or other causes. Man found the lands already covered with them and began using them because they led him to water and to salt licks and other places where the primal necessities — water, food, and materials for clothing — could be obtained. Later they became media of friendly or hostile communication between the people themselves.

"There was far more travel among the Indians than is usually supposed. This was sometimes for barter-commerce, sometimes for visits of a social, friendly, or religious character, and sometimes for war or adventure.

"There are well-authenticated cases of Indians having gone on visits to a series of distant friendly tribes, covering from 1,000 to 2,000 miles, and being absent from home for two months or more. A friendly visitor with a new sacred or social dance was always welcome in any Indian village, and great pains were taken to learn it.

"In times of war or when on special missions they went much farther. For example, Tecumseh, or his agents, covered the entire country from the Seminole of Florida to the tribes on the headwaters of the Missouri River. 'The Iroquois of central New York were familiar with the country as far west as the Black Hills of Dakota, whence they returned with prisoners; the same Indians went from New York to South Carolina to attack the Catawba and into Florida against the Creeks . . . .'[1]   . . .

"Gabriel Arthur, who was captured by some Indians of upper East Tennessee, probably somewhere on the French Broad River, claimed to have accompanied them in a raid on the Spaniards in Florida. After their return and a short rest they raided an Indian town near the present site of Port Royal, S. C., and after another short rest they went on a visit to a friendly tribe on the Great Kanawha, about a day's march from the place where it empties into the Ohio. When they started on their return trip they could not resist the temptation to go out of their way to attack a Shawnee village near the present site of Portsmouth, Ohio. Thus, from December, 1673, to May, 1674, or a little over five months, they went from the French Broad to Florida, a distance of about 450 miles; from the French Broad to Port Royal, a distance of about 350 miles; and from the French Broad to Portsmouth, Ohio, a distance of about 200 miles. They also made a long hunting trip of about 200 miles by canoe during this period. Nothing in the story of these forays indicates that the Indians regard them as extraordinary.

"Less conspicuous historically, but probably of greater importance in the long run were trading expeditions. In prehistoric America, as now, each section produced some desirable products which the others did not have. In the Mounds of Ohio, Tennessee, and elsewhere objects from the Atlantic, the Gulf of Mexico, and the Pacific, and from nearly every section of the interior of the United States have been found obsidian from the Rocky Mountain region, pipestone from the great red pipestone quarries of Minnesota or Wisconsin, steatite and mica from the Appalachians, copper from the region of the Great Lakes and elsewhere, shells from the Gulf of Mexico and the Atlantic, dentalium and abalone shells from the Pacific coast, and now and then artifacts which at least hint at some remote contact with Mexican Indian Culture.

---

[1] Hodge, 1912, Part 2, p. 800.

"The Cherokee region of the Appalachians yielded steatite admirably suited to the manufacture of fine pipes. There are many authentic records of Cherokee carrying quantities of pipes to distant regions for sale or barter, and these are found at many points in the middle southern United States.   . . .

"Before the Indians obtained horses from the Spaniards the prehistoric trader, when traveling by land, was forced to carry his stock in trade on his back, a laborious process which necessarily limited the amount. Some tribes, notably the Plains Indians, used the dog as a pack animal and also worked him to the travois, and elsewhere he was worked to sleds; but the Indians of the Southeast do not appear to have used the dog for any of these purposes.   . . .

"It was the wide commercial-barter travels which gave the Iroquois their close acquaintance with the northern central United States; and when they received firearms from the Dutch about 1620 they quickly conquered a large portion of what had once been their commercial territory, extending from the Great Lakes to northern Tennessee on the south, and to the Mississippi River on the west. As we have seen, some of their war parties reached the Black Hills of South Dakota.   . . .

"Lawson relates the following in regard to barter-commerce in the Carolinas:

'The women make baskets and mats to lie upon, and those that are not extraordinary hunters, make bowls, dishes, and spoons, of gumwood, and the tulip tree; others, where they find a vein of white clay, fit for their purpose, make tobacco-pipes, all which are often transported to other Indians, that perhaps have greater plenty of deer and other game.'[2]

"Cabeza de Vaca, in relating his experiences as a barter trader among the Indians along the Gulf coast about 1535, doubtless gives a reasonably accurate picture of the life of native Indian merchants in that region. He was practically a prisoner, defenseless and without European articles of barter, and had only such objects as any Indian trader might have carried. He says:[3]

'I was obliged to remain with the people belonging to the island more than a year, and because of the hard work they put upon me and the harsh treatment, I resolved to flee from them and go to those of Charruco, who inhabit the forests and country of the main, the life I led being insupportable. Besides much other labor, I had to get out roots from below the water, and from among the cane where they grew in the ground. From this employment I had my fingers so worn that did a straw but touch them they would bleed. Many of the canes are broken, so that they often tore my flesh, and I had to go in the midst of them with only the clothing on I have mentioned.

'Accordingly, I put myself to contriving how I might get over to the other Indians, among whom matters turned somewhat more favorably for me. I set to trafficking, and strove to make my employment profitable in the ways I could best contrive and by that means I got food and good treatment. The Indians would beg me to go from one quarter to another for things of which they have need; for in consequence of incessant hostilities, they cannot traverse the country, nor make many exchanges. With my merchandise and trade I went into the interior as far as I pleased, and travelled along the coast forty or fifty leagues. The principal wares were cones and other pieces of sea-snail, conchs used for cutting, and fruit like a bean of the highest value among them, which they used as a medicine and employ in their dances and festivities. Among other matters were sea-beads. Such were what I carried into the interior; and in barter I got and brought back skins, ochre with which they rub and color the face, hard canes of which to make arrows, sinews, cement and flint for the heads, and tassels of the hair of deer that by dyeing they made red. This occupation suited me well; for the travel allowed me liberty to go where I wished, I was not obliged to work, and was not a slave. Wherever I went I received fair treatment, and the Indians gave me to eat out of regard to my commodities. My leading object, while journeying in this business, was to find out the way by which I should go forward, and I became well known. The inhabitants were pleased when they saw me, and I had brought them what they wanted; and those who did not know me sought and desired the acquaintance, for my reputation . . . .'   . . .

"Farther on he thus refers to barter in bows:[4]

'These people speak a different language, and are called Avavares. They are the same that carried bows to those with whom we formerly lived, going to traffic with them, and although they are of a different nation and tongue, they understand the other language.'

"And still farther on he says:[5]

'I bartered with these Indians in combs that I made for them and in bows, arrows, and nets. We made mats, which are their houses, that they have great necessity for; and although they know how to make them, they wish to give their full time to getting food, since when otherwise employed they are pinched with hunger. Sometimes the Indians would set me to scraping and softening skins; and the days of my greatest prosperity there, were those in which they gave me skins to dress. I would scrape them a very great deal and eat the scraps which would sustain me two or three days. When it happened among these people, as it had likewise among others whom we left behind, that a piece of meat was given us, we ate it raw; for if we had put it to roast, the first native that should come along would have taken it off and devoured it; and it appeared to us not well to expose it to this risk; besides we were in such condition it would have given us pain to eat it roasted, and we could not have digested it so well as raw. Such was the life we spent there; and the meagre subsistence we earned by the matters of traffic which were the work of our hands.'   . . .

"Some authorities seem to believe that those engaged in barter-commerce were given free passage among the tribes, possibly even in times of war.[6] We can find no authentic instance of immunity granted to Indians engaged in commerce who belonged to a hostile tribe, unless from considerations having no relation to their occupation.   . . .

[2] Lawson, 1714, p. 338. [3] The quotation from Cabeza de Vaca is quoted by permission from Barnes and Nobles, Inc., and is from their "Original Narrative Series," SPANISH EXPLORERS IN THE SOUTHERN UNITED STATES, 1528-1543, edited by F. W. Hodge and T. H. Lewis; Hodge edited the narrative by Cabeza de Vaca. Copyright 1907, New York. [4] Ibid., p. 73. [5] Ibid., pp. 81, 82.
[6] Jones, C. C., 1873, pp. 243-244; Mason, O. T. in Hodge, 1912, Pt. 1, p. 332.

" . . . we read that De Soto found natives around the saline springs making salt which they carried elsewhere to exchange for skins and shawls. [7] There are many accounts of a similiar aboriginal barter in salt in many portions of the United States. The salt springs and licks were highly valued and much resorted to.   . . .

"Hundreds of . . . references to the joint use of trails by man and beast are scattered throughout the records of the early settlers. [8] It is well known that the Murfreesboro and Franklin Turnpike now leading into Nashville followed substantially the animal trails to the salt licks in Sulphur Spring Bottom at Nashville, the old French Lick. Haywood [9] says:

'The land adjacent to the French Lick, which Mr. Mansco in 1769 called an old field, was a large, open piece frequented and trodden by buffalos, whose large paths led to it from all parts of the country, and there concentrated.'   . . .

"In considering the ancient Indian trails we should bear in mind the life, habits and surroundings of the Indian. These trails followed the lines of least resistance; they avoided rough, stony ground, briars, and close undergrowth such as is formed by laurel. This was to prevent undue wear on clothing or footgear and to save time.

"In the wooded or mountainous regions of the central southern United States the Indians were forced to go in single file, and the paths were usually from 18 to 24 inches in width. On the open, grassy prairies of the Middle West, however, where there were no special obstacles, they proceeded en masse in such formation as suited their pleasure, and thus often made wide trails.

"In the mountains, trails often led along the higher grounds and ridges where the undergrowth was not so dense and there were fewer and smaller streams to cross. There, too, the road rose and fell less and the outlook for game and for enemies was wider. Where possible, trails passed through the lower gaps in the mountain ranges.   . . .

"Over much of the southeast water routes existed alongside of land trails, sometimes supplementing them, sometimes paralleling them, sometimes practically excluding them. The Mississippi River and its branches, the Pascagoula, the Mobile, including the Tombigbee and Alabama, the Apalachicola, the Altamaha, Savannah, Santee, and many minor streams were all utilized, as were the coasts of the Gulf of Mexico and the Atlantic Ocean, especially where there were series of lagoons protected by outside islands or bars, as along the northwest and east coasts of Florida and the coast of Georgia. On some of the more rapid interior streams water transportation was only in one direction, in which case canoes of elm or cypress bark, or even of hickory and other trees, or buffalo skins over a wooden framework, often took the place of the more substantial but heavier dugouts elsewhere universal." [10]

WOODLAND TRADE

Quotation from James B. Griffin, "Culture Periods in Eastern United States Archeology," ARCHEOLOGY OF EASTERN UNITED STATES, Edited by James B. Griffin, University of Chicago Press, 1952, pp. 360-361. Quoted by permission from the University of Chicago Press. Copyright 1952 by the University of Chicago.

"Wide-flung trade or cultural connections of the Hopewellian people, particularly in the Ohio area indicates a considerable knowledge of the entire area east of the Rocky Mountains. There was fairly extensive contact with the far southeast and probably the Florida area, for it was from this general region that most of the large, marine busycon and cassis shells have come. The cassis shell is almost a time marker in the Hopewellian horizon. Its live range is from Cape Hatteras down the east coast of the United States and on into the West Indies. It is not found on the Gulf Coast of Florida. It is reasonable to suppose that the barracuda jaws, the shell of the sea tortoise, spade fish, and live shark's teeth were derived from the cultural connection into the northern and northwestern Florida area. Santa Rosa-Swift Creek probably received the copper earspools, copper breastplates, the copper so-called pan pipes, the idea of utilization of platform pipes, stone imitation carnivore teeth from the Ohio center. Also in this same general direction of course were the mica mines of Virginia and North Carolina which were so extensively worked by peoples on a primitive level with probably

[7] Hodge and Lewis, Op. Cit., p. 218. [8] "Of the Big Bone Lick, in Boone County, Ky., and its ancient salt-making trails, Mr. J. Stoddard Johnston discusses as follows: 'Salt was manufactured at Big Bone Lick by the Indians before 1756, and by the whites as late as 1812. It required five or six hundred gallons of water to make a bushel of salt.' (Johnston, First Explorations of Kentucky in Journals of Walker and Gist, p. 47.)"

[9] Haywood, 1823, p. 108. [10] Myer describes in detail 125 native trails in the Southeastern United States. Excerpts from the general introduction only are included herein.

most of the utilization of this mineral being made in the Hopewellian culture. Another time marker for this period was the extensive utilization of obsidian, particularly in Ohio Hopewell, and this is a very distinctive time marker. Obsidian also appears in some ten or twelve Illinois Valley Hopewell sites, although mostly in the form of flakes. It is not known where the source was for this material, whether in the northern Rockies, the southern Rockies in eastern Arziona and New Mexico, or in Middle America. Obsidian has not been found in the southeast, the lower Mississippi Valley, or the Caddoan area. The grizzly bear teeth were also extensively utilized by the Hopewell peoples and even ivory is reported. Additional examples of the connection between Ohio Hopewell and the southeast are the presence of simple stamp, check stamp, and complicated stamp impressions on a small percent of the pottery. There are also such vessel shapes as that called the T-shaped lip and the vertical compound vessels which connect Ohio Hopewell into the Florida area.

"These extensive trade relations are sometimes spoken of as though they were conducted on a rather drab economic level, whereas it would appear that the primary purpose for the acquisition of these materials was for their ceremonial utilization by the living people, and then placement with the honored dead in their large and complicated burial tumuli. There would seem to have been a religious motivation for their acquisition, for certainly the majority of the specimens had practically no utilitarian importance or significance. It was not acquisition of materials for exchange in order to build wealth for handing down to one's descendants, but rather the accumulation of such items perhaps for prestige value which would be accorded to those who were dead and to those close relatives who were still living. It has been suggested many times that these trade connections seem to indicate trips of individuals into the far southeast, or into the Plains, or into the northern Mississippi Valley and Lake Superior area, and that they were on regular, definite missions to obtain these raw materials. It may have been because of the common cultural foundation which existed through the Hopewellian period that such individuals were welcomed in foreign tribal groups while on such a mission to obtain these raw materials and it is likely that these travelers would take along with them some of the finished products from the Ohio area associated with the ceremonial complexes which were dominant at the time."

MISSISSIPPI TRADE

During the Mississippi Culture Period, the list of native trade items found at habitation sites of the Southeast was approximately the same as that for the Woodland Period.[11] However, the quantities of the materials were far greater, and the articles into which they were fabricated were more specialized, varied and intricate in design. In addition to other items listed, galena or lead ore was also traded in the Woodland and Mississippi Periods. It is thought to have originated in the Joplin, Missouri, district. Though pottery is difficult to transport, it nevertheless was exchanged in limited quantities during both the Woodland and Mississippi Periods. Gordon R. Willey in ARCHEOLOGY OF THE FLORIDA GULF COAST, records many examples of trade or exchange of pottery among sites in the Gulf Coast and near area. Moundville-type sherds have been found at a number of Southeastern sites, and as far away as Kincaid, Illinois.[12] In some instances the presence of isolated pottery sherds of an "outside culture" at a particular site, may have resulted from the exchange of ideas rather than actual pottery vessels; however, there are many definite proofs of the exchange of vessels during the Woodland and Mississippi Periods.

The following quotations regarding Late Mississippi or Historic Period trade refer not only to traffic in durable-type objects, but also to exchange of many perishable-type articles, some of which were doubtless traded in prehistoric times.

HISTORIC TRADE

Quotation from John R. Swanton, THE INDIANS OF THE SOUTH-EASTERN UNITED STATES, Bureau of American Ethnology, Bulletin 137, 1946, pp. 736-742 (Quoted courtesy Smithsonian Institution, Bureau of American Ethnology).

"Du Pratz speaks of a Yazoo who asserted he had been as far west as the shores of the Pacific, [13] some

[11] Archeological publications are full of references to exotic material found at native sites throughout the Southeast. Ford and Webb (`95.) discuss many native trade goods found at Poverty Point, Louisiana. Ford and Willey (1940, p. 131) report trade materials at the Woodland Period Crooks site, Louisiana; these included conch shells, copper, galena, quartz crystal, pumice, and volcanic tuff. Shetrone and Greenman (1931, p. 423) report pipes of southern origin in the fill of one of the Seip mounds, Ohio. Setzler (1940, pp. 260, 263-264) refers to a variety of Southeastern trade goods found at mound, village, and burial sites in the Northern Mississippi Valley. Many archeological publications have recorded evidence of the general and widespread native trade beginning as early as the Late Archaic Period and increasing in the Woodland and Mississippi Periods. [12] Cole, Fay-Cooper and others, 1951, p. 354. [13] Le Page du Pratz, 1758, Vol. 3, pp. 89-128.

Chickasaw are said to have reached Mexico, and we know that they constantly crossed the Mississippi to make war on the Caddo. General Milfort claims to have taken a band of Creeks far up Red River to a place where they believed their ancestors formerly lived,[14] but in his time the western emigration of the southern Indians due to the pressure of the whites and the attractiveness of western hunting fields had already begun. In late colonial times there appears to have been a Chickasaw settlement in Pennsylvania, and in the early part of the eighteenth century the Iroquois on one side and the Cherokee and Siouan Indians on the other maintained a bitter war. Most of this, however, was at a relatively late period.

"Trade is determined to a considerable extent by the distribution of raw materials which have a demand value at a given place and time . . . . we have noted two general drifts of trade, from the coast inland and vice versa, and between the mountains or uplands and the plains, of which the intercourse between the tribes of the lower Mississippi and the Caddo may be regarded as a special case.

"Cabeza de Vaca gives some interesting information relative to the trade carried on by coast and interior peoples of Texas between the Brazos and Guadalupe Rivers, a trade in which he himself took part.[15] In the territory now embraced in the State of Louisiana there was regular traffic between the Chitimacha and Atakapa Indians and the Avoyel, the Opelousa tribe acting as middlemen. The last named obtained fish from the Chitimacha and Atakapa, which they exchanged with the Avoyel for flints. Although it is said that flint was abundant in the Avoyel country, it seems probable that they got much of it still farther inland, at the novaculite quarries about Hot Springs, Arkansas. Some of the flints which the Atakapa obtained in this manner were passed on to the Karankawa, and the Karankawa supplied them with globular or conical oil jugs. It is also said, though this may apply to a later period, that the Atakapa carried moss and dried smoked fish to Galveston Island. It would hardly seem as though the last-mentioned article would be in demand with a people such as the Karankawa, themselves coastal. The Atakapa are also said to have gotten most of their pots either from the Karankawa, as just mentioned, or from the inland tribes, and they probably obtained skins from the inland tribes as well. To the latter they gave in exchange sharks' teeth, 'marine curios,' dried or smoked fish, and feathers of birds.[16] We may suspect that they got this pottery not only from the Avoyel but from the Caddo tribes, who were noted pottery makers, but it may have come from sources as distant as the Quapaw, who are said to have traded in pots.[17] The Chitimacha claim that they formerly got stone beads as well as arrow points from the inland tribes.[18] We may suspect that the coast Indians also got bowwood from the Caddo in the same way, since tribes came to the Caddo from long distances to secure it.[19] There are records that the Tewa obtained bows from this section through the medium of the Comanche.[20] The Quapaw exchanged earthen vessels, canoes, and wooden platters with the Caddo for bows and arrows and for salt.[21] When De Soto was at Pacaha in 1541, 'he met with eight Indian merchants who traded (salt) through the provinces' and said that it was to be found in the mountains 40 leagues from Pacaha. Some of the Spaniards set out with them to purchase salt, and to get specimens of a yellow metal which they supposed to be gold but actually proved to be copper, and the Pacaha chief supplied them with pearls, deerskins, and beans with which to make the trade. They returned in 11 days with six loads of 'fossil salt' and some copper.[22] Later on they themselves found salt in the provinces of Colima and Cayas. These places were in what is now Arkansas, but other salt provinces, Chaguete and Aguacay, were evidently in Louisiana.[23] When the French entered the country, trade in salt was still active but most salt seems to have been extracted in northern Louisiana. The Tunica Indians are particularly mentioned in connection with it, but the Koroa, Washita, and Natchitoches were also concerned in it, and the Cahinnio were active as middle men. The principal outlets on the Mississippi appear to have been the Taensa and Quapaw towns.[24] Smaller centers of trade were the town of the Namidish and the Chitimacha country. The Natchez are said to have obtained pearls for their Sun caste from the upper course of Pearl River.[25] Still farther east, on the lower Tombigbee, we find the Tohome tribe exploiting a small salt lick.[26] Some of this salt may have found its way to the Mississippi, since it appears from an early French narrative that the Yazoo sometimes went as far as the River of Mobile for shells.   . . .

"Although, as already noted, the inhabitants of Florida obtained much of their flint without going outside

[14] Milfort, 1802, pp. 86-111. [15] Cabeza de Vaca, Bandelier ed., 1905, pp. 74-75.
[16] Dyer, 1917, pp. 6-7. [17] Margry, 1875-86, pp. 412, 424, 442-443. [18] Swanton, 1911, pp. 345-347. [19] Margry, 1875-86, vol. 3, p. 412.
[20] Robbins, W. W., J. P. Harrington, and others, 1916, p. 68. [21] Margry, 1875-86, vol. 3, pp. 442-443. [22] Garcilaso, 1723, pp. 187-188.
[23] Garcilaso, 1723, p. 189; Bourne, 1904, vol. 2, pp. 147-148; Robertson, 1933, pp. 192-193, 237-238.
[24] Margry, 1875-1886, vol. 3, pp. 442-443; vol. 4, pp. 432, 435; Cox, 1905, vol. 1, p. 45. [25] Hennepin, 1698, p. 177; Jones, C. C., 1873,
p. 470. [26] See De Crenay map in Swanton, 1922, Pl. 5.

the peninsula, the early French and Spanish narratives give evidence that stone for various purposes was obtained from Flint River and in the Appalachian Mountains, and that copper was imported from the latter country. [27] When De Soto was in the Apalachee country, Garcilaso tells us that a youth was brought to him who had traveled far inland in Florida, meaning the North American continent in general, with traders.   He said that they obtained at Cofitachequi a yellow metal, evidently copper, which they carried long distances in trade. In southern Florida we are told that the natives traded in fruit and the kunti flour obtained from a Zamia. Later they bartered 'skins, mocking birds, and pet squirrels' at Havana for guns, ammunition, and clothing. [28] About 1774 Bartram tells us the coast Indians of Florida would give two or three buckskins for a single root of Angelica. [29] And Catesby says regarding the Ilex Vomitoria:

'This medicinal shrub, so universally esteem'd by the Indians of North America, is produced but in a small part of the continent, confined by northern and western limits, Viz. North to lat. 37, and west to the distance of about fifty miles from the ocean: yet the Indian inhabitants of the north and west are supplied with it by the maritime Indians in exchange for other commodities. By the sour faces the Indians make in drinking this salubrious liquor, it seems as little agreeable to an Indian as to an European palate, and consequently that the pains and expences they are at in procuring it from remote distances, does not proceed from luxury (as tea with us from China) but from its virtue, and the benefit they receive by it.'[30]

"According to the same writer Indians as far away as Canada were supplied with bills taken from the ivory-billed woodpecker.[31]

"As we pass northeast along the Atlantic coast, we seem to discover more evidence of trade. It is several times intimated that Cofitachequi was a considerable mart, and this was in the neighborhood of Augusta, Georgia. About 60 years after the time of De Soto, the Spanish explorer Ecija reports that Indians were in the habit of descending the Santee River with cloaks 'and many other things' and also copper and 'plata blanca,' probably mica, which they exchanged with the coast Indians for fish and salt.[32]   . . .

"In the region about Chesapeake Bay, the sounds of North Carolina, and among the Tuscarora and the Siouan tribes in their vicinity, references to native trade become more numerous. Lederer speaks of Katearas, chief residence of the Tuscarora head chief, 'as a place of . . . Indian trade . . . .'[33] . . . Farther on he met some Cheraw Indians who had gone to trade with the Ushery (probably the Catawba). As media of exchange he mentions 'small shells . . . roanoack or peack,' and also pearls, vermilion, and pieces of crystal. . . . The peack or peak had been introduced into the South from New Netherlands and New England, but the roanoke was a truly local and oboriginal medium of exchange and was used for all purposes, as Lawson states at considerable length.[34] . . . The Powhatan Indians brought corn in baskets to sell to the Virginian colonists.[35]

"As is common the world over, feasts and ceremonies were made occasion for trading. 'They meet,' says Lawson, 'from all the towns within fifty or sixty miles round, where they buy and sell several commodities, as we do at fairs and markets.[36]

"Marginella shells were also obtained in the Sound country to trade with the interior Indians, and the effects of this trade are noted when archeologists lay open mounds and burials along the Mississippi and Ohio Rivers.

"From beyond the limits of this area catlinite pipes were obtained as already noted, along with much of their copper. In later times, gold and silver were picked up on the Florida coast from wrecked Spanish treasure ships, and the Choctaw got silver by raiding the Caddo Indians after they had taken it from the Spaniards. By this Red River route the famous Chickasaw horses were also brought into the country.[37] But trade across the southern Plains had been established before white contact, for De Soto's party found blue stones, evidently turquoises, and shawls in a province called Guasco west of the Mississippi, and the trade in Caddo bows seems to have extended to the Pueblo country in prehistoric times.[38] A European product much more serious for the Indians was rum, which also was distributed in part through native channels.

"The following interesting view of the changes introduced by white contact is given by Catesby:

'Before the introduction of fire-arms amongst the American Indians, (though hunting was their principal employment) they made no other use of the skins of deer, and other beasts, than to cloath themselves, their carcasses for food, probably, then being of as much value to them as the skins; but as they now barter the skins to the Europeans, for other cloathing and utensils they were before unacquainted with, so the use of guns has enabled them to slaughter for greater number of deer and other animals than they did with their primitive bows and arrows. This destruction of deer and other animals being chiefly for the sake of their skins, a small part of the venison they kill suffices them; the remainder is left to rot; or becomes a prey to the wolves, panthers, and other voracious beasts. With these skins they purchase of the English, guns, powder, and shot, woollen cloth, hatchets, kettles, porridge-pots, knives, vermilion, beads, rum, etc.' "[39]

[27] Le Moyne, 1875, p. 7; Fontaneda, 1854, p. 20. [28] Garcilaso, 1723, p. 104; Swanton, 1922, p. 344. [29] Bartram, 1792, p. 325; 1909, pp. 46-47. [30] Catesby, 1731-43, vol. 2, p. XV. [31] Ibid. [32] Lowery ms. [33] Alvord, 1912, p. 225. [34] Lawson, 1860, pp. 314-317. [35] Smith, John, Arber ed., 1884, p. civ. [36] Lawson, 1860, p. 288. [37] Swanton 1946, p. 348. [38] Robertson, 1933, p. 256. Caddo trade is discussed in Swanton, 1942, pp. 192-203. [39] Catesby, 1731-43, vol. 2, pp. XI-XII. For more about trade see Swanton, 1946.

ABOVE. Cache of projectile points found with a burial in a truncated mound; longest is about 1-1/16''; two appear to be made of obsidian. Elmore County, Alabama. The turtle in the center is about 1-⅝'' long. Montgomery County, Alabama. All of these were probably products of native trade (Courtesy, Wiley Hill, III). Flint, chert, quartz, novaculite, and similar materials were frequently traded. Traffic in stone began as early as the Late Archaic Period (Ford and Webb, 1956).

BELOW. LEFT. Side and top views of a redstone disk pipe about 3½'' diameter, found at Moundville, Alabama. This style of workmanship and stone (catlinite) is typical of the Oneota Culture Focus of the Mississippi Period in the Upper Mississippi Valley. This type pipe is sometime referred to as a "Siouan disk" pipe. The flat disk around the bowl rests on a tapering, flat, angular stem. A similar disk pipe was also found at the Spiro Mound, Oklahoma, where, as at Moundville, it represented an outside source of trade. See Hamilton, 1952, p. 39 and Pl. 22 (Courtesy, Alabama Museum of Natural History). Redstone and objects made of it were items of prehistoric and historic trade. UPPER. RIGHT. Birdstone of banded slate, about 5½'' long. This was found at an Indian site in North Alabama. It was doubtless an item of trade, for such artifacts are typical of certain Woodland culture sites in the New York, Ontario, and near areas. They are rarely found in the Southeast; the stones occur in the named areas in a variety of similar shapes and represent remarkable workmanship; their purpose is problematical (Courtesy, Helen Keller Birthplace Museum and R. B. Martin collection). LOWER. Conch shell dipper or cup, 10'' long; these are particularly characteristic of the Woodland and Mississippi Periods. Conch shell beads found at many late Archaic sites give evidence of the early beginning of coast to interior trade (Courtesy, Lt. T. F. Moebes).

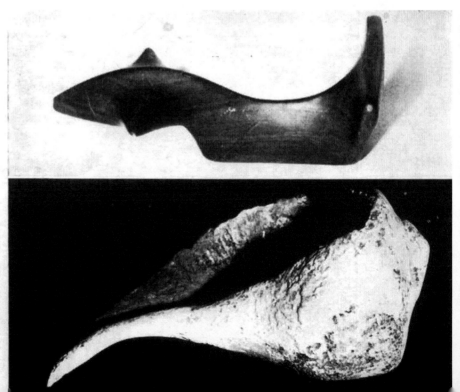

NATIVE TRADE

Plates 15 and 16

RIGHT. "Map illustrating the distribution of certain natural resources in the Southeast drawn upon by the Indians" (After John R. Swanton, 1946, map 13, face p. 254. Reproduced courtesy, Smithsonian Institution, Bureau of American Ethnology).

Swanton's map, as he explained, does not attempt to show all types of articles traded, nor all sites of the sources of various products listed. It serves to emphasize the wide-spread possibilities for regional trade.

BELOW. LEFT. Stone tools —roller-pestle, celt—6" long, chisels, and two pitted stones or drill sockets. Stone for making such tools and also some of the finished tools were items of interior to coast trade. These were found in the Mobile County, Alabama Gulf Coast Area (Courtesy, City of Mobile).

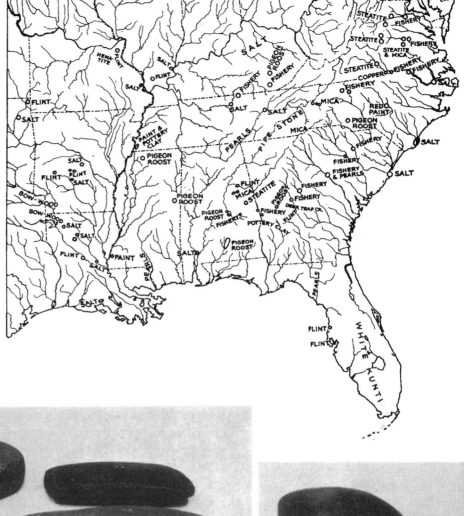

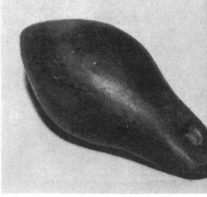

RIGHT. Problematical stone—net sinker, weight, or ornament? Drilled at the top for suspension. Made of iron carbonate, partially altered to iron hydroxide; 3.3" long. Probably an item of native trade. Mobile County, Alabama (Courtesy, Mrs. W. L. Durant).

BELOW. LEFT. Chunk of galena or native lead, diameter, 2-¾"; worked around sides. Galena has often been found at Woodland and Mississippi Period sites. Much of the galena found in the Southeast is believed to have originated in the Joplin, Missouri, area. This was found in Marshall County, Alabama (Madison County Chapter, Alabama Archaeological Society). CENTER. Fragments of mica, longest 4¼". Mica was a trade item originating in the Appalachian region. These fragments were found with cave burials, Morgan County, Alabama (Courtesy, Lt. T. F. Moebes). RIGHT. Chunk of native copper, about 4" long and ¼" to ½" thick; copper occurs in relatively pure malleable form in the Lake Superior area. Nuggets are sometimes found in the Appalachian range. Copper beads have been found at some Late Archaic sites in the Southeast; these indicate the probability of a very early beginning of north-south trade. From a native site in Alabama (Courtesy, T. J. DeJarnette).

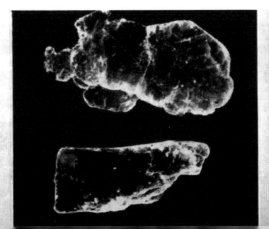

Chapter 3

CEREMONIAL COMPLEX

Quotation from A. J. Waring, Jr. and Preston Holder, "A Pre-historic Ceremonial Complex in the Southeastern United States," AMERICAN ANTHROPOLOGIST, Vol. 47, No. 1, January-March, 1945, pp. 1-34. Quoted by permission from Dr. A. J. Waring, Jr., M. D., Dr. Preston Holder, and the AMERICAN ANTHROPOLOGIST.*

"Since the archeological investigations of the sites of Etowah and Moundville, it has been apparent that there exists in the southeastern United States a complex of specific motifs and ceremonial objects. The recent discoveries at Spiro, Oklahoma,[1] and the reappearance of Cushing's Key Marco photographs[2] reem-phasize the presence of this complex throughout the Southeast, extending from Oklahoma to Florida, from the Gulf to the Great Lakes.

"Unfortunately, the bulk of this material has never been subjected to adequate analysis. It has been handled as exotic, introduced by trade from some foreign source, or it has been accepted as indigenous but has been left undiscussed beyond the mention of a few parallels or has been made the subject of purely distributional studies. It is the purpose of this paper to investigate the similarities in material from widely separated sites and to interpret them in the light of recently-established chronological sequences. We will also attempt to suggest the nature of this complex and to come to some conclusions as to factors determining its spread.

"In our efforts to demonstrate the existence of this complex it is necessary to examine carefully those sites which contain sufficient amounts of the material for systematic analysis. Our main considerations, therefore, will be Etowah (Georgia), Moundville (Alabama) and Spiro (Oklahoma). Material from other sites will also be used; notably from the Hollywood Mound (Georgia), the Citico Mound and Castalian Springs (Tennessee), Mount Royal and Key Marco (Florida) and Pecan Point and the Menard Mound (Arkansas). The three first-mentioned sites alone, however, are adequate to demonstrate the main points of this paper: (a) that the motifs and ceremonial objects appear as a cult complex in association with platform mounds, (b) that the complex is found virtually intact over a wide geographic area, and (c) that the complex is chronologically late.

"In a presentation of this material it will be necessary to outline as briefly as possible the following groups of elements: I. MOTIFS, II. GOD-ANIMAL REPRESENTATIONS, III. CEREMONIAL OBJECTS and IV. COSTUME.

I. MOTIFS

"The motifs have been chosen according to the following criteria: (a) that each is sufficiently specialized as to preclude casual delineation, (b) that each, from its appearance in association with other motifs and elements of the complex, is unquestionably a part of the complex, and (c) that each carried sufficient ceremonial significance to be used alone on cult objects.

"On the basis of the foregoing criteria the following motifs have been selected: (1) the CROSS, (2) SUN CIR-

*(Dr. A. J. Waring, Jr., M. D., Savannah, Georgia, and Dr. Preston Holder, Professor of Archeology, Washington University, St. Louis, Missouri.—Ed.)
[1] "The Spiro Site is situated in Oklahoma on the Arkansas River about fifteen miles from the Arkansas state line. The activities of a group of relic hunters in a burial structure at this site resulted in the dispersal of one of the most amazing caches of ceremonial material ever found in the mound area.
"The chief public collections of this material are located in The Museum of the American Indian, The Museum of the University of Arkansas and the Nebraska State Historical Society. Later work at the site under the direction of Dr. Forrest Clements resulted in the dis-covery of further material which is now among the collections of the University of Oklahoma." (Dr. R. E. Bell, Department of Anthropology, University of Oklahoma, also has promoted the investigation, preservation, and study of Spiro material.—Ed.)
"A fine privately-owned collection is that of Mr. H. M. Trowbridge of Bethel, Kansas." (Now a part of Kansas City.—Ed.)
"We are greatly indebted to the Museum of the American Indian and to Mr. Kenneth Miller, for extending every aid to us and allow-ing us to use its material.
"Mr. Trowbridge allowed us to use some of his material and went to considerable trouble in making tracings of some of the designs upon his conch bowls available to us, and we are deeply grateful to him.
"Our thanks are also due to A. T. Hill of the Nebraska State Historical Society for allowing us to reproduce designs from bowls in his society's possession."
[2] ". . . M. W. Stirling, Chief of the Bureau of American Ethnology."

CLES, (3) the BI-LOBED ARROW, (4) the FORKED EYE, (5) the OPEN EYE, (6) the BARRED OVAL, (7) the HAND AND EYE and (8) DEATH MOTIFS. (For examples see Figure I.)

"The CROSS includes the Greek Cross and the swastika. It is usually enclosed in a Sun Circle but frequently appears separately. It apparently had the same value as the Sun Circle since the two seem interchangeable on otherwise rigidly specialized objects (notably serpent & scalloped-circle gorgets and on the copper Symbol Badges).

"The SUN CIRCLE includes various forms of rayed and scalloped circles. They may undergo modifications, however, and the center may contain concentric circles, a spiral, the Cross, or the Open Eye. The commonest appearance of this Motif is on the familiar Middle Mississippian painted bottle forms. [3]

"The BI-LOBED ARROW consists of two kidney-shaped lobes separated by a down-pointing arrow. The edges of the lobes may be plain or scalloped. A band connects the lobes at the mid-point, and a line, presumably representing a bowstring, passes from the apex of each lobe to the butt of the arrow shaft. The significance of this motif is particularly perplexing. It is found as a sheet-copper hair ornament at Etowah [4] and at the Citico Mound [5] and appears in the hair knot of the Eagle Being throughout the area. [6] As a matter of fact it seems to be quite intimately associated with the Eagle Being. It also occasionally appears as an isolated motif, as on the grave wares at Moundville.

"The FORKED EYE occurs in innumerable variations. It is characterized by a circumocular marking which may be bi-forked, tri-forked or even with the zig-zag lines down the face which MacCurdy has suggested might represent tears. [7] This last variation is interpreted by Wintemberg as representing the flashing eye of the Thunder Bird. [8] These are interesting speculations. We should like to point out, however, that Yacovleff has held that closely similar eye-markings in Peruvian art were derived from the natural eye-markings of members of the FALCONIDAE. [9] It seems possible that we might have a parallel of this in the Southeast for the following reasons: the eye is almost invariably seen on the Eagle Being or on the Bird-Serpent Composite; also, the eye-markings of the Duck Hawk, Peal's Falcon and the Peregrine Falcon closely resemble the conventional motif, and the range of these birds includes the whole of the southeastern United States. On rare occasions this motif appears as an isolated design. [10]

"The HAND AND EYE consists of an extended hand containing a naturalistic eye in the center of the palm. Both nails and volar markings are frequently shown upon the same example. The eye may be replaced by a cross in a circle. [11]

"The OPEN EYE is the term we have applied to the motif seen in Fig. Iv. This motif was first recognized by Moore on specimens from Moundville. While it has not yet been reported from Etowah or Spiro, its common occurrence at Moundville and throughout the Mississippi Valley seems sufficient to justify its inclusion. [12]

"The BARRED OVAL consists of an oval with a longitudinal bar inside. There are several examples from both Moundville and Spiro. It is seen in profile under the tails of cat figures on a conch bowl from Spiro and repeated in full face on the flanks of the same figures. [13] It is seen both under the tail and on the wings of a woodpecker figure from Moundville. [14] Thus, from its context on both sites it would appear to represent either an anus or vagina. It also appears quite commonly as a marking on the rattlesnake's body [15] and also, of course, as a separate motif.

"DEATH MOTIFS include representations of the skull, femur or the fleshed radius and ulna, separately or in combinations. Occasionally a skeletal hand and eye are found attached to the radius and ulna. These motifs occur at Spiro, rarely in the Mississippi Valley and are quite common at Moundville. [16]

II. GOD-ANIMAL REPRESENTATIONS

"The foregoing motifs appear both as attributes and as paraphernalia of the following God-Animal Beings: 1. BIRDS (a) the Eagle, naturalistic[17] and anthropomorphized;[18] (b) the Pileated (or Ivory Billed)

[3] Holmes, 1903, Plate XVII and XXXVIII. Willoughby, 1897. Fig. 1 and 2. [4] Moorehead, 1932. Fig 20b. [5] M. A. I. Cat. No. 15/868. [6] Starr, 1897. Page 57. Fig. 5i, this paper. Thruston, 1892. Moorehead, 1932. Figs. 13, 14, and 15. [7] MacCurdy, 1917b. P. 73. [8] Wintemberg, 1923. [9] Yacovleff, 1932. [10] Fig. 2 d and e. Conch bowl (Sipro). M. A. I. Cat. No. 18/9119. [11] Thruston, 1890. Fig. 40. [12] Fig. 3 o and c. Moore, 1907. Figs. 42 and 100. [13] Conch bowl (Spiro). M. A. I. Cat. No. 18/9124. [14] Fig. 4e. [15] Fig. 4 j, k and l. Fig. 5 h. [16] Fig. 1 (VIII). [17] Fig. 4 b and c. Fowke, 1910. Plates XVI, XVII, XVIII, and XIX. Moorehead, 1932. Figs 9, 10 and 11. [18] Fig. 4 a and d. Fig. 5 a, b, c and f. Moorehead, 1932. Figs 12, 13, 14, 26 a and b, 27, 29 and 30. M. A. I. Cat. No. 18/9309 and 18/9125. [19] Fig. 4 e, f, g, h and i. Moorehead, 1932. Figs. 31 and 32 a, b, c, d and e. [20] Moorehead, 1932. Fig. 32c. Jackson, 1935. 18/9125.

Woodpecker, always naturalistic;[19] (c) the Turkey, always naturalistic.[20] 2. The RATTLESNAKE, naturalistic,[21] horned,[22] plumed,[23] winged,[24] anthropomorphized[25] or in any combination of these. 3. The CAT, always naturalistic.[26] These conclude the animals, but it should be noted that several of the bird, serpent and human figures are antlered[27] raising the question whether the deer should not be included. 4. HUMAN. Many of these figures probably represent completely anthropomorphized Animal Beings. The only sub-type that appears with any clarity is that of the Chunkee Player.[28] Considerations of dress, paraphernalia and stance lead one to feel that many of these figures either reflect or represent the practice of god-impersonation.

"Dual figures are seen, notably in Tennessee,[29] at Etowah[30] and at Spiro.[31] Usually these represent individuals in combat, either eagles (naturalistic or anthropomorphized) or human beings. There is also a dual anthropomorphized serpent representation from Spiro; the figures, however, are not shown in combat.[32]

III. CEREMONIAL OBJECTS.

"A group of ceremonial objects is associated with these motifs and god-animal beings. As a matter of fact we have derived the two preceding groups of elements from figures engraved or embossed on the surfaces of these ceremonial objects. From the nature of the workmanship, material and associations it seems that the function of the objects was truly ceremonial and not domestic.

"The specific ritualistic use is beyond any but the vaguest conjecture, but some hints may be had from their appearance as costume or paraphernalia of the beings described above.

"These objects are as follows:

(1) GORGETS	b. the Plume	(13) EFFIGY PIPES
a. shell	c. the Baton	a. squatting humans
b. copper	(8) EAR SPOOLS	b. human figure with bowl
(2) OBLONG GORGETS OF COPPER	a. wood	c. cat pipes
(3) MASK GORGETS	b. stone	(14) NOTCHED STONE DISCS
(4) COLUMELLA PENDANTS	c. copper-covered wood	(15) DISCOIDAL STONES
(5) EMBOSSED COPPER PLATES	d. copper-covered stone	(16) CONCH SHELL BOWLS
a. Head Plates	(9) THE HAFTED CELT	(17) CEREMONIAL FLINTS
b. Eagle Plates	(10) THE PIERCED CELT	(18) BOTTLES
(6) COPPER SYMBOL BADGES	(11) THE MONOLITHIC AXE	a. painted
(7) SHEET COPPER HAIR EMBLEMS	(12) THE BATON	b. bipartite
a. the Bi-lobed Arrow		c. tripartite

"CIRCULAR GORGETS OF SHELL were divided by Holmes[33] into the following categories: (1) the Cross, (2) the Scalloped Disc, (3) the Bird, (4) the Spider, (5) the Serpent and (6) the Human figure. The basic or central design is usually a cross. Thus, in the Serpent Gorget, the conventionalized coiled body of the rattlesnake is held to the plain outer band by four tangs forming the cross. Both the Serpent and the Spider Gorgets seem to be distributed over a limited area, namely Holmes' Southern Appalachian, but like many of these elements there are areal variations which cannot be discussed here. Holmes' categories have proved valid in the light of newer material, but additional categories should be added such as the Turkey Gorget, the Pileated Woodpecker (in which the two woodpeckers sit facing one another on the transverse arms of the cross), the Antlered Bird-Being (in which the figure is conventionally shown seated cross-legged) and the Fighting Eagle-Beings. The Chunkee Player Gorget seems to be a valid category. The figure in this type is seen in special costume crouched in the throwing position with a biconcave chunkee stone in its hand.[34]

"CIRCULAR GORGETS OF COPPER have appeared both at Etowah and at Moundville.[35] They are somewhat larger than the shell gorget and contain a central cross or swastika surrounded by embossed concentric circles. They are pierced for suspension.

"OBLONG GORGETS OF COPPER consist of small, tapering pendants of sheet copper perforated at the larger end for suspension. The larger end typically contains an embossed circle in the center of which are variations of the cross or sun-circle. In some specimens there are a series of circles diminishing in size, each of which contain swastikas. These have been described from Etowah and Moundville.[36]

[19] Fig. 4e, f, g, h and i. Moorehead, 1932. Figs. 31 and 32a, b, c, d and e. [20] Moorehead, 1932. Fig. 32c. Jackson, 1935. Plate I. [21] Gorget (Spiro). M. A. I. Cat. No. 18/7915. Webb, 1939. Plate 95. [22] Fig. 3 u. Fig. 4 j. Conch bowl (Spiro). M. A. I. Cat. No. 18/9309. [23] Fig. 4 k. Fig. 3 v Conch bowl (Spiro). M. A. I. Cat. No. 18/9082. [24] Fig. 4 k. Moore, 1907. Figs. 51-65. [25] Fig. 4 l. Fig. 5 h. Science News Letter, 1938. [26] Moore, 1905. Figs. 1, 2. 3 and 166. Lemley and Dickinson, 1937. Plate V 1 and 2. Plate VI 3. [27] Fig. 4 j and l. Wooden mask (Spiro). M. A. I. Cat. No. 18/9036. MacCurdy, 1913. Fig. 77. Moorehead; 1932. Figs. 26a and 29. [28] Fig. 5f. MacCurdy, 1913. Figs. 70, 71 and 73. [29] Holmes, 1883. Plate LXXIV. Several additional examples have been found during the course of recent work under T. M. N. Lewis. [30] Moorehead, 1932. Figs. 9 and 28. [31] Shell gorget (Spiro). M. A. I. Cat. No. 18/9186. [32] Fig. 5h. [33] Holmes, 1883. Pp. 267-305. [34] Vide supra. Also Fig. 5g. [35] Fig. 3 p and q. [36] Fig. 3 m, n and o.

"COLUMELLA PENDANTS are made from the columella and terminal whorl of the large conch. The tip of the columella is drilled for suspension. This type of pendant has appeared at Etowah,[37] and Spiro,[38] and from two sites in the Wheeler Basin which contained other comparable material.[39] It seems likely, in view of the fact that these unusual pendants are found in close association with other material of the complex, that these are the objects which appear suspended around the necks of the god-animal beings[40] rather than the gourd rattles which Willoughby suggests.[41]

"The MASK GORGET, called by Holmes the 'Human Face Gorget,' is typically pear-shaped with the two eyes pierced through. The circumocular marking is usually an elaboration of the Forked Eye. The mouth and nose are rudimentary. This type of gorget has a tremendous distribution, from southern Manitoba[42] to Alabama.[43]

"COPPER SYMBOL BADGES are small, sheet-copper bangles pierced for suspension and shaped like the Baton, the Bi-lobed Arrow and arrowheads with human heads embossed on them. Anywhere from one to thirty of the identical pattern may be found in a single grave.

"SHEET COPPER HAIR EMBLEMS consist of sheet copper representations of the Bi-lobed Arrow,[44] the Baton,[45] or large, curved plumes.[46] They have a bone pin attached at the base for insertion into the hair knot. They are often depicted as hair ornaments or gorgets and copper plates.[47]

"EMBOSSED COPPER PLATES are divisible into three types. (1) HEAD PLATES are typically square or slightly elongated and bear on the surface the embossed representation of a human head with a beaded forelock and Forked Eye. They are usually pierced along the edge for attachment to some object or material.[48] These artifacts occur in the graves of apparently important individuals. Since they are usually found lying in contact with the frontal area of the skull, they probably formed part of a ritualistic headdress.[49] (2) EAGLE PLATES refer to those embossed copper plates which are shaped like an eagle. Some are purely naturalistic while others show a tendency towards anthropomorphization which reaches its most striking form in the Etowah Plates, one of which is shown in Fig. 5a. These plates are widely distributed and yet are closely similar in design and technique. Fowke reports an impressive group of them from Southern Missouri.[50] From Spiro comes a specimen quite similar in design but not in execution to the anthropomorphized eagles of Etowah. Unfortunately the upper portion of this figure is missing, but enough remains, including the fringed apron, the sash, the beaded wristlets and anklets, the trophy head held in one hand, the wings and the triangular base of the Baton to permit a positive identification.[51] At Etowah these plates were found wrapped in skins and textiles and placed beneath the heads of certain individuals. The absence of perforations makes it doubtful that these were attached to any costume, but these plates probably served an important ceremonial function. (3) Another type of plate, known only by two examples, has appeared from Mount Royal (Florida) and Spiro (Oklahoma).[52] It is a square plate with four Forked Eyes and four oblong elements arranged around central concentric circles. The Florida specimen was found lying on top of skull fragments and superimposed on a backing of reeds. Possibly these should be classed with the Head Plates, but the absence of perforations makes this arrangement doubtful.

"EAR SPOOLS invariably appear in the ears of god-animal beings. In these representations a short string of beads or a tassel is frequently seen attached. Ear spools also appear in the large ceremonial burials found at sites where elements of the complex appear. At Spiro[53] ear spools were found bearing the cross, the Forked Eye, and the square with looped corners which appears on the Bird Gorgets. These ear spools are of the "collar button" type and are made of wood or stone. They may or may not be covered with copper.

"By CELTS OF STONE OR COPPER we do not mean the ordinary utilitarian celt found on late sites throughout the Southeast. We refer to a class of finely made artifacts generally occurring in association with other elements of the complex. These implements were made of thin, soft copper, friable claystones, and other materials, but they are all alike in that their general structure and the usual absence of a cutting edge

[37] There is an example in the Etowah case at the United States National Museum, presumably from Mound C. Although the eyelet is broken off, the work on the rest of the specimen makes positive identification possible. [38] Fig. 3s. (M. A. I. has two examples from Spiro.) [39] Webb 1939. Plates 94a and 109b. [40] Fig. 5 a, b and f. [41] Willoughby, 1932. P. 40. [42] Montgomery, 1910. Plate III. [43] Brannon, 1935. [44] Moorehead, 1932. Fig. 20 a and b. Nashville, Tennessee, M. A. I. Cat. No. 15/868. [45] Jackson Co., Ala., M. A. I. Cat. [46] Moorehead, 1932. Fig. 19. (The manner of wearing is erroneously represented). Jackson Co., Ala. M. A. I. Cat. Spiro, Okla. M. A. I. Cat. No. 20/706 and 20/707. Moore, 1905. Fig. 45. [47] Moorehead, 1932. Figs. 12, 13, 14 and 15. [48] Fig. 2 a, b and c. [49] Moore, 1915. Fig. 52. [50] Fowke, 1910. Plates 15-19. [51] Fig. 5c. [52] Fig. 2 d and e. [53] Fig. 3 f and g.

make their utilitarian value doubtful. The Pierced Celt and the so-called 'Spud' also should probably be included here. The wide spatial and temporal distribution of this class of implements in the New World leaves the problem of origins still open, but it also strengthens its claim for inclusion as a ceremonial element of the complex under consideration.

"The MONOLITHIC AXE should be discussed under the heading of Hafted Celt, but because of its distinct and separate character as an artifact it is treated separately. It is obviously non-utilitarian and serves as a most interesting example of the integration and ramifications of the complex. It appears at Moundville, Etowah and Spiro and always represents a hafted celt.[54] A very significant detail is the eyelet which is always present at the butt of the handle. This eyelet also occurs on the wooden hafts of the copper axes from Spiro[55] which were additionally carved at the insertion of the blade to represent the head of a pileated woodpecker, mouth open, tongue protruded, crest erect and with eyes of inlaid shell. While with one exception the monolithic specimens were not so elaborate, the eyelet is invariably present. The copper blades of the Spiro specimens are so delicate and slender that they could never have been put to domestic use. In addition, in mounting them in a haft, durability had been sacrificed for ornament.

"The BATON, also often referred to as the 'Mace,' was first noted at Etowah where it appeared in the hand of the Eagle Being on the Etowah Plates. It is usually portrayed with a cross on its flat surface and two tassels dangling from it. Examples with terraced edges are seen from Moundville, Etowah and Spiro. It is represented in the large ceremonial flint forms from Tennessee[56] and Spiro.[57] Specimens from the latter site were found painted half red and half white. The Baton appears in polished stone from Louisiana.[58] Small copper bangles were found in its shape at Etowah.[59] It is portrayed on shell gorgets from New Madrid, Mo.[60] and Castalian Springs, Tenn.[61] It appears on copper plates from Etowah, Illinois,[62] and Spiro[63] and as sheet copper Hair Emblems from Alabama.[64] It is also found on the engraved conch bowls from Spiro.[65] Cushing found an example of the Baton itself preserved in the muck at Key Marco. It was about two feet long, was made of wood, and terminated in a 'grooved knob or boss to which tassel cords had been attached.'[66]

"There has been much speculation about this artifact. Its shape is suggestive of Middle American representations of the ceremonial atlatl, as has been pointed out by Nuttall.[67] All agree that its function was highly symbolic, and certainly it is one of the most constant elements of the ceremonial complex we are tracing. Because of its great importance we have included it as a ceremonial 'object' although in all cases except one it survives in representations only.

"EFFIGY PIPES seem to run with the complex. In general three types are recognizable. They are (a) the squatting human figure, (b) the human figure holding a receptacle and (c) the 'cat pipes' so familiar at Moundville and along the Lower Mississippi. Other types which seem to be related to this material include copulating humans and frogs and the human head pipes of the Georgia type .

"SCALLOPED STONE DISCS appear both at Etowah and Moundville in conspicuous numbers. They have been variously referred to as paint palettes, 'sun circles' and even calendar stones.[68] Several bear complex elements engraved on their surfaces. At present it is futile to suggest a function for these objects.

"DISCOIDAL STONES, both plain and concave, have been found at Etowah, Moundville and Spiro. Their presence in the hands of the figures on the Chunkee Player Gorgets as well as the appearance of the artifact itself at all three sites seems adequate to justify its inclusion.

"CONCH BOWLS appear at all sites at which this material is found. Engraved conch bowls of the elaborately figured type, however, appear only at Moundville and Spiro. At Moundville only a single example has been found.[69] Spiro, on the other hand, has produced the amazing series of over one hundred of these containers. Most of the designs from Spiro which are shown in this paper are taken from the surfaces of these vessels. Their significance raises an interesting point. Several of the Heye Museum specimens show an old

[54] Moore, 1905. Fig. 6. Moorehead, 1932. Fig. 52. Spiro: Two examples are reported to be from Spiro. One is in the Maffenbier Collection (Newark, N. J.). The other is in the Museum of the American Indian. The former is an almost exact duplicate of one from Tennessee (Fig. 2j). The authenticity of the latter has been questioned. [55] Fig. 2k. [56] Fig. 3a. Seever, 1897. Fig. III No. 12, 13, 14 and 15. Thruston, 1890. Fig. 151 and Plate XIV. [57] Fig. 2t and u. Spiro: Other flint Batons from this site are in the collections of John Maffenbier (Newark, N. J.), H. M. Trowbridge (Bethel, Kan.), and J. G. Braeklein (Kansas City, Mo.). [58] Ascension Parish, La. M. A. I. Cat. No. 7098. [59] Fig. 2 m and n. [60] Thruston, 1890. Plate XVII. [61] Myer, 1917. P. 102. [62] Thomas, 1891. Fig. 85. [63] Fig. 5c. This restoration is based on the butt which is the only remaining portion of the Baton. [64] Fig. 2 o and p. [65] Fig. 2 r and s.
[66] Fig. 2 q. [67] Nuttall, 1932. Page 140. [68] Holmes, 1906. Moore, 1905. Figs. 4, 5, 7, 19, 23, 65, 66, 103, 110, 111, and 116. Moore, 1907. Figs. 87 and 88. Etowah. Fragments in the U. S. National Museum. Figs. 3 t, u and v. [69] Moore, 1905. Fig. 34.

fluid level, as if they had been buried containing a liquid. The taking of the Black Drink among the Muskhogeans was traditionally done from conch shell bowls and had the most basic ceremonial significance. Possibly these containers were prototypes of those in use in historic times.

CEREMONIAL FLINTS include various long blade forms and the Baton representations. Tennessee has yielded other related forms including aberrant blade forms, the turtle, the disc, the human head, the hafted celt and an odd wrench-like form which probably represents an eagle's claw. The great cache from the stone grave cemetery on the Duck River, Tennessee,[70] contained every variety of flint-form mentioned, and with it were found two stone figures (male and female) of the type found by Moorehead at Etowah.

"Certain BOTTLE FORMS seem to run with the complex. They are all types which are typically Middle Mississippian, and appear regardless of the basic ceramic complex. The three types found most commonly are: (a) the SIMPLE BOTTLE with variations of the Cross, the Sun Circle, the Bi-lobed Arrow, Death Motifs or the Hand and Eye done in Applique, red or black paint, engraved, or by the lost-color technique; (b) BIPARTITE bottles with a stirrup spout, occasionally with figure modelling at the junction of the spout; (c) TRIPARTITE BOTTLES with a triple stirrup spout. The three containing elements in the last-mentioned type may be modeled in the form of human heads. The first-mentioned form is familiar throughout the whole area. The second is the least common of the three, one example coming from Etowah and the rest from the Mississippi Valley. The third type is more generally distributed with examples from Spiro, [71] Moundville, [72] and t h e Hollywood Mound. [73] Again, the use of these vessels is not known. The only three examples from Etowah[74] came from the same stone-box graves in which were found the embossed coppers already discussed.

IV. COSTUME

"Specific elements of costume constitute a group of elaborate identities between these widely-separated sites. They appear on the various god-animal representations and survive in their non-perishable parts with the burials themselves. The group of elements which we recognize is as follows:

HEAD-DRESS AND HAIR ORNAMENT	BODY ORNAMENT AND SKIRT	PARAPHERNALIA
1. occipital hair knot	8. beaded bands on arms and legs	15. The Baton
2. tasseled head tablet	9. necklace	16. flint knives
3. ear spools (usually tasseled)	10. necklace with columella pendant	17. the Human Head
4. Bi-lobed Arrow Hair Emblem.	11. beaded choker	18. the Hafted Celt
5. Copper Plume Hair Emblem.	12. beaded belt	
6. antlered head-dress	13. knotted sash	
7. beaded forelock	14. the Fringed Apron	

All of these elements with the exception of numbers 5, 6, 11, 16 and 18 appear on the larger of the two Etowah Plates. Certain of the elements are invariably present. These are the hair knot, ear spools, beaded bands, the beaded belt and the knotted sash. The beaded forelock, the Bi-lobed Arrow, the Hair Emblem, the columella pendant and the Fringed Apron are so individual and necessary a part of the costume as to be diagnostic. The Hair Emblem has been described. The beaded forelock is that spikelike, beaded object seen hanging from the forehead of the figures. The Fringed Apron is a very complex affair, consisting of a large heart-shaped apron suspended in front from a fringed sash. Its edge is always fringed and the center contains a peculiar, rectangular figure divided into three zones by two transverse lines. Short strings of beads are sewn around the edges of the zones.

"The Head-dress varies from the simple occipital knot stuck with the Plume or the Bi-lobed Arrow to the elaborately crested types and those with the tasseled tablets such as are seen at Etowah. The beaded forelock is always present.

"The Fringed Apron and the columella pendant occur almost invariably on the Eagle Being as well as on the Chunkee Player. The Eagle Being occasionally appears without the Fringed Apron but with a breech clout and knotted sash.

"As we indicate above, elements of the ceremonial costume appear with burials, presumably those of important individuals. These burials, as at Etowah, are frequently intrusive into the floors of temple structures on platform mounds. Burials were found there with bead bands at the wrists, elbows, knees and ankles, with

---

[70] Seever, 1897. Fig. 3.   [71] M. A. I. Cat. No. 20/742.   [72] Moore, 1905 Fig. 172.   [73] Thomas, 1891. Fig. 199.   [74] Figs. 3 h, k and l.

gorgets and columella pendants at their necks and with Copper Plume and Bi-lobed Arrow Emblems in place behind their skulls. [75] A monolithic axe, as well as several ceremonial flints and the much-discussed copper plates, were also found with these burials. When burials are found in which the individuals have been interred wearing the same ornaments and clothing and with the same paraphernalia which one sees on representations of the god-animal beings, some type of god-impersonation is certainly indicated. When, as at Etowah, this material is restricted to those burials found in a single platform mound and not with the burials occurring in the village site, the evidence is suggestive of god-impersonation by a restricted group. The fact that cult material appears in the graves of women and infants as well as men suggests that class factors are involved.

"Motifs, God-Animal Representations and ceremonial objects occur at Etowah, Moundville and Spiro in quantities large enough to be subjected to a tabular analysis. The following table has been constructed to show the relative occurrence of this material on these three sites.[76]

TABLE I	Etowah	Moundville	Spiro		Etowah	Moundville	Spiro
MOTIFS				(26) the Pierced Celt	X	X	X
				(27) the Monolithic Axe	X	X	X
(1) the Cross	X	X	X	(28) the Baton	(X)	(X)	(X)
(2) Sun Circles	X	X	X	(29) Effigy Pipes			
(3) the Bi-lobed Arrow	X	X	X	a. squatting humans	X	X	X
(4) the Forked Eye	X	X	X	b. human with bowl	X	X	X
(5) the Open Eye*		X		c. cat pipes		X	
(6) the Barred Oval		X	X	(30) notched stone disc	X	X	
(7) the Hand and Eye		X	X	(31) discoidal stones	X	X	X
GOD-ANIMAL REPRESENTATIONS				(32) conch shell bowls			
(8) the Eagle	X	X	X	a. plain	X	X	X
(9) the Woodpecker	X	X	X	b. engraved		X	X
(10) the Turkey	X	X	X	(33) ceremonial flints	X	X	X
(11) the Rattlesnake				(34) bottle forms			
a. horned		X	X	a. simple painted	X	X	
b. plumed	X	X	X	b. bipartite	X	X	
c. winged		X	X	c. tripartite*	X	X	X
d. anthropomorphized			X				
(12) the Cat		X	X	**COSTUME**			
(13) the anthropomorphized Eagle	X	X	X	**HEAD-DRESS AND HAIR ORNAMENTS**			
(14) the Chunkee Player			X	(35) occipital hair knot	X	X	X
(15) Dual Figures	X		X	(36) tasseled head tablet	X	X	
CEREMONIAL OBJECTS				(37) ear spools	X	X	X
(16) circular gorgets of copper	X	X		(38) Bi-lobed Arrow Hair Emblem	X	X	X
(17) circular gorgets of shell	X	X	X	(39) Plume Arrow Hair Emblem	X	X	X
(18) oblong gorgets of copper	X	X		(40) antlers	X		X
(19) Mask Gorgets	X	X		(41) beaded forelock	X	X	X
(20) columella pendants	X	(X)	X	**BODY ORNAMENT AND SKIRT**			
(21) Emposed Copper Plates				(42) beaded bands	X	X	X
a. Eagle Plates	X		X	(43) necklace	X	X	X
b. Head Plates	X		X	(44) necklace with columella pendant	X	X	X
c. Forked Eye Plates			X	(45) beaded choker			X
(22) sheet copper hair emblems				(46) beaded belt	X	X	X
a. the Bi-lobed Arrow	X	(X)	(X)	(47) knotted sash	X	X	X
b. the Plume	X	X	X	(48) Fringed Apron	X	X	X
c. the Baton			X	**PARAPHERNALIA**			
(23) ear spools	X	X	X	(49) the Baton	X	X	X
(24) copper symbol badges	X	X		(50) the Human Head	X		X
(25) copper ceremonial celt	X	X	X	(51) flint knives	X	X	X
(26) stone ceremonial celt	X	X	X				

X means the occurrence of the object itself under the heading CEREMONIAL OBJECTS. (X) under the same heading means the object occurs in representation only. *(Open Eye—Etowah, Pl. 109; Spiro, Pl. 28. R. E. Bell does not associate the tripartite with Spiro).

"So far the question of style has not been touched upon. This paper cannot possibly go into the many ramifications of style and technique into which a thorough discussion would lead. The material from Spiro

[75] Moorehead, 1932. P. 68. [76] "It will be observed that all elements appear on at least two sites, with the exceptions of the Cat Pipe and the Forked Eye Plate. From this table it will be seen that 52% of these 51 elements appear at all three sites. Many which do not appear at Moundville appear at Etowah and Spiro, and many not found at Etowah are found at Moundville and Spiro. In fact, 83% of the group appear at Spiro and also at one or both of the more easterly sites. Thus such elements of the complex as we are able to recognize are distributed at least 83% intact over the entire Southeast. Undoubtedly, if the quantity of material from Etowah and Moundville equalled that of the Spiro loot, the number of elements in common would be even higher.

"The correspondence between this material is even more striking than a simple tabular form can show. Many of the elements given a weight of one in the above calculations are elaborately specialized. Some represent in themselves a complex of specialized elements. A case in point is the Eagle Plate. Another is the remarkable Forked Eye Plate with almost identical specimens from Spiro and Mount Royal, Florida."

is in many ways radically different from that of Etowah and Moundville. Design elements which are used throughout the rest of the Southeast with considerable conventionality and restraint are used at Spiro with what appears to be utter capriciousness and abandon. Such technical innovations as full face representation, bas-relief, and shell carving in the round are seen. Many of the old, familiar elements are distorted into new and bizarre forms. Thus we see serpents with seven deer's heads, copper-covered wooden representations of flint knives and human beings with serpent bodies issuing from their backs. The designs on the conch shell bowls are completely wild and many strange and unrelated elements appear. Bison representations are seen, and such naturalistic subjects as speared fish and uprooted pine trees with woodpeckers on their branches add a note completely foreign to the late phase of Southeastern ceremonial activity. The bulk of material from each of the three great sites could not possibly be confused with another. Nevertheless, and this is an extremely important point, there exists at the core a basic group of elements and a basic stylistic similarity in all of the material. The same motifs, the same god-animal representations and the same ceremonial objects are present. The same conventionalization of the rattlesnake are seen, the same drafting of the human profile, the same ear treatment and the same treatment and grouping of motifs.[77]

"The motifs appear disproportionately from site to site. For example, only a single representation of the Hand and Eye and two of the Bi-lobed Arrow have come from Spiro, while at least twenty of each have appeared from Moundville. The same may be said of the winged serpents which appear twice from Spiro and not at all from Etowah. In addition, the actual distribution of the material is different from site to site; as has been stated, at Etowah all of the ceremonial material came from the stone graves in a single platform mound. At Spiro they came from a series of log-roofed chambers in a small conical mound near a platform mound. At Moundville the designs were used freely on the engraved grave wares in village site burials as well as mound burials throughout the site. This difference in distribution of material in the burials suggests that the complex had a slightly different social integration in the different areas, that in one area ceremonial practices were in the hands of a small group while in another they were used more or less by the whole community. This is what one would expect to find in a spreading cult.

"There are two further points regarding this material: The fact that the elements are widely distributed, and the fact that the material invariably appears in close association with platform mounds. The problem of ceremonial centers marked by platform mounds is one of considerable interest. The mounds themselves are truncated pyramids of earth upon the summits of which ceremonial structures were erected. Frequently the actual evidence of habitation upon the site seems superficially inadequate to account for the labor necessary to pile up structures containing over a million cubic feet of earth. This fact suggests that such sites are indeed CENTERS and that they served an area appreciably larger than the confines of the site itself.[78]

"We now turn to a chronological consideration of the complex in the light of recent archeological evidence from Georgia, Tennessee, Alabama, Florida and Louisiana. In doing so, each area will be discussed separately.

"GEORGIA: The Georgia chronology has been established in preliminary form by A. R. Kelly, [79] Gordon Willey and Charles Fairbanks in central Georgia and by Holder, Waring and Caldwell [80] on the Georgia coast. In central Georgia the Napier period, which was a late development out of Swift Creek, was interrupted by a Middle Mississippian complex of an early type, namely Macon Plateau. [81] On the coast, the sequence was interrupted by the intrusion of a people from the north who made a crude, sherd-tempered, cord-marked ware (woodland), who made clay platform pipes, who used projectile points of bone and who probably retained the use of the weighted atlatl.

---

[77] "It may be argued that such identities in widely separated material may represent trade from the same center; that the products of a relatively few cult centers, widely bartered, give a false extent of the culture area proper. In answering such an argument it may be pointed out that although the shell from which one object is made comes from the Gulf and the copper for another may come from Lake Superior, the finished ceremonial objects usually shows the characteristics of the stylistic sub-area in which it is found, and, within limits, could not be confused with material from another area. Along the same line of thought it might be pointed out that the greater part of the motifs from Spiro appear on the 100-odd engraved conch bowls, while beyond one isolated example from Moundville no other comparable specimen has been found in that area. The motifs from Moundville are mostly seen on the engraved grave-wares which have a relatively localized distribution."

[78] "Before turning to a consideration of the chronological position of the complex, it should be noted that there existed an earlier level of ceremonialism, namely that typified by a group of burial customs seen throughout the Southeast, of which the 'Hopewell Culture' may well be the culmination. Examples in the archeology of the area are Webb's 'Copena Complex' in Northern Alabama (Webb, 1939) and the burial customs of the Marksville Period in Louisiana as typified at the Crooks Mound. (Ford, 1940). There is evidence of similar levels in Kentucky, (Webb, 1941), Georgia and Florida. Work is as yet too incomplete to make any definite statements, but when the definitive synthesis of archeological evidence of late Southeastern ceremonialism is finally written, we feel that cognizance of the earlier level will have to be taken in the interpretation of many of the later aspects."

[79] Kelly, 1938.   [80] Caldwell, 1941.   [81] Kelly, 1939.

"This point in the Georgia sequence is of particular interest to us, since it marks the first appearance of unmistakable evidence of the ceremonial complex under discussion. The tentative date set for this Middle Mississippian intrusion is later than 1400 A. D. The situation at Macon is that of a large mound site surrounded by a series of fortifications. Mounds A and B are large platform mounds which have not been excavated. Mound C is a platform mound composed of superimposed temple structures and contained numerous burials, intrusive and otherwise, at all levels. Some of them were quite elaborate, but none contained material typical of later ceremonial manifestations. Mound D is a large, low mound. The old surface at its base was marked by two low mounds with wattle-and-daub structures on their summits, surrounded by the well-preserved rows of an ancient corn field. These had been carefully covered by eight feet of mound fill and new structures erected on the surface. It is tempting, in the light of later Muskhogean ceremonial, to assume that the corn field had a particular significance and that the preservation of the furrows was not entirely fortuitous.

"The most important structure at Macon is the ceremonial earth lodge. This was found under a low mound, the borders of which were contiguous with Mound D. It is a semisubterranean, circular earth lodge with a tunnel entrance. Around the wall is ranged a bank of raised clay seats, and opposite the entrance is a raised dais in the shape of an eagle with a Forked Eye plainly puddled in the baked clay. [82] This is the earliest appearance of a cult element reported from Georgia.

"The Macon Site is of particular importance, since it shows the complex in an early and formative stage and also points unmistakably to a Mississippian origin of the ceremonial. It is of additional interest that many earlier elements still persisted. Fairbanks has remarked upon the 'Adena-like' appearance of the trait list of Mound C. [83]

"Etowah (Mound C) may be placed later than Macon. The Etowah site shows much evidence of fusion of older Georgia traits with those introduced in the Mississippian push. This is particularly striking in the ceramics, where one sees the old stamping techniques (chiefly Napier) applied to shell-tempered vessels of Middle Mississippian form. The ceremonial activity was elaborate and fully developed and similar to that at Moundville and Spiro. The Hollywood Mound belongs to this period.

"Elements of the complex are still present in the Lamar period. Serpent and mask gorgets are found, and effigy water bottles shaped like a dog with Sun Circles painted on their sides have been found at three 'Lamar' sites, namely the Bull Creek cemetery near Columbus, Georgia,[84] the Nacoochee Mound,[85] and the Neisler Site.[86]

"TENNESSEE: The Tennessee material is as yet mostly unpublished, but much that is pertinent is present in the archeological work conducted under T. M. N. Lewis of the Division of Anthropology, University of Tennessee. * Work in Hamilton and Jefferson Counties and at Hiawassee Island has resulted in the discovery of a number of engraved shell gorgets along with a complete account of their archeological associations and provenience. [87] On sites 1 and 3 in Hamilton County a series of forty gorgets have been found. They include such designs as the Scroll and Circle, the Rattlesnake, the Mask, the Turkey Cock, the Bird Design, the Fighting Warriors and the Kneeling Human Figure. In several cases burials were found with shell bead bands at the ankle, wrist, knee and elbow. Ceremonial objects were frequently found in association; these are conch bowls, 'water bottles,' ear spools, gorgets and ceremonial celts. From site 1 Ha 3 came a monolithic axe found with a group burial in the late levels of a mound composed of a series of superimposed structures. The axe was accompanied by an eight inch celt and a pair of copper-on-wood ear spools. Space is not available to present an adequate analysis of the Tennessee material. Suffice it to say that it has a stratigraphic occurrence in the upper horizons. A figured gorget was found in the latest level at Hiawassee Island, a site which showed an appreciable amount of European trade material. In no instance was material found in the early levels in Tennessee which could be regarded as developmental.

"LOUISIANA: In Louisiana, the chronology has been worked out by James A. Ford and his associates. [88] Unlike other areas in the Southeast, Louisiana reflects few cultural cross-currents. From the earliest to the latest there is an orderly development, both in ceramics as well as ceremonial. The latter was related to the

[82] Kelly, 1938, P. 11. [83] Fairbanks, Mound C Trait List. (MS) Fairbanks, 1956—Ed.).
*(Since this article was written, Lewis and Kneberg have published a number of books and articles regarding archeological remains of the Tennessee area.—Ed.)
[84] Kelly, The Bull Creek Cemetery. (MS) [85] Heye et al 1918. Plate V. [86] On the Flint River, Georgia. [87] "We are much indebted to Andrew Whiteford for assembling this material for us and to T.M.N. Lewis for permission to use it." [88] Ford, 1936. Ford, 1940.

Hopewell of Ohio. It is interesting that the earliest appearance of the burial mound in the Southeast is in the late Tchefuncte Period. Thus, when the late ceremonial complex under discussion enters the area, it is particularly striking against this background of orderly development. Elements of the complex appear only in the historic phase and even then only sporadically. The most interesting occurrence of a single artifact in the area is at the Fatherland Plantation Site, which has been identified as the site of the Grand Village of the Natchez. Here in a platform mound, upon which stood the mortuary temple of the Natchez, was found a human head of stone incised with the Forked Eye. Along with it were found numerous burials and much European trade material.

"FLORIDA: A chronological outline for northwest Florida was worked out by Gordon Willey and R. B. Woodbury during the summer of 1941. [89] Elements of the cult period do not appear until protohistoric and historic levels. The final period, Ft. Walton, was marked by a degeneration of the older styles and the appearance of shell-tempered ware along with effigy forms which have obvious affinities with Moundville. To this last period belong the platform mound at Camp Walton, the bird and human effigy forms and the stylized Hand-and-Eye and Skull designs on bowls. Evidence that these sites are late is to be had, not only in the stratigraphy, but also in the fact that fragments of Spanish olive jars are not uncommon on them.

"ALABAMA: The cultural sequences in Northern Alabama have been worked out by Webb, DeJarnette and their co-workers. [90] The final period is characterized by shell-tempered wares. To this period are assigned those sites which contain ceremonial material belonging to the complex. Two such sites are Lu 21 (Seven Mile Island) and Lu 92 (Kogers Island). The former was a platform mound composed of several rectangular, superimposed platforms of clay on the surfaces of which were built wattle-and-daub structures. Intrusive burials had been made into these floors at all levels. Material found with these burials included notched stone discs, greenstone celts, a stone pendant of the Cross and Circle and Hand type found at Moundville, embossed copper ear spools, zoomorphic effigy bottles (painted and unpainted) and an engraved bottle bearing on its surface the flying rattlesnake. A sherd of ware foreign to Alabama but typical of the Lamar period in Georgia served as additional evidence for the late dating of this site.

"The Kogers Island Site had no mound but consisted of a village site and cemetery. Material belonging to the complex found here included notched stone discs, a dog effigy pipe, copper Emblem Badges, embossed copper-on-wood ear spools, conch shell gorgets and ceremonial bottle forms. The Emblem Badges were of two types, one shaped like a projectile point and bearing the eye design, the other shaped like a miniature Baton with the cross embossed on its surface. Several of the latter were found and are almost identical with those found at Etowah. The Gorgets were of two types, one bore a central Cross surrounded by a series of scallops, the other was the Bird Design, consisting of a central Cross and Sun Circle surrounded by a square with looped corners and four pileated woodpecker heads. The ceremonial bottles were chiefly engraved and bore the flying rattlesnake with the Forked Eye and Hand and Eye designs.

"This material from Northern Alabama serves to date Moundville as belonging to the protohistoric period in Alabama. In addition, at the Charlotte Thompson Place in central Alabama,[91] cult material was found in good association with European trade material.

"Thus, from an examination of the archeological sequences in Georgia, Tennessee, Louisiana, northwestern Florida and northern Alabama, one arrives at the same conclusions. In all areas these elements appear late. In no area, except Georgia, are developmental forms seen. In Georgia the first appearance of the complex is at the Macon Site which has been shown to be pure, transplanted Middle Mississippian. If Spiro may be judged by what few ceramic specimens we have seen from it and by analogy with the related Gahagan Mound,[92] the pottery bears many resemblances to the Caddoan wares of the Lower Valley and is correspondingly late.

"Since the occurrence of this material is unquestionably late, it may be assumed that examination of the ethnographic accounts of the area would show evidence of an organized group of ceremonials which can be correlated with this archeological complex. This is indeed the case. The Creek, the Natchez and the Chickasaw possessed what once must have been a common ceremonial. In ETOWAH PAPERS Willoughby makes

[89] Willey and Woodbury, 1942. (Willey, 1949—Ed.) [90] Webb, 1939. Webb and DeJarnette, 1942. [91] Moore, 1899. Pp. 319-333. [92] Webb and Dodd, 1939.

much of this fact and comes to the conclusion that the Etowah material represents proto-Muskhogean ceremonial Paraphernalia and formed a connecting link between Creek and Natchez ceremonial. Whatever the early form of the ceremonial complex was, it reached the historic level in an altered form. This may be seen from the archeological evidence as well as from the ethnological evidence. Swanton, approaching this problem from the ethnological side in 1927 before much of the archeological material now at hand was availaible wrote:

'Among the Creek Indians, however, the term "green corn dance" applies specifically to the busk, or posketa, meaning the "fast," which occurred when the first flower corn of the season was ready for consumption, between the middle of July and the middle of August. In the course of my investigations among these Indians, about 15 years ago, I learned that the busk was not an isolated ceremony. It was the most important ceremony of the year, that indeed with which the new year began, but it was the fourth of a series of rituals spaced about a month apart and, hence, beginning in April or May. The first three were rather local in character and prepared the way for the main ceremonial to which many persons of related or friendly towns were invited. Following the busk, particularly if the food were plentiful, came a succession of social gatherings extending into the late fall and commonly called the "raccoon dance" or the "old people's dance," the only one in which masks were worn. One Creek informant declared this to be the most sacred ceremonial of all. The religious side of some of these dances was not always conspicuous, but we know them only in their decadence, and it seems to be a universal truth that when ceremonials decay the social elements become progressively more pronounced, while those having an esoteric or sacred import are gradually abbreviated. As far back as the middle of the 18th century Adair observed this process taking place. There are, then, so far as the Creek Indians are concerned, good indications of a long summer ceremonial season, and it would have taken comparatively little elaboration of known ritual to produce a pageant imposing and intricate enough to match any mound group of which we have knowledge, even Cahokia itself.

'We may conclude, then, by saying that the historic ceremonies and ceremonial mounds of our Southeastern Indians, or of the Creeks alone suggest psychical and technical forces sufficient to account for all the mounds of the Mississippi Valley and the districts north of the Gulf of Mexico.' [93]

"To orient Dr. Swanton's conclusions with the complex in question, it should be recalled that the Macon Site is the 'Ocmulgee Old Fields' of Bartram and that Creek tradition points to that site as one of the first points of occupation and fortification after their migration from the Red River region where they acquired their ceremonial and the four medicines. We cannot discuss historic ceremonial in the Southeast at this time.

"To summarize the chronological aspects of the complex: these elements appear suddenly and late. When they appear, Macon excepted, they are apparently fully elaborated. No developmental sequences of the elements are traceable. Such Hopewellian traits as the serpent representations, the ceremonial celt and the omnipresent conch bowl might be regarded as suggesting a background of ceremonialism upon which the complex proper might develop. The gap between the two is wide, none the less.

"Another important point is the ubiquitous manner in which elements of the complex appear again and again in the midst of otherwise unrelated groups. When one compares the ceremonial elements one finds the usual high correlation in the several localities, but when one compares other traits, the correlation is almost nil. Thus, comparing Etowah, Moundville, and Spiro on the basis of ceramics is an unrewarding task. Aside from the ceremonial bottle forms, the presence of shell as an aplastic and the appearance of the strap handle on the domestic ware, few points in common can be found. At Etowah stamping had reached a high plane of technique and had a local tradition and development that went back to the late archaic. At Moundville stamping was absent. Both ceramic traditions are completely different from that in the Lower Mississippi Valley to which Spiro is said to be related. The basic cultural dissimilarity extends further to include house-type and most domestic artifacts. It is interesting to see elements crop up at Key Marco against a cultural background that suggests primitive survivals dating back to Southeastern archaic levels.

"Thus it would seem that the complex represents something late and specialized, something which could reappear essentially intact in unrelated groups a thousand miles apart. In short, the complex reflects the existence of a pre-Columbian cult which swept through the late prehistoric Southeast very much as the Ghost Dance swept from tribe to tribe across the Plains in the late nineteenth century.

"The subject of Mexican influences frequently arises. Certainly, two periods of possible Mexican influence can be recognized. The first period was at the close of the Southeastern archaic when the basic economy shifted from a hunting-fishing-gathering economy to an agricultural one. This is presumably the time of the introduction of maize. At this period the bicymbal copper ear-spool, the copper celt and the burial mound idea appear in the Southeast and are found first in the Lower Mississippi Valley. These are possible Mexican importations. It will be noted that with these exceptions, the complex outlined above embraces partically all of the Mexicanoid elements which have been recognized in Southeastern archeology. In a recent paper Phillips has outlined many of these elements and has pointed out their late relationship.[94] He feels that they

[93] Swanton, 1927.   [94] Phillips, 1940.

are actually of Mexican origin. Unfortunately, when one looks for Mexican sources one is hampered by two factors: in the first place, while archeology of the Huastec area is a virtual blank, yet tantalizing details are known; the presence of vessel forms belong to Vaillant's 'Q Complex,' ceremonial mounds of earth, and a shell-work technique which may well have connections with the engraved shell gorgets which are such a striking element in the cult complex in the Southeast. In the second place, when one looks for sources in the ceremonial material of highland Mexico, one strikes difficulty because this material has been neither organized nor interpreted. The temple mound, the bird-serpent composite, the Hand and Eye, the human head held by the hair, the ceremonial hafted celt and possibly the Baton all have close counterparts in the Mixteca-Puebla 'culture.' The feel of the cult material under discussion is Middle American rather than Southeastern. Since none of these Mexicanoid elements appear in the earlier Southeastern levels and since they arrive in a body, suddenly and late, it seems most likely that they are of Mexican origin. Also, both in Mexico and in the Southeast, these elements were bound in with a late ceremonial complex. Since diffusion from the Southwest, from the West Indies or from the North cannot be demonstrated, it seems inescapable, J. Alden Mason to the contrary notwithstanding, that the route of ingress lay along the Texas Coast.

"Phillips writes: 'We are evidently concerned with the transmissions of a cult (or a group of associated cults) rather than culture in a more general sense.' With this we are in entire agreement. He does not feel, however, that these similarities are best explained on the basis of elaboration of the cult within the Middle Mississippi Valley and spread from the Source. He feels that such sites as Moundville, Etowah and Spiro have simply come under the same influence, that 'waves' of Middle American influence striking these centers of population gave rise to the complex as we see it. We feel that there are at least two fundamental objections to this attitude. In the first place, no single artifact of Mexican manufacture has been reported north of Texas to our knowledge. The second objection lies in the fact that these elements resolve into a basic and essentially un-Mexican core complex which this paper has outlined. It is too much to believe that these widely separated sites in the Southeast would select the same elements from those waves of influence, and not only select the same elements but modify and elaborate them in the same manner.

"There were probably at least two mechanisms by which the complex spread: (1) by rapid diffusion from group to group and (2) carried by moving peoples. In most instances the spread was cross-cultural. However, it should be remembered that the three great cult sites lie on the peripheries of the Middle Mississippi expansion, and that great movement of population certainly served to introduce the cult into Georgia and Alabama. Because of the nature of the complex and because of the fact that its spread seems to be to a great degree linked to the movements of Middle Mississippian groups, we feel that the spread of the complex from a single Southeastern community or group of communities is strongly suggested.

"One further point is to be made. The sites at which the complex is strongest lie in rich, fertile bottom lands. The distribution along the spine of the Mississippi-Missouri Rivers and on the South Atlantic and Gulf drainage coincides with the distribution of the most markedly horticultural communities. It should be noted that Strong figures an antler bracelet from Nebraska which bears the Hand and Eye motif,[95] indicating a considerable spread of the complex along the river bottoms far out into the Plains. At Spiro, motifs and other elements are found associated with maize representations in at least five instances. At Key Marco, a community of hunters and fishers whose roots lie in the earliest levels of the Southeastern cultures, the cult had such vigor that elements could be grafted directly onto a basically non-agricultural ceremonial complex.

"We feel that it is possible to account for all the above facts by the following hypothesis: There existed in the prehistoric Southeast a highly-developed cult or cult complex, integrated with and fundamentally dependent upon a horticultural base. This cult was synthesized within the southeastern United States in a single community or restricted group of communities at a relatively late date from elements introduced from Middle America. This integration probably took place in the Middle Mississippi Basin. From this center the cult spread rapidly, crossing tribal boundaries, flowered abruptly and passed almost as quickly, reaching historic levels only in an attenuated form. Local variations in the complex are explicable in terms of the previous ceremonial life and basic economics of the subareas under consideration. These variations, the attenuated forms and the probable nature of the original cult will be considered in a subsequent paper."

Bibliography is included in the general bibliography in the back of the book.

[95] Strong, 1935. Plate 10 No. 2.

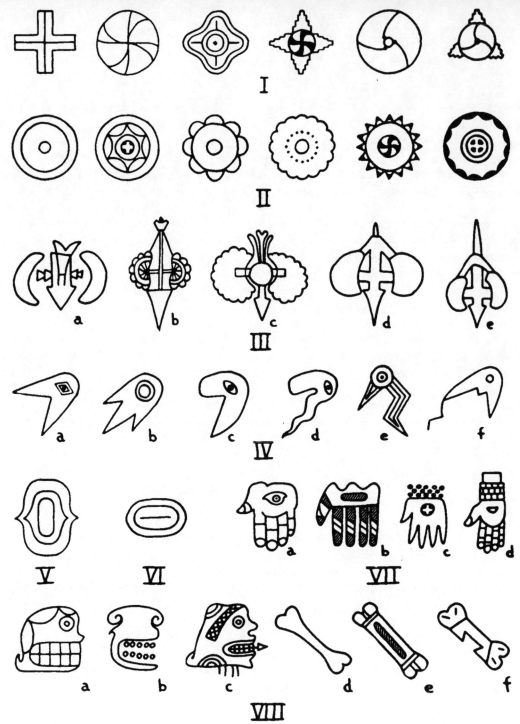

MOTIFS

Plate 17

ABOVE. "Figure 1. (Waring and Holder, 1945): I. the Cross. II. the Sun Circle. III. ~~the~~ Bi-lobed Arrow. IV. the Forked Eye. V. the Open Eye. VI. the Barred Oval. VII. the Hand and Eye. VIII. Death Motifs. (I and II: examples from Willoughby, 1897 and Holmes, 1903. III a: Moundville, engraved on bowl. Moore, 1907, Fig. 39. III b: Moundville, engraved on stone disc. Moore, 1905, Fig. 5. III c: Moundville, engraved on jar. Moore, 1905, Fig. 87. III d: Etowah, copper hair ornament. Moorehead, 1932, Fig. 20 b. III e: Spiro, see Fig. 5 d. IV a: Spiro, shell gorget. M. A. I. Cat. No. 18/7914. IV b: Etowah, copper plate. Willoughby, 1932, Fig. 11 a. IV c and d: Spiro, shell gorget. M. A. I. Cat. No. 18/9084. IV e: Ely Mound, Virginia. Carr, 1881. IV f: Calf Mountain Mound, Manitoba. Montgomery, 1910, Pl. III. V: Moundville, copper gorget. Moore, 1905, Fig. 102. VI: see Fig. IV e. VII a: Moundville, engraved on bowl. Moore, 1907, Fig. 62. VII b: Moundville, engraved on bowl, Moore, 1907, Fig. 45. VII c: Nashville, Tenn., painted bottle. Thruston, 1890, Fig. 40. VII d: Spiro, shell gorget. Science News Letter. VIII a: Moundville, engraved on bowl. Moore, 1905, Fig. 62. VIII b: Central Mississippi, painted bottle. Shetrone, 1930. Fig. 242. VIII c: Walls, Miss., engraved jar. Brown, 1926. VIII d: Pecan Point, Ark., applique on bottle. Moore, 1910. Fig. 225. VIII e: Moundville, engraved on bowl. Moore, 1907. Fig. 45. VIII f: Spiro, conch shell bowl. M. A. I. Cat. No. 18/9082.)" M. A. I. abbreviation for: Museum of the American Indian.

Figure I and the following figures in this chapter are from the article quoted in this chapter. This article by Dr. A. J. Waring, Jr., and Dr. Preston Holder is entitled "A Prehistoric Ceremonial Complex in the Southeastern United States;" it is from the AMERICAN ANTHROPOLOGIST, Vol. 47, No. 1, 1945. The article, figures, and diagrams are reproduced herein by permission from Dr. A. J. Waring, Jr., Dr. Preston Holder, and the AMERICAN ANTHROPOLOGIST.

LEFT. Burial and accompanying artifacts including a pottery bottle, stone celts, and other broken pottery vessels. Cultura Arcaica Tlatilco, Edo. de Mexico (Cortesia del Museo Nacional de Antropologia, de Mexico).

BELOW. Funeral urn of modeled pottery, representing the God, Xipe; he wears elaborate paraphernalia, holds a baton in one hand and a head with long hair in the other. Monte Alban, III, Oaxaca (Cortesia del Museo Nacional de Antropologia, de Mexico).

CENTRAL AMERICAN SIMILARITIES

Plate 18

Bar gorgets, drilled beads, boatstones, rudimentary zoomorphic forms, pottery, stamped decoration, circular ear spools, burial mounds, and celts of the Woodland Period (some Late Archaic also) are similar to certain Central American objects, styles, and techniques. Even more noticeable similarities are found in the Mississippi Period "symbols;" ceremonial paraphernalia; truncated earth mounds; planned agricultural villages; and certain artifacts—burial urns, long-neck pottery vessels, painted, engraved, and black-filmed pottery, modeled effigy vessels and vessel handles; and stone forms—celt, spatulate object, roller-pestle, paint palette, image, bowl, and monolithic ax.

There has been frequent speculation as to a probable relationship be'ween the Middle Mississippi Period Culture of the Southeastern United States and cultures of Central America. Holmes referred to this (1883) and to possible Caribbean influences (1894). Cushing (1896) expressed belief in the latter. After finding ceremonial pottery at Moundville, Moore (1905) mentioned the possibility of Central American influence; other authors have briefly discussed or mentioned this. Waring and Holder (1945) and Krieger (1945) stimulated further debate; Lewis and Kneberg (1954) compared engraved shell disks; Rands (1957) continued a discussion which will provoke further debate.

BELOW. "Petroglyphs on a boulder on the ranch of Rudy Zapata—the San Carlos Ranch—some thirty miles over almost impassable desert south from the Arizona-Mexico border at Sasabe. This is in Sonora, about eighty miles east of the Gulf of California. The boulder, of a greyish-tan granite, measures about 6 feet by 8 feet in lateral and longitudinal diameters, respectively. The face, on which the petroglyphs are pecked to a depth of about one-eighth inch, inclines approximately twenty degrees from the horizontal.

"The motifs on the rock, some of which may be better comprehended from the accompanying line drawing, are quite different from any heretofore reported from this region. No interpretation of these designs is offered at the present time. All of the motifs may be found in the Eastern United States, the Valley of Mexico, or the U. S. Southwest, though not necessarily in the particular combination shown here or in any one given locality." (Courtesy, Carl B. Compton and William J. Schaldach, Instituto Interamericano, Denton, Texas).

CEREMONIAL OBJECTS

Plates 19 and 20

BELOW. "Figure II (Waring and Holder, 1945): Ceremonial Objects. a-e: examples of the embossed Copper Plate. See also Fig. IV a-c and Fig. V a. f-j: Monolithic Stone Axe. k: hafted copper celt from Spiro showing similarity to the monolithic forms. l-w: examples of the Baton from widely separated sites throughout the Southeast. l, r, s and w are taken from copper plates and engraved conch shell bowls. m and n are Copper Symbol Badges. o and p are Sheet Copper Hair Ornaments. t, u and v are in chipped flint. q is the only example of the baton extant, having come from the Key Marco muck. x, y and z are Copper Symbol Badges in the shape of stylized feathers.

"(a. Spiro. M. A. I. Cat. No. 20/699. b. Spiro. M. A. I. Cat No. 20/700 c. Etowah, Mound C. Willoughby, 1932. d. Mount Royal, Florida. Moore, 1894. Vol. I. e. Spiro. M. A. I. Cat No. 20/701. f. Hamilton County, Tenn., U. of Tenn. Museum. g. Etowah, Mound C. Moorehead, 1932. Fig. 52. h. Moundville Moore, 1905. Fig. 6. i. Tennessee? Peabody Museum, Yale University. Cat. No. 3701. j. Nashville, Tenn., Thruston, 1890. k. Spiro. wooden hafted axe in form of pileated woodpecker with blade of copper and eye of shell. One of a bundle of several of identical pattern. M. A. I. Cat. No. 18/9077. l. Etowah, Mound C. Thomas, 1891. Plate XVII. Detail from embossed copper plate. m. Etowah, Mound C. Sheet Copper Symbol Badge. Willoughby, 1932. Fig. 17. n. Etowah, Mound C. Sheet Copper Symbol Badge. Willoughby, 1932. Fig. 18. o. Moundville, Sheet Copper Hair Emblem in shape of Baton. Moore, 1905. Fig. 105 p. Jackson Co., Ala., sheet copper Hair Emblem in shape of Baton. M. A. I. Cat. No. 7960. q. Key Marco, Fla., wooden Baton. Cushing, 1896. Fig. 4. S. r. and s. Spiro. Engraved on conch shell bowl. H. M. Trowbridge Collection. t. Spiro. The Baton in chipped flint, painted red and white. M. A. I. Cat. No. 18/9334. u. Spiro. Baton in chipped flint. Remnants of paint present. M. A. I. Cat. No. 18/9335. v. Tennessee. Baton in chipped flint. Moorehead, 1910. w. Union Co., Ill., detail from embossed copper plate. Thomas, 1891. Fig. 85. x. Etowah, Mound C. Sheet Copper Hair Emblem in shape of a plume. Thomas, 1891. Fig. 188. y. Spiro. M. A. I. Cat. No. 20/706. z. Jackson Co., Ala., M. A. I.)" Reproduced by permission from Dr. A. J. Waring, Jr., Dr. Preston Holder, and the AMERICAN ANTHROPOLOGIST.

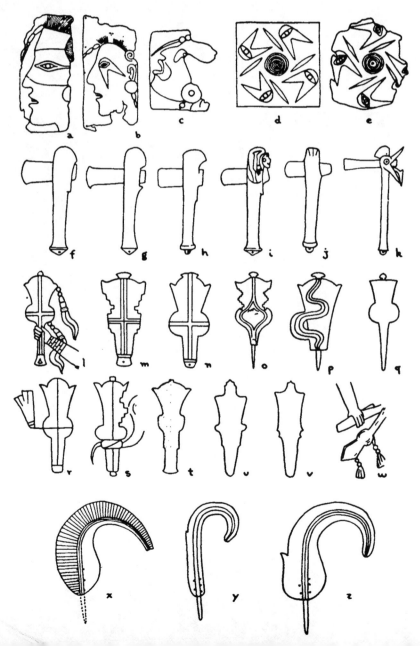

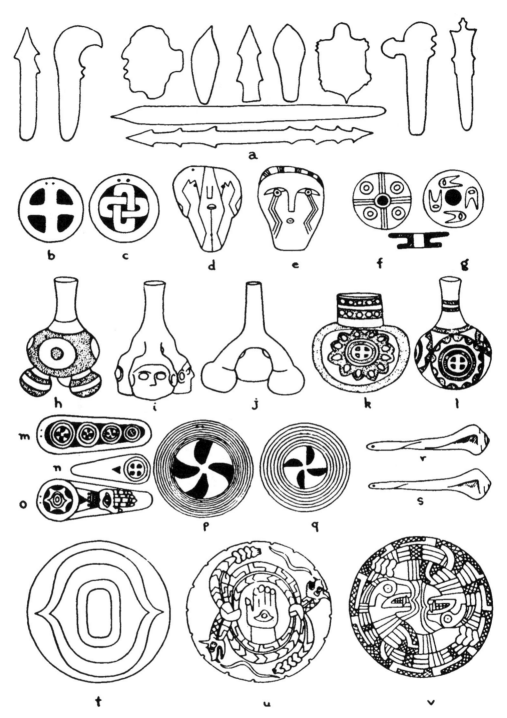

ABOVE. "Figure III (Waring and Holder, 1945): Ceremonial Objects. a: variations in the ceremonial flint forms from Tennessee and Georgia. b and c: circular gorgets of shell. Simplest form. d and e: mask gorgets. f and g: copper-covered ear-spools of stone. h, i and j: tripartite bottles. k and l: painted bottles (Cross and Sun Circles). m, n, and o: oblong gorgets of copper. p and q: circular gorgets of copper. r and s: columella pendants. t, u and v: engraved stone discs.

"(a: Moorehead, 1910. Vol. I, Figs. 157-162. 1932. Fig. 55. b: Charlestown, Mo., Holmes, 1883. Pl. LI. c: Missouri. Mac-Curdy, 1913. Fig. 62. d: Turkey Island, Ark., Moore, 1910 Page 321. e: Acquia Creek, Va. Holmes, 1883. Pl. LXVII. f and g: Spiro, M. A. I. Cat. No. 18/6521-2. h, k and l: Etowah, Mound C. Moorehead, 1932. Fig. 33. i: Hollywood Mound, Ga. Thomas, 1891. Fig. 199. j: Spiro. M. A. I. Cat. No. 20/742. m: Etowah, Mound C. Moorehead, 1932. Fig. 23. n: Moundville. Moore, 1905. Fig. 102. o: Moundville. Moore, 1907. Fig. 100. p: Moundville. Moore, 1905. Fig. 134. q: Etowah, Mound C. Moorehead, 1932. Fig. 22. r: Wheeler Basin, Ala. Webb, 1939. Pl. 109b. s: Spiro. M. A. I. t: Menard Mound, Arkansas. Stoddard, 1904. Page 153. u: Moundville. Moore, 1905. Fig. 7. v: Mississippi. Holmes, 1906. Fig. 1.)" Reproduced by permission from Dr. A. J. Waring, Jr., Dr. Preston Holder, and the AMERICAN ANTHROPOLOGIST.

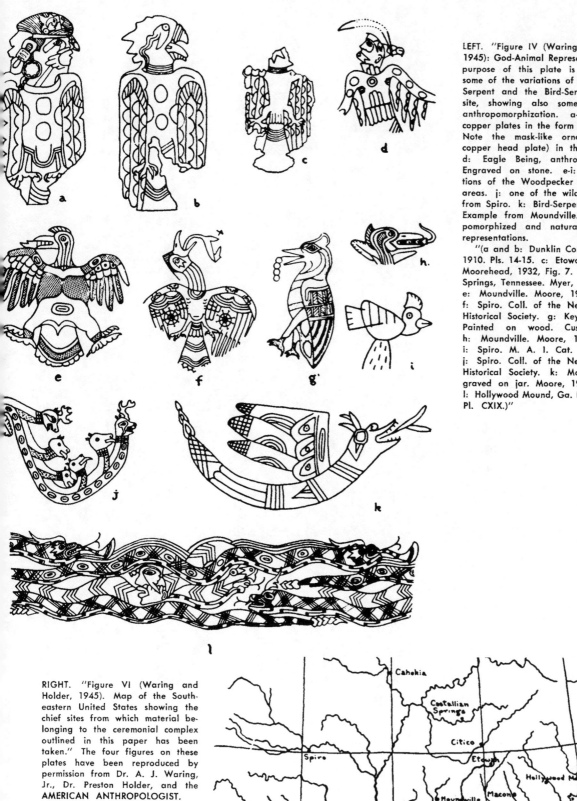

LEFT. "Figure IV (Waring and Holder, 1945): God-Animal Representations. The purpose of this plate is to illustrate some of the variations of the Bird, the Serpent and the Bird-Serpent Composite, showing also some degree of anthropomorphization. a-c: embossed copper plates in the form of the Eagle. Note the mask-like ornament (sheet copper head plate) in the hair in a. d: Eagle Being, anthropomorphized. Engraved on stone. e-i: Representations of the Woodpecker from various areas. j: one of the wilder variations from Spiro. k: Bird-Serpent Composite. Example from Moundville. l: Anthropomorphized and naturalistic serpent representations.

"(a and b: Dunklin Co., Mo. Fowke, 1910. Pls. 14-15. c: Etowah, Mound C. Moorehead, 1932, Fig. 7. d: Castalian Springs, Tennessee. Myer, 1917. Fig. 2. e: Moundville. Moore, 1907. Fig. 38. f: Spiro. Coll. of the Nebraska State Historical Society. g: Key Marco, Fla. Painted on wood. Cushing, 1896. h: Moundville. Moore, 1905. Fig. 9. i: Spiro. M. A. I. Cat. No. 18/912. j: Spiro. Coll. of the Nebraska State Historical Society. k: Moundville. Engraved on jar. Moore, 1907. Fig. 58. l: Hollywood Mound, Ga. Holmes, 1903. Pl. CXIX.)"

RIGHT. "Figure VI (Waring and Holder, 1945). Map of the Southeastern United States showing the chief sites from which material belonging to the ceremonial complex outlined in this paper has been taken." The four figures on these plates have been reproduced by permission from Dr. A. J. Waring, Jr., Dr. Preston Holder, and the AMERICAN ANTHROPOLOGIST.

LEFT. "Figure V (Waring and Holder, 1945): God-Animal Representations. a, b, c and f: variations of the anthropomorphized Eagle Being from Etowah and Spiro. Note the interesting correspondence in detail in the copper plate from Etowah (a) and the plate from Spiro (c). d, e, g, h and i: representations from Spiro. Note Chunkee Player (g).

"(a: Etowah, Mound C. Thomas, 1891. Pl. XVII. b: Spiro. Engraved on conch shell bowl. M. A. I. Cat. No. 18/9121. c: Spiro. Embossed copper plate. M. A. I. Cat. No. 18/9332. d: Spiro. Engraved on fragment of conch shell bowl. H. M. Trowbridge Collection. Cat. No. 2634. e: Spiro. Engraved on conch shell bowl. M. A. I. Cat. No. 18/9123. f: Etowah, Mound C. Engraved on conch shell gorget. Moorehead, 1932. Fig. 26a. g: Spiro. Engraved on conch shell gorget. M. A. I. Cat. No. 18/7913. h: Spiro. Engraved on conch shell bowl. M. A. I. Cat. No. 18/9083. i: Spiro. Conch shell gorget (in partial bas-relief). M. A. I. Cat. No. 18/9085.)"

GOD-ANIMAL REPRESENTATIONS AND CULTURE PERIODS

Plates 21 and 22

RIGHT: "Figure VII (Waring and Holder, 1945). Chronological arrangement of the ceramic periods in the Southeastern United States in their probable temporal relationship, demonstrating the late occurrence of the ceremonial complex. The stippled area represents periods in which elements of the complex have appeared. See text for bibliography of the above arrangement."

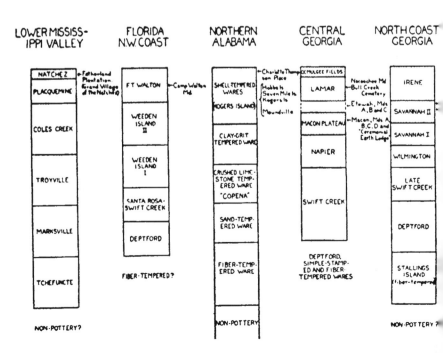

Chapter 4

SYMBOLISM

Quotation from Charles C. Willoughby, "Notes on the History and Symbolism of the Muskhogeans and the People of Etowah." From the ETOWAH PAPERS 1: EXPLORATION OF THE ETOWAH SITE IN GEORGIA by Warren K. Moorehead. Published for Phillips Academy by the Yale University Press. Copyright 1932. Quoted by permission from Yale University Press and the Robert S. Peabody Foundation for Archaeology, Phillips Academy, Andover, Mass.

"THE EAGLE AMONG THE MUSKHOGEANS. [1] The eagle was regarded among the Muskhogeans as a mighty bird (great king). The symbolic meaning of its white tail feathers is made plain by a passage in a speech delivered by Tomochichi, a Creek chief, when presented to King George II, by Governor Oglethorpe, during their visit to England in 1734:

'These are the feathers of the eagle, which is the swiftest of birds, and who flieth all around our nations. The feathers are a sign of peace in our land, and have been carried from town to town there; and we have brought them over to leave with you, O great king, as a sign of everlasting peace.' [2]

"When the portrait of this chief and his nephew was painted in London, the latter was represented holding an eagle in his arms. The golden eagle was esteemed by many American tribes for its tail and wing feathers, and for its fluffy white under feathers. Adair says that a whole Creek town would contribute to the value of 200 deerskins to the killing of a large eagle, and the man who killed one received an honorary title for his exploit. Eagle feathers are often spoken of as red or white. Of course they are red only when artifically colored. The tips of the white feathers and most of the darker feathers of the tail of the golden eagle are brown or gray shading into black. The peace calumet of the central and southern tribes was ornamented with about seven tail feathers of the golden eagle arranged fanwise. Du Pratz makes it clear that the feathers of this bird were on the peace calumets of the Natchez. The peace calumet was changed to a war calumet by staining the white portions of the feathers red. The red feathers of the flamingo were sometimes used on war calumets of this tribe. According to Bartram, the Creeks and Muscogulges made their royal standard (which resembled a calumet with the pipe-bowl removed) of the tail feathers of the painted vulture. This was called by a name which signified eagle's tail. When carried in battle it was painted with a zone of red within the brown tips. [3] These vulture feathers were probably used only as a substitute for the less easily procured eagle feathers which they resembled. White indicated peace; red the color of blood, symbolized war. The division of both Creek and Natchez into war and peace parties, distinguished by the red and white plumes worm by the warriors; and the separation of the Creek districts into war and peace (red and white) towns, all tend to show the regard in which these symbolic colors were held. Chekilli's migration legend tells us that 'If an enemy approaches with white feathers and a white mouth and cries like an eagle, they dare not kill him.'

"The importance of the eagle as a symbol among the tribes is manifest. At the annual celebration of the posketv (green corn dance) a wooden image of it was erected. Adair saw in several ceremonial grounds two white painted eagles carved out of poplar wood, with their wings stretched out, and raised five feet off the ground standing at the corner and close to the red and white imperial seats. This writer also tells us that a pole was commonly fixed at the apex of the roof of the winter hot house that displayed on its top the figure of a large carved eagle. [4]

"The temples of the Natchez group were surmounted by two or three large wooden eagles looking toward the rising sun. In describing those of the Natchez proper Du Pratz says, 'the wing feathers are large and very distinct. The ground color is white mingled with feathers of a beautiful red color.' This bird, however, was not always a symbol of peace. It was so considered only when its feathers remained white. When its feathers were red it became an emblem of war. The Creek war chief who led the revolt against the Americans in 1813-14, bore the name Lamhi-tchati, which signifies Red Eagle. Swanton says that according to the late

---

[1] Willoughby, 1932. Eagle, pp. 33-38. Woodpecker, pp. 57-59. [2] D. G. Brinton, NATIONAL LEGEND OF THE CHAHTA-MUSKOXEE TRIBES, p. 12. [3] Bartram, 1792, p. 151. [4] Adair, 1775, pp. 30, 419.

Judge James R. Gregory, who belonged to the town of Ocmulgee, each talwa, or town, or at least the more important of them, anciently had a special emblem entirely distinct from the totems of the clans. He stated that the Coweta emblem was a wooden eagle marked like a spotted eagle . . . with drops of blood represented issuing from the corners of its mouth. Whenever an important council was to be held it was brought out and set up in the ground in front of the miko's seat, facing east. Coweta was a red or bloody town where the chiefs and warriors assembled when war was proposed.[5]

"That the eagle also filled an important role in the life of the people who built the Etowah mounds is shown by the copper plates bearing representations of this bird which were taken from the temple mound (C) by the Bureau of American Ethnology . . . in 1885, and by the Phillips Academy at Andover during its recent explorations (1932). The spotted eagle may well have been the emblem of this important town. It should be borne in mind that these plates of polished copper were originally red, that oval spots appear on the bodies of the birds, and that the wing feathers bear semi-oval markings . . . . The design surrounding each eye is characteristic of the spotted war eagle; it usually has two points, though sometimes three . . . .

"It is at once apparent that the representations of the eagle in embossed sheet copper from the Etowah group, and those from Illinois and Missouri . . . are intended for the same bird. The oval spots on the body, the markings on the quill feathers of the wings, and the design around the eye, show this conclusively. In some 26 representations of the spotted eagle which we have examined, the eye is surrounded by this design, having either two or three projections. In a few examples it is not shown. It also occurs in pictures of the combined eagle and serpent, the two chief war patrons of the Muskhogean people. Several water bottles from Moundville, Alabama, show incised drawings of this dual being. It is also a distinguishing mark in personifications of this bird as in . . . (the human figures on copper plates from Etowah) and in some of the shell gorget 'masks' from western Virginia, southern Ohio and Tennessee. One of the gorgets was found with a burial in the Etowah village site, but it lacked the surrounding eye pattern. One of the finest copper plates secured by Mr. Moore . . . shows four eyes each surrounded by one of these designs, each eye alternating with what seems to be intended to represent a flint sword.[6] The occurrence of this eye design ranges from Madisonville, southern Ohio, to Florida, and from western Virginia to Missouri. In one or two examples from the north of the area, one of the arms of the design merges into a lightning line in . . . (one from Peoria, Illinois, in the collection of the Bureau of American Ethnology). This merging is also shown in some of the shell gorget 'masks' figured by Holmes. These recall the lightning flashes from the eye of the thunderbird, a being common in the mythology of many northern tribes. The thunderbird seems to have been unknown, however, among the Muskhogeans . . . .

"THE WOODPECKER.—. . . occupied a prominent place in the ceremonies and symbolism of many tribes in the . . . southern . . . United States. This bird's head or tail appears incised on no less than six water bottles . . . (and) a shell gorget from Moundville. (He refers to its appearance on several Etowah Shell gorgets —1932, Fig. 32). . . . A combination of woodpecker heads and the sun or world symbols (sometimes with the "looped band") appear on shell gorgets from Tennessee. . . . These . . . may well have been clan symbols.

"In the Peabody Museum at Cambridge, are two very old calumets, on the upper side of the stems of which are fastened several upper mandibles of . . . (the woodpecker) with scalp and crest attached. The mandibles are turned backward over the scalp which is tightly bound to the pipestem. One of the pipes is a war calumet with the pendent attached of eagle feathers stained red. The other is a peace calumet with eagle feathers unstained. The stem and appendages of the calumet all had their symbolic meanings, and together formed one of the most highly organized ritualistic emblems known.

"THE SWASTIKA-CROSS SYMBOL.[7] (Regarding a breastplate or circular gorget of copper found at Etowah with an excised swastika surrounded by eight embossed circles — see Waring and Holder, Fig. III q — Willoughby states:) The central portion shows one form of swastika and probably symbolizes the moving winds; the whole symbol being a variant of the straight armed cross within a circle which is so characteristic of this region. During Mr. Moore's exploration of the group of mounds near Moundville, Alabama, previously referred to, he found with a burial in Mound O, nearly a duplicate of this breast plate."

(He further refers to a copper pendant — see Waring and Holder, Figure III o — showing four excised

[5] Bartram, 1792, p. 389. [6] Moore, 1894, Pt. I, frontispiece. A similar plaque was found at Spiro; see Waring and Holder, 1945, Figure II, d, and e.—Chapter 3 herein. [7] Willoughby, 1932, pp. 44-45.

swastikas with concentric circles around them, and states:) "Mr. Moore found several pendants of this same material (copper) and similar shape at Moundville four of which had a swastika of the same pattern at the larger end, below which was a triangular opening.

"It is very probable that these interesting ornaments were symbols of the wind clan, which was one of the most important of the Muskhogean people. There are various stories concerning the origin of this clan, most of which relate to the dispersing by the winds, of the thick fog which orginally covered the earth, and which led to the appearance of light and the sun. Before the coming of the winds the Indians had been unable to see, and were dependent on their other senses, especially that of touch, in their efforts to obtain subsistence.[8]

"THE COSMIC OR WORLD SYMBOL. [9] It may be well to speak more specifically of the cosmic or world symbol, which, in itself or in some of its parts, formed so important a part of the symbolism of the Muskhogean tribes. It was by no means confined to this area, but in no other section of America does it seem to have occupied so conspicuous a place in the culture of the people. To the Indian the world was a body of land like a great island entirely surrounded by water; this was covered by a great dome, across which the sun took its daily course from east to west. The water extended to the lower edge of this sky dome, which formed a great circle enclosing both water and land. The four cardinal points were determined by the course of the sun, and the direction of the winds, which came from the north, south, east, and west. The Indians therefore graphically represented the world by one or more circles enclosing a cross, and with or without a central circle, which symbolized the sun in the zenith, at the period of its greatest power. This doubtless explains why in so many representations of the sun, there is a cross in its center; it is the meeting point of the lines of the four directions. Excellent pictures of the sun showing the central cross appear on two of the three water bottles from the temple mound (Etowah—see Waring and Holder, Figure III, h, k, I). We find in the rituals and legends of the Indians generally, considerable data bearing on this subject but it is usually fragmentary. The Cherokee thought the earth was a great island floating in a sea of water, and suspended at each of the four cardinal points by a cord hanging down from the sky vault, which was of solid rock.[10] . . . The sun as we have seen, was the supreme diety of the Natchez, and the perpetual fire, so carefully preserved by various tribes of this region was derived from the sun and was the symbol of the great luminary. In the Creek migration legend, the Kasihta, Coweta, and Chickasaw, when at the forks of the Red River, were at a loss for fire. They were visited by the Hayayalgi, four men who came from the four corners of the world, who started it for them. In explaining the above Gatschet writes: 'The Hayayalgi, coming from the four corners of the world to light the sacred fire, the symbol of the sun, are the winds fanning it to a higher flame.'

"It will be remembered that the personal standard of Tascaluca, the Choctaw chief, was a circular, umbrella-like affair, divided into four quarters by a white cross, against a background of black or red. The baton of the master of ceremonies of the Natchez was a cross, and small white crosses, probably peace tokens, were presented by the Natchez chief, to Iberville, to his brother, to Sieur Dugnay, and to the Jesuit father who accompanied them, upon their visit to the Natchez in 1700.

"The national, or sacred fire of the Creeks was maintained by four logs placed in the form of a cross. As their inner ends were consumed by the smoldering fire the logs were pushed inward. Although the Creeks had different traditions regarding the origin of this fire, its symbolism is obvious.

"An interesting incident in connection with the symbol of the cross, occurring during the feast held by the Natchez in the month of the deer is given by Du Pratz. The Great Sun came out of his house and took the road to the temple:

'He stops in the middle of the open space opposite the temple, before which he makes a kind of obeisance, bending very low, and without bending his knees he takes up a little earth which he throws on his head, and then turns successively towards the four quarters of the earth, doing the same thing in each direction. Then, without changing his position, he looks fixedly at the temple, which he has to the south of him, he extends his arms horizontally (or in a cross) and remains without more movement than a statue. He remains in this attitude for about half an hour. Then the grand master of ceremonies comes to relieve him and do the same thing. This one is himself relieved at the end of a similar period of time by the great war chief who remains there equally long. [11]

"SERPENT SYMBOL. [12] So far as the present writer has been able to learn, no serpent gorgets have been taken from the temple mound (Etowah). [13] This seems to indicate that the tattooed or spotted serpent was not a patron of the royal family at Etowah. Among the Natchez, however, the serpent seems to have held a place very near to the sun, for Tattooed-serpent was evidently the hereditary title of the great war chiefs. To the

8 Swanton, 1928, pp. 110-112.   9 Willoughby, 1932, pp. 59-62.   10 Mooney, 1900, p. 239.   11 Swanton, 1911, p. 112, quotes Du Pratz.
12 Willoughby, 1932, pp. 62-63.   13 In the collection of the United States National Museum there is a serpent gorget which is catalogued "the Temple Mound C, Etowah." See the Etowah Plates shown herein for a photograph.

north of Georgia in eastern Tennessee many serpent gorgets have been found, also a considerable number of the scalloped shell discoidal gorgets the significance of which is not altogether clear . . . .

"Several serpent gorgets, however, were found with burials in the village site to the east of the great mound of this group (Etowah) during the Andover explorations, and they are not uncommon in other sections of northern Gegoria. . . .

"These show the spotted serpent coiled in the center of the disc. The four horns, so characteristic of the serpent deity north of Mexico appear as curved lines on the upper jaw. These vary in the different gorgets both in number and design, but they can usually be recognized. The outer circle of the gorget represents, of course, the horizon or outer limit of the Indian's world, within this outer circle the four ends of the cross connect it with the serpent. The cross, though usually present, is sometimes missing. The finest representations of the horned serpent in combination with the world symbol, in the north, are the work of the Great Earthwork Builders of Ohio, the most notable example being the serpent mound of Adams County. [14]

"The Cherokee who overran eastern Tennessee and northern Georgia at a period probably not long antedating the arrival of the Spaniards, have legends relating to their encounters with this serpent, which was said to dwell in the mountains. It was called Uktena, and was as large as a tree trunk. It had horns on its head and a bright blazing crest like a diamond on its forehead. It had rings or spots of color along its whole length, and could only be wounded in the seventh spot from the head, because under this spot were its heart and its life. This serpent was so deadly that even to see it asleep was death, not to the hunter himself, but to his family. [15] These legends show conclusively that this serpent was not a patron of the Cherokee, but an enemy to be overcome and destroyed. It seems probable that these serpent gorgets may be attributed to the Natchez, as Tattooed-serpent was the title of the war chief, and it may well have been the patron of some of the war towns. Upon the body of the serpent in nearly all of these gorgets there are four or five spots made up of concentric circles with a central dot, separated by crosshatched oval spots.[16]   . . .

"THE SUN. [17] All accounts agree in attributing to them (the Natchez) an extreme form of sun worship. Their ritual was highly developed. The position of the head chief, known as the Great Sun, was somewhat different from that among other tribes. He seemed to have absolute power over the lives and property of his subjects. When he died his wives and principal servants gave up their lives so that their spirits might accompany his in its journey to the spirit world. Children were sometime voluntarily sacrificed at his death by their parents. . . .

"Le Petit says (regarding the Natchez) [18]

'The sun is the principal object of veneration to these people; and as they cannot conceive of anything which can be above this heavenly body, nothing else appears to be more worthy of their homage. It is for the same reason that the great chief of the nation, who knows nothing on earth more dignified than himself, takes the title of Brother of the Sun, and the credulity of the people maintains him in the despotic authority which he claims. To enable them (the Sun and great chief) better to converse together they raise a mound of artificial soil on which they build his cabin, which is of the same construction as the temple. The door fronts the east, and every morning the chief honors by his presence the rising of his older brother, and salutes him with many howlings as he appears above the horizon. Then he gives orders that they shall light his calumet; he makes him an offering of the first three puffs which he draws; afterward raising his hand above his head, and turning from east to west, he shows him the direction which he must take in his course.'

"Penicaut informs us that the mound on which the house of the Great Sun was built is larger than the other mounds, and the sides are steeper. The following is an extract from Iberville's account of his visit to the Natchez in 1700;

'We repaired to his (the Chief's) cabin which is raised to a height of ten feet on earth brought thither, and is 25 feet wide and 45 feet long. Near-by are eight cabins. Before that of the chief is the temple mound which forms a round, a little oval, and bounds an open space about 250 spaces wide and 300 long.'[19]

"Charlevoix says the chief's cabin was larger and higher than the others and was very neatly plastered on the inside. Le Petit writes that the interior was furnished with a number of beds on the left as you enter the door, but on the right was only the bed of the great chief which was ornamented with different painted figures. According to Du Pratz the house of the head chief (Great Sun), and that of the great war chief (Tattooed-serpent), and also the temple, were on the public square. . . . [20] The house of the Great Sun faced the east and was on the highest mound. The temple also faced the east and the mound on which it was built stood upon the western side of the public square. The house of the Tattooed-serpent, the great war chief, also stood at one side of the square. His name, like that of the Great Sun was apparently hereditary. His house does not seem to have been built upon a mound, although in former times it may well have been so placed."

[14] Willoughby, 1919, pp. 153-163. [15] Mooney, 1900, pp. 297-298. [16] One of the serpent gorgets found at the Etowah village site has a swastika in one of the typical serpent's spots. Willoughby shows a drawing of it.
[17] Willoughby, 1932, pp. 22-24. [18] Swanton, 1911, p. 102, quotes Le Petit. [19] Shipp, 1881, p. 628. [20] Swanton, 1911, p. 148.

PREHISTORIC DESIGNS—SPIRO

Plates 23 and 24

These are shell gorgets from the Craig Burial Mound—Spiro Mound—Le Flore County, Oklahoma (Courtesy, University of Oklahoma, Stovall Museum). Such gorgets were cut from the outer whorl of marine univalve shells; designs were often engraved on the concave or inner side of the shell which has a natural smoothness, gloss, and often rose-tinted surface. UPPER. LEFT. Dancing figure gorget, 14.6 cm. diameter; sun circles; forked eye—short on one side; hair crest; flint dagger; shell ornaments and other ceremonial regalia. RIGHT. Raccoon gorget, 17.9 cm. diameter. Raccoon at center top and others hanging from sides of the figures; note, markings on face, tail, and body, and sex symbol? Note, other symbols—cross, swastika, sun circles; moccasins and other clothing; headdress may imitate a bird. CENTER. LEFT. Spider-hand gorget. This may represent the palm? of the hand with shell beads at wrist. Spider is carefully depicted with eight legs. Concavity of shell is pronounced. Hamilton, 1952, pictured several designs with spider motifs; others with hands and a variety of cult symbols. LOWER. LEFT. Hand and eye gorget. Sun circles are separated by parallel, excised spokes; the outside is scalloped. RIGHT. Woodpecker gorget, 9.7 cm. diameter. Note, long bill, crest, and symbol (turkey-like) at throat; the latter emphasizes the swastika design. The bird may be a composite representation. It is similar to certain shell gorget designs from the North Alabama-Tennessee area.

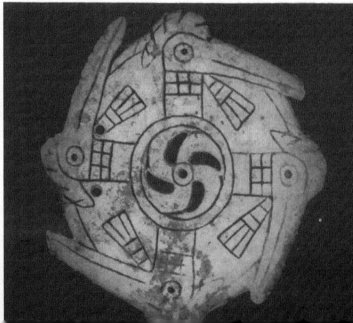

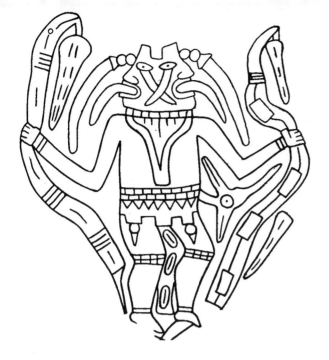

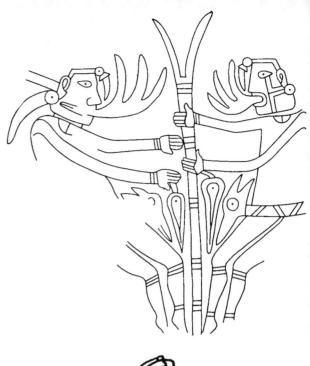

These designs were engraved on the outer surface of giant marine univalve shells, 12" to 15" long. The narrow part of the design is found at the small end of the shell and the widening design spreads around the expanding upper whorl. Spiro designs are the most elaborate found in or near the Southeast. They appear to depict life-activities or ceremonials. (The designs on this plate are pictured, Courtesy, Museum of the American Indian, Heye Foundation, and are from shells in their collection. Museum numbers are indicated. For other Spiro designs see E. K. Burnett, THE SPIRO MOUND COLLECTION IN THE MUSEUM, 1945). Dimensions refer to length. UPPER. LEFT. Masked snake dance, 11⅝" (18-9122). Note, speech symbol at mouth; barred oval; and deer's head at belt? RIGHT. "Choosing sides for the busk or green corn ceremony" (18-9123), see also Hamilton, 1952. Note, markings on faces—these occur on other similar designs; typical Spiro ear; large speech symbols. CENTER. RIGHT. "The Runner" (18-9085). This design is from a shell gorget rather than the outside of a shell "cup." The gorget is about 5" diameter. Note, eye at elbow joint; shoulder decorations or paintings; gorget or chunkey stone at neck? LOWER. LEFT. Masked eagle dancer, 13" long (18-9121). Note, round object at neck; unusual breechclout, shaped like the dorsal part of the spider depictions; rectangle or opening in the apron; tail and wing feathers with barred oval on wing; step design overhead. RIGHT. Snake dancer, 12⅜" (18-9083). Elaborate design of remarkable symmetry, showing action; probably exemplifying a ceremonial activity. Note, flint daggers? and regalia.

ABOVE. Design from whorl of giant marine univalve shell. Bi-lobed symbol headdress and forked eye are similar to Etowah copper plate designs. Note, bi-fork human eye and tri-fork serpent eye; clothing; and broken stick held in man's hand ? which appears to represent or symbolize the same object as depicted on chunkey-player shell gorgets—Spiro, Kentucky, and Missouri— pictured herein (Courtesy, Lightner Museum of Hobbies; collection on loan to Smithsonian Institution, United States National Museum; drawing courtesy, USNM 411901-411903).

PREHISTORIC DESIGNS—SPIRO

Plates 25 and 26

BELOW. Masked dancers. LEFT. Man in deer mask with antler, 13-1/16" length of shell. Note, shell ornaments, bow in hand, speech symbol, round symbol at neck. Objects hanging from arms may be leaves of corn or busk symbols? or pelts? RIGHT. Ceremonial performer, 11¼". Elaborate ornaments; speech symbol; head effigies, masks, or decapitated human heads? above arms. This may represent a dancer in a sacrificial ceremony (These are two of many designs found on giant conch shells in the Spiro collection owned by H. M. Trowbridge—2632 and 2630. These are pictured in Hamilton, THE SPIRO MOUND, 1952, and were reproduced from that publication, Courtesy, The Missouri Archaeological Society and H. M. Trowbridge. Hamilton, 1952, pictured several dozen designs and artifacts from the H. M. Trowbridge collection. He also included many others from other sources).

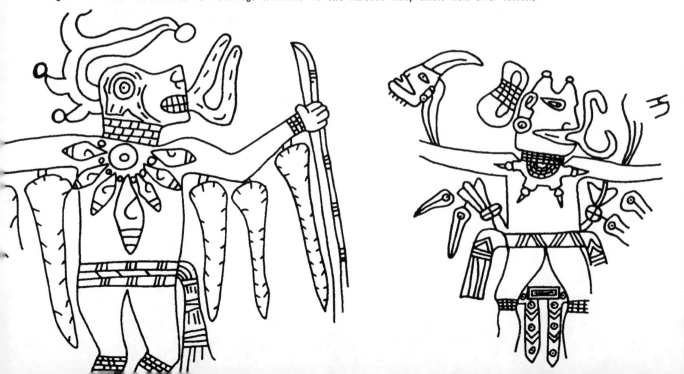

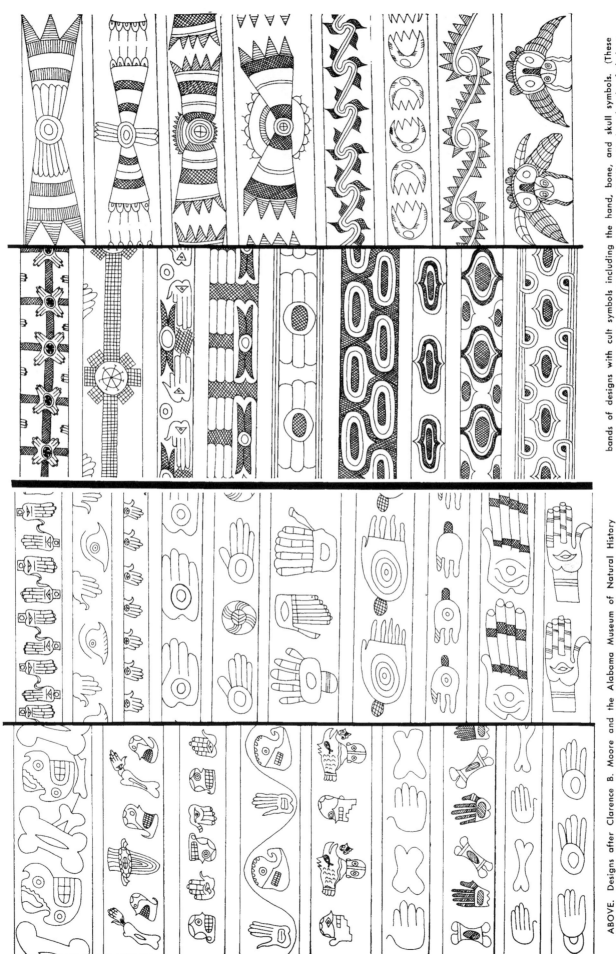

ABOVE. Designs after Clarence B. Moore and the Alabama Museum of Natural History collection, Mound State Monument, Moundville, Alabama. These are not tracings; they are only quickly made free-hand drawings, but they are closely representative, and show the variety of typical cult designs and combinations of designs used at Moundville. LEFT. Various bands of designs with cult symbols including the hand, bone, and skull symbols. (These include, Moore, BWR 22, 63, 147, 153, and MR 45, 46. RIGHT. Various bands of designs showing the ogee or open eye (or female symbol?), and wings. (These include, Moore, BWR 17, 30, 64, 74, and MR 41 and 42). Drawings by Ed.—ELF.

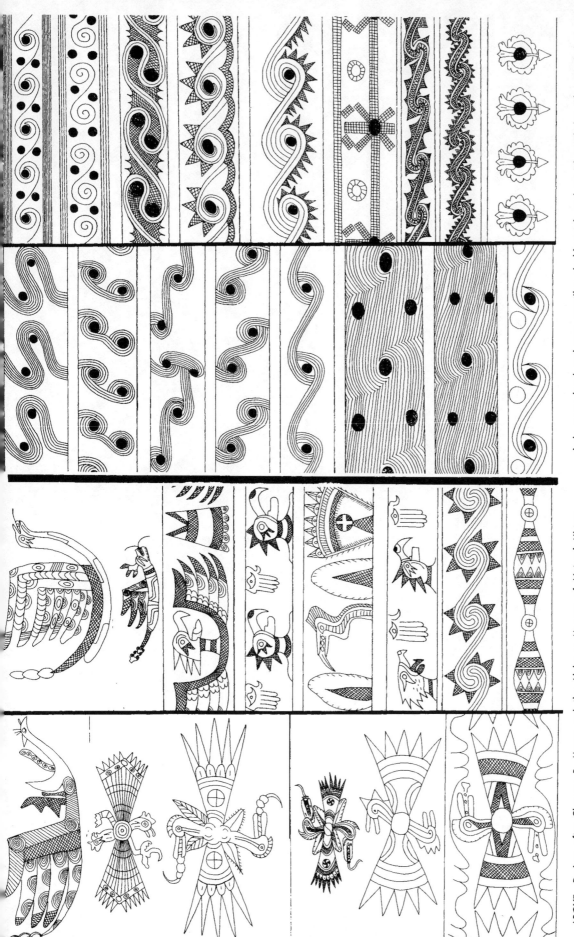

ABOVE. Designs after Clarence B. Moore and the Alabama Museum of Natural History collection, Mound State Monument, Moundville, Alabama. These are not tracings; they are only quickly made free-hand drawings, but they are closely representative, and show the variety of typical cult designs and combinations of designs used at Moundville. LEFT. Various bands of designs with symbols, including, serpent—winged, plumed or horned—with leg symbols; double-bird; bi-fork and tri-fork eye; abstract serpent or snake; eagle, heron, and duck; cross; hand and eye; swastika; double oval; and speech symbols. (These include, Moore, BWR 9, 113, 152, and MR 79. RIGHT. Various bands of designs including, thumb-print designs combined with incised lines, abstract serpent, arrow, and other. (These include, Moore, BWR 148 and MR 69). These designs usually cover the entire surface of the vessels below the neck.

These are designs from the sides of large marine shells. UPPER. LEFT. Serpent, 11" x 7". RIGHT. Serpent, 9" x 6½". CENTER. RIGHT. Serpent, 10" x 7". Note, cult symbols: skull, bones (ulna and radius), hand, cross, sun circles, barred oval, horned, plumed, and winged serpents with rattles, leg, and other symbols; forked eye; and speech symbols (Courtesy, University of Arkansas Mueseum, B. Sp. 103, 105, and 100). LOWER. LEFT. Puma with eagle claws, 8½" length of shell. Note, barred oval—Waring and Holder, 1945, interpreted this as probably a symbol for the vagina or anus; it also may be a male sex symbol; it might have had a variety of meanings, as do some recorded Southwestern Indian symbols. CENTER. Crested birds on conventionalized tree, 10¼" length of shell. Nature designs are very rare in primitive art. This design is from the Museum of the American Indian, Heye Foundation, 18-9124, as are others below. The fragment of a similar design is found in the collection of the University of Oklahoma; instead of a bird, there is the profile of the body and head of an animal, standing lengthwise on each conventionalized limb of a similar tree. RIGHT. Fish and arrows, 9¾" length of shell. Curved lines on side of fish may be water symbols; arrows possibly indicate a method of native fishing; some of them seem to have pierced deep enough to show the feather and nock; the arrow near the head may have pierced the fish or gone through (Courtesy, Museum of the American Indian, Heye Foundation; left, 18-9120 and right, 18-9308).

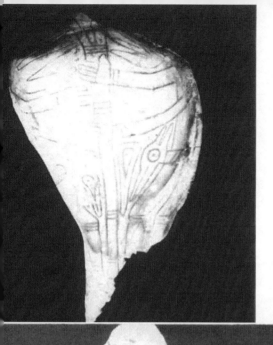

PREHISTORIC DESIGNS—SPIRO

Plates 27 and 28

LEFT. Engraved conch shell, 14⅝" long. "Choosing Sides" or busk design (Courtesy, H. M. Trowbridge collection, 2635. Figure 92, Hamilton, 1952. Reproduced Courtesy, Missouri Archaeological Society, H. M. Trowbridge, and H. W. Hamilton).

BELOW. Fragments of engraved shells. CENTER. LEFT. Hand showing nails, joints, abstract eye, wrinkles at wrist, and shell beads. RIGHT. Fragment of engraved shell dipper or ceremonial cup, 9" diameter; tattooed human figure and symbols. LOWER. LEFT. man in a boat, 14.3 cm. x 9.8 cm. Unusual figures at each side with cross-hatched, half-circles beneath; these figures may represent growing plants. Note, shape of paddle, hair crest, ear spool, and other ornaments. RIGHT. Bi-lobed arrow which seems to be pointing upward, or the reverse direction of several of the bi-lobed arrows engraved on Moundville pottery vessels; fragment about 8" long (Courtesy, University of Oklahoma, Stovall Museum). An illustration depicting the culture traits of the Craig Burial Mound—Spiro— is found in J. B. Griffin, 1952, Fig. 136).

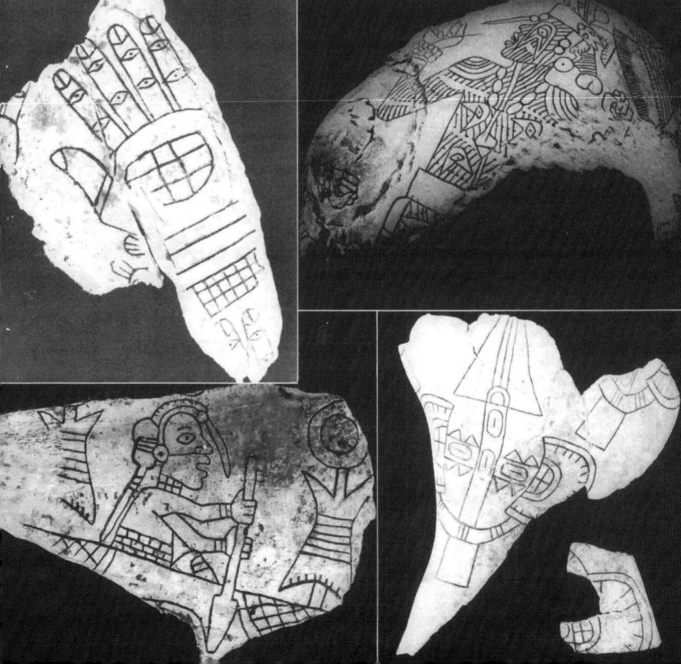

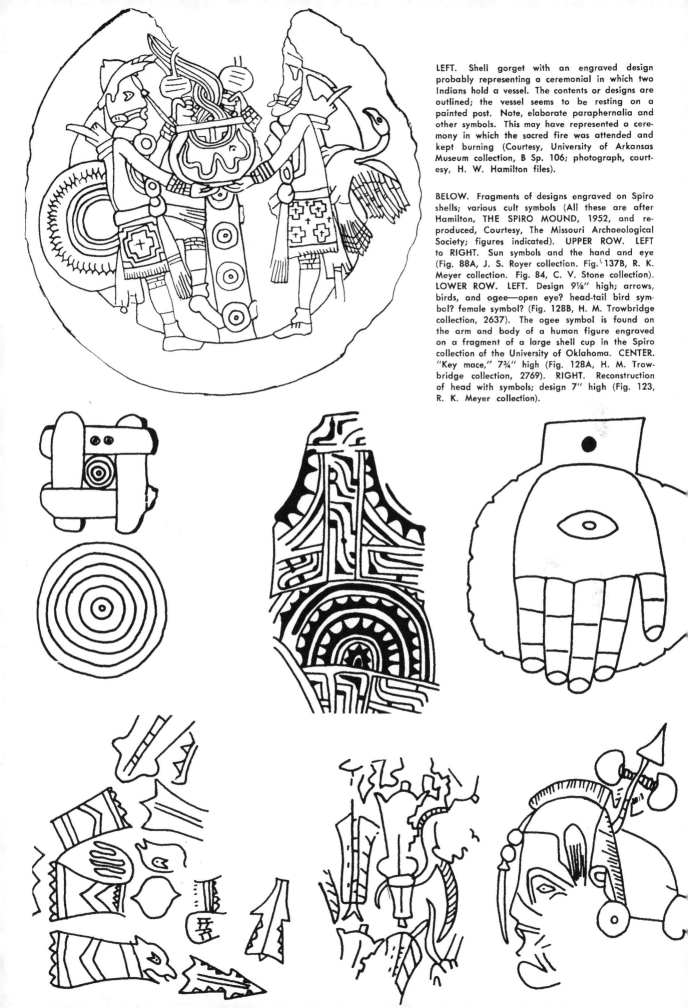

LEFT. Shell gorget with an engraved design probably representing a ceremonial in which two Indians hold a vessel. The contents or designs are outlined; the vessel seems to be resting on a painted post. Note, elaborate paraphernalia and other symbols. This may have represented a ceremony in which the sacred fire was attended and kept burning (Courtesy, University of Arkansas Museum collection, B Sp. 106; photograph, courtesy, H. W. Hamilton files).

BELOW. Fragments of designs engraved on Spiro shells; various cult symbols (All these are after Hamilton, THE SPIRO MOUND, 1952, and reproduced, Courtesy, The Missouri Archaeological Society; figures indicated). UPPER ROW. LEFT to RIGHT. Sun symbols and the hand and eye (Fig. 88A, J. S. Royer collection. Fig. 137B, R. K. Meyer collection. Fig. 84, C. V. Stone collection). LOWER ROW. LEFT. Design 9⅛" high; arrows, birds, and ogee—open eye? head-tail bird symbol? female symbol? (Fig. 128B, H. M. Trowbridge collection, 2637). The ogee symbol is found on the arm and body of a human figure engraved on a fragment of a large shell cup in the Spiro collection of the University of Oklahoma. CENTER. "Key mace," 7¾" high (Fig. 128A, H. M. Trowbridge collection, 2769). RIGHT. Reconstruction of head with symbols; design 7" high (Fig. 123, R. K. Meyer collection).

PREHISTORIC DESIGNS—ETOWAH

Plates 29 and 30

The Etowah site is located near the Etowah River in Bartow County, northwestern Georgia, three miles from Cartersville. The first extensive exploration of the site was conducted by the Bureau of American Ethnology in 1885 and the results were published by Cyrus Thomas in the Bureau's 5th Annual Report in 1887. The next significant exploration was done in the late 1920's under the supervision of W. K. Moorehead for the Phillips Academy, Andover, Massachusetts. The Georgia Historical Commission is presently excavating and accumulating information and artifacts at the site. L. H. Larson, Jr., Archaeologist-in-charge, reports that several fragmentary copper plates have been discovered which bear the following symbols: sun circles, cross, ogee or open eye, man-eagle, and eagle; in addition several engraved shell gorgets have been found which are very similar to Willoughby (1932) Figures 26a, 28, and 29; and another has circles and a cross. They also discovered a hafted copper celt, several carved stone images, a carved wooden mask with antlers, a monolithic axe, and other objects of the Southern Ceremonial Complex. It is their belief that the Temple Mound (C), which is smaller than the great mound, was the site of a mortuary temple, hence the many burials with fine artifacts associated. The primary culture traits of Etowah are summarized in J. B. Griffin, 1952, Figure 159.

A number of textile fragments with stamped Cult designs were found by Moorehead; several painted pottery water bottles were decorated with the cross and sun circles. Although some of the Etowah pottery was shell-tempered, it was not predominantly so, as at Moundville; the many sherds of stamped ware found there, also reflect their South Appalachian pottery traditions brought forward from the Woodland period. In addition to the stamped designs, however, there were incised geometric band designs which resembled some of the protohistoric-historic Creek designs of the Coosa-Tallapoosa River area of Alabama and the Lamar and Irene cultures of the Georgia area.

As at Spiro, though with less diversification of subject, Etowah designs emphasize the human figure more than do the designs of Moundville, where animals and birds were the primary subjects of representation.

The designs on these pages are from Charles C. Willoughby, "Notes on the History and Symbolism of the Muskhogeans and the People of Etowah," from Warren K. Moorehead, ETOWAH PAPERS, EXPLORATION OF THE ETOWAH SITE IN GEORGIA, published for the Department of Archaeology, Phillips Academy, Andover, Massachusetts, by Yale University Press, New Haven, copyright 1932. Reproduced here by permission from the Yale University Press and the Robert S. Peabody Foundation for Archaeology, Phillips Academy, Andover, Massachusetts.

OPPOSITE PAGE. LOWER FIGURES. Human figures in elaborate eagle paraphernalia; these were found during the exploration of the Bureau of American Ethnology. (The line drawings are from Willoughby, 1932, Figures 14 and 15; after the BAE). These copper plates were found beneath the skull of a skeleton in a stone-lined grave in the Temple Mound (C); adhered to the copper plates were scraps of leather, beneath which were fragments of cane; in this same grave was a crescent-shaped copper headdress, two pottery vessels, and many shell beads. LEFT. Plate 16" long. RIGHT. Plate 20" long. The hooked nose and forked tongue or beak representation on the cheek are embossed in copper, and may indicate a mask. Eagle feathers project from the shoulders and a large tail hangs in the background. Note, elaborate shell headdress; bi-lobed ornament; baton with cross marking and ornaments attached ("badge of office"?); shell beads at arm, leg, waist, and hair; shell beads and a columella pendant with end of whorl attached. Part of hair seems braided. Figures wear a breechclout which Cushing (1897, p. 432) suggests may be a "girdle-pouch of fur" with an opening at the rectangular center design; he suggests that the short lines around the edge are indications of hair or fur. Note, the shape and markings of decapitated heads or masks held in the hands; they resemble the heads of the figures shown on the opposite page, and the heads or masks held by the figures on the shell gorgets.

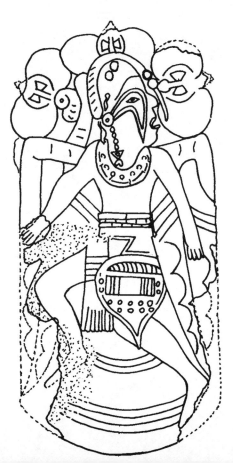

Dancers in eagle paraphernalia found in two small stone-lined graves in the Temple Mound (C) during the Moorehead excavation. LEFT. Copper plate 15½" long (Willoughby, 1932, Figure 13). Note, wings project from shoulders; forked eye; semi-oval quill marks on wings. Across crown from front to back is a curved crest or feather-type object, possibly the same type object as found by the Bureau of American Ethnology (See outline in Waring and Holder, 1945, Ceremonial Objects). Note, bi-lobed ornaments in hair and shell-shaped hair knot? RIGHT. Copper plate 10½" high (Willoughby, 1932, Figure 12). Crudely made plate of two thin pieces of copper riveted together near the middle. Large nose and marks on face indicate the figure may be masked; bi-lobed or winged object above head; hair crest with feathers protruding from either side.

RIGHT. Four shell gorgets; anthropomorphic representations or ceremonial activities? Black areas indicate excised areas; the lines were engraved. The two on the left were discovered by BAE and the two on the right by Moorehead. (All drawings are from Willoughby, 1932, Figures 28, 26b, 26a, and 29). They were found with burials in Temple Mound (C). LEFT. UPPER. Fragment showing two men in conflict—one knocked backward; 5″ diameter. Note, face and body markings; knee bands; and ornaments hanging from hair crest in front. LOWER. Badly weathered; 2½″ diameter. Eagleman with antler headdress; forked design around mouth; ear spools, sash, and beaded breechclout. RIGHT. UPPER. Man with flint dagger in one hand and head or mask in other; 2⅝″ diameter. Willoughby suggests that it may "commemorate a conflict between the spotted eagle people and the followers of this mythical blue bird in which the latter are overcome. . . ." LOWER. Shell gorget 4¾″ diameter. Note, short wings; long, curved tail; eagle claws; bi-lobed symbols above arms; and shell decoration on breechclout. Willoughby suggests that this may "represent the personified blue, long tailed King of Birds, who according to Creek tradition, came everyday and killed and ate the people." The man above holds a similarly marked head.

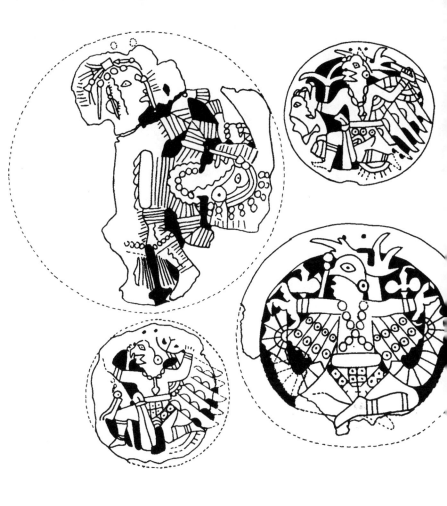

PREHISTORIC DESIGNS—ETOWAH AND OTHER SITES IN GEORGIA

Plates 31 and 32

OPPOSITE PAGE. UPPER ROW. Spotted eagles embossed on copper plates found with burials in the Temple Mound, Etowah (Willoughby, 1932, Figures 7 and 9). LEFT. Found during Bureau of American Ethnology excavation; 14" x 7½". RIGHT. Fighting eagles; 10½" long; found by Moorehead. This is an excellent example of inverted symmetry. Willoughby (p. 14) states that various Creek towns had emblems, separate from the clan symbols or totems. Swanton (1928, p. 243) states that the eagle was the emblem of historic Coweta; Willoughby suggests that the spotted eagle may have been the emblem of Etowah, and since the copper was reddish in color, it may have been considered a war eagle. Note, oval marks on body and semi-oval feather markings on wings. In addition to these eagles in profile, he shows fragments of another plate in which the eagle is face-front with tri-fork eyes and a mouth indicated by a parallel-line oval enclosing a zigzag line; one fragment of which has part of a bone pin still attached. These are similar to the eight copper eagle plates found in a cache at Malden, Missouri, reported by Gerald Fowke (1910).

ABOVE. RIGHT. Typical rattlesnake or serpent gorget; Etowah; 4⅝" x 4⅛". Note, mouth and teeth in center; body of snake in circular design around head; rattles to left above eye; cross design joins snake to outer circle. Such gorgets, some more conventionalized, are found over a wide area of the Southeast at late prehistoric-protohistoric sites. This gorget is reported to have come from the Temple Mound (C), Etowah, though Moorehead's exploration did not reveal serpent gorgets in the Temple Mound, but rather in the village site near (Courtesy, Smithsonian Institution, USNM, 170834, Steiner collection).

ABOVE. Shell gorgets; excised areas are in black; single lines are engraved. LEFT TO RIGHT. Cross, scallops, and circles in a design similar to that found on negative-painted pottery; 3⅛" diameter. Stalling's Island Mound, Columbia County, Georgia (After Claflin, Plate 44, Papers of the Peabody Museum, Harvard, Vol. 14, No. 1). SECOND. Serpent, forked eye, cross, and circle; 2.4" diameter; in an infant burial; unusual because of direction of serpent's head. Creighton Island, Georgia (After, C. B. Moore, 1897, Figure 18). THIRD. Three concentric circles with irregular incisions; 3.8" diameter; cross and small circle in center are semi-perforations. Creighton Island, Georgia (After C. B. Moore, CERTAIN ABORIGINAL MOUNDS OF THE GEORGIA COAST, 1897, Fig. 19). Other cult designs from the Georgia coast which Moore shows in this volume are: Figure 36—pipe with several incised representations of the barred oval; Plate XIV; barred oval incised in band design on pottery vessel; and Plate XVI, conventionalized hand incised on pottery vessel. At Mississippi Period mound sites along the Georgia coast Moore found pottery similar to that reported at Lamar and Irene sites in the Georgia interior; some of which was stamped; some incised with geometric band designs; some combined both methods of decoration. RIGHT. Triskel and scallops; 3½" diameter; a design frequently found in eastern Tennessee. Ocmulgee, Georgia (After, Pope, 1956, p. 43).

OPPOSITE PAGE. CENTER ROW. Designs engraved on shell gorgets found with burials in the Temple Mound, Etowah (Willoughby, 1932, Figure 32). LEFT. Woodpeckers standing on pottery vessel ? and cross-bar; 1⅞" diameter. CENTER. Spider and sun circles, 2" diameter. RIGHT. Turkey on lowered bar of cross; 1⅝" diameter. Excised areas, indicated in black, were probably carved to enhance the effect of the design. LOWER ROW. Designs from artifacts found in the Temple Mound, Etowah (Willoughby, 1932, Figures 33c and 31). LEFT. Design from a negative-painted, long neck, pottery bottle. Such designs were often applied two to four times around the body of the bottle. It is a sun circle and cross or cosmic or world symbol. RIGHT. Woodpecker gorget with long bill and crest; also cross and world symbol; about 3½" diameter. (All designs on the opposite page are reproduced by permission from the Yale University Press and the Robert S. Peabody Foundation for Archaeology, Phillips Academy, Andover, Massachusetts, copyright 1932. The drawings are from C. C. Willoughby's article in W. K. Moorehead, ETOWAH PAPERS, 1932).

PREHISTORIC DESIGNS—MOUNDVILLE

Plates 33 and 34

The prehistoric Indian site at Moundville, Alabama, is located on the Black Warrior River in Hale County. More than two dozen truncated earth mounds were built there by the Indians. The first extensive excavation at this site was directed by Clarence B. Moore. It was recorded in the Journal of the Academy of Natural Sciences of Philadelphia, which published two volumes dealing primarily with Moundville. They were, ABORIGINAL REMAINS OF THE BLACK WARRIOR RIVER. . . . 1905 (BWR) and MOUNDVILLE REVISITED. . . . 1907 (MR). Moore excavated aboriginal sites throughout the Southeast and wrote some two dozen books, illustrating in photographs and drawings, hundreds of the remarkable artifacts which he discovered. His books are a monumental work on Indian Art of the Southeast. Their illustrations have never been excelled. Moore's field notes, original volumes, and many of the artifacts he collected, are now owned by the Museum of the American Indian, Heye Foundation. The site is now a State Monument under the custody of the Alabama Museum of Natural History, University, Alabama. A museum and research center have been established at Mound State Monument. A summary depiction of Moundville culture features is found in J. B. Griffin, 1952, Figure 151.

As Spiro excelled in shell engraving, Etowah in copper repousse, and Key Marco in wood carving, so Moundville excelled in engraving (cutting or scratching) symbolic designs on the outside of shell-tempered, post-fired, black-filmed pottery vessels. These usually covered the entire body of the vessel. In addition to the engraved designs, there were incised designs—drawn or trailed into many pre-fired plastic-clay vessels; these designs were usually geometric and often in narrow bands about the neck or shoulder of the vessel. The high gloss of the finest vessels, doubtless resulted from careful polishing; the black finish may have resulted from smudge firing (baking the vessel the usual length of time, then covering the fire to hold the smoke in until the carbon condensed into the porus clay) or may have been a prepared paint or wash; the fact has not been definitely established. The best of the pottery has been found with burials, as if placed there as a mortuary tribute; it may also have served ceremonial and domestic purposes. The incised and plain ware was probably primarily domestic in use though it is also found in burials; it may have been placed there as food containers.

Designs engraved on Moundville pottery are generally simpler than those engraved on Spiro shells. Although this, in part, may have resulted from the difference in technique and material used, the Spiro designs generally appear to be more advanced in craftsmanship and combination of symbols. The editors have not seen any human figures incised on Moundville pottery or copper pendants, and very few on Moundville engraved shells; at Spiro the human figure is recorded in many forms and situations; their serpents are also more complicated in design and more formal in style. Moundville excels in animal representations and especially in modeled pottery effigies of animals and humans. Designs at both sites include the same basic symbolic motifs and express symmetry and rhythm (All of the designs recorded on these two pages are after the books of Clarence B. Moore as indicated, and they are designs engraved on pottery vessels).

BELOW. TOP TO BOTTOM. LEFT. Conventionalized serpent (MR-67). Abstract tree or nature design? 4¾" wide (MR-32). Ogee or open eye, 5" wide (BWR-122). Bi-lobed arrows pointing downward; thumb-print in center; about 6" wide; applied to side of short-neck water bottle (BWR-88). Fish heads or wings? swastika-circle inside; teeth, hair or feathers indicated by short marks at notches (BWR-90). RIGHT. Swastika and cross of four directions, 4½" wide (MR-5). Crosshatched, cross-ray design and sun circles, with three fingers (BWR-54). Skull and hand and eye; about 3½" wide, on entire side of cup (BWR-62 and 63). Bone, hand, skull, cross, arrow-type object, and star in oval (BWR-147).

RIGHT. TOP TO BOTTOM. LEFT. Cross and swastika design with eagle heads, about 4¾" diameter; applied on bottom and up sides of vessel (MR-8). Highly conventionalized serpent design around shoulder of vessel (MR-71). RIGHT. Eagle and barred oval design; applied to bottom and sides of vessel (MR-38) Hand and sun circle-ray design (BWR-126).

Symbols which Moore found engraved on Moundville pottery, embossed on copper, or engraved on shell were: the hand; hand and eye; variations of the eye (fork, loop, circle, slant); death symbols (skull and bone—radius and ulna and long bone); sun circle; star; cross; crescent or moon; swastika; step; spiral; bi-lobed arrow; ogee or open eye; barred oval; and a variety of animal designs including: birds—double and composite types, woodpecker, duck, heron, eagle, and turkey; the bird wing in pairs and single; winged serpent; serpent with forked eye, plumes or horns, leg symbols, and rattles; conventionalized serpent; and a variety of decorative geometric designs.

BELOW. TOP TO BOTTOM. LEFT. Winged serpent with leg-symbols (MR-53). Conventionalized serpent, showing merging of designs; about 15" long around vessel (MR-44). Turkey, 4½" high (MR-11). Plumed serpent, 8¼" long (MR-59). Ivory-bill woodpecker—double-bird; an example of inverted symmetry; 4½" x 7½". Often there are two double-birds or two serpents on a vessel, and the total design covers the circumference (MR-36). RIGHT. Winged serpent with leg symbols (MR-52). Winged serpent with rattles replaced by bird's tail (MR-64). Serpent disarticulated, 3½" x 15"; design around vessel (MR-161). Serpent, plumed and horned, 8½" long (MR-58). Double-bird, heron? 5½" x 10" (BWR-118).

ABOVE. Typical Moundville pottery vessels which have been restored. Duck effigy bowl; long-neck bottle—8⅝" high; and short-neck bottle. There are two serpents or snakes on the center vessel, one following the other around the bottle; the design was engraved—cut or scratched in after firing; the vessel is polished black-filmed ware; the engraved lines were chalked by the Museum to show the design (Courtesy, Smithsonian Institution, United States National Museum).

LEFT. CENTER. Two views of a pottery beaker with skull and bone design; about 4½" high (Courtesy, Alabama Museum of Natural History, Museum Paper 20, p. 11).

PREHISTORIC DESIGNS— MOUNDVILLE

Plates 35, 36, 37, and 38

LEFT. LOWER. Pottery bottle, 5¾" high with double-bird design; an example of inverted symmetry; the design is repeated on the opposite side of the vessel. Though some of the designs of primitive artists are very similar to each other, they are never exactly the same, for the designs were doubtless free-hand work, applied without the aid of a pattern. C. B. Moore described pottery shapes at Moundville as predominantly, "pot, bowl, and bottle." (Courtesy, Museum of the American Indian, Heye Foundation, 18-432).

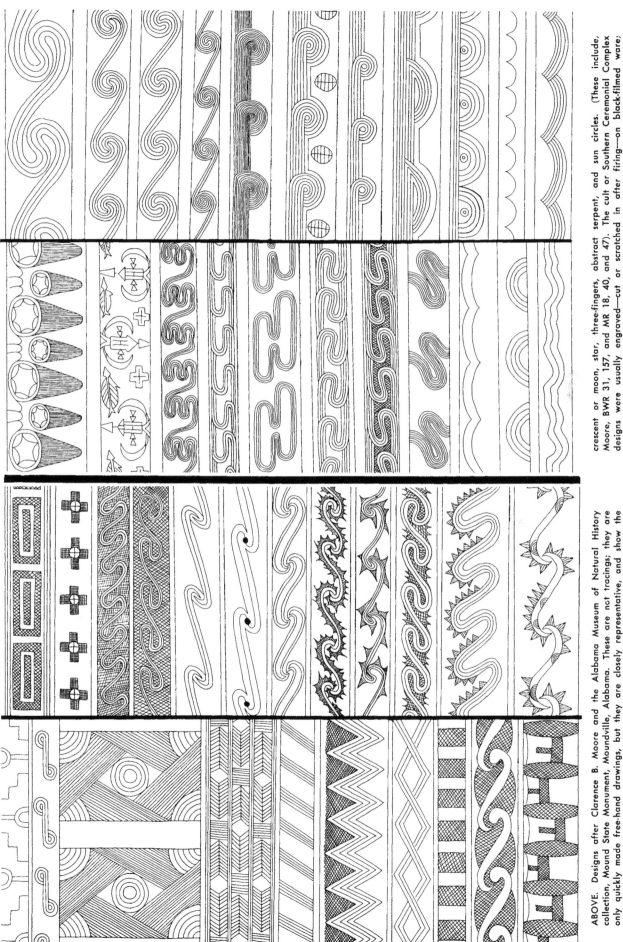

ABOVE. Designs after Clarence B. Moore and the Alabama Museum of Natural History collection, Mound State Monument, Moundville, Alabama. These are not tracings; they are only quickly made free-hand drawings, but they are closely representative, and show the variety of typical cult and geometric designs applied to Moundville vessels. LEFT. Various bands of designs showing the cross, sun circles, abstract serpent, barred rectangle (variation of barred oval?), step, fishbones, and other geometric designs. (These include, Moore,

crescent or moon, star, three-fingers, abstract serpent, and sun circles. (These include, Moore, BWR 31, 157, and MR 18, 40, and 47). The cult or Southern Ceremonial Complex designs were usually engraved—cut or scratched in after firing—on black-filmed ware; they are sometimes also found on plain pottery—without paint or wash—and were incised—trailed or traced into the soft clay before firing. The geometric designs were usually incised on plain pottery.

BURIAL URNS—
ALABAMA RIVER AREA
Plates 39 and 40

LEFT. Burial urn covers from the lower Tallapoosa and upper Alabama River areas. These are drawings by Dr. R. P. Burke, M. D., Montgomery, Alabama. Half of the covers are tuck-in type; the others, flare-rim type. These are shell-tempered; the tuck-in types pictured ranged from 8″ to 13″ rim diameter. Flare-rim covers often ranged from 10″ to 20″ in rim diameter. The vessel on the third row, right, covered an urn containing an adult skeleton; found with this burial were 30 small wheel-shaped beads; two round ear plugs; one iron knife, and a piece of sheet iron. Several vessels pictured were from Taskigi (Courtesy, Dr. R. P. Burke, M. D.; photograph by Alex L. Bush). BELOW. LEFT. Burial urn with a tuck-in type cover; urn cover is about 14″ maximum diameter (Courtesy, J. P. Daole; photograph by Jack D. Ray). RIGHT. Burial urn with a flare-rim cover, about 20″ rim diameter (Courtesy, Alabama Department of Archives and History, Brannon collection).

RIGHT. Shell-tempered pottery vessels from the Alabama-Lower Tallapoosa River areas, found at urn-burial sites (Drawings Courtesy, Dr. R. P. Burke, M. D.).

P. A. Brannon (1935, pp. 31-32) states:

"In view of the fact that out of more than two thousand evidences of Urn-Burial at Taskigi, (lower Tallapoosa area) nine cases have shown blue glass beads and one or two pieces of iron, it must be held that the custom extended down to the historic period. . . . I cannot believe that the custom existed later than 1700. France established a post at this place in 1715. Had the custom been in vogue then, there would have been much evidence of trade material in these urn." He believes the burial urns belonged to the Alibamos, who "stopped at what we have termed Koasati Town and in subsequent years branched out their settlements. It is not unreasonable to assume that these settlements extended all the way south to the Tensas country. There is scattered indication here and there on the upper Tombigbee, and a few even up the Black Warrior. . . ."

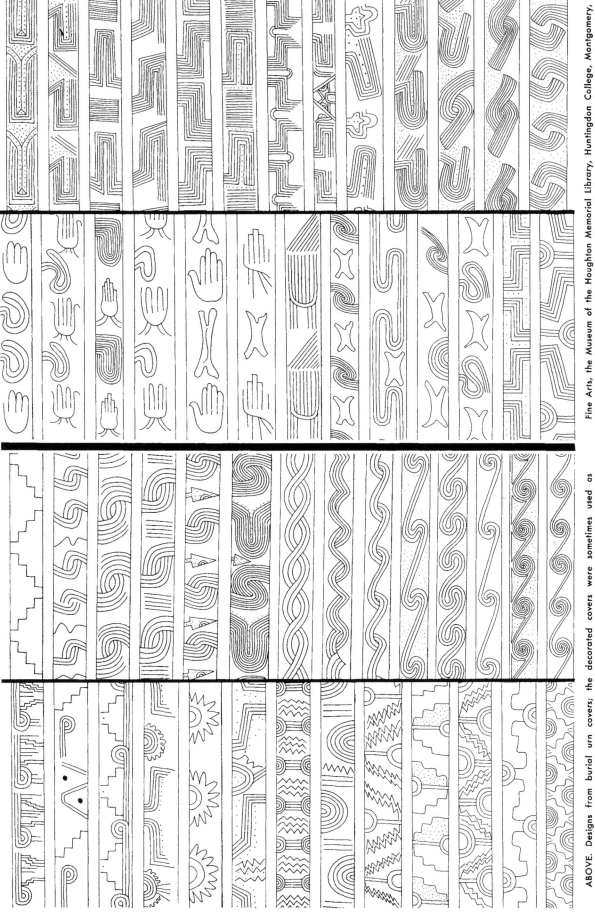

ABOVE. Designs from burial urn covers; the decorated covers were sometimes used as receptacles for the bones, but they were generally used as covers for the plainer receptacles. Although the designs shown above are not tracings but only free-hand drawings they are good representations of the variety and type of designs found on burial urns from the Alabama River and near tributary areas. The drawings are after designs found on Fine Arts, the Museum of the Houghton Memorial Library, Huntingdon College, Montgomery, Alabama, and four are after Moore, 1905. The hand, sun circle, step, the zigzag line or lightning? and bone seem to be the only designs of the Southern Ceremonial Complex used in burial urn decorations (Drawings by Ed.—ELF). For other designs found on burial urns and other vessels of the Coosa-Tallapoosa Valley, see Burke, 1936, AP 21:5-6:4-20.

ABOVE. LEFT. Drawing of a human figure on a fragment of conch shell, probably part of an engraved dipper; maximum width 5½". Note, hair crest and nose to ear mark. RIGHT. Shell gorget engraved to represent a man's head decorated with elaborate paraphernalia; 3¾" diameter. (Both of the above shell artifacts are from Moundville, Hale County, Alabama, and are pictured, courtesy, Museum of the American Indian, Moore collection, 17-1044 and 17-1043).

PREHISTORIC DESIGNS—MOUNDVILLE AND THE ALABAMA RIVER

Plates 41 and 42

Though the depictions of the human head shown in the drawings above do not appear to be "flattened heads," purposed deformation of the head was practiced by some of the natives at Moundville. It has been described as follows (Alabama Museum of Natural History, Museum Paper 20, 1942, p. 3—published by Alabama Geological Survey):

"Head-flattening was caused by strapping the young Indian to a wooden cradle board. The pressure of the leather thongs on the soft bones of the baby's head caused a flattening which remained throughout life. Such a head seems to have become a mark of good rearing, and greatly to be desired, for many mothers went so far as to strap sand bags on their children's heads to induce this flattening."

A concise and illustrated description of Moundville characteristics is presented in Museum Paper 20. The following statements are made regarding ornamentation at Moundville (p. 4):

"Leather and fabrics woven of vegetable fibers were fashioned into garments. In extremely cold weather robes made of feathers were worn over the rest of their clothing.

"The Moundville Indians, both men and women, were fond of personal adornment. They wore ear plugs, bracelets and arm bands of copper, and beads and pendants of bone, stone, shell and copper. . . . Long hair-pins were made of bone, and considerable time was devoted to hairdressing."

BELOW. LEFT. Shell gorget 3" diameter. Conventionalized design of kneeling man with animal features, doubtless symbolic, note, tri-fork eye, heart-shaped object at hip, circles (eyes?) at joints and on body, and other symbols. Moundville, Alabama (Courtesy, Museum of the American Indian, 17-1042). CENTER. Abstract serpent or bird-man ? 3⅝" diameter. Moundville (Redrawn after a photograph of the Museum of the American Indian, 17-1037). RIGHT. Shell gorget with cross, scallops, and circle design; 2" diameter. Found near a child burial; this burial had been disturbed by an adult burial in which Moore found a copper fishhook—unbarbed but grooved for a line—and two wooden beads overlaid with copper; the latter were on the vertex of the skull of the adult. (Moore, 1905, BWR, p. 233).

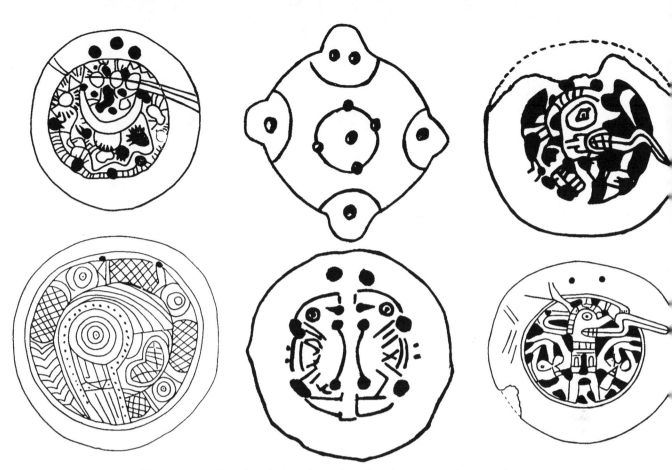

ABOVE. Group of shell gorgets made from the whorl of the conch shell; such ornaments often ranged in diameter from 2" to 6". The design was usually engraved on the concave or inner surface which is smooth and somewhat colorful. Frequently holes were carved at various points to enhance the design. These are black. Lines indicate engraving. UPPER ROW. These three are after C. B. Moore, ALABAMA RIVER, (1899, Figures 56, 56a, 54 and 53, 53a). LEFT. "Blowing-God or Warrior surrounded by one of the typical gorget serpents" (p. 338); 2¾" diameter. CENTER. Circle, quarter circles, and semi-perforations; 1.8" x 1.6". RIGHT. Kneeling human figure with baton in one hand and other on flexed knee; 2" diameter; masked head; long nose; protruding tongue; "double-beaded forlock, common to certain warrior figures on shell gorgets and copper plates" (p. 336). LOWER ROW. LEFT. Rattlesnake or serpent gorget from an urn-burial site on the Lower Tallapoosa River, Alabama; 4½" diameter (After ARROWPOINTS, P. A. Brannon, Vol. 22, No. 1 & 2, Fig. 6, p. 26, 1937; gorget in Brannon collection). CENTER. Two birds standing on a lowered cross-bar facing each other; 2" diameter (After Moore, 1899, Fig. 55, p. 337). RIGHT. Bird-man; two similar gorgets were found by C. A. Jones at a site two miles south of Line Creek, Montgomery County, Alabama; other similar gorgets have been found at urn-burial sites in the Upper Alabama River area; 4⅝" (Redrawn from photograph, ARROWPOINTS, Vol. 5, No. 5, p. 89, 1921. Also in an article by P. A. Brannon, "A Tallapoosa Bird Concept," ARROWPOINTS, Vol. 22, No. 1 & 2, Figure 10, 1937).

BELOW. LEFT. Shell gorget; bird-man; 4½" diameter; Central Alabama. (Drawing by Dr. R. P. Burke, M. D., from a gorget in his collection; reproduced, courtesy, Dr. R. P. Burke) RIGHT. Shell gorget; very concavo-convex and very large—about 6½" x 6½"; bird-man design. Central Alabama (Courtesy, T. L. DeJarnette).

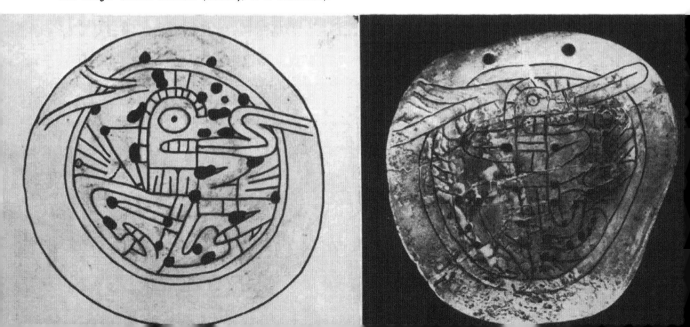

ABOVE. Shell gorgets. UPPER. Cross or cardinal points design and sun circles, 4" diameter; this was found under a small shell-tempered bowl at the head of an extended burial; the concave shape is evident in the photograph. Limestone County, Alabama (Courtesy, Dr. F. J. Soday). LOWER. LEFT. Ivory-bill woodpecker or turkey cock? about 4" diameter. Similar gorgets have been found in northern Mississippi, Alabama, and in Tennessee. The basic square with side spirals occurs over a wider southeastern area and in Central America. This design is often engraved on the convex or outside of the shell-whorl. Limestone County, Alabama (Courtesy, James Ratliff). RIGHT. Shell gorget, 3½" diameter. Jackson County, Alabama (Courtesy, Museum of the American Indian, Heye Foundation, 17-929).

PREHISTORIC DESIGNS—NORTH ALABAMA AND TENNESSEE

Plates 43 and 44

BELOW. Shell gorgets. LEFT. Spider, scallops, sun circles; 2.3" diameter; found in a burial with three greenstone celts, shell-tempered water bottle and bowl, ground facets of galena and shell beads. Jackson County, Alabama. CENTER. Bird-man similar to designs found at Etowah, Georgia, and in Eastern Tennessee; 3½" diameter; found in a grave, which was lined with limestone slabs; other associations were cylindrical and disk shell beads; limestone discoidal; and shell-tempered pottery. Jackson County, Alabama. (These two photographs, Courtesy, Alabama Museum of Natural History; permission also from University of Kentucky Press, Webb, 1951, GUNTERSVILLE BASIN, Plates 75 A and B). RIGHT. Gorget showing barred oval, cross, and sun circles. A number of similar gorgets have been found in Northern Alabama, Tenessee River area, at Mississippi Period sites; 2½" diameter (Courtesy, Alabama Museum of Natural History).

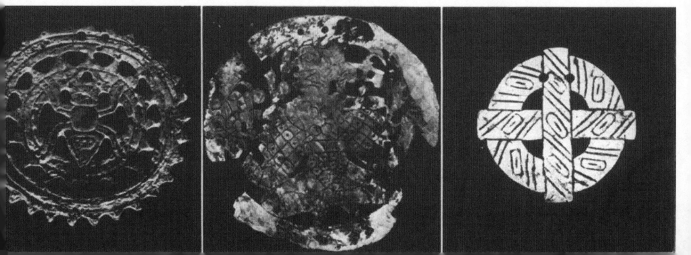

ABOVE. Shell gorgets showing variations of the cross. LEFT. Modified cross design. CENTER and RIGHT. After Holmes, 1883, Pl. LII, Fain's Island and Lick Creek, Tennessee. LOWER ROW. LEFT. Design from gorget from Hamilton County, Tennesse (collection, University of Tennessee, after Lewis and Kneberg, 1954, p. 110). CENTER. Rattlesnake design with cross in position of head; Jonesboro, Tennessee (Redrawn after Lewis and Kneberg, 1954, p. 110, from a gorget in the collection of the American Museum of Natural History). RIGHT. Marion County, Tennesse (After Moore, 1915, Fig. 74).

BELOW. LEFT. Bird-man; Big Toco Mound, Monroe County, Eastern Tennessee (Redrawn by permission; Moorehead, 1932, Fig. 30—Willoughby shows its comparison with Etowah designs). The fragment of this gorget is owned by the National Museum, and is pictured by Wilson in "The Swastika." CENTER. Fragment of gorget showing men with wings, plumes, and eagle talons; profile faces; figures seem to be in serious conflict, and have in one hand a long flint knife, and in other hand, near face, a weapon with a crook; about 5" diameter; McMahan Mound, Sevierville, Tennessee. This is in the collection of the National Museum; is pictured by Holmes, 1883, Pl. LXXV-1 (62930). (Redrawn by permission from Yale University Press and Peabody Museum, Phillips; from Moorehead, 1932, Fig. 27, where it is compared with human designs from Etowah). RIGHT. Bird-man. University of Tennessee collection from Tennessee (Redrawn from Lewis and Kneberg, 1954, p. 187).

Lewis and Kneberg give the following description of Tennessee shell gorgets: —"disks cut from the walls of large marine conchs." —"Method of decoration . . . shallow, fine-line engraving is combined with small, circular, drilled pits and cut-out portions to form the designs. The engraving technique, since it is widely used as a method of decorating bone, stone and pottery, is less significant when considered alone than when in combination with the other two techniques. . . ." (In this article they point out the similarities between certain Mexican—Huastec—engraved shell disks and those of Tennessee). "The cutting out of portions of the background to emphasize the design is comparable, not only in effect produced but also in the way it was accomplished. In both regions most of the apertures were started with holes drilled from the reverse side of them and then finished from the front side. This is shown by the circular perforations which are nearly always larger on the reverse side. To remove large pieces, several small borings were made and the section sawed out between the holes. Then the sharp edges were ground smooth up to the margins of the design. Thus the techniques of the decoration point to a common tradition of craftsmanship. . .

"Surface used for decoration. With a few exceptions, Tennessee shell gorgets are decorated on the concave surface . . . . the interior (concave) surface of a conch shell has a natural luster which would influence its selection for ornaments, not to mention avoiding the necessity of artificially polishing the exterior. Nevertheless in the case of shell vessels, a few gorgets, and particularly shell masks, the exterior (convex) surface was polished and decorated. . . .

"Style of decoration . . . . the heads of figures are disproportionately large . . . . the heads and legs are always shown in profile, while the torsos and arms almost invariably are shown in front or three-quarters view." (quoted by permission; Lewis and Kneberg, TEN YEARS OF THE TENNESSEE ARCHAEOLOGIST, pp. 185-186).

ABOVE. UPPER. Three serpent gorgets. McMahan and Lick Creek mounds, Tennessee (After Holmes, 1883, Pl. LXV). LOWER. Three bird—woodpecker or turkey—gorgets. LEFT. From a stone grave near Nashville. CENTER. Gorget 2½" diameter. Cumberland River, Tennessee. RIGHT. From a stone grave in Old Town, Tennessee (After Holmes, 1883, Pl. LIX; several gorgets used in his study were from the Peabody Museum).

BELOW. UPPER. Two spider gorgets and a bird-man gorget. LEFT. Spider gorget 3" diameter. New Madrid, Missouri. CENTER gorget 2½" diameter. Fain's Island, Tennessee (After Holmes, 1883, Plate LXI—1 & 4). RIGHT. Bird-man gorget 6¾" diameter. Tennessee (After Lewis and Kneberg, 1954, p. 186; University of Tennessee collection). LOWER. Bird designs. LEFT. Turkey or woodpecker? on a lowered cross-bar; 2" and 2½" diameter. Hamilton County, Tennessee (After Lewis and Kneberg, 1954, p. 111). RIGHT. Bird-man. McMahan Mound, Tennessee (After Holmes, 1883, Pl. LXV).

ABOVE. LEFT. Unusual double-serpent gorget—two tails and two open mouths with teeth. 5½" diameter. Hamilton County, Tennessee (Courtesy, Museum of the American Indian, 4-9252). RIGHT. Snake motif, 4" diameter, Hamilton County, Tennessee (Courtesy, Chicago Natural History Museum, 205705). (Moore, 1915, pictures in Figures 91 and 92, snake gorgets from Citico Mound, Hamilton County, Tennessee).

PREHISTORIC—PROTOHISTORIC DESIGNS—TENNESSEE

Plates 45 and 46

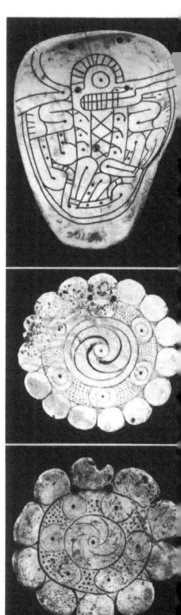

RIGHT. UPPER. Bird-man. From a mound on the north bank of the Hiwassee River, Meigs County, Tennessee, about 5½" long (Courtesy, Peabody Museum, Harvard University, 20124). TWO LOWER GORGETS. Scallops, sun circles and triskel design. 4" and 3¼"; Tennessee, probably Dallas Focus (Courtesy, Rochester Museum of Arts and Science, AR 462 and 443).

Holmes (1883, pp. 290-291) describes the snake design on shell gorgets as follows: "Among the thirty or forty specimens that I have examined, the engraving of the serpent is, with one exception, placed upon the concave side of the disk, which is, as usual, cut from the most distended part of the Busycon perversum, or some similar shell. The great uniformity of these designs is a matter of much surprise. At the same time, however, there is no exact duplication; there are always differences in position, detail, or number of parts. The serpent is always coiled, the head occupying the center of the disk. With a very few exceptions the coil is sinistral. The head is so placed that when the gorget is suspended it has an erect position, the mouth opening toward the right hand.

"The saucer-like disks are almost circular, the upper edge being mostly somewhat straightened—the result of the natural limit of the body of the shell above. All are ground down to a fairly uniform thickness of from one-eighth to one-fourth of an inch. The edges are evenly rounded and smooth. Two small holes for suspension occur near the rim of the straighter edge, and generally on or near the outline of the engraved design, which covers the middle portion of the plate. The diameter ranges from one to six inches.

"To one who examines this design for the first time it seems a most inexplicable puzzle; a meaningless grouping of curved and straight lines, dots and perforations. We notice, however, a remarkable similarity in the designs, the dies being radically the same in all specimens, and the conclusion is soon reached that there is nothing haphazard in the arrangement of the parts and that every line must have its place and purpose. The design is in all cases inclosed by two parallel border lines, leaving a plain belt from one-fourth to three-fourths of an inch in width around the edge of the disk. All simple lines are firmly traced, although somewhat scratchy, and are seldom more than one-twentieth of an inch in width or depth.

"In studying this design the attention is first attracted by an eye-like figure near the left border. This is formed of a series of concentric circles, the number of which varies from three in the most simple to twelve in the more elaborate forms. The diameter of the outer circle of this figure varies from one-half to one inch. In the center there is generally a small conical depression or pit. The series of circles is partially inclosed by a looped band one-eighth of an inch in width, which opens downward to the left; the free ends extending outward to the border line, gradually nearing each other and forming a kind of neck to the circular figure. This band is in most cases occupied by a series of dots or conical depressions varying in number from one to thirty. The neck is decorated in a variety of ways; by dots, by straight and curved lines, and by a cross-hatching that gives a semblance of scales. A curious group of lines occupying a crescent-shaped space at the right of the circular figure and inclosed by two border lines, must receive particular attention. This is really the front of the head—the jaws

(continued on Plate 48)

ABOVE. UPPER ROW. LEFT. Human in ceremonial regalia holds head or mask by the hair; note, forked eye; bi-lobed symbol in hair; and mace in left hand; 3⅞" diameter. Sumner County, Tennessee (Courtesy, Museum of the American Indian, Heye Foundation, 15-853). RIGHT. Bird—ivory-bill woodpecker, heron, swan, turkey ? 4¼" diameter; design on convex side of shell. Mississippi (Holmes, 1883, Pl. LVIII) He describes it: "A square framework of four continuous parallel lines, symmetrically looped at corners, enclose a central circle, the inner line touching the tips of the pyramidal rays . . . . outside are four symbolic birds' heads placed against the side of the square opposite the arms of the cross . . . . drawn after what the artist considered a well-recognized model . . . . mouth open and mandibles long, slender and straight." He further states (p. 280) "With all peoples the bird has been a most important symbol. Possessing the mysterious power of flight by which it could rise at pleasure into the realms of space, it naturally came to be associated with phenomena of the sky—the wind, the storm, the lightning, and the thunder. In the fervid imagination of the red man, it became the actual ruler of the elements, the guardian of the four quarters of the heavens. As a result the bird is embodied in the myths, and is a prominent figure in the philosophy of many savage tribes. The eagle, which is an important emblem with many civilized nations, is found to come much nearer the heart of the superstitious savage; its plumes are a badge of the successful warrior; its body, a sacred offering to his deities, or an object of actual veneration. The swan, the heron, the woodpecker, the paroquet, the owl, and the dove were creatures of universal consideration. Their flight was noted as a matter of vital importance as it could bode good or evil to the hunter or warrior who consulted it as an oracle."

SOUTHEASTERN DESIGNS

Plates 47 and 48

LEFT. Five shell gorgets with designs engraved on concave side and showing excised areas. Two spider-circle designs; one turkey or bird; one scallop-triskel; one human effigy—note: conch columella pendant, earspools, weapons, antler headdress, and wing and tail feathers, shell beads at wrist, knee and ankle. Largest 4½"; smallest 1⅝" diameter. Tennessee, Dallas Culture (Courtesy, University of Tennessee). Regarding the spider gorget, Lewis and Kneberg (1954, pp. 114-115), say: "The spider is occasionally depicted on Tennessee shell gorgets. The small gorget was found in Hamilton County. It is apparent that the Indian artist was not particularly concerned with the idea of realism from the fact that he has shown somewhat more than the eight legs with which nature has endowed this creature. On other gorgets as few as four legs are shown." (See J. B. Griffin, 1952, Fig. 109, for a picture of features of the Dallas Culture. Lewis and Kneberg, 1946, discuss Dallas culture features).

"Many of the late prehistoric tribes of the Southeast had special designs which were restricted to ceremonial use. They were rarely used on pottery vessels and never on utilitarian objects. Similarly, the Navaho use a certain set of designs for their ceremonial sand paintings and an entirely different set for their blankets. In one case the designs are symbolic and in the other, decorative. Thus, we find spiders, rattlesnakes, turkeys, pileated woodpeckers, fantastic human figures and certain geometric symbols engraved upon shell gorgets.

"We do not know what meaning the spider had in the religious symbolism of the Indians who used this design on their gorgets. One of the Osage Indian clans looks upon the spider as the symbol of life, and it is depicted with a cross in the center of the body, very much like the Tennessee gorget in the accompanying illustration. One of the Pueblo groups regards the spider as the first living creature and the creator of all other living things." (Quoted by permission from Dr. T. M. N. Lewis).

OPPOSITE PAGE. CENTER. Two snake gorgets. LEFT. 5" x 6", McMahan Mound, Sevierville, Tennessee. (Holmes, 1883 LXIII). RIGHT. 4½", Washington County, Virginia (Courtesy, Smithsonian Institution, USNM, 37-176). Similar serpent gorgets have been found over a widespread area of the Southeast. They also lead in frequency of occurence.

(continued from Plate 46)

and the muzzle of the creature represented. The mouth is always clearly defined and is mostly in profile, the upper jaw being turned abruptly upward, but, in some examples, an attempt has been made to represent a front view, in which case it presents a wide V-shaped figure. It is, in most cases, furnished with two rows of teeth, no attempt having been made to represent a tongue. The space above and below the jaws are filled with lines and figures, which vary much in the different specimens; a group of plume-like figures, extends backward from the upper jaw to the crown, or otherwise this space is occupied by an elongated perforation. The body is represented encircling the head in a single coil, which appears from beneath the neck on the right, passes around the front of the head, and terminates at the back in a pointed tail with well defined rattles. It is engraved to represent the well-known scales and spots of the rattlesnake, the conventionalized figures being quite graphic. . . . In some cases one or more incised bands cross the body in the upper part of the curve. . . . The body is in many cases nearly severed from the rim of the disk by four oblong perforations, which follow the border line of the design, (forming a cross, connecting the serpent with the outer circle). In most cases three other perforations occur about the head; one represents the mouth, one defines the forehead and upper jaw, and the third is placed against the throat. These may be intended merely to define the form more clearly. The curious plume-like figures that occur upon the heads of both varieties may indicate the natural or reputed markings of the animal represented. It is possible that (some of them) may be intended to represent the common yellow rattlesnake, the Crotalus horridus, of the Atlantic slope, the characteristic markings of which are alternating light and dark chevrons, while the diamond rattlesnake, the Crotalus adamanteus, of the Southern States may have served as a model for the other group." (Holmes, 1883, pp. 290-291).

OPPOSITE PAGE. LOWER. RIGHT. Design on shell gorget which represents a human throwing a chunkey stone; note, costume and stick in left hand; about 4" diameter. Eddyville, Kentucky. (Redrawn after MacCurdy. National Museum, 14640).

RIGHT. UPPER. Two snake designs; shell gorgets. North Carolina (After Rights). CENTER ROW. Two cross-circle-scallop designs, about 4" diameter, Foster Place, Arkansas (After Moore, 1912. Red River Sites, Figures 94 and 95). LOWER ROW. LEFT. Limestone disk, star design; probably part of an earspool; about 3" diameter. Arkansas (After Moore, 1912, Figure 97). RIGHT. Cross design from shell gorget. North Carolina (After Rights).

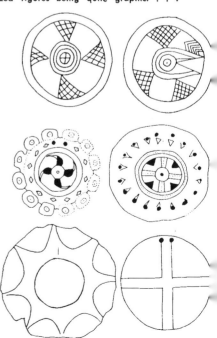

LEFT. Snake gorget; 4¼" x 3½"; Mississippi County, Missouri (Courtesy, B. W. Stephens).

OPPOSITE PAGE. UPPER. These drawings show designs from six of eight shell gorgets found in same native cemetery in Perry County, Missouri. These are pictured in an article by George G. MacCurdy entitled, "Shell Gorgets from Missouri," AMERICAN ANTHROPO-LOGIST, Vol. 15, No. 3, 1913, pp. 395-414. They are in the collection of Yale University; the gorgets were secured by Professor O. C. Marsh in 1871. The drawings and quotations from this article which appear herein, are published, courtesy, AMERICAN ANTH-ROPOLOGIST. UPPER LEFT. Man in position to hurl a chunkey stone; 5" diameter; note, bent or broken stick in left hand. A similar gorget has been found at the Spiro mound (Burnett, 1945). Another weathered gorget of the same Yale collection, not pictured here, has an upright figure with a chunkey stone in the left hand. RIGHT. Masked figure with antler headdress; he appears to be suspended with his arms thrust through the center of two stars; fragments of two similar stars are opposite the hips; three arrows pierce the left foot, side, and head; one is shown on the right at the foot; others have probably weathered away; this may represent a rite of sacrifice. MacCurdy describes such a rite of the Indians of the Plains. Also shown are two spider—cross designs; MacCurdy refers to the fact that some spiders have a natural cross on the under side of their body; all have eight legs; and the head-downward position is that of repose. He also discusses the spider in Central American mythology. The cross-circle design is shown on two gorgets. The cross is one of the most repeated of all symbols; it is found on gorgets, vessels, gamestones, and fabrics. It is even found on some pipes, as on the sides of a clay pipe from Southeastern Missouri (USNM, 72134).

OPPOSITE PAGE. LOWER. Two human figures engraved on shell gorgets; about 4½" diameter. Note, similar treatment of the border with parallel lines. LEFT. This design has weathered and some of the features are lost. The figure appears to be wearing a mask and has a prominent proboscis; note, mace with cross in background; long braid of hair; frame on headdress; bilobular symbol in hair; shell-beaded band at waist; sash; pouch or bag with rectangular opening; round object on chest—similar round copper gorgets have been found at certain Middle Mississippi sites as Moundville, Alabama; it has also been suggested that it might be a chunkey stone, but the former seems more likely. MacCurdy suggested that the long nose might be the representation of an eagle beak (p. 410) (After MacCurdy, 1913, and Thruston, 1890, Pl: XVII). The shell is from New Madrid County, Missouri, and at the time it was represented by Thruston was in the collection of A. E. Douglass, and displayed at the American Museum of Natural History. J. M. Goggin and Stephen Williams, in the 1956 bulletin, "The Long Nosed God Mask in Eastern United States" also illustrate this gorget. They describe this as a figure with "a long, curved-under nose," and state, "The rest of the symbols and objects shown are those of the Southern Cult, and in one hand the figure is holding what may be a hafted spud. It is interesting to note that the eye is represented as a diamond, and that a circular ear spool also occurs. No site provenience can be established, but the artifact more than likely came from one of the four major Mississippian sites on Sikeston Ridge (Potter, 1880, pp. 11-19) in northern New Madrid County." They further state, "The New Madrid portrayal on shell is very similar to human figures on two of the copper plates from Mound C at Etowah, Georgia (Willoughby, 1932, Figs. 12 and 15); there are analogies in the headdress as well as in many other details of apparel and ornament. The New Madrid figure has the largest nose, but the individual on one of the Etowah plates does have the suggestion of a nose which is larger than usual and may indicate that the 'warrior' is wearing an eagle mask. Another copper plate from Etowah (Willoughby 1932, Fig. 12), less well executed than the other two, also has a nose longer than usual. In these Etowah representations, other charateristic features held in common are: the diamond-shaped eye, often with weeping eye symbol; and circular ear spools." (Quoted by permission from the Missouri Arch-aeological Society and The Missouri Archaeologist—Vol. 18, No. 3, October 1956).

BELOW. Three examples of the spotted eagle; embossed on thin sheet copper and cut into shape; in order to have a sheet large enough for the design, the natives often riveted two or more pieces together. Left and Center are two of eight eagle-plates found near Malden, Dunkl:n County, Missouri, in a cache, as if they had been wrapped together and buried or lost there. These are now in the Wulfing collection, Washington University. The third or right eagle was obtained by the Bureau of American Ethnology in an exploration at Peoria, Illinois; they also found a similar fragment in Union County, Illinois. (These drawings are reproduced from Moorehead (Willoughby) 1932, Figure 8, where they are shown for comparison with the Etowah specimens; he drew the Missouri eagles after G. Fowke's, BAE, Bull. 37. The drawing presented here is reproduced, courtesy, Yale University Press and Pea-body Museum, Phillips Academy). Virginia D. Watson, 1950, published THE WULFING PLATES, with photographs and careful descriptions of the eight Wulfing copper plates. The eagle on the left is unique, because it has easily recognizable human features at the head, and many character-istics of the Southern Cult, as the "occipital hair knot;" beaded forelock; ear-spools; hand-over-mouth;- e-laborate headdress; hair-crest; quill mark-ing; long tail; and sqread wing.

PREHISTORIC DESIGNS—MISSOURI

Plates 49 and 50

BELOW. RIGHT. Shell gorget design showing a human figure holding a mask or head with long hair; the feet of the figure are parted as if in walking; an unusual vessel-shaped object is behind the standing figure. Note, object in right hand; diamond-shaped eye with conical pit in center; sash hanging from arm between legs; pouch shaped like spider-back representations on shell and with a rectangular opening? It has short lines which may be fur or hair marks. Southeastern Missouri. (Holmes, 1883, Pl. LXXIII). See James B. Griffin, 1952, Fig. 120, for culture traits of the New Madrid Focus, Sikeston Ridge area.

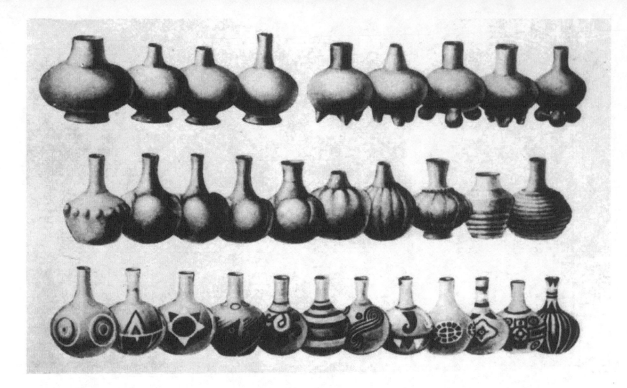

ABOVE. Various forms of bottles showing pottery design and decoration; the latter was often applied with red and white paint. (Holmes, 1903, "Aboriginal Pottery of the Eastern United States," Plate XVII).

PREHISTORIC DESIGNS—MIDDLE MISSISSIPPI VALLEY

Plates 51 and 52

LEFT. Decorative designs from the Middle Mississippi Valley showing variations in symbols—circle, cross, swastika, triskel, steps, spiral and scallops. These are often placed on vessels by the application of red, white or black paint; the tan or yellowish color of the clay in the vessel, sometimes was used to form a part of the design. Others were incised before firing and engraved after the surface was baked (Holmes, 1903, Ibid, Plate XXXVIII). Holmes makes the following observation: "From the beginning of my rather disconnected studies of the ornamental art of native tribes, I have taken the view that, as a rule the delineative devices employed were symbolic; that they were not primarily esthetic in function, but had a more serious significance to the people using them. When vases were to be devoted to ceremonial ends, particular forms were made and designs were added because they had some definite relation to the uses of the vessels and were believed to add to their efficacy. . . . Stellar and lobed figures and circles probably represent the stars, the sun, or the horizon circle. The cross, the various forms of volutes and scrolls, and the stepped figures represent the four winds, the clouds, and rain; and the reptiles, quadrupeds, birds, men, and monsters are connected with the same group of phenomena. The vessels marked with these figures were no doubt devoted to particular functions in the ceremonial activities of the people. . . . The same region furnishes many symbols engraved on shell, bone, stone." (pp. 100-101).

In 1897 Charles C. Willoughby discussed "Decorations Upon Pottery from the Mississippi Valley." Regarding the "cross symbol" on artifacts from Tennessee, Lewis and Kneberg (1954, p. 109) state:

"It is found on shell and stone gorgets, pottery vessels, and frequently on small stone and pottery discs. In . . . Central American regions the cross was a symbol of the god of fertility and rain. . . . The early French missionaries who visited various North American Indian tribes described a ceremony in which the high priest faced the rising sun, saluted it with a torch and in turn waved the torch toward the four points from which the winds blew. In so doing, the path of the torch conformed to a cross. The same ceremony was performed with a tobacco pipe by some groups. . . ."

ABOVE. Shell-tempered pottery bottles. UPPER ROW. Three bottles with designs painted in red and white on buff colored clay vessel. Center bottle is 9" high and 8½" diameter. Mississippi. CENTER ROW. Four bottles. Three are Nodena, red and white. Left of first, 7" high; five "hands" are painted around the vessel; the neck appears to have been broken and resmoothed by the native. Second 9⅜" high; four alternating up-and-down heads are painted around the bowl. Third, has a swastika swirl on the body and steps on the neck. Fourth, the red paint is applied to a buff-colored vessel, 9" high; it appears to be negative painting, or else, the red paint was scraped off the buff surface, leaving the diamond design, and the band around the neck. Arkansas. LOWER ROW. Eight Nodena red and white bottles showing a variety of swirl designs; they are 7¾" to 9¾" high. Note, bottle, center rear, has a swirl design on the neck rather than the usual solid red, horizontal stripe or step designs. Front center bottle—swirl does not cross at center as is customary on such bottles, but forms a loop. Bottle at right of center—depicts infrequent left-hand swirl. Arkansas. (All bottles shown on this page are in the collection of Frank, Frank, Jr., and Robert H. Morsat; photographs by Jack D. Ray).

SOUTHERN CULT MOTIFS ON WALLS-PECAN POINT POTTERY

Plates 53 and 54

ABOVE. Illustrations of pottery vessels from the Walls-Pecan Point area showing cult motifs. The photographs have been roughly retouched to emphasize the designs. These depict three methods of decoration—incised lines, modeled forms and features, and applique or fillet. These illustrations were reproduced by permission; they are from an article by Dr. Robert L. Rands, "Southern Cult Motifs on Walls-Pecan Point Pottery," AMERICAN ANTIQUITY, Vol. 22, No. 2, Part 1, October 1956, pp. 183-186. BELOW. The article is quoted by permission from Dr. R. L. Rands and AMERICAN ANTIQUITY—publication of the Society for American Archaeology. Dr. R. L. Rands, Department of Anthropology, University of Mississippi, described this as a "Paper read at Eleventh Southeastern Archaeological Conference, Moundville, Alabama, November 1954. These remarks form part of a study aided by a Faculty Research Grant of the University of Mississippi." January 1955.

"Certain published designs from Walls-Pecan Point phase pottery are strikingly in the tradition of the so-called 'Death Cult' of the Southeastern United States. Particular reference is made to 2 Walls Engraved bottles, illustrated by Phillips, Ford, and Griffin (1951, Fig. 111 g) and by Calvin Brown (1926, Fig. 278). The first of these, showing a winged serpent almost identical to those of Moundville, is at the University of Arkansas. The second, depicting skulls, long bones, and hands with oval markings at the palms, is at the University of Mississippi. The way in which these 2 vessels fit into the art of the Southern Cult is striking, but even casual examination shows that this holds true for the pottery of the phase as a whole to a markedly smaller degree. At most it appears to be 'attenuated,' or perhaps 'undeveloped,' Cult.

"The remarks which follow are based upon an examination of over 1100 complete or virtually complete vessels. As far as I can tell, these are all from sites belonging to or closely connected with the Walls-Pecan Point 'phase' or 'focus,' a cultural manifestation lying in small portions of eastern Arkansas, northwestern Mississippi, and southwestern Tennessee. The majority of the vessels were dug by amateur collectors, and so it is possible that in a few cases proveniences are wrongly given. Due, apparently, to the greater amount of digging in the more southerly sites, the material is especially representative of the Wallslike components. By and large, however, the assemblage of pottery seems generally characteristic of the phase.

"The description by Waring and Holder of a decade ago (1945) is used as a guide to the Cult motifs. Because of the somewhat divergent nature of the Walls-Pecan Point designs, however, the classification of 8 motifs made by these writers is expanded slightly. Attention is thereby focused more effectively on those general correspondences which do exist.

"The virtual absence of Cult designs on objects other than pottery should be stressed. In addition, the great importance of the bottle as a ceramic object on which Cult motifs occur (Waring and Holder 1945: 14) holds true to only a limited degree for the bulk of the Walls-Pecan Point material. Rather the motifs occur, often as minor elements, on effigy bowls, particularly those of serpents and human figures.

"As one of the God-Animal beings associated with the Cult, 'The RATTLESNAKE, naturalistic, horned, plumed, winged, anthropomorphized' is named by Waring and Holder (1945: 5). The horned snakes of the Walls-Pecan Point potters typically lack rattles, as well as numerous other features found at such Cult centers as Moundville or Spiro. A slight tendency is shown, however, for the so-called horned serpent to be associated with the few 'pure' Cult designs which do occur. For this reason it deserves special mention.

"Another feature of some interest which is held to be associated with the Cult is the 'occipital hair knot' (Waring and Holder 1945: 15). Of the more than 1100 vessels examined from Walls-Pecan Point sites, 18 are human effigy bowls. Predominantly they are Bell Plain. Of these 18, 13 show the characteristic rolls of hair, either realistically or else suggested in a more conventionalized fashion. The percentage occurrence of this Cult feature is, then, a high one (72% of the human effigy bowls).

"Turning to the 8 'motifs' recognized by Waring and Holder (1945: 3), we find the following situation (occurrences refer only to the complete vessels which I have examined):

"1. The CROSS. Very rare except as a minor element in the form of a swastika spiral or triskele, usually enclosed in a circle. As such, the cross occurs in 2 principal locations: (a) toward the shoulder of Rhodes Incised jars and, rarely, bottles (the body decoration is of an allied form) (Fig. 1 a); (b) on the back or top of serpent heads, on rim effigy bowls (Fig. 1 b, c). The spiral cross was noted on 9 Rhodes Incised vessels and 6 serpent effigies. One-third of the 18 Bell Plain and Walls Engraved serpent effigies showed this feature 33%). However, it was not seen on any of the 7 Neeley's Ferry Plain serpents.

"2. SUN CIRCLES. Absent.

"3. The BILOBED ARROW. One possible example; very generalized in nature, however.

"4. The FORKED EYE. Ten examples, five of them associated with serpents (Fig. 1 c-e). But as a total of 28 vessels occurs showing beings of the sort usually referred to as serpents, the consistency of the association is not a high one (18%). The forked eye also occurs on non-serpentine subjects.

"5. The OPEN EYE, or 'ogee symbol.' Ten or 11 examples, mostly on the shoulders of Bell Plain bottles (Fig. 1 f). Less frequently, the rims of shallow bowls, as seen from above, take on this characteristic shape. The motif is frequently on Moundville pottery, being one of the several links between that site and the Walls-Pecan Point phase (Griffin 1952: 236). Attention might be called therefore, to a somewhat similar design, suggesting a variation on the 'ogee' symbol, which occurs both at Moundville (Moore 1905, Fig. 7) and in southwestern Tennessee (Fig. 1 e). In each case, interlaced or superimposed serpents form an outline quite comparable to that of the 'ogee' motif. The Tennessee example is of interest in that it is placed on the shoulder of a bottle in a way characteristic of the regular motif.

"6. The HAND AND EYE. Strictly speaking, no examples of this motif are found in the vessels under consideration. Apparently related Cult designs do occur in which the eye is replaced by a cross in a circle or by an ovate element (Waring and Holder 1945, Figs. 1, 7, b-d). Even if these are included as variants of the hand-eye motif, however, the occurrence on Walls-Pecan Point pottery is not much more impressive. A single specimen, a Walls Engraved bottle, shows an oval area at the palm of the hand.

"7. The BARRED OVAL. Absent, although suggested by the marking in the palm of the hand in the last-mentioned example.

"8. DEATH MOTIFS. Again it is necessary to subdivide the motif. The 2 variants of particular interest here are the skull and the long bones. The former is of limited occurrence, just 2 examples (Walls Engraved) being known. Bones occur with slightly greater frequency, once on a Walls Engraved bottle, in connection with skulls, and 3 times modeled on Bell Plain bottles.

"This completed the motifs specifically mentioned by Waring and Holder. A few additional observations need to be made, however. While the hand and eye motif is very rare, plain hands, without markings at the palm, occur somewhat more frequently (10 vessels). For the most part, these examples are modeled on Bell Plain bottles. In 3 of these cases, the hands occur in association with bones.

"It has been pointed out that the forked eye is quite rare on the Walls-Pecan Point pottery. A much more usual facial treatment consists of grooves below but not contacting the eyes—as much associated, let us say, with the mouth or nose as with the eye (Fig. 1 c, d). In some cases, to be sure, the appearance of the grooves approaches atypical examples of the so-called 'weeping eye.' The grooves in question occur on 19 of the 28 vessels showing serpents (68%).

"Finally, mention should be made of the 'horned' nature of the serpents shown on Walls-Pecan Point pottery. Deer antlers are absent from the collections examined. Difficulty sometimes exists in determining whether a supposed set of horns is prominent and clearly hornlike (Fig. 1 b) or reduced and perhaps earlike (Fig. 1 c). I would, however, state the situation somewhat as follows: of the 19 'snakes' which show protuberances on the head, only 4, all examples of Bell Plain, have truly 'prominent' horns (21%). This is to say that horns appear to be emphasized on only 14% of the 28 vessels showing 'serpents.' A general lack of emphasis on the 'horned' concept is suggested which is in sharp contrast to the situation at, say, Moundville or Spiro.

"Any conclusions to be drawn from the preceding observations would have greater reliability if the sample were larger. General trends, however, should be indicated. None of the Cult motifs occur with great frequency. Those which are present tend to be simplified in form or to lack a prominent position. The small spiral crosses at the back of the serpent heads might be remembered in the latter connection. Hands occur with some frequency but almost always as plain, unelaborated motifs. The occasional association of hands and long bones does suggest the concept of the Death Cult, however. The horned serpent appears but generally lacks the specific features and elaboration likely to be found at the large Cult centers. And so on.

"The problem of particular interest in all this was alluded to in the opening remarks, when the Walls-Pecan Point material was described as, at best, either an 'attenuated' or 'undeveloped' Cult. Does the small amount of art comparable to that from the Cult centers reflect a 'watering down' of the Cult as it spread out from these centers? Or did the Walls-Pecan Point potters share widespread religious concepts out of which the Cult crystallized in certain sites and areas? Perhaps both factors were involved, but the degree to which each was present remains a significant problem. It cannot be answered on the basis of present data. However, similar analyses of other phases in the Southeast, which show both resemblances to and divergences from the great Cult centers, should be useful. These, together with more intensified investigations of Cult materials in the large centers — studies on the order of that by Waring and Holder but done quantitatively — should help shed light on the nature and origin of the Southern Cult."

Bibliography: C. S. Brown, 1926; J .B. Griffin, 1952; C. B. Moore, 1905; P. Phillips, J. A. Ford, and J. B. Griffin, 1951; A. J. Waring, Jr., and P. Holder, 1945.

PREHISTORIC DESIGNS—WALLS-PECAN POINT

Plate 55

LEFT. Engraved designs found on pottery from the Walls, Mississippi, area showing several symbols of the Southern Ceremonial Complex—hand, bone, skull, wing, cross, swastika swirl, swastika in a circle, abstract serpent, and cross-hatching (Courtesy, Mississippi Geological Survey, after Brown, 1926, Figures 279, 280, 282, and 301). For more pottery from the Walls, Mississippi-Memphis, Tennessee-Pecan Point and St. Francis, Arkansas area, see J. B. Griffin, 1952, Figs. 124-128. Also, Phillips, Ford, and Griffin, 1951.

OPPOSITE PAGE. UPPER RIGHT. Limestone slab about 15" x 19" with carving on each side; the engraved lines on the obverse side depict six human figures engaged in ceremonial activities; on the reverse side are two persons, one with his bow drawn is shooting an arrow. Note, man on left side of this drawing appears to wear an antler headdress and hold a hafted axe, similar to the copper axes found at Spiro; the sun-circle is a prominent decoration on the garments and bodies; the figure in the frame is smoking an elbow pipe; the man with the square shield wears an elaborate headdress; the shield is decorated with concentric circles and what may be snake symbols. The figure on the lower right seems to have a crest or roach of hair, feathers, or copper. This stone was first pictured by Thruston, 1890; it is now owned and located at the Tennessee Historical Society's Museum in Nashville; this drawing is after M. Parker, "A Study of the Rocky Creek Pictograph," Lewis and Kneberg, 1954, pp. 87-91. This stone is from a site in Sumner County, on Rocky Creek near Castalian Springs, near the Cumberland River, northeast of Nashville. (Redrawn from Lewis and Kneberg, 1954, by permission from Dr. T. M. N. Lewis, Editor the TENNESSEE ARCHAEOLOGIST).

BELOW. UPPER ROW. Two shell-tempered pottery vessels. LEFT. Pottery head-pot about 6" high. This is an unusual type of bottle, relatively rare in occurrence and characteristic of northeastern Arkansas and southeastern Missouri. St. Francis area, Arkansas (Courtesy, G. E. Barnes). RIGHT. Pottery vessel from Fuller site near Memphis, Tennessee; 10¼ cm. Notched rim with applique arcades, and punctates around neck. The body of the vessel is decorated with four deeply incised swastika swirls and with four triskeles, each enclosed in a circle near the neck between the swirls (Courtesy, G. E. Barnes). LOWER ROW. LEFT. Shell-tempered pottery vessel with incised design applied while clay was soft. Rim is arcaded and decorated with applique and punctates. Maximum height 10 cm. (Courtesy, University of Mississippi, Davies Collection). RIGHT. Water bottle; maximum height about 18½ cm. Fillets of clay have been appliqued to the surface of the bottle in reproduction of cords; such were presumably used to suspend pottery vessels. Walls, De Soto County, Mississippi (Courtesy, University of Mississippi, Davies Collection).

BELOW. Groups of designs —cross, snake, turkey tracks, arrows, half-moon, and others—from the face and sides of a large boulder located in a huge rock shelter in a mountainous area of the William B. Bankhead National Forest, Lawrence County, Alabama. These and other petroglyphs in the forest were found by Spencer A. Waters in 1956. He describes the rock shelter as a part of an enormous sandstone bluff which can be approached by two paths. Carved footholds or steps made by the Indians lead up the bluff to a slanting ledge which extends to the top; also, a natural crevice stretches diagonally down the bluff. Artifacts have been found inside the shelter; these include fragments of stone bowls and sherds of pottery tempered with fiber, sand, limestone, and shell; this variety indicates the probability of long habitation (Courtesy, S. A. Waters).

PICTOGRAPHS

Plate 56

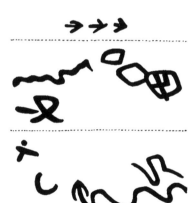

In an article entitled, "The Importance of Petraglyphs in Tennessee," Robert M. Tatum defines the pictograph area of the Southeast, and describes some of the symbols and subjects found:

"Although the big areas of petroglyphs are in the Southwest, many do occur in the eastern half of the country, and Tennessee seems to be the center of one of these areas. Because of the sandy soil of many southern states we do not find any free rock surfaces where designs could be incised or painted . . . . Tennessee . . . is an important link between the states of Missouri and Arkansas where we find a large number of designs, and the eastern states where fewer designs are located." (On an accompanying map he shows the petroglyph areas of Tennessee, North Carolina, Southwest Virginia, North Georgia, Arkansas, and Missouri).

"Within the State of Tennessee the author has, with the gracious aid of Professor T. M. N. Lewis and others, been able to locate three regions of sites. All of these are in the northern half of the state where suitable terrain makes their presence more likely. One area is in the region of Dickson, Davidson and Cheatham Counties. The second is formed by Roane County, and the third by Campbell County . . . .

"A glance at the map of Tennessee and the nearby states will immediately show the geographical distribution has as a center the North Carolina and Tennessee state line. About this line is a region of dense petroglyph distribution. In northern Georgia are incised drawings of men, deer, buffalo, turkey, snakes, hands, footprints, tracks, as well as circles and half moons. In eastern North Carolina we find use of red paint to make pictures of men, and geometric designs. In other sections we find circles, triangles, ladders, wheels, hands, snakes, and numerous deeply incised cups. Virginia has many examples of red paintings of humans, animals, circles, sun disks, and also red and black designs of diamonds.

" . . . it is obvious that a high correlation between the sites in the four states exists. In all of them the color red is predominant. (other colors he mentions are: yellow, blue, black, white and orange paint). The use of the circle is common to all four, deer to three, buffalo to two, humans to four, and animals to four. The presence of lines, wheels, bows, etc. is enough to let us conclude that the sites are related . . . .

"Missouri is the center of a Middle West petroglyph area. In this state we find examples of normal hands and six-fingered, deformed hands, as well as bird designs. In the Tennessee area we also find such hands and birds but their presence is not noticed any farther north than New Jersey. The presence of these designs in Tennessee might well mark an extension from Missouri. The bow, connected circles, star and moon are other designs thus far limited to either the southwest or middlewest and seldom found in the east." (Excerpt from an article in Lewis and Kneberg, 1954, pp. 40-41; quoted courtesy, Dr. T. M. N. Lewis. Mr. Tatum's work in investigating the petroglyph area was "supported by grants from the Penrose Fund of the American Philosophical Society and by the Washington Academy of Science; permission to quote granted by each).

Although the designs shown on this page are rock carvings—engraved or cut into the surface of the rock — many of the pictographs in the Southeast were painted; others were pecked; and some combined these methods.

Chapter 5

KEY MARCO

Quotation from Frank Hamilton Cushing, "Exploration of Ancient Key Dwellers' Remains on the Gulf Coast of Florida," PROCEEDINGS OF THE AMERICAN PHILOSOPHICAL SOCIETY. Paper read before the Society, November 6, 1896, Vol. XXV, December 1896, No. 153. Printed April 20, 1897, Philadelphia, pp. 329-432 and Plates XXV-XXXV. Excerpts. (Quoted by permission from the American Philosophical Society.)[1]

"I was not much delayed in securing two men and a little fishing sloop, . . . and in sailing forth one glorious evening late in May, with intent to explore as many as possible of the islands and capes of Charlotte harbor, Pine Island South, Caloosa Bay and the lower more open coast as far as Marco, some ninety miles away to the southward. . . .

"The astonishment I felt . . . on penetrating into the interior of the very first encountered of these thicket-bound islets, may be better imagined than described, when after wading ankle deep in the slimy and muddy shoals, and then alternately clambering and floundering for a long distance among the wide-reaching interlocked roots of the mangroves . . . I dimly beheld, in the sombre depths of this sunless jungle of the water, a long, nearly straight, but ruinous embankment of piled-up conch-shells. Beyond it were to be seen . . . other banks, less high, not always regular, but forming a maze of distinct enclosures of various sizes and outlines, nearly all of them open a little at either end or at opposite sides, as if for outlet and inlet.

"Treading this zone of boggy bins, and leading in toward a more central point, were here and there open ways like channels. They were formed by paralleled ridges of shells, increasing in height toward the interior, until at last they merged into a steep, somewhat extended bench, also of shells, and flat on the top like a platform. Here, of course, at the platform, the channel ended, in a slightly broadened cover like a landing place; but a graded depression or pathway ascended from it . . . . In places off to the side on either hand were still more of these platforms, rising terrace-like, but very irregularly, from the enclosures below to the foundations of great, level-topped mounds, which, like worn-out elongated and truncated pyramids, loftily and imposingly crowned the whole, some of them to a height of nearly thirty feet above the encircling sea. . . .

"The bare patches along the ascents to the mounds were, like the ridges below, built up wholly of shells, great conch-shells chiefly, blackened by exposure for ages. . . .

". . . the surface below, like the bare spaces themselves, proved to be also of shells, smaller or much broken on the levels and gentler slopes, and mingled with scant black mold on the wider terraces, as though these had been formed with a view to cultivation and supplied with soil from the rich muck beds below. Here also occurred occasional potsherds and many worn valves of gigantic clams and whorls of huge univalves that appeared to have been used as hoes and picks or other digging tools, and this again suggested the idea that at least the wider terraces—many of which proved to be not level, but filled with basin-shaped depressions or bordered by retaining walls—had been used as garden plats, some, perhaps, as drainage basins. But the margins of these, whether raised or not, and the edges of even the lesser terraces, the sides of the graded ways leading up to or through them, and especially the slopes of the greater mounds, were all of unmixed shell, in which, as on the barren patches, enormous nearly equal-sized whelks or conch-shells prevailed. . . .

". . . Like the pelicans . . . they (the natives) had at first merely resorted to low outlying reefs in these shallow seas as fishing grounds, but ere long had built stations there, little shelters, probably, on narrow platforms held up by clumsy piles. . . . The shells of the mollusks they had gathered for food had naturally been cast down beside these lengthy platforms, until they formed long ridges that broke the force of the waves when storms

[1] Excerpts from: Reconnaissance (pp. 331-360). Piles and Timbers (pp. 362-363). Furniture (pp. 363-364). Navigating Apparatus and Fishing Gear (pp. 364-367). Tools and Implements (pp. 367-371). Weapons (pp. 371-374). Personal Ornaments and Paraphernalia (pp. 374-378). Miscellaneous Ceremonial Appliances (pp. 378-387). Masks and Figureheads (pp. 388-394). In addition paragraphs from General Conclusions (pp. 394-415—paragraphs: pp. 400-401, 402, and 411). The Key Marco exploration was jointly sponsored by the Smithsonian Institution, Bureau of American Ethnology, and the University of Pennsylvania, Department of Archaeology and Palaeontology. Artifacts recovered are in the United States National Museum, and the University Museum, University of Pennsylvania. See also J. A. Mason, 1950.

swept by. Thus, I fancied, these first builders of the keys had been taught how to construct with special purpose sea-walls of gathered shells, how to extend the arms of the reefs, and to make other and better bayous or fish-pounds within them by forming successive enclosures, ever keeping free channels throughout for the driving in of the fish and the passage of their canoes. And when the innermost of the enclosures became choked by drift and other debris they had filled them with shell stuff and mud from the surrounding sea, and so of some had made drainage-basins to catch rain for drinking water, and of others, in time, little garden plats or fields.

"Thus it was that the erstwhile stations had become better and better fitted as places of longer abode; and yet others of the enclosures or courts farthest in had become filled, and were in turn wrought into basins and gardens to replace the first that had been made; for these were now covered over and piled higher to form wide benches whereupon the long mounds or foundations might be erected. Finally, aloft on these greater elevations strong citadels of refuge alike from foe and hurricane; storehouses, dwellings of chiefs or leaders, and assembly-places and temples had been builded. . . . "

(After this general description of the "artificial shell islands," Cushing described the features of many of the individual islands. He concludes the section:)

". . . there were, in Charlotte Harbor, Pine Island South, Caloosa Entrance and Matlatcha Bay alone, more than seventy-five of them (ancient artificial shell islands). Forty of this number were gigantic, the rest were representative of various stages in the construction of such villages of the reefs. . . .

"Key Marco, water-courts, canals, elevations, central mounds, cistern holes, garden terraces and all, was . . . but another such as were the keys further north. . . ."

(Regarding the artifacts found at the various islands, including his more extensive work at Marco, he states:)

"The objects found by us in these deposits were in various conditions of preservation, from such as looked fresh and almost new, to such as could scarcely be traced through or distinguished from the briny peat mire in which they were embedded. They consisted of wood, cordage and like perishable materials associated with implements and ornaments of more enduring substances, such as shell, bone and horn—for only a few shaped of stone were encountered during the entire search.

"Articles of wood far outnumbered all others. I was astounded to find that many of these had been painted with black, white, gray-blue, and brownish-red pigments; . . . owing to the presence in these pigments of a gum-like and comparatively insoluble sizing, the costings of color were often relatively better preserved than the woody substance they covered, and enabled us the more readily to distinguish the outlines of these painted objects. . . .

"Some of the things thus recovered could be preserved by very slow drying, but it soon became evident that by far the greater number of them could not be kept intact. No matter how perfect they were at first, they warped, shrank, split, and even checked across the grain, like old charcoal, or else were utterly disintegrated on being exposed to the light and air if only for a few hours. . . .

"From the fact that many of the objects lay suspended, as it were, in the mud above the bottom, I judged that when these remains were thrown down into the little water court, the spaces between the house-benches and around the borders of the quays at least, must have been already choked up somewhat with debris or refuse and slime or mud; for out in the middle of the court where the deep open space occurred throughout the channel between the two canals, little was found in the way of art remains, except such as lay directly upon, or very near to, the bottom.

ANCIENT ARTIFACTS FROM THE COURT OF THE PILE DWELLERS. KEY MARCO.

"PILES, TIMBERS, etc.—None of the piles found by us exceeded six and a half feet in length. . . . the greater number of them were less than three and a half feet long . . . . They were tapered toward the bottom and bluntly pointed, rudely squared or hollowed out at the tops as though to support round, horizontal timbers; and they were bored or notched slantingly here and there through the edges . . . for the reception of rounded braces or cross-stays of poles or saplings . . . . Some of the piles were worn at the points . . . as though they had rested upon, but had not been driven into, the solid shell and clay-marl benches . . . . The longer piles were, on the contrary, round. They were somewhat smaller, quite smoothly finished, and had been . . . actually driven into the bottom. It therefore appeared to me that they had been made so as to be thus driven into the edges of the benches at either side of the peg-supported platforms, in order to keep these from swerving in case an unusual rise in the waters caused them to float. There were other pieces equally long, but broken off near their points. They were slightly grooved at the upper ends and tied around with thick, well-twisted ropes or cables made of cypress bark and palmetto fibre, as though they had served as mooring-posts . . . . I found abundant broken timbers, poles, and traces of wattled cane matting as well as quantities of interlaced or latticed saplings—laths evidently, for they seemed to have been plastered with a clay and ash cement—and quantities also of yellow marsh-grass thatch . . . . Here and elsewhere along the edges of the benches occurred fire-hardened cement or mud hearth-plastering, mingled with ashes and charcoal—which indeed occurred more or less abundantly everywhere . . . .

"FURNITURE, etc.—Here and there were found curious wooden seats—more or less like ancient Antillean stools (Plate No. 59), . . . flat slabs of wood from a foot to more than two feet in length, slightly hollowed on top from end to end as well as from side to side, with rounded bottoms and substantial, prong-like pairs of feet near either end, from two to three inches long. Some of these stools had the feet level; others, so spread and beveled that they would exactly fit the hollow bottoms of canoes. Others still were smaller . . . so diminutive, in fact, that they could have served no purpose else . . . than that of head-rests or pillow-supports. We found . . . examples of what might have been the pillows used in connection with these rests. They were taperingly cylindrical, made of fine rushes, and showed a continuous four-ply plat, so that, like cassava strainers, they were flexible and compressible, yet springy, and they had probably been filled with Florida moss or deer hair . . . . Portions of mats, some thick, as though for use as rugs, others enveloping various objects and others still of shredded bark in strips so thin and flat and closely platted that they might well have served as sails, were frequently discovered. Yet except for masses of the peat or mud upon which the remains of this matting lay and which therefore when dry showed traces of its beautifully and variously formed plies, naught of them could be preserved. It was obvious . . . that the peoples who had inhabited the court understood well, not only platting, but weaving and basketry-making too.

"POTTERY AND UTENSILS.—A few examples of pottery were discovered lying always on or near the bottom, and with one exception invariably broken. All of these vessels, notwithstanding the fact that some of them had their rims more or less decorated, showed evidence of having been used as cooking bowls or pots. Associated with them were household utensils—spoons made from bivalves, ladles made from the greater halves of hollowed-out well-grown conch shells; and cups, bowls, trays and mortars of wood . . . . They ranged in size from little hemispherical bowls or cups two and a half or three inches in diameter, to great cypress tubs more than two feet in depth, tapering, flat-bottomed, and correspondingly wide at the tops. The smaller mortar-cups were marvels of beauty and finish as a rule, and lying near them and sometimes even within them, were still found their appropriate pestles or crushers (Plate No. 59) . . . .

"The trays were also very numerous . . . ; comparatively shallow, oval in outline and varying from a length of six and a half or seven inches and a width of four or five inches, to a length of not less than five feet and a width of quite two feet. The ends of these trays were narrowed and truncated to form handles, the upper faces of which were usually decorated with neatly cut-in disc-like or semilunar figures or depressions . . . . I was impressed with their general resemblance to canoes . . . .

"NAVIGATING APPARATUS AND FISHING GEAR.—This inference was strengthened by the discovery here and there of actual toy canoes . . . . There were six or seven of these, and while they generally conformed to a single type, . . . the dugout, they differed very materially in detail. Three of them were comparatively flat-bottomed. One, about five inches in length by two in breadth of beam and an inch in depth, was shaped . . . like a . . . flat-bottomed row boat . . . . Another of these . . . was much sharper and higher at the stem and stern, had very low gunwales, and was generally narrower . . . . Yet another looked like a clumsy craft . . . was comparatively wide, and its ends also quite broad. All except one of these, I observed, were decorated at one end or both, with the same sort of semilunar or dics-like devices, that were observable on the trays.[2]

---

[2] "Two others of the toy canoes . . . were not more than three inches broad by nearly two feet in length, . . . tapered cleanly toward the forward ends, which were high and very narrow, yet square at the sterns, which were also high. We found them almost in juxta-position. . . . Little sticks and slight shreds of twisted bark were lying across them and indicated to me that they had once been lashed together, and, as a more finished and broken spar-like shaft lay near by, I was inclined to believe that they represented the sea-going craft of the ancient people here; . . . vessels . . . made double—of canoes lashed together, catamaran fashion—and propelled not only

". . . splintered gunwales and a portion of the prow of a long, light cypress-wood canoe, and . . . fragments . . . of a large . . . clumsier boat . . . were found down toward the middle of the court. Not far from the remains of these I came across an ingenious anchor. It consisted of a bunch of large triton-shells roughly pierced and lashed together with tightly twisted cords of bark and fibre so that the long, spike-like ends stood out radiatingly, like the points of a star. They had all been packed full of sand and cement, so as to render them thus bunched, sufficiently heavy to hold a good-sized boat. Near the lower edge of the eastern bench lay another anchor. It was made of flat, heart-shaped stones, similarly perforated and so tied and cemented together with fibre and a kind of red vegetable gum and sand, that the points stood out radiatingly in precisely the same manner. Yet another anchor was formed from a single boulder of coraline limestone a foot in diameter. Partly by nature, more by art, it was shaped to resemble the head of a porpoise perforated for attachment at the eye-sockets. Balers made from large conch shells crushed in at one side, or of wood, shovel shaped, or else scoop shaped, with handles turned in, were abundant; as were also nets of tough fibre, both coarse and fine, ... To the lower edges of these, sinkers made from thick, roughly perforated umboidal bivalves, tied together in bunches, or else from chipped and notched fragments of heavy clam shells, were attached, while to the upper edges, floats made from gourds, held in place by fine net-lashings, or else from long sticks or square-ended blocks, were fastened.[3]

"We found four or five fish-hooks. The shanks or stems of these were about three inches long, shaped much like those of our own, but made from . . . curved main branches of the forked twigs . . . . These were cut off at the forks in such manner as to leave a portion of the stems to serve as butts, which were girdled and notched in, so that the sharp, barbed points of deer bone, which were about half as long as the shanks and leaned in toward them, could be firmly attached with sinew and black rubber-gum cement. The stems were neatly tapered toward the upper ends, which terminated in slight knobs, and to these, lines . . . were tied by half-hitches . . . . Little plug-shaped floats of gumbo-limbo wood, and sinkers made from the short thick columellae of turbinella shells—not shaped and polished like the highly finished plummet-shaped pendants we secured in great numbers, but with the whorls merely battered off—seemed to have been used with these hooks and lines. That they were designed for deep-sea fishing was indicated by the occurrence of flat reels or spools . . . . There were also shuttles or skein-holders of hard wood, six or seven inches long, with wide semicircular crotches at the ends. But these may have served in connection with a double kind of barb, made from two notched or hooked crochet-like points or prongs of deer bone, that we found attached with fibre cords to a concave round-ended plate, an inch wide and three inches long, made from the pearly nacre of a pinna shell . . . .

"TOOLS AND IMPLEMENTS.—The working parts of the various instruments of handicraft that we found were not of stone, but almost exclusively of hard organic substances—shell, bone, horn, and teeth—principally those of sharks—with their various kinds of wooden appurtenances or haftings, sometimes intact, sometimes merely indicated by the presence of fragments or traces . . . . as a rule, the lashings by which they had been bound together . . . of rawhide thongs or of twisted sinew or fishgut—had wholly dissolved . . . . Such bindings had, however, in many instances been reinforced with cements of one kind or another—a sticky red substance, . . . or else rubber-gum, asphaltum, or a combination of rosin and beeswax and rubber, which still endured and retained perfect impressions of the fastening cords . . . .

"Large clam shells, deeply worn at the backs, as well as showing much use at the edges, seemed to have

[3] "Around the avenues of the court I was interested to find netting of coarser cordage weighted with unusually large-sized or else heavily bunched sinkers of shells, and supplied at the upper edges with long, delicately tapered gumbo-limbo float-pegs (3½" to 8" long), those of each set equal in size, each peg thereof partially split at the larger end, so as to clamp double half-turns or ingeniously knotted hitches of the neatly twisted edges-cords with which all were made fast to the nets . . . they would turn against the current of the tide . . . and would continuously bob up and down on the ripples, . . . in such manner as to frighten the fish that had been driven, or had passed over them at high tide, when, as the tide lowered, they naturally tried to follow it. In connection with these nets we found riven stays, usually of cypress or pine, such as might have been used in holding them upright. Hence I inferred that they had been stretched across the channels not only of the actual water courts of residence, like this, but probably also, of the surrounding fish-pounds; . . ."

with paddles, but also, perhaps, by means of sails, made probably from the thin two-ply kind of bark matting . . . of which there were abundant traces near the mid-channel, associated with cordage and with a beautifully regular, and much worn and polished spar . . . . Jonathan Dickinson . . . narrates how, just two hundred years ago, he and his companion voyagers were shipwrecked on the Florida shore. He clearly describes such a double canoe . . . when he tells how a Cacique, into whose hands they fell, went to wrest back the plunder that had been taken from them by earlier captors. The Cacique—to quote the author freely—came home in great state. He was nearly nude and triumphantly painted red, and sitting cross-legged on their ship's chest, that stood on a platform midway over two canoes lashed together with poles . . . .
"Two tackle-blocks, real prehistoric pulleys, that we found, may have pertained to such canoes as these. Each was three inches long, oval, one side rounded, the other cut in at the edges, or rabbetted . . . . The tenon-like portion was gouged out midway, transversely pierced, and finished with a smooth peg or pivot over which the cordage turned . . . . a paddle (was found) near the mouth of the inlet canal. . . ."

served both as scrapers and as digging implements or hoes; for some of them had been hafted by clamping curved sticks over the hinge and over the point at the apex or umbo—where it showed wear—precisely in such manner as Le Moyne seems to have attempted to show in his representation—published in De Bry and other early works—of Indians planting corn.

"Picks, hammers, adzes and gouges made from almost entire conch shells were found, . . . the conch-shell heads of these tools were most ingeniously hafted. The whorl was usually battered away on the side toward the mouth, so as to expose the columella. The lip was roundly notched or pierced, and the back whorl also perforated oppositely. Thus the stick or handle could be driven into these perforations, past the columella in such a manner that it was sprung or clamped firmly into place. Nevertheless it was usually further secured with raw-hide thongs—now mere jelly. . . . Several very ingenious hacking tools or broad-axes had been made merely from the lips and portions of the outer or body-whorls of these conchs. They were simply notched at the ends so as to receive correspondingly grooved or notched sticks which were bound to their inner sides with thongs passed around the ends and over the backs. The wide, curved, natural edge of the lips, had then been neatly sharpened. . . . In addition to these cutting tools, celts, or rather celt-shaped, but curved adze-blades, two of them in connection with their handles—which were made from forked branches, one limb cut short and shouldered to receive the blade, the other left long, . . . as the handle (were found). True celts were found too, made from the heavy columellae of triton shells. One of them was accompanied by a pierced handle, the most elaborately decorated object of its kind thus far found in our country. It was superbly carved from end to end with curved volute-like decorations, concentric circles, ovals, and overpliced as well as parallel lines, regularly divided by encircling bands, as though derived from ornate lashings; while the head or extreme end was notched around for the attachment of plumes or tassels, and the opposite or handle-end furnished with an eyelet to facilitate suspension. Numbers of carving adzes, . . . were also secured. . . . Each consisted of a curved or crozier-shaped handle of hardwood about a foot in length, sharply crooked toward the head, which consisted of a perfectly fitted, carved, polished and socketed section of deer horn . . . . shaped as to receive . . . little blades made either from bits of shell, the sharp ventral valves of oysters . . . or sometimes, from very large shark or alligator teeth. These peculiar little hand-adzes . . . . were elaborately carved. All had eyes, mostly protuberant, just above the sockets, and one, for example, was slightly crooked from side to side, and shaped to represent a fanged serpent; another had carved near its head, a surprisingly realistic horned deer's head. . . .

"Cutting and carving knives of shark's teeth, varying in size from tiny straight points to carved blades nearly an inch in length and in width of base were found by hundreds. Some were associated with their handles . . . five to seven inches in length by not more than half or three-quarters of an inch in diameter . . . . Some were slightly curved, others straight . . . . All were furnished with nocks at the lower ends which were also a little tapered—for the reception of the hollow bases of the tooth-blades that had been lashed to them and cemented with black gum. Not a few of these doubly-tapered little handles were marvels of finish, highly polished, and some of them were carved or incised with involuted circlets or kwa-like decorations, or else with straight or spiral-rayed rosettes and concentric circles, at the upper ends, as though these had been used as stamps in the finishing of certain kinds of work. The other class of handles . . . was designed for receiving one or more of the shark-tooth blades, . . . at the sides of the ends, . . . They were nearly all carved; a few . . . elaborately; and they ranged in length from the width of the palm of the hand to five or six inches . . . . (see Plate 57).

"I found these diminutive shark-tooth blades . . . by far the most effective primitive carving tools I had ever learned of, and therein perceived one of the principal causes of the preeminence of the ancient key dwellers in the wood carver's art . . . . There were girdling tools or saws—made from the sharp, flat-toothed lower jaws of king-fishes—into the hollow ends of which curved jaw-bones, the crudest of little handles had been thrust and tied through neat lateral perforations . . . I found not a few examples of work done with them, in the shape of round billets that had been severed by them and spirally haggled in such a way as to plainly illustrate the origin of one of the most frequent decorations we found on carved wood works, the spiral rosette just referred to. There were minute little bodkin-shaped chisels of bone and shell, complete in themselves; and there were, of course, numerous awls and the like, made from bone, horn and fish spines. Rasps of very small, much worn and evidently most highly prized fragments of coral sandstone, as well as a few strips of carefully rolled-up shark skin, told the story of how the harder tools had been edged, and the polished wood—, and bone-work finished, here.

"WEAPONS.—It was significant that no bows were discovered in any portion of the court, but of atlatls or throwing sticks, both fragmentary and entire, four or five examples were found. Two of the most perfect of these were also the most characteristic, since one was double-holed, the other single-holed . . . . Arrows about four feet in length, perfectly uniform, pointed with hard wood, the shafts made either of a softer and lighter kind of wood or of cane, were found. The nocks of these were relatively large. This suggested that certain curved and shapely clubs, or rather wooden sabres —for they were armed along one edge with keen shark-teeth—might have been used not only for striking, but also for flinging such nocked spears or throwing-arrows . . . .

"War clubs proper, that is, of wood only, were found in considerable variety. The most common form was that of the short, knobbed bludgeon. Another was nearly three feet long, the handle rounded, tapered, and furnished at the end with an eyelet for the wrist cord. The blade was flattish, widening to about three inches at the head, and it was laterally beveled from both sides to form blunt edges and was notched or roundly serrated . . . . The type was obviously derived from some pre-existing kind of blade-set weapon. This was also true, in another way, of the most remarkable form of club we discovered. It was not quite two feet in length, and made of some dark-colored fine-grained kind of hard, heavy wood, exquisitely fashioned and finished. The handle was also round and tapering, the head flattened, symmetrically, flaring and sharped-edged, the end square or but slightly curved, and terminating in a grooved knob or boss, to which tassel-cords had been attached. Just below the flaring head was a double blade, that is, a similunar, sharp-edged projection on either side, giving the weapon the appearance of a double-edged battle-axe set in a broadened club. This specimen . . . was absolutely identical in outline with the so-called batons represented in the hands of warrior-figures delineated on the shell gorgets and copper plates found in the southern and central Mississippi mounds . . . . It not only recalled these, but also typical double-bladed battle-axes or clubs of South and Central American peoples . . . .

"I must not fail to mention dirks or stilettos, made from the foreleg bones of deer, the grip ends flat, the blades conforming in curvature to the original lines of the bones from which they were made. One of them was exquisitely and conventionally carved at the hilt-end to represent the head of a buzzard or vulture, the which was no doubt held to be one of the gods of death by these primitive key-dwellers. There were also striking-and thrusting-weapons of slender make and of wood, save that they were sometimes tipped with deer horn or beautifully fashioned spurs of bone, but they were so fragmentary that I have thus far been unable to determine their exact natures. (See Plate 57).

"PERSONAL ORNAMENTS AND PARAPHERNALIA.—Numerous objects of personal investure and adornment were collected. Aside from shell beads, pendants and gorgets, of kinds found usually in other southern relic sites, there were buttons, cord-knobs of large oliva-shells, and many little conical wooden plugs that had obviously formed the cores of tassels; sliding-beads, of elaborately carved deer horn . . . and one superb little brooch, scarcely more than an inch in width, made of hard wood, in representation of an angle-fish, the round spots on its back inlaid with minute discs of tortoise shell, the bands of the diminutive tail delicately and realistically incised, and the mouth, and a longitudinal eyelet as delicately incut into the lower side. There were very large labrets of wood for the lower lips, the shanks and insertions of which were small, and placed near one edge, so that the outer disc which had been coated with varnish or brilliant thin laminae of tortoise shell, would hang low over the chin. There were lip-pins too; and ear buttons, plates, spikes and plugs. The ear buttons were chiefly of wood, and were of special interest—the most elaborate articles of jewelry we found. They were shaped like huge cuff buttons—some, two inches in diameter, resembling the so-called spool-shaped copper bosses or ear ornaments of the mound builders. But a few of these were made in parts, so that the rear disc could be, by a partial turn, slipped off from the shank, to facilitate insertion into the slits of the ear lobe. The front discs were rimmed with white shell rings, within were narrower circlets of tortoise shell, and within these, in turn, little round, very dark and slightly protuberant wooden bosses or plugs, covered with gum or varnish and highly polished, so that the whole front of the button exactly resembled a huge round, gleaming eyeball . . . . some having been overlaid in front with highly polished concavo-convex white shell discs, perforated at the centers as if to represent eye pupils . . . .

"There were still other ear buttons, however, elaborately decorated with involuted figures, or circles divided equally by sinusoid lines, designs that were greatly favored by the ancient artists of these keys. The origin of these figures, both painted as on the buttons—in contrasting blue and white—and incised, as on discs, stamps, or the ends of handles, became perfectly evident to me as derived from the 'navel marks,' or central involutes on the worked ends of univalvular shells; . . . That the ear buttons proper were badges, was indicated by the finding of larger numbers of common ear plugs; round, and slightly rounded also at either end, but grooved or rather hollowed around the middles. Although beautifully fashioned, they had been finished with shark-tooth surface—hatching, in order to facilitate coating them with brilliant varnishes or pigments. The largest of them may have been used as stretchers for ordinary wear; but the smaller and shorter of them were probably for ordinary use . . . and had taken the place of like, but more primitive ornaments made from the vertebrae of sharks . . . .

"I could not quite determine what had been the use of certain highly ornate flat wooden discs. They were too thin to have been serviceable as ear plugs, or as labrets. But from the fact that they were so exquisitely incised with rosettes, or elaborately involuted, obliquely hatched designs, and other figures—the two faces different in each case—and that they corresponded in size to the ear buttons and plugs, I came to regard them as stamps used in impressing the gum-like pigments with which so many of these ornaments had been quite thickly coated . . . . Very long and beautifully finished, curved plates of shell had been used probably as ear ornaments or spikes, also; since they exactly resembled those depicted as worn transversely thrust through the ears, in some of Le Moyne's drawings . . . . and many of the plummet-shaped pendants I have before referred to, must have been used after the manner remarked on in some of the old writers, as 'ear weights' or stretchers, and some, being very long, not only thuswise, but also as ear spikes for wear after the manner of using the plates just described. While certain crude examples of these curious pendants had been used apparently as wattling bobbets, still others, better shaped, had as certainly served as dress or girdle pendants . . . some of tthe cruder and heavier of these shell, coral, and coral-stone plummets, must have served purely practical ends . . . . as wattling weights and netting bobbetts, . . . Others, . . . as fish-line weights. Still, several of the more elaborate of them were not only decorated, but were so beautifully shaped and so highly polished that they could have been employed only as combined stretchers and ornaments or as insignia of a highly valued kind.

"The remains of fringes and of elaborate tassels, made from finely spun cords of the cotton-tree down— dyed, in one case green, in another yellow—betokened high skill in such decorative employment of cordage. The remains, too, of what I regarded as bark headdresses quite similar to those of Northwest Coast Indians, were found. Associated with these, as well as independently, were numbers of hairpins, some made of ivory, some of bone, to which beautifully, long flexible strips of polished tortoise shell . . . had been attached. One pin had been carved at the upper end with the representation of a rattlesnake's tail, precisely like those of Cheyenne warriors; another, with a long conical knob grooved or hollowed for the attachment of plume cords. Collections of giant seacrab claws, still mottled with red, brown, orange, yellow and black colors of life, looked as though they had been used as fringe-rattles and -ornaments combined, for the decoration of kilts. At all events their resemblance to the pendants shown as attached to the loincloth of a man, in one of the early paintings of Florida Indians . . . was perfect. Here and there, bunches of long, delicate, semi-translucent fish-spines indicated use either as necklaces or wristlets; but generally such collection were strung out in a way that led me to regard them as pike-, or shaft-barbs.

"Certain delicate plates of pinna-shell, and others of tortoise-shell, square—though in some cases longer than broad—were pierced to facilitate attachment, and appeared to have been used as dress ornaments . . . Similar plates . . . seemed to have been inlaid . . . .

"Considerable collections or sets of somewhat more uniform tortoise-bone and pinna-shell plates, from an inch and a half to nearly three inches square, were found closely bunched together, in two or three separate places. None of them were perforated. Moreover, nearly all were worn smooth on both faces, and especially around the edges, as though by much handling . . . . In each collection, or set, which consisted of from twenty or more to forty or more pieces, a small proportion were distinguished from the others by difference in length or in material or in surface treatment . . . . I judged that possibly these sets of the plates, at least, had been used in sacred games . . . .

". . . By far the greater number of the articles of personal adornment described . . . were more than this . . . . They may . . . be regarded as having been especially sacred, used as amulets, and in many cases, as . . . badges of office, birthright, or priestly rank . . . . The ear buttons already described illustrate this, as well as certain of the gorgets. These were about three inches in diameter, discoidal, and each cut out from the labrum of a pyrula or conch, to represent a broad circle enclosing a cross. Above the end of the upper arm of this cross, four holes were drilled (instead of one), for suspension. The margin of the inner side was, moreover, scored with definite numbers of notches . . . the circle represented the horizon surrounding the world and its four quarters—typified by the cross as well as the four holes or points—the notches in its rim, the score of sacred days in the four seasons pertaining to the four quarters thus symbolized . . . .

"MISCELLANEOUS CEREMONIAL APPLIANCES: SACRED AND SYMBOLICAL OBJECTS: CARVINGS AND PAINTINGS.—Less difficulty attended the determination of other than the strictly personal appliances of ceremonology which we found . . . . This was particularly the case with a heterogeneous collection of things I discovered close under the sea wall, at the extreme western edge of the court. I regarded its contents as having constituted the outfit of a 'Medicine man,' or Shamanistic priest. It contained several articles of a purely practical nature . . . two or three conch-shell bailers; one or two picks or battering tools of conch-shell . . . a hammer . . . made from a large triton-shell . . . several hollow shaving-blades or rounding-planes, made from the serrate-edged dental plates or mandibles of the logger-head turtle, and some shell chisels and cutters of various other sorts. (Other articles were) several natural but extremely irregular pearls; peculiarly shaped, minute pebbles and concretions; water-worn fragments of coral exhibiting singular markings, such as regular lines of star-like or radiate dots; more than twenty distinct species of small, univalvular shells, and half as many of small bivalves— . . . These were mingled with oliva-shell buttons and pendants, and pairs of sunshells (solenidae), two of which had been externally coated with a bright yellow pigment, and others of which had once been painted, inside, with symbolic figures or devices in black . . . There were a number of interesting remains of terrestrial animals. One was the skull of an opossum. It had been carefully cleaned, and cut off at the occiput, and to the base thus formed, the under jaw had been attached frontwardly at right angles, in such manner that the object could be set upright. The whole had been covered with thick, white pigment, and on this background lines in black, representative of the face marks or features of the living animal, as conventionally conceived, had been painted, doubtless to make it fetishistically 'alive and potent' again. Another skull, that of the marten or weasel, occurred in this little museum of a primitive scientist; . . . both the opossum and the weasel were favorite 'mystery animals' of Indian Shamans elsewhere . . . . There were kilt-rattles, made from peculiarly mottled claw shells of both the smaller sea-crab and the great king-crab; and a set of brilliant colored scallop shells, and another set of larger pecten shells, all in each set perforated, obviously for mounting together on a hoop, to serve as castanets, precisely as are similar shells among the Shamans of the far-away Northwest coast. There was still another kind of rattle—duplicated elsewhere—made from the entire shell or carapace of a 'gopher,' or land-tortoise, . . . there were, in addition, a beautiful little sucking tube made from the wing-bone of a pelican or crane, and near at hand a sharp scarifying lancet of fish bone set in a little wooden handle, of precisely the kind described by old writers as used by the Southern Indians in blood letting and ceremonial skin-scratching.

"In addition to these . . . there were a number of highly artificial things. Most interesting of these and conclusively significant of the nature of the find, was what I regarded as a set of 'Black Drink' appliances. It consisted of a gourd, the long stem of which had been perforated at the end and sides; of a tall wooden cup or vase—brewing-churn and drinking-drum, in one; of a toasting tray of black earthenware punctured around the rim to facilitate handling when hot, and of a fragmentary, but nearly complete, sooty boiling-bowl or hemispherical fire-pot, also of black earthenware. Near by were two beautifully finished conch-shell ladles or drinking cups, both rather smaller and more highly finished than others found in different parts of the court. The larger one was still stained a deep reddish brown color inside . . . .

"Three other objects in the curious lot of sacerdotal things I have been describing were especially typical; . . . . One was a small, square, paddle-like tablet, about six inches long, three inches wide, and five-eights of an inch thick. At one end presumably the lower, was a sort of tenon; that is, the board was squarely cut in from either side to the middle, where a projection about an inch wide and a little more than an inch long was left, as though either for insertion into a mortice, or to facilit...e attachment to something else . . . . A much larger tablet or board, an inch thick and six to seven inches wide, by nearly two feet in length, also tenoned in like manner at the lower end, lay on edge near by. Along the middle of one face of this tablet, two elongated figures were cleanly cut in or outlined, end to end, figures that seemed to represent shafts with round terminal knobs—indicated by circles—the sides of the shafts being slightly incurved, so that the figures as a whole greatly resembled the conventional delineations of thigh bones as seen in the art-works of other primitive peoples—in, for example, the codices, and on the monuments, of Central America. Another tablet of this sort, somewhat wider, longer, and more carefully finished by the shaving down of its surfaces with shark-tooth blades, showed likewise along the middle of one face similar devices, carved, however, in relief, as though to represent a pair of thigh bones laid lengthwise and end to end upon, or rather, set into the center of one side of the board.

"Near the first described of these curious objects which I regarded as probably mortuary, was another tablet, . . . more elaborate . . . . (See Plate 59). These curious tablets, tenoned at the lower ends, notched in midway, and terminating in long shovel-shaped extensions beyond the necks thus formed, were represented by no fewer than ten or twelve examples . . . . But they varied in size from a foot in length by three inches in width, to nearly five feet in length, by more than a foot in width . . . . On the obverse or flat under surface of the tablet were painted equidistantly, in a line, four black circles enclosing white centres, exactly corresponding to other figures of the sort found on various objects in the collections, and from their connection, regarded by me as word-signs, or symbols of the four regions.

"That these curious tablets were symbolical—even if designed for attachment to other more utilitarian things —was indicated by the fact that various similar objects, too small for use otherwise than as batons or amulets, were found. Several of these were of wood, but one of them was fine-grained stone and all were exquisitely finished. Those of wood were not more than eight inches in length by three inches in width; and they were most elaborately decorated by incised circles or lenticular designs on the upper convex sides— still more clearly representing eyes — and by zigzag lines around the upper margins as clearly representing mouths, teeths, etc., and on the same side of the lower portions or bodies by either triangular or concentric circular figures; while on the obverse or flat side of one of them was beautifully incised and painted the figure of a Wheeling Dolphin or Porpoise, one of the most perfect drawings in the collection . . . . The moderately small, highly fin- ished wooden figures of this kind, seemed also to have been used more as portable paraphernalia—as batons or badges in dramatic or dance ceremonials perhaps—than for permanent setting up or attachment. That this may have been the case was indicated in the finding of a 'head-tablet' of the kind. It was fifteen inches in length by about eight inches in width, although wider at the somewhat rounded top than at the bottom. On the flatter, or what I have called the under side of the lower portion or end, this tablet was hollowed to exactly fit the forehead, or back of the head, while on the more convex side, it was figured by means of painted lines, almost precisely as were the upper surfaces of the small wooden batons or miniature carved tablets . . . .

". . . the larger of them may have been used in other ways; as, for example, on the prows of canoes, or at the ends of small mortuary structures—chests or the like—or they may have been set up to form portions of altars. But in any one of these uses they might well have served quite such a symbolic purpose as I have sug- gested; for they were obviously more or less animistic and totemic, and it is for this reason that I have pro- visionally named the larger of them 'Ancestral Tablets,' and look upon the smaller of them as having been used either as amulets or to otherwise represent such tablets in the paraphernalia of sacred ancestoral cere- monials . . . .

"In addition to the head tablet I have spoken of, various thin, painted slats of wood were found in two or three places. They were so related to one another in each case, that it was evident they had also formed por- tions of ceremonial head-dresses, for they had been arranged fan-wise as shown by cordage, traces of which could still be seen at their bases. Besides these, other slats and parts of other kinds of head-dresses, bark tassels, wands—one in the form of a beautifully shaped spear, and others in the form of staffs— were found; many of them plainly indicating the practice of mimetically reproducing useful forms, and especially weap- ons, for ceremonial appliance.

"Perhaps the most significant object of a sacred or ceremonial nature, however, was a thin board of yellowish wood . . . . an elaborate figure of a crested bird was painted on one side of it, in black, white, and blue pigments (See Plate 59). Although conventionally treated, this figure was at once recognizable as representing either the jay or the king-fisher, or perhaps a mythologic bird-being designed to typify both . . . . It will be observed, however, not only that considerable knowledge of perspective was possessed by the primitive artist who made this painting, but also that he attempted to show the deific character of the bird he here represented by placing upon the broad black painted-band beneath his talons (probably symbolic of a key), the characteristic animal of the keys, the raccoon; by placing the symbol or insignia of his dominion over the water—in form of a double-bladed paddle—upright under his dextral wing; and to show his dominion over the four quarters of the sea and island world thus typified, by placing the four circles or word-signs, as if issuing from his mouth,—for in the original, a fine line connects this series of circlets with his throat, and is further continued downward from his mouth toward the heart . . . .

"Other, smaller, thin painted boards were found, but it was evident that they were lids or other portions of boxes, —some of which, indeed, we found nearly complete. . . . It was enfolded within decayed matting containing a bundle or pack, in which were also nine ceremonial adzes, a pair of painted shells, a knife with animistically carved handle, and other articles—all evidently sacred, or for use in the making of sacred objects . . . . The little figure of the crocodile (was) painted on this lid . . . . Upon another box-lid or tablet was painted in outline, a graceful and realistic figure of a doe, and along the middles of the ingeniously rabbetted sides and ends of these boxes—whether large or small—were invariably painted double lines, represented as tied with figure-of-eight knots, midway, or else fastened with clasps of oliva shell—as though to mythically join these parts of the boxes and secure their contents. (See Plate 59).

"The painted shells I have referred to as contained in the pack just described, were those of a species of Solenidae, or the radiatingly banded bivalves that are locally known in that portion of Florida as 'sun-shells.' Each pair of them was closed and neatly wrapped about with strips of palmetto leaves that were still green in color, but which of course immediately decomposed on exposure to the air. On opening this pair of them, I found that in one of the lids or valves, the left one, was a bold, conventional painting, in black lines, of an outspread hand. The central creases of the palm were represented as descending divergingly from between the first and middle fingers, to the base (thumbs crooked down). This was also characteristic of the hands in another much more elaborately painted shell of the kind . . . As may be seen (in Plate 59), this painting represented a man, nearly nude, with outspread hands, masked . . . and wearing a head-dress consisting of a frontlet with four radiating lines—presumably symbolic of the four quarters—represented thereon, and with three banded plumes or hair-pins divergingly standing up from it . . . .

"As evidenced by the exquisite finish and ornamental designs of so many of the implements, weapons and utensils I have described, the ancient key dwellers excelled especially in the art of wood-carving. While their arts in paintings were also of an unusually highly developed character,—as the work of a primitive people— their artistic ability in relief-work was preeminently so. This was further illustrated in a little wooden doll, representing a round-faced woman wearing a sort of cloak or square tunic, that was found near the southernmost shell-bench along the western side of the court . . . . Near this little figure was a superbly carved and finished statuette in wood, of a mountain-lion or panther-god—an outline sketch of which is given in (Plate 58).

"MASKS AND FIGUREHEADS . . . The masks were exceptionally well modeled, usually in realistic representation of human features, and were life-size; hollowed to fit the face, and provided at either side, both above and below, with string-holes for attachment thereto. Some of them were also bored at intervals along the top, for the insertion of feathers or other ornaments, and others were accompanied by thick, gleaming white conch-shell eyes that could be inserted or removed at will, and which were concave—like the hollowed and polished eye-pupils in the carving of the mountain-lion god—to increase their gleam. Of these masks we found fourteen or fifteen fairly well-preserved specimens, besides numerous others which were so decayed that, although not lost to study, they could not be recovered. The animal figureheads, as I have called them, were somewhat smaller than the heads of the creatures they represented. Nearly all of them were formed in parts; that is, the head and face of each was carved from a single block; while the ears and other accessory parts, and, in case of the representation of birds, the wings, were formed from separate pieces. Among these animal figureheads were those of the snouted leather-back turtle, the alligator, the pelican, the fish-hawk and the owl; the wolf, the wild-cat, the bear and the deer. But curiously enough, the human masks and these animal figureheads were associated in the finds, and by a study of the conventional decorations or painted designs upon them, they were found to be also very closely related symbolically, as though for use together in dramaturgic dances or ceremonials.   On one or two occasions I found the masks and figureheads actually bunched, just as they would have been had they thus pertained to a single ceremonial and had been put away when not in use, tied or suspended together.   In case of the animal figureheads the movable parts, such as the ears, wings, legs, etc., had in some instances been laid beside the representations of the faces and heads and wrapped up with them. We found two of these figureheads—those of the wolf and deer—thus carefully wrapped in bark matting, but we could neither preserve this wrapping, nor the strips of palmetto leaves or flags that formed an inner swathing around them.   The occurrence of these animal figureheads in juxtaposition to the human masks which had so evidently been used ceremonially in connection with them, was most fortunate; for it enabled me to recognize, in several instances, the true meaning of the face-paint designs on the human masks thus associated with these animal figures . . . .[4]

"Near the northernmost shell bench . . . was found, carefully bundled up, . . . the remarkable figurehead of a wolf with the jaws distended, separate ears, and conventional, flat, scroll-shaped shoulder-or leg-pieces, designed for attachment thereto with cordage . . . . (See Plate 60).

"In another portion of the court the rather diminutive but exquisitely carved head, breast and shoulders (with separate parts representative of the outspread wings, near by) of a pelican, was found, and in connection with this, a full-sized human mask of wood, also . . . . (See Plate 60).

". . . To such a people, of course, form, semblance, aspect, is therefore all important; and they naturally think that by reproducing a given form or appearance which of itself gives rise to a certain effect, they may

[4] "Nothing short of a full treatise on this primitive philosophy of analogy, and the relation hereto of maskology or disguise by costuming, painting, tatooing, bodily distortion or mutilation and the like, as a means of becoming actually incarnated with the spirits of ancestors, mythic beings, and animals, or totem gods, would fully explain the significance of the bunched animal figureheads and animistically painted human masks that we found. I may add, however, that one can see how far reaching was this primitive conception of the life-potency of form, or expression, by examining any sorts of ancient vessels that are decorated with maskoids or diminutive representations of human or semi-human countenances. Almost always these maskoids—whether found on mound-builder vessel, Central American jar, ancient Peruvian vase, or even Etruscan urn—are characteristic, according to the style of expression they represent, of some particular kind or use of the vessel they occur on . . . .

"A strikingly perfect example of the kind of animal carving I have earlier characterized, was the figurehead of a deer . . . . (See Plate 58).

"A mask of purely human form was also found not far away. It had evidently been associated with the figurehead in such ceremonials as I have referred to. At any rate, like the figurehead itself, it had over the eyebrows a crescent-shaped mark—which seems, by the way, to have been the forehead-symbol of all sorts of game-animals amongst these people, as betokened by its presence on the forehead of the rabbit carving and of other similar animal carvings. It also had the tapered, sharp-pointed white marks or patches along either side of the nose above the nostrils, observable on the snout of the deer head, and the four sets of three lines radiatingly painted around the eyes to represent winkers. This latter characteristic in the eye-painting of the deer figurehead, is very noteworthy; for it would seem that it was intended to symbolize, by means of the four sets of three lines, not merely the eyelashes of the deer, but also rays, of the 'eye of day' or the sun. This I infer the more unhesitatingly because, according to the accounts given by more than one early writer on Florida, the deer must have been regarded among some of the Floridian tribes as one of the gods of day or of the dawn—as indeed is both the antelope and the deer among the Zunis. In such event they symbolize—just as do similar sets of radiating lines around paintings of the Zuni sun-god—the four sets of the sun's rays that are supposed to correspond to the four quarters of the world, as well as to the four sets of three months in the corresponding four seasons of the year over which the sun god is believed to have dominion—since he creates all the days thereof.

"Not only were the human masks associated with their animal counterparts, but sometimes two or more of the human masks were found in one such group. In two or three instances we found multiple sets of them. In such case they were superimposed, as though they had been tied or wrapped, one inside of the other, and thus hung up or laid away, and had fallen so gently into the water-court that their relation to one another had not been disturbed thereby. A notable example of this kind was found in the association of two masks—one lying directly over the other, the faces of both turned upward—that lay not far away from the turtle-figurehead that I have already described. The painted lines on the lowermost of these masks were indicative that it was designed to represent the man-turtle or man-turtle god; whilst the lines upon the superimposed mask seemed, from their general resemblance to the face marks painted upon the bear-figurehead I have also described, to indicate that they were designed to represent the same sort of human presentmentation of the bear. I am at a loss to account for this singular consociation of the two masks—the turtle-man mask and the bear-man mask—unless by supposing that the ancient people who made them, regarded the somewhat sluggish turtle as the 'bear of the sea,' and the bear, whose movements are also awkward, as one of his 'brother-turtles of the land,' or that they otherwise mythically related them.

"We found several human masks by themselves. One was clearly, from the length of its sharp nose and the painted lines upon its features, designed to represent the cormorant; another, from the oblique or twisted form of its mouth, its nose awry, and its spiral or twisted face-marks or bands, as plainly represented the sun-fish or some other slant-faced fish. I regarded a third one of these masks as that of the man-bat-god. It was of especial interest, not only on account of its associations, but also on account of its general resemblance to the face of the bat-god of night conventionally depicted so frequently on Central American monuments. Still another mask was of equal interest, for it represented unmistakably, in a half-human, half-animal style, the features of the wild-cat; and the curiously doubled paint lines with which its cheeks were streaked downwardly below the eyes, although strictly regular and conventional, were singularly suggestive of the actual face-markings of the wild-cat, and thus enable us to understand the significance of like lines that are incised upon certain purely human-faced figures characteristic of many of the maskoidal pipes from mounds of the Ohio and Mississippi valleys.

"I would once more call attention to the association in groups or sets, of the animal figureheads and especially of the masks, as affording still further proof of similarity, if not identity, in key-dweller art and mound-builder art, and as thus affording also a satisfactory explanation of certain points observable in delineations I have so often heretofore referred to as occurring upon the shell gorgets and copper-plates of the ancient mounds of Georgia and other Southern States. Almost always, in these delineations of the mythic human figure, it may be observed that while upon the face, a mask is plainly portrayed, yet, in one or other of the hands is as distinctly represented another mask—not a head, as has frequently been supposed,—and I am therefore inclined to believe that, as with the key dwellers, so with these peoples of the mounds, dramas representative of the transformation of gods from animal into human form, and from one human character into another human character, were probably attempted in their sacred dances.

"The so-called baton, held in the right hand of the figure on the Etowah copper plates . . . may be seen to correspond very closely to the war-club which we discovered in the court of the pile dwellers . . . . It may be seen, too, that the winged god here portrayed wears not only a beaked mask, but also a necklace of oval beads, and an elongated pendant depending there from, like those we so frequently found; an ear button, also exactly like those we found; that around the wrists, arms and legs of this primitive portrait are represented reticulate or plaited bands, as around the wrists and legs of the figure painted in the sacred shell I have described and . . . finally, this character bears in his left hand a mask, the face lines and ear plug of which . . . closely resemble those that we actually found in the court of the pile dwellers." (pp. 391-394).

again and unerringly produce, or help to reproduce the same effect, with the form of their own making . . . ."

(In further explanation of the forms of artifacts, Cushing (pp. 400-414) states:)

". . . It must be constantly borne in mind that these ancient theorists believed their implements and weapons and amulets to be alive, and felt that the powers of these things were not only strengthened, but were also restricted to or rendered safe for, special uses, as well as made to be related to their makers, by their forms or by the decorations or figures placed upon them, especially when these were highly symbolic. It is for this reason more than any other, that primitive peoples cling so to forms, and are so chary of borrowing new forms of implements or weapons, etc. When they do borrow the fashions of such things, they proceed at once to cover or invest them with the peculiar decorative or symbolic devices that they are accustomed to associate with the same kinds of things in time-honored use among themselves. It is chiefly due to this tendency that we have kept inviolate for us everywhere in the primitive world, signs on the relics we find, of what have been termed cultural areas or areas of art-characterization. And so, while the extensive and long-continued intercourse in the barter of the far-southern peoples of Florida and the keys, with more northern peoples . . . will account for much in this spread of identical art forms, nevertheless it does not, I am inclined to think, explain the whole. (pp. 400-401).

"I would again mention the wide prevalence in the keys, of the distinctively conventional treatment of carved and incised work,—whether on shell, bone, or stone,—illustrated by so many specimens in our collection, in connection with its almost equally wide prevalence on figures found in the mounds; which art-vogue was, it would seem, more at home in the keys—more in accordance with a seaside environment that appears to have originated these conventional forms and modes of treatment—than in the lands of the north. (p. 402).

". . . Their art is not only an art of the sea, but it is an art of shells and teeth, an art for which the sea supplied nearly all the working parts of tools, the land only some of the materials worked upon. A study of these tools of shell and teeth furnishes us with an instructive lesson as to the ingenuity of primitive man, as to his capability of meeting needs with help of what would at first seem to be impossible, or but very indifferent means; and as to the effect of this on derived art in general. . . . I have found that teeth and shell, wherever suitable kinds of these natural tools of the animals themselves could be secured, have played a far more important part, even in the arts of peoples who had abundance of excellent material for stone implements at hand, than has hitherto been realized. (p. 411).

". . . The abnormally high development in government, indicated by great public works on the keys and among the mounds, and in a measure by historic records, is, as we have seen, paralleled in the arts of the keys, for in them we found, along with an exceedingly high growth of the conventional side of art, an artistic freedom on the aesthetic side that I have not seen equaled in any of the primitive remains of this continent, elsewhere, save alone perhaps, in those of Central America. This gives good ground for another generalization; that while the desert of the land, with its scant vegetation and scanter animal life, leads naturally, yet through the technique involved, to formal conventional art, the desert of the sea, teeming with growth and quick with animal life in untold variety, beauty, and abundance, leads as in this case, and for like reasons, not to formal, but to highly realistic conventionalization. In the one art, that of the land desert, may be found abundant textile and basketry forms of decoration. There, life seems to have been held so dearly that only in angular or geometric style, or by means of pure symbols rather than by direct representation, were animistic qualities attributed to things made; so that above any other art, the art of the arid desert may be called attributive art. But here in the sea wastes, where life so abounded, the forms, alike of animals and of men, were lavishly, most realistically and gracefully represented, and the commonest tools were shaped over with quite unmistakable life-marks and other added features, and were thus, while conventionally, withal realistically and fearlessly invested, with their animistic and specialistic powers. So, in contrast to the art of the inland desert, this of the sea may be called an art of investure . . . there is scarcely a primitive kind of art, ancient or modern, which cannot be measurably interpreted by comparative study of the one kind (the conventional and attributive) and the other kind so clearly illustrated by our collection (the realistic and the conventionally investive). In this, then, as in its exemplification of man's direct relationship in cultural and even perhaps in racial development, to his environment, our study of the ancient key remains, takes its place in the general study of the Science of Man. (p. 414).

PREHISTORIC DESIGNS—KEY MARCO, FLORIDA

Plates 57 and 58

"It (Demorey's Key) was in some respects the most remarkable key encountered during the entire reconnaissance . . . . The lower end or point of this key consisted of an imposing massive and symmetrical sea wall, of conch-shells chiefly, ten or twelve feet high, and as level and broad on top as a turnpike . . . . This wall . . . merged in the second and third of a series of broad terraces . . . . Occupying a point midway along the inner curve of this elevation . . . directly up from the mangrove swamp it encircled . . . stood a lofty group of five elongated mounds . . . divided from the embracing terraces by a long, deep, and very regular graded way, which led up from a canal . . . to the highest of the terraces, the one forming the wide central elevation. Another and much steeper and shorter graded way led up from yet another parallel canal . . . and joined this longer graded way near its ascent to the high central terrace . . . . The most remarkable feature of this key was a flat, elongated bench, or truncated pyramid, that crowned the middle elevation . . . . this platform . . . was almost vertically faced up with conch-shells; their larger, truncated and spiral ends, laid outward and in courses so regular, that the effect was as of a mural mosaic of volutes . . . . Thus was revealed . . . a parallelo-grammic and level platform, some three and a half feet high and twelve yards in width, by nearly thrice as many in length. It was approached from the inner side by a graded way that led obliquely along the curved ascent up from the mangrove swamp, to a little step-like, subsidiary platform half as high and some twelve feet square, which joined it at right angles . . . . The top of this lesser step, and the approaches to either side of it, were paved with very large uniform-sized clam-shells, laid convex sides upward, and as closely and regularly as tiles." Cushing suggests that because of its central position and regularity of work and graded ways leading to it, this was probably the temple mound.

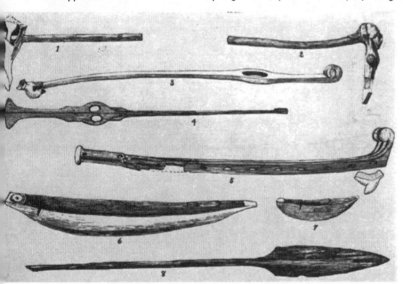

LEFT. "Tools and Weapons. 1. Hafted busycon,—or conch-shell gouge, adze or agricultural implement; buttonwood handle 15" long; shell head or armature, 7" long. 2. Handle of a carving-adze of hard, dark wood, like madeira in appearance; handle 12"; head, from crook to inter-section of socketed blade-receptacle of deer horn, 5" long; ingenious bit-holder, 3" long; it was found with eight other similarly crooked and socketed adze-handles; note carved rodent gnaw-ing at stick on top of crook; others depicted other animals. 3. Single-hole atlatl or throwing-stick, 18" long; it is figured upside down; the tail of the rabbit-carving on the end was skillfully designed as the propelling spur—the rabbit tail is erect, as in the act of thumping, forming a spur for the nock of the dart; it was found, associated with the plugged and hollowed or 'footed' shaftment of an elaborate cane throwing-spear. 4. Double finger-hole atlatl or spear-thrower, 16" long; as other, it is dark, red-brown, flexible wood—may be iron-wood; fitted with a short groove and carved with edge lines. 5. Unusual and highly finished hard-wood sabre-club armed with shark teeth (one showing); several were found which were from 24" to 30" long. 6. Toy canoe of cypress wood, 19¾" long. It was found with another of like proportions, to which it had been attached, (probably in imitation of sea-going catamaran-canoes, of the ancient key (dwellers) by means of cross-stays. 7. Toy canoe; flat-bottom of the type probably used in canals, bayous and other shoal waters. 8. Hardwood paddle, end of handle was burned off; found sticking through muck, in the mouth of the inlet-canal. Blade is leaf-shaped and tapered to sharp point; flat or convex on one side, and flat or slightly concave on other." (Cushing, Plate XXXII, p. 423).

In addition to the above types of tools, Cushing describes others:

"Of course scrapers and shavers of various kinds abounded. . . . The most elaborate objects of this kind were, however, cer-tain flat-hinged bivalves or arca shells, about three and a half or four inches long. The umboidal apices of these had been broken away and strips of bark and . . . leather, had been so passed back and forth through the apertures, and platted along the hinges or straight backs, as to afford excellent grasp. All of them were crenulate at the edges and some of them were . . . made of two shells tightly tied together, one inside the other, . . . Several draw-knives made from split leg-bones of the deer sharp-ened to beveled edges from the inside; some ingenious shaving-knives, made from the outer marginal whorls of the true conchs—the thick indented or toothed lips of which formed their backs or handles, the thin but strong whorl-walls being sharpened to keen straight edges—completed the list of scraping and planing tools." (p. 370).

RIGHT. Figurehead of a deer—a mask or ceremonial object. This is from a painting made by Wells Sawyer while the specimen was fresh; the painting is owned by the National Museum. The artifact is owned by the University Museum, University of Pennsylvania. This photograph has been reproduced, courtesy, Smithsonian Institution, Bureau of American Ethnology. The full-face drawing below found in Cushing, Plate XXXV, gives another view of the mask. He describes it as follows:

"This represents the finest and most perfectly preserved example of combined carving and painting, that we found —unless the figurehead of a great sea turtle and its companion masks be exempted. In form, or mere contour, it portrayed with startling fidelity and delicacy, the head of a young deer or doe, a little under life-sized; that is, in length, from back of head to muzzle, 7½"; in breadth across forehead, 5½"; the bases of the ears were hollow and tubular; they were transfixed with pegs to facilitate attachment by means of cords passed through bifurcate holes at the back edge of the headpiece; they were also relatively large, and were fluted, and their tips were curved as in nature, only more regularly; they were painted inside with a creamy pink-white pigment to represent their translucency; and the black hair-tufts at the back were neatly represented by short, double black streaks of paint, laid on lengthwise and close together. On the crown of the head were two slight, flat protuberances, with central peg-holes, for the attachment of small antlers, probably imitative, for they had disappeared, as actual horns would not have done.

"The slime of the tortoise-shell eyes still remained in place, and the combined bees-wax and rubber-gum cement with which they had been secured was still intact when the specimen was found. The whites of the eyes had consisted of some very bright gum-like substance, and the front corners or creases of the eyes had been filled with black gum and varnish, highly polished, so that, save for the four conventional sets of equidistantly radiating winker-marks they gave a surprisingly life-like realistic and timid or appealing, yet winsome expression, to the whole face. The muzzle, nostrils, and especially the exquisitely modeled and painted chin and lower jaw, were so delicately idealized that it was evident the primitive artist who fashioned this masterpiece, loved, with both ardor and reverence, the animal he was portraying.

"The face-markings were perfectly symmetrical. Those in white are sufficiently shown in the drawing. The cheeks or jowls were gray-blue, merging upwardly into black, and the two central and lateral bands over the forehead were divided by a deep black band, and were themselves of a deeper blue. The face, below the forehead-crescent, and between and to either side of the white nose-marks, was painted a dull black; while the nozzle was covered with an intensely black and gleaming varnish, and the nostrils, which were outlined in black, were deeply cut in and partially filled with a thick dead black substance, to make them appear still deeper.

"I need only add that all the face-marks were not only delicately outlined with black, but were edged with fine, regular hair-marks; and that like marks, as well as minute stipplings, covered all the blue, and lighter black areas of the face and sides, while along, and to the rear, of the upper lip, the hair-warts were represented by neat, oval and regularly disposed, thick or protuberant dots of black gum or varnish.

"Although so much of the line-painting on this figure was as fine as though made with a camel's-hair brush, it was evident, as on other painted specimens, that points and spatulae of some kind—probably of wood—as well as brushes of human hair, had been employed in much of the work; for the paint was mixed thickly with gum-sizing,—such as we found many lumps of, in several shells filled with both the black kind, and the less permanent white and blue kinds of pigment . . . . The ear-pieces had been attached to the back of the head by means of cords passing over pegs thrust through them and then through bifurcated holes at the points of attachment to the head-piece, in such a manner that they could be used as pulleys for the realistic working of these parts; and the unpainted edge, as well as peg-holes all around the rearward portion of the head, plainly indicated that the skin of a deer or some flexible substitute therefor, had been also attached to it, the more perfectly to disguise the actor who no doubt endeavored in this disguise to personate the character of the deer-god or dawn-god, the primal incarnation of which this figure was evidently designed to represent." (Cushing, Plate XXXV, pp. 429-432).

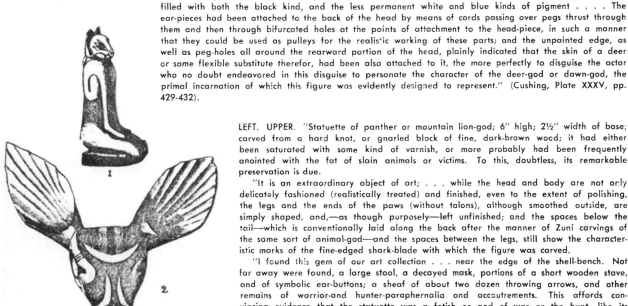

LEFT. UPPER. "Statuette of panther or mountain lion-god; 6" high; 2½" width of base; carved from a hard knot, or gnarled block of fine, dark-brown wood; it had either been saturated with some kind of varnish, or more probably had been frequently anointed with the fat of slain animals or victims. To this, doubtless, its remarkable preservation is due.

"It is an extraordinary object of art; . . . while the head and body are not only delicately fashioned (realistically treated) and finished, even to the extent of polishing, the legs and the ends of the paws (without talons), although smoothed outside, are simply shaped, and,—as though purposely—left unfinished; and the spaces below the tail—which is conventionally laid along the back after the manner of Zuni carvings of the same sort of animal-god—and the spaces between the legs, still show the characteristic marks of the fine-edged shark-blade with which the figure was carved.

"I found this gem of our art collection . . . near the edge of the shell-bench. Not far away were found, a large stool, a decayed mask, portions of a short wooden stave, and of symbolic ear-buttons; a sheaf of about two dozen throwing arrows, and other remains of warrior-and hunter-paraphernalia and accoutrements. This affords convincing evidence that the statuette was a fetish or god of war or the hunt, like its clumsier stone analogues in Zuni land." (Cushing Plate XXXV). The artifact is displayed at the National Museum.

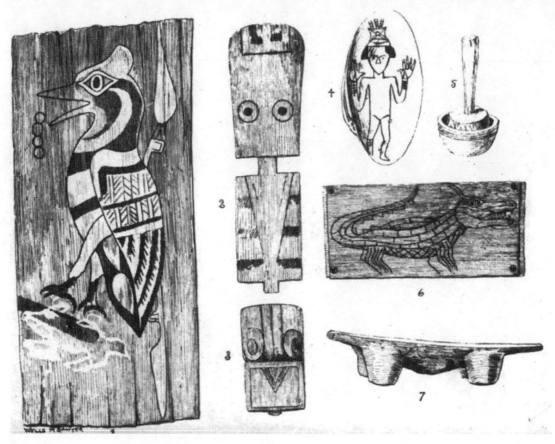

ABOVE. "Painted Tablets and Shell (symbolic or sacred) and utensils. 1. Tablet of rivean cypress wood, shaved with shark-tooth blades to a uniform thickness of less than half an inch,—the characteristic marks of this work being visible all over the unpainted portions of both sides of the board. It was found standing slantingly upright, the painted side fortunately protected by its oblique position. It was marvelously fresh when first uncovered,—the wood, of a bright yellowish-brown color, and the painting vivid and clear. It is 16½" in length by 8½" in width, and was slightly concavo-convex from side to side. Upon the hollow side is painted the figure of a crested bird, with four circlets falling from his mouth. A black bar, and over it the outlines, in white, of an animal, is represented as under the talons; it had a long and faintly ringed tail, which extended nearly to the lower paddle blade, and enabled me to identify it, in turn, as a picture of the raccoon. A long, double-pointed object,—probably a double-bladed paddle,—is borne aloft under the right wing of the figure.

PREHISTORIC DESIGNS—KEY MARCO, FLORIDA

Plates 59 and 60

"The drawing shown does not show some of the minutest, yet most significant details; the bands and spaces of white on the figure, enclosed very significant zones of clear light blue,—on the crest, neck, body and wings; they made it possible to identify this primitive bird painting as that of the jay, or else of the king fisher, or more probably still of a crested mythic bird or bird-god combining attributes of both. (Professor W. J. McGee, Bureau of American Ethnology, made the following statement to Cushing) '. . . it is a well-known fact that certain classes of men among the Southern tribes,—notably those of the Maskokian confederacy, the Creeks especially,—wore the hair in erect crests, cropped and narrow in front, broadening rearwardly to the back of the head, where it was allowed to grow to the normal length, and whence it depended in each case, either naturally like a tail, or bound about with fur or stuffs, to form the so-called scalp-lock. The researches of Gatschet make it evident that this was the special hair-dress of the Warrior-class (see portrait of Tomochichi, a Yamasee war-chief, in Urisperger, vol. 1). He finds that in the Creek language, Tas-sa (Hichiti Tas-si), signifies alike 'Jay or king-fisher' ('crested bird') and 'hair-crest;' while Tas-sika-ya signified 'Warrior;' (lit., 'crest standing up'—that is, 'he of the erectile crest'). From other sources it appears that as the jay was regarded as more powerful in resisting even birds of prey than were any other birds of his kind,—as was also the king-fisher, so nearly resembling him, more powerful than other birds of his kind,—because of their shrill and startling cries and their habits of erecting their hair-like crests when alarmed in defending, or wrathful in offending their kind. Wherefore, the crest of the Jay and of the male king-fisher—who were probably bird-gods of war,—came to be imitated . . . in the head-dress (or aspect) of the Warrior — the Wrathful Defender of his People and their Homes.' (Passage later published, American Anthropologist Vol. X, pp. 17-18)

"All of the main outlines of this primitive painting,—the crest, neck, breast, shoulder, and oblique end of the tail, were delicately spaced, so as to produce the effect of double outlining and so as to enhance both the beauty and the perspective of the figure. The centres of the circlets falling from the open beak were filled with pigment—originally blue, white, and probably red,—and a tongue-like line of white extended from the mouth to the circlets and was oppositely continued in black, into the throat of the figure —enabling me to identify it as the heart-line, and these circlets as 'living,' or 'sounding' breaths or words—symbolizing the 'commands of the four quarters.' 2. One of several mysterious objects, 'altar-' or 'ancestral-tablet'. It was painted on both sides,—in black and white on the side here shown, and with four round marks of white enclosed and dotted in black, centrally and equidistantly disposed along the other side. It was made of light wood,—pine or cypress;—2' 3½" x 10"; flat, and 1" thick below the shoulders, and nearly 3" thick in the middle of the convex shovel-shaped head or nose. 3. Coral limestone amulet 2" long. This and figure 2, seem to be two highly conventionalized representations of some kind of monster of the deep—like the alligator, or cayman or American crocodile. 4. Painted figure—probably with a mask since no mouth is represented; elaborate headdress; prominent hands; painted on the concave or inner valve of a pair of sun-shells, which were found tightly closed together, and near some symbolic head-slats, on which a bird-god (like the one just described) had been painted. 5. Beautiful little pestle and bowl of mastich-wood found together as here shown, although tilted over. The pestle was six and a half inches high; the bowl, three and a quarter inches in diameter. Both were handsomely polished and were reticularly decorated with incised lines, so delicate as to almost escape detection. 6. A little jewel-box lid or bottom, of hard, dark brown wood, 8" x 4"; the ends were rabbetted and drilled for attachment (with sinew and black gum, traces of which remained), to the ends of the box, and the ends themselves were in juxtaposition. Each end was four inches long and of corresponding width, and painted lengthwise on the outside, with mythic tie-cords and shell-clasp figures. The bottom and the other parts were missing, save for fragments. With these fragments, however, were some of the most superb ear jewels and plugs, shell beads and pearls, among all our findings. Curiously enough, the remarkable outline of a horned crocodile, painted on this little lid as here shown, occurred on the inside, and this plainly indicates the sacred nature of the box and its contents. (Note careful leg treatment, serrated tail and scales on back and under belly). It is interesting to note that the horned crocodile (or alligator) was seen by William Bartram, painted on the facades of the great sacred houses of the Creek Indians, when he visited their chief towns more than a hundred years ago. This specimen was found with a ceremonial pack and painted shell. 7. Wooden stool, 17" long and 6" to 7" wide at one end and 5" wide at other; 6" high. It was blocked out with shell adzes—as shown by traces of hacking still visible on its under side, then finished with shark tooth knives,—from a piece of hard, yellowish wood, probably buttonwood . . . . It is sloped . . . . This indicates that it was designed for use astride . . . as is also indicated in other, even unsloped specimens, by the slant of the pegs or feet, which adapted some of these stools for use in canoes, lengthwise, but not crosswise. It is well known that the Antilleans, whose stools . . . . were not unlike them in style, had a fashion of sitting astride or lengthwise of them . . . . " (Cushing, Plate XXXIV, pp. 426-428).

BELOW. Masks and figureheads. Animal figureheads with correspondingly painted human masks. Many such pairs were found together; some more striking or perfect examples than these; these are shown because they illustrate particularly well the singular relations and meanings of these peculiar objects of art. 1. Wolf figurehead, put together as the relations of the perforations and cord fragments therein indicated they were originally joined; when found, ear-pieces were back to back, and were thrust through the

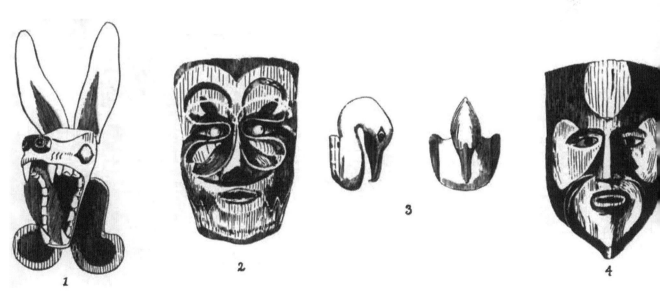

hollow head-piece and open mouth; the conventional, scroll-like shoulder and leg-pieces, were laid together in like manner, and were neatly bound, with strips of palmetto, or flag-leaf-still green in color—to the side of the head; head-piece, 6½" long; spread of jaws, 5⅞"; ear-pieces, 6" long; leg and shoulder-pieces, 4-6/8" long. 2. Human featured mask associated with wolf figurehead; 9" x 6". The general aspect and face-markings do not show well in a black and white drawing, since the color-designs were in black, brown, gray-blue and white. In full color, there is an unmistakable correspondence between the figurehead and mask. Note face-markings: black ear-marks over the eyes; black, indented stripe under and around the nostrils; the scroll-like outlines of the shoulder-pieces (in white lines over all the other markings in the middle of the face), and the zigzag lines representative of the gnashing teeth or tusked jaws of the wolf (across the cheeks toward the mouth of the mask). 3. Pelican figurehead (two views), 4½" high by 3" width of shoulders; a graceful and realistically painted carving; "near it were thin slats, admirably cut and painted to represent the wings of the bird; and they were pierced, as were the incut shoulders of the figurehead itself, for attachment thereto." 4. Human-featured, pelican mask found near the figurehead; 9-⅛" x 5-¼"; "it was unquestionably designed to represent the human, or man-god counterpart of this bird; for not only was the chin protruded and the under lip pouted to symbolize the pouch of the pelican, but also, the rear and tail of the body (painted in white on the chin), trailing legs (in gray-blue and white lines, descending from the nostrils around the corners of the mouth), the wings and shoulders, (in dappled white over the cheeks), and the huge bald head (in white on the forehead of the mask), were all most distinctly suggested. Moreover, on the upper edge of the mask (at the terminal point of the bird head painted on the forehead), were perforations, indicating that either an actual beak, or an appendage representative thereof, had been attached. With this in mind, if the mask be reversed and a comparison of the design on it be made with the figure-head, or with the imagined form of a flying pelican seen from above, the almost ludicrous resemblance of the design to its supposed original will readily enough be seen." (Cushing, XXXIII, pp. 424-425).

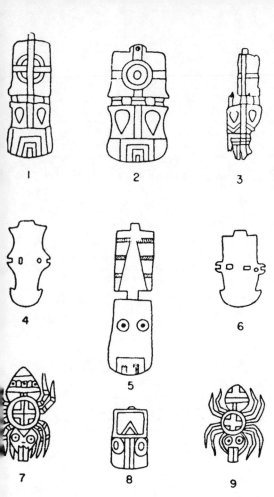

1 2 3 4 5 6 7 8 9

LEFT. Illustration of designs from Indian artifacts found in Florida. Reproduced from an article by John Wallace Griffin, "Historic Artifacts and the 'Buzzard Cult' in Florida," FLORIDA HISTORICAL QUARTERLY, April 1946, pp. 296-301. BELOW. The article explaining the designs is quoted by permission from J. W. Griffin and the FLORIDA HISTORICAL QUARTERLY.

"An extensive literature on the archaeology of Florida has been amassed over a considerable number of years. By far the greater part of this literature is purely descriptive, and it is the purpose of this paper to take some of the older materials and interpret them in the light of current archaeological knowledge; knowledge which has advanced at an almost breathtaking rate in the past decade. For our purposes we shall select seven related artifacts from southern Florida; made of gold, silver, brass, stone and wood.

"The small gold ornament, shown as figure 2 in the accompanying plate, was described by A. E. Douglass in 1890. It was found on an island in the Kissimmee river near Fort Bassinger (Basinger) and is two and a quarter inches long, one and a quarter inches broad and the thickness of a half dollar. Tests showed it to be sixty percent gold, thirty percent copper and ten percent silver; doubtlessly representing a post-contact source of metal. It consists of two main segments separated by a depressed area containing two holes. One of the segments bears a projection, bored for suspension. The obverse is decorated with incised lines as shown in figure 2, while the reverse has incised crescents in the upper left and lower right quarters, and incised vertical lines in the other two quarters.

"C. B. Moore . . . discovered two small metal ornaments with burials in the Gleason mound on the east bank of the Banana river in Brevard county. One of them is of brass (figure 4) and is about one and three-quarters inches long, while the other (figure 6) is of silver and is about one and one-half inches long. Also found with burials in this mound were three large glass beads and three silver beads, apparently of European make. The general outlines of these two small gorgets are similar to the gold ornament discussed above, but either they bore no ornamentation or the oxidation of the metal had obliterated it.

"Two wooden plaques from South Florida have been published by J. W. Fewkes (figures 1 and 3). Figure 1 is eight and one-quarter inches high by three inches wide; figure 3 is nine and three-quarters inches long by three and one-fifth inches wide. Both were removed by dredge from below a shell mound west of Fort Myers on the Calocsahatchee river, and were presented to the National Museum by Mr. George Kinzie. (Fewkes did not publish the sizes of the objects or their find-spot; the writer is indebted to Joseph R. Caldwell of the U. S. National Museum for this information.)

"The famous Key Marco site, excavated by Cushing, provides us with our final set of data. The wooden example shown as figure 5 was made of pine or cypress, was two feet three and one-half inches long, ten inches wide, three inches thick in the middle of the head and one inch thick on the flatter upper portion. The design is painted in black and white and the reverse had four round marks of white enclosed and dotted in black. No fewer than ten or twelve of these objects were uncovered by Cushing; probably all had been painted, although the evidence was lacking on most. In size they ranged from slightly over one foot to nearly five feet in length. Various similar objects, several of wood, one (figure 8) of stone were found. They were decorated by incising with eyes, zig-zags for mouths, and triangles or concentric circles on the bodies. The example figured is of coral limestone, about two inches long, and is grooved for suspension.

"There are as many interpretations as to what the designs are meant to depict as there are finders and writers, and the explanation offered in this paper differs from all of them. Douglass interpreted his gorget (figure 2) as representing a cross with the cross rests was a crude representation of the gradines which the two pear-shaped figures he took to be hearts, representing down and thought that the projections and round hole in figure and gave no indication of what he thought they represented; he, too, figures his specimens upside down, from our point of view. Cushing felt that the design of figure 5 represented an alligator or similar creature. had the most ingenious, and the least tenable, theory. He interpreted his gorget (figure 2) as representing a cross with the Orbis Mundi at the intersection of the arms; the base on which characterize the Spanish-American mounting of the cross. The two thieves crucified with Jesus. Moore figured his gorgets upside 6 represented a duck head. Fewkes merely called his 'altar slabs'

"The writer is of the opinion that the designs on these Florida artifacts are intended to represent the spider. Figures 7 and 9 are spiders from incised round shell gorgets from Missouri and Illinois. The holes in the gorgets (not shown in these drawings) make it certain that the spider hung head downwards, which is not an abnormal position for a spider. If these spiders are closely compared with the Florida materials it will be noted that many similarities exist, despite the lack of legs and the generally more conventionalized appearance of the Florida examples. The division of the artifacts into two segments may be taken to represent the cephalothorax and abdomen of the spider; the shell gorget examples have the cross and circle superimposed at the juncture of these two segments. The cross and circle motif occurs on at least two of the Florida examples, and on all of the decorated examples the eyes and the rectangularly shaped mouth parts are evident. Furthermore, the lateral protrusions at the middle of several of the Florida examples might conceivably be taken to represent, in a rudimentary fashion, the legs which are fully represented on the carved shell examples.

". . . we have seen that the artifacts described seem to represent the spider, which is a 'Buzzard Cult' motif, that two of them display the cross and circle, another cult motif, and that others come from Key Marco which is an acknowledged 'Buzzard Cult' site. This is of interest since three of the objects are of metals which must have come from White sources. The metals could date from a time shortly after the discovery, say the first quarter of the sixteenth century, since we know from Fontaneda's memoir that the Calusa of South Florida had access to such metals from wrecked Spanish ships. This, however, sets the maximum, not the minimum age. In this connection it is of interest to note that John Davides in his HISTORY OF THE CARIBBY ISLANDS published in 1666 tells of pile dwellings near the sea among the Indians 'beyond the Bay of Carlos and Turtugues' (Cushing, p. 403). The Key Marco site is of course in the correct area for this statement, and it was built on piles. Ford and Willey gave a 'guess date' of from 1600 to 1700 for the 'Buzzard Cult', while Waring and Holder, without stating any definite dates, would seem to incline toward a slightly earlier dating. The evidence presented here, together with some not presented here but which the writer hopes to publish soon, strongly suggests that the seventeenth century dating is correct; that the 'Buzzard Cult' falls definitely into historic times in Florida." (One paragraph, not included here, discusses Southeastern culture periods).

Bibliography: F. H. Cushing, 1897; A. E. Douglass, 1890; J. W. Fewkes, 1928; J. A. Ford and G. H. Willey, 1941; C. B. Moore, 1922; A. J. Waring and P. Holder, 1945.

PREHISTORIC, PROTOHISTORIC, AND HISTORIC DESIGNS FLORIDA

Plates 61 and 62

RIGHT. Wooden ceremonial slab. Obverse and reverse sides. Southern Florida. (Courtesy, Smithsonian Institution; Miscellaneous Collections, Vol. 80, No. 9, Pl. 2. USNM 329,599). This is Fig. 1 on the opposite page. Two crudely similar objects are reported from the Thomas Mound, Hillsborough Co., Fla. (Florida Geological Survey Museum). One is of copper (4.5 cm. high x 2.8 cm. wide); the other, of silver. These are described by Goggin (1947) and pictured in outline by Willey (1949, pp. 124-125).

BELOW. From an engraving by De Bry, after a drawing by Le Moyne, who visited Florida in 1564-65. Timucua Tribe. It pictures natives making an offering to the sun. The painter explained that the natives stuffed the skin of a deer with edible roots, decked it with garlands of fresh fruits, and placed it on top of a tree in a position in which it faced the rising sun. The chief and medicine man are near the pole and the other natives are around; they are imploring the sun to give them the foods of field and forest abundantly in the coming year, as they offer in abundance here. The natives are showing the scene to the Frenchmen. Note: body painting, the shell plummets? on the waist girdle and the beads around the knee. (Photograph from book in Rare Book Room, New York Public Library.

"The sun and moon were considered the abodes of powerful beings, or at least as connected with such beings; the former was evidently associated with the chief deity of the southern Indians . . . . Tukabahchee miko quoted the old people to the effect that the sun must be a great way off, 'for if it came near it would burn everything up.' When the sun or moon was eclipsed they said that a great toad (sabakti) was about to swallow it, and in order to help drive it away they discharged their guns at it and shot at it with arrows until they 'hit' it . . . . (Swanton 1928, p. 479).

"Adair gives the Chickasaw name of the supreme deity as 'Loak-Ishto-hoollo-Aba' . . . which appears to signify 'the great holy fire above,' and indicates his connection with the sun. Adair adds that he 'resides as they think above the clouds, and on earth also with unpolluted people. He is with them the sole author of warmth, light, and of all animal and vegetable life.' (Adair, 1775, p. 19). His name at once suggests the Uwa shil ('Big fire') of the Natchez, which was their name for the sun, the highest object of their worship, or rather the abode of that highest object, and a connection between the Chickasaw and Natchez conceptions is thereby indicated." (Swanton, 1928, pp. 479, 482). Bartram (1909) stated that the Indians at treaties, councils, and other important occasions blew a smoke tribute toward the sun, and looked at it in reverence.

"The captaine bad the boy ask him what he thought became of them after their death . . . to which he answered . . . that after they are dead here, they goe up to a top of a high tree, and there they espie a faire plaine broad path waye, on both sides whereof doth grow all manner of pleasant fruicts, as mulberies, straberries, plombes, etc. In this pleasant path they rune toward the rising of the sun, where the godly hare's howse is . . . ." Strachey (1849, pp. 98-100; Swanton, 1946, p. 749).

Chapter 6

STONE AND COPPER

Quotation from John R. Swanton, THE INDIANS OF THE SOUTHEASTERN UNITED STATES, Bureau of American Ethnology, Bulletin 137, 1946, pp. 541-549—excerpts. Quoted courtesy, Smithsonian Institution, Bureau of American Ethnology.

"It might be supposed that the Florida Indians would have been under the necessity of importing most of their flint, and, indeed, some of the Frenchmen with Laudonniere reported that a certain stone used in northwestern Florida for arrow points and wedges with which to split wood was found 'at the foot of the mountains,' by which he meant the Appalachians.[1] But Europeans were then unaware of the extent of country between Florida and these mountains and the quarries in between, so that little reliance can be placed upon the statement. On the other hand, we are informed that all of the arrowheads of southern Florida were made of material obtained near Ballast Point, about 5 miles below Tampa. Farther north, on a small stream known as Trouble Creek . . . is an outcrop of blue flint which was also worked by the aborigines.[2]

". . . C. C. Jones mentions quarries as existing along the Oconee, Ocmulgee, Flint, Chattahoochee, and other southern streams, and states more specifically that there were a number of open-air workshops along the line of Savannah River and especially that portion which formed the eastern boundary of the counties of Richmond, Columbia, Lincoln, and Elbert, and in the counties of South Carolina on the opposite side.[3] . . . .

"Beverley[4] quotes Alexander Whittaker, Minister of Henrico, to the effect that 'Twelve miles from the Falls (of James River, Virginia), there is a Chrystal Rock, wherewith the Indians do head many of their Arrows.'

"In Alabama there was a quarry on the southeastern side of Story's (or Storees) Mountain, . . . east of Youngsboro. . . . Another was at the eastern end of Cedar Ridge in Talladega County. . . .

"West of the Mississippi about Hot Springs, Ark., were extensive novaculite quarries, and quarries were reported . . . in Montgomery County, and near Magnet Cove in Hot Springs County.[5]

"At some time in the past steatite, or soapstone, was used considerably. This was a favorite material for pipes even in late times, and steatite pots, or fragments of pots, have been found on known Creek sites along Tallapoosa River (Alabama). Bushnell has located several quarries in Virginia, and there was one near Dudleyville, Tallapoosa Co., Ala., . . .[6]

"Muscovite mica mines were worked in Clay Co., Ala. . . . and in Talladega County . . . . A mica mine is also reported from Hall County, Ga., but the most extensive workings were in Mitchell and Yancy Counties, N. C.[7]

"Flint arrow points are mentioned as in use throughout almost the whole Gulf region, but flint seems to have been used nowhere to the exclusion of other material. As we have specific mention of flint, or at least 'stone,' arrow points in Florida and the seacoast section of Louisiana where it must have been hardest to get, we may feel sure that there was practically no exception to the universality of its employment. . . .[8]

"Other stone objects[9] (in addition to arrow points, axes, pipes, and chunkey stones)[10] known to have been used in the Southeast were mortars for cracking nuts and grinding paint, and, in prehistoric times in the mountain country, mortars for grinding corn. These were sometimes made of separate blocks of stone and

---

[1] Laudonniere, 1586, p. 8. [2] Walker, S. T., 1880, p. 394. [3] Jones, C. C., 1873. Swanton also refers to a flint quarry 2 miles above Columbus, Ga., in Muscogee County (Brannon, P. A., 1909, p. 194), and 'a great flint implement factory at Albany, Dougherty County, (Georgia), near Flint River . . . .' [4] Beverley, 1705, bk. 2, p. 11.
[5] Thomas, 1891, p. 15; Holmes, 1903, pp. 196-200. [6] Tuomey, 1858, p. 46. [7] Thomas, 1891, p. 15; Holmes, 1919, pp. 241-252.
[8] Hakluyt, 1847-89, vol. 3, p. 613; Robertson, 1933, p. 37; Swanton, 1922, p. 357; 1911 p. 347. Swanton, states (1946, p. 543-544) "Flint was employed in the manufacture of one other weapon, though there were few notices of it anywhere but in Virginia. It is described as a wooden sword the edges of which were set with sharp stones more likely to have been of flint than anything else. (Smith, John, Tyler ed., 1907, p. 14). It is rather remarkable that the only description of anything similar is in Garcilaso's account of the images about the door of the temple of Talimeco. Two of these are said to have been armed with 'copper axes, the edges of which are of flint.' (Garcilaso, 1723, pp. 130-137). . . . [9] Swanton (1946, pp. 548-549). [10] These subjects are discussed individually by Swanton (1946, pp. 544-548).

sometimes worked in the living rock. In the Tennessee country and neighboring sections stone images have been found. We know that wooden images were in use among the Virginia and Carolina Indians and even the Creeks, but there is no certain mention of stone images in literature. The only possible exception is the sacred stone preserved by the Natchez in their temple, though it is not positively known that this was worked. Finally we may add two wholly different ways in which stones or rocks were utilized. One was in the formation of fishweirs. These were either inland, like the one on the falls of James River, into which fish were carried by the descending current, or coastal, like that reported by Garcilaso at Tampa Bay, which caught fish as they swam shoreward.[11] Along most of the lower Atlantic and Gulf coasts, however, fishweirs were made of wooden piles interwoven with flexible withes. Still another use of rocks was as altars. The early writers on Virginia speak of these as if they were common in the Algonquian country, one consisting of a solid block of crystal being particularly noteworthy,[12] but fewer were mentioned in the rest of the region under discussion. . . ."

GREENSTONE AND STEATITE

Quotation from Walter B. Jones, "Geology of the Tennessee Valley Region of Alabama. . . ." From William S. Webb, AN ARCHAEOLOGICAL SURVEY OF WHEELER BASIN ON THE TENNESSEE RIVER IN NORTHERN ALABAMA, Bureau of American Ethnology, Bulletin 122, 1939, pp. 16-18. Quoted courtesy, Smithsonian Institution, Bureau of American Ethnology.[13]

"GREENSTONE. This is a metamorphic rock, rather soft and fine grained, susceptible of taking a very good polish. Very little is known about the original source of this material, although it is widely distributed throughout the Tennessee Valley, in mounds, cemeteries, and villages of all types and ages. Greenstone was in common use by the aborigines, mostly for objects of a useful or ceremonial nature. Axes, celts, and spades range in size from 1 to 24 inches in length, and from less than one-half inch to several inches in thickness. The material in the long spades or agricultural tools is usually schistose, and gray-green in color. In these there are frequently thin bands or streaks of a darker material, which is dark green to almost black. In spite of the wide distribution and diffusion of greenstone, there is a rather striking uniformity in the color and texture of the material.

"Little has been published on the subject. Tuomey[14] called it 'trap dykes.' S. J. Lloyd[15] thinks it corresponds with 'greywache' of the older geologists. T. N. McVay[16] identified some as 'clinochlore.' Gunter Glass[17] compared a number of samples of Hillabee schist and greenstone artifacts, and noted the great similarity. The Hillabee formation is a chlorite schist, green to gray in color, schistose to massive, and usually fine-grained. The beds occupy a narrow belt extending from Clanton in Chilton County northeastward through Coosa, Clay, and Cleburne Counties. The Coosa River runs through the belt at a point a few miles east of Clanton. The Tallapoosa and Little Tallapoosa cut through it in Cleburne County, the rest of the belt is about halfway between these river systems. The average width of the belt is about 1.5 miles, while the maximum is about 4 miles, in the southwestern portion of Clay County. Even though the outcrop of the Hillabee is narrow, there was plenty of material available, and, furthermore, it was readily accessible.

"It is apparent that other formations in the Piedmont area in other States are similar to the Hillabee and could have furnished greenstone. The wide use of the material makes it evident that there were many sources of supply. Unfortunately no greenstone quarries attributable to the aborigines have been observed. However, it is the writer's opinion that the lack of positive evidence does not detract from the accuracy of the statement that the Alabama source of greenstone was the Hillabee schist.

"No suggestion can be made as to the routes of travel by which the aborigines of the Valley reached the source of supply, or even whether the supply came from Alabama or elsewhere in the Piedmont plateau. . . .

"SOAPSTONE (STEATITE). This material occurs abundantly in various parts of the crystalline area in Alabama, particularly in Chilton, Tallapoosa, and Chambers Counties. Seldom are the beds massive, usually occurring more in the form of talc (soapstone) schists. In this account the term 'soapstone' means those beds

---

[11] Garcilaso, 1723, p. 94. [12] Beverly, 1705, bk. 2, pp. 10-11. [13] Dr. Walter B. Jones, State Geologist of Alabama. [14] Tuomey, Michael, Geology of Alabama, 1850. Glossary. [15] [16] [17] Personal communication.

of steatite, serpentinic or talcose rocks which are sufficiently soft and massive to be used for the manufacture of artifacts by the aborigines.

"Fragments of vessels made of this material are widespread, though seldom abundant, in the Tennessee Valley. In addition to its use in the manufacture of culinary vessels, such as pots and bowls, the latter up to 18 inches in diameter, the aborigines also used soapstone extensively for pipes. The soft and tough nature of the material made it very well adapted for the latter purpose, as is well proven by the size and elaborate design of some of the pipes which have been found.

"Because of the near coincidence of Tuomey's early work as State geologist and the actual Indian occupation of the soapstone region, his pen pictures of aboriginal quarrying are more accurate than could be written at the present time. They are as follows:[18]

'North of the falls the rocks become talcose, and on a little stream, called Coon Creek, beds of hornblende and soapstone occur. In a hollow, near the creek, a bed of soapstone of great thickness is found. This seems to have been well known to the Indians, who resorted to the spot for the purpose of manufacturing culinary utensils. Excavations of considerable extent were made in the best portions of the rock and the sides of the excavations are curiously pitted where the vessels have been cut out. It appears to have been their practice to inscribe on the rock the circumference of the pot or bowl to be cut out, and then to excavate around it until sufficient depth was attained, after which the mass was split off and finished. Occasionally, when failure in splitting off the mass ensued, pieces remain attached to the rock. Everywhere the impression of the bottom of the vessel is left on the face of the quarry. The rock is calcareous, effervescing with acid. Crystals of pyrites are abundant, but no other minerals, excepting actynolite and talc, are found here.

'These Indian excavations have deceived many inexperienced persons, who supposed that they were made for the precious metals. The soapstone of this locality extends across the county into Chambers, and at intervals throughout this extent it is perforated by such excavations. This is the locality which excited so much interest as the Tallapoosa Silver Mine.

'From Fitzpatrick's to Dudleyville the rocks become slaty; the village stands upon a bed of geneiss. Beyond the village two shafts were sunk in search of copper. One was induced by a vein of cellular quartz, that once contained iron pyrites; and the other is in a trap dyke, on the side of which was cut a vein of asbestos and talc, 1 foot thick. Parallel with these slates is a noble bed of soapstone, the strike of which is indicated by numerous Indian excavations.

'On the way to the Morgan Gold Mine, on Tallapoosa, a powerful trap dyke was examined, at Perry's Mill, and further on the soapstone is excavated, to a greater extent than I have seen elsewhere. These quarries must have been worked for ages. Numerous unfinished and broken pots and bowls were found here.

'Everywhere in the South, fragments of soapstone vessels are found with other Indian remains; but Alabama is the only State in which I have met with these excavations. It would appear that a considerable trade was carried on at these localities.'

"These statements were corroborated by Eugene A. Smith[19] in his field notes for October 14, 1874. Smith adds:

'This soapstone, which seems to be a soft serpentinic rock, light green and granular, is in beds striking NNE. and dipping 85° to ESE. Part of these strata are very thick and massive, showing no traces of stratification, save being enclosed between laminated beds of the same material. It is from the granular massive variety that the Indians seem to have worked out their utensils.'

"From the statements of these two close observers it is apparent that the objects were at least 'roughed out' at the quarries, and either finished there or later at the villages. There is no evidence available as to whether the Valley tribes went to the quarries by land or by water. The relative abundance of the material in the Valley would make it obvious that trade alone could scarcely account for all of it. The Valley peoples must have both known of and visited the quarries of the Tallapoosa River area."

STEATITE (SOAPSTONE)

Quotation from David I. Bushnell, Jr., "The Use of Soapstone by the Indians of Eastern United States," The Smithsonian Institution, Annual Report, 1939, Publication 3555, Washington, 1940, pp. 471-490—excerpts. Quoted courtesy, Smithsonian Institution.[20]

"Steatite, generally called soapstone, is a variety of talc usually of a gray, grayish green, or brownish color. It varies in hardness according to its purity and composition and occurs in many localities from Georgia and Alabama in the south to the New England States, thence northward to the Arctic coast, and in Newfoundland. The composition and physical properties of soapstone vary greatly . . .[21]   . . .

"WORK AT THE QUARRIES. In some localities rough, irregular pieces of stone were taken from the quarries, then trimmed and reduced to the desired size, and later fashioned into smoothed vessels. This appears to have been the practice when a new site was discovered, where pieces of stone protruded from the surface and

[18] Tuomey, Michael. GEOLOGY OF ALABAMA. 2nd Report, 1858 (written about 1854), pp. 46, 63-64.
[19] State Geologist of Alabama, 1873-1927.
[20] Several sources of quarry investigations are cited by Bushnell.
[21] He quotes Laddo (1925), explaining that talc, the main mineral component of soapstone, if present in sufficient amount, makes it feel soapy. It may also contain dolomite, calcite, quartz, magnetite, pyroxene, tremolite, and chlorite; a high content of chlorite makes it easier to cut.

were easily detached, but the same method was sometimes followed even though it was necessary to cut blocks from the solid mass.   . . .

"The second and more characteristic way of shaping and removing the blocks was practiced when the stone was compact, relatively soft, and easily worked with the primitive tools. A spot was selected on the exposed surface of the soapstone, and the outline of the desired block was channeled, or rather grooved, by the use of stone implements. The groove was widened and deepened to the depth of the piece to be removed. During the preliminary cutting the block assumed the form of the intended vessel, often with projections at the ends which were later fashioned into lugs or handles.

"Many stone implements have been discovered in the vicinity of the quarries which had been used in preparing the blocks of stone and later in trimming and shaping the utensils. Some are deeply weathered, indicative of age. A large number of the objects are made of quartzite, often crudely flaked boulders with slight secondary chipping. These differ in size; some are rather massive and heavy, and others are slender, chisellike implements. They appear crude, but were so formed to serve definite purposes during the process of shaping and reducing the blocks of stone.

"FINISHING THE VESSELS. After the outside of the vessel had been roughly shaped, the more difficult process of hollowing the inside was begun. This work resulted in many pieces being broken and abandoned as useless. It is evident that few, if any, vessels were carried from the vicinity of the quarry until after they had been entirely formed and were in a condition to be used, although the surfaces, both inside and outside, remained very rough and irregular. The finishing of the surface was accomplished at the village, after the return from the quarry, and obviously much of the smoothing resulted from the long use of the vessel.

"The majority of the vessels from many quarries are rather long and narrow, having a length greater than the width, and being less in depth, with rounded sides and bottom. Handles extend from the narrow ends, some being placed well below the upper edge while others are at or very near the top."

(Bushnell mentions quarries in Virginia, the District of Columbia, Maryland, New York, the Connecticut Valley, Rhode Island, North Carolina, South Carolina, Tennessee, Alabama, and Georgia and adds:)

"Soapstone or steatite does not occur in situ in Florida, and the nearest deposits are northward in central Alabama. Consequently, all soapstone vessels found in Florida had been carried from some distant point."

(Bushnell describes several quarry sites in Virginia and the District of Columbia:)

"Amelia County.—Shallow excavations 10 to 70 feet in diameter,[22] filled with vegetal mold, indicated the quarries of the Indians. A space about 40 by 60 feet was cleared, and

'. . . everywhere over the rock surface, thus exposed, he found grooves and hollows made by the Indians in taking out sugarloaf-shaped masses of the rock; and throughout the soil removed he found numerous fragments of the masses mostly hollowed as the beginning of pots, together with numerous quartz picks, some broken axes and mauls, and a few hammers of soapstone, which had been used in quarrying and working the material.'

"Goochland County.— . . . At that time, 1881, part of the surface of the quarry had been cultivated, but much of it remained covered with brush. Many specimens, some of which were in a more finished condition than usual, were found in the vicinity of the quarries. One bowl, recovered from the bed of the creek, was 15 inches in length and weighed about 40 pounds. There was likewise discovered 'an axe and a broken bowl lying just as they had been left by the Indians.'

"Albemarle County— . . . site . . . on the James River.[23]

'. . . For a distance of nearly a thousand feet along the ridge it is possible to trace pits dug by the Indians, generations ago, when getting soapstone. More than 20 such excavations were discovered, the majority being within the northern half of the distance, and becoming less clearly defined southward. They vary in diameter from 10 to 30 feet and at present are from 2 to 4 feet in depth, some are distinctly separated while others merge and may in reality be parts of a greater excavation. The surface surrounding the pits is covered with pieces of stone which had evidently been rejected and thrown from the quarries . . . .'

"Fairfax County.—One of the most interesting ancient quarries in Virginia, and certainly the one most carefully examined and studied was about 2 miles northwest of Clifton. . . .[24] The examination of the quarry was begun late in March 1894—

'. . . and in a few weeks a most striking illustration of the enterprise and skill of our aboriginal tribes was exposed to view. A trench or gallery some 25 feet wide and reaching in places a depth of 16 feet had been carried into the face of the hill to a distance of 60 to 70 feet, and a second pit, inferior in dimensions, had been opened beyond this. Almost the entire excavation had been carved out of the solid steatite by means of stone picks and chisels, and all the evidence of the cutting and sculpturing—even the whitened surfaces of the tool marks—were as fresh as if the work of yesterday. . . .

'Much impure stone had been cut away in efforts to reach the purer masses, and this was a most laborious work . . . . The whole surface, with its nodes and humps and depressions, covered everywhere with the markings, groovings, and pitting of the chisel, presented a striking example of the effectiveness of native methods and persistence of native effort.' "

[22] Cushing, 1877.   [23] Bushnell, 1926; quoted from JOURNAL OF THE WASHINGTON ACADEMY OF SCIENCES.   [24] Holmes, 1897.

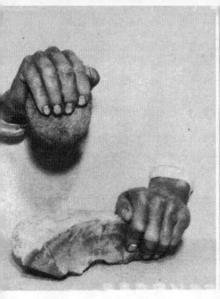

ABOVE. Fracturing (chipping or flaking) stone. LEFT. Percussion fracture. The large, quarried mass of stone or boulder from a stream-bed was broken into workable size by blows of a hammerstone. CENTER. Percussion fracture. Smaller cores or pebbles were fractured by successive blows of a hammerstone; flakes were produced as blanks were chipped into basic shapes desired for various tools and points. Specialization of shapes was sometimes carried further by percussion fracture. This method was extensively employed at quarry sites. It greatly reduced the weight of raw materials which were to be transported to other sites for finishing. Caches of percussion-shaped blanks have been found at quarry and village sites; they were doubtless deposited by a native trader or stone-worker to hide or preserve them from exposure in an attempt to keep the stone fresh and easily workable as it was when first quarried. RIGHT. Pressure fracture. Blank forms of tools and points which had been roughed-out by percussion (as well as many flakes), were often further refined or reworked by pressure flaking with a bone or antler tool; animal teeth also were used as flakers to thin, shape, notch, or serrate a projectile point or tool. This work was done in the hand or by resting the object upon a support. The finest tools and points made by the Indians often show evidence of secondary chipping by pressure. A Museum Diorama (Courtesy, Lookout Mountain Museum, Rock City Gardens, Inc., Lookout Mountain, Tennessee).

FRACTURING, PECKING, ABRADING, AND DRILLING STONE

Plate 63

BELOW. LEFT. UPPER. Pecking or battering followed fracturing in the process of manufacturing ground and polished stone objects. A harder stone was struck against a softer stone with appropriate force, so that it gradually wore off the surface of the latter; it was a very exacting process whereby the chipped article was slowly shaped into a more specialized form, with a uniformly textured though slightly rough surface. This process was used to achieve the detailed primary shape of the polished tools and ornaments. LOWER. Abrading, grinding or polishing was a further refinement of the stone's surface. One stone was rubbed against another, often taking off particles of both, but wearing the softer stone first. Abrading followed the processes of fracturing and pecking. It was used to sharpen points or edges of polished tools and ornaments, to smooth and polish entire surfaces, and even to polish the drill and ream bores of some finely made pipes. Sand mixed with water or grease, and used beneath a wood, leather, or stone buffer was an often used abrasive. In addition to the three herein mentioned and illustrated methods of working stone objects, there was another process; a stone in crude or polished form might be incised or carved. The engraving of designs by means of scratched or cut-in lines, and later the sculpturing of stone objects in low and high relief and in the round was practiced by craftsmen of the advanced primitive cultures.

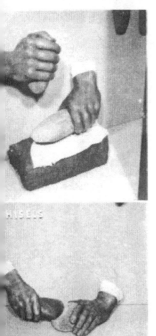

RIGHT. UPPER. Flint drill. The hand drill or reamer was the forerunner of the shaft drill. Even after the latter came into general use, there was still a place for the hand drill. It was used to make the initial indentations in wood, stone, shell, bone or other material, so that the shaft drill could easily take-hold without slipping from the selected place of bore. The hand drill was also convenient for many quick jobs and for work where much manual pressure had to be applied. The hand drills and reamers were sometimes hafted. LOWER. Shaft drill. This example shows a hollow cane drill being used on a stone which appears to be a primary form of bannerstone, or throwing stick weight. The example is not entirely realistic, in that the stone being drilled would doubtless have to be secured in some manner. It is said that a partially split log, was sometimes wedged open, then the stone inserted, and the wedge removed; this allowed the log to close on the stone, thereby, creating a natural vise. The feet and knees of the craftsman probably served as another natural vise. Some stones to be drilled were doubtless lashed or glued into place in a secure spot. The hollow cane drill was often used with moistened sand as an abrasive; the hole resulted in a slightly conical bore and a core. This doubtless was a very early form of shaft drilling, for the evidence of it is found on bannerstone remains throughout the Southeast, some of which have an incomplete bore with part or all of the core still attached, as in the example above the hands. Other types of shaft drills are shown in a following plate. For further explanation of working stone see: Holmes, 1897 and 1919—BAE, Bull. 60, Pt. 1.

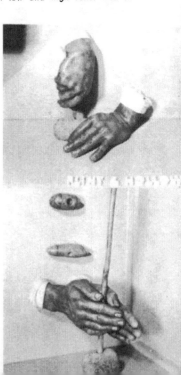

Artifacts were made from a variety of stones. J. M. Kellberg (1955) discusses the properties of and ways to identify the most frequently found stones, including: limestone, dolomite, mudstone, slate, shale, flint, quartz, quartzite, chert, sandstone, granite, talc schist, hematite, and others. He adds:

"There is no distinct line of demarcation among most of the common types of rocks found in the southeastern United States. One rock type often grades into another, either due to conditions in initial deposition in the case of sedimentary rocks, to varying intensities of metamorphism in metamorphic rocks, or to a combination of both processes. Variation in depositional conditions is reflected in the graduation from limestone to shaly limestone to calcareous shale to shale to sandy shale to shaly sandstone to sandstone. Graduation caused by increase in metamorphism is evidenced by the change of shale to siliceous slate to schist and finally to gneiss as the material is subjected to increased heat and pressure during periods of intense deformation of the earth's crust." (Quoted by permission from the TENNESSEE ARCHAEOLOGIST).

a. "The fire-drill, consisting of shaft, and base block."
b. "Wooden shaft with narrow, stone drill-point."
b¹. "Wooden shaft with wide, bevelled stone drill-point or reamer."
c. "Wooden shaft with wooden drill-point, to be used with sand and water."
d. "Wooden shaft with tubular, wooden or cane drill-point."
e. "Wooden shaft with tubular drill-point of copper."
f. "Pump drill (probably brought to North America by Europeans—West, p. 348)."
g. "Strap drill (used along northwest coast of North America—West, p. 350)."
h. "Bow drill (an improvement over strap drill)."
i. "Solid copper drill-point."

RIGHT. Illustration and explanation reproduced from George A. West, TOBACCO, PIPES, AND SMOKING CUSTOMS OF THE AMERICAN INDIANS, Parts I and II. Bulletin of the Public Museum of the City of Milwaukee, Vol. XVII, Plate 251, 1934. Illustration and quotation below are reproduced by permission from the Milwaukee Public Museum).

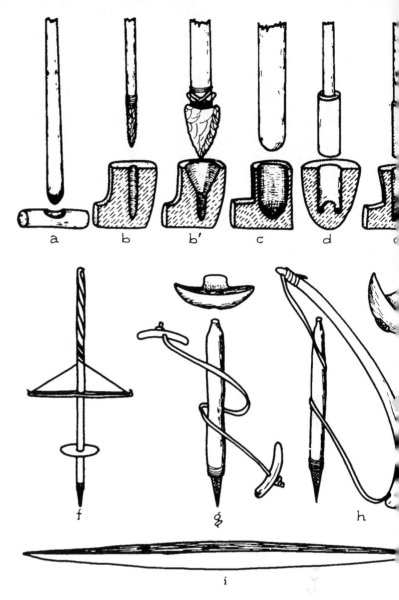

DRILLS USED IN MAKING ABORIGINAL PIPES

Plate 64

"In the fabrication of aboriginal pipes the making of the stem and bowl cavities required the greatest of skill, patience and good judgment. The exterior of a pipe, whether it be effigy in form or not, could be executed without the use of specialized tools. The work consisted of pecking, scraping, and abrasion by the use of sandstone, and sand-and-water. The pipe-maker, however, had in his kit chipped stone scrapers and other tools that, when attached to a handle, gave the carver a better tool than a scale of chert would be. In excavating the stem and bowl holes prepared tools were necessary. These consisted of drills, gouges, and reamers. The first drill used was usually made of chert, very slim and expanded at one end into a flat handle to be held between the thumb and fingers when in use. This drill was followed by another stone drill of greater diameter. To make the excavations cone-shaped, the gouge was brought into play, followed by the reamer which left the holes circular and smooth. In some cases as many as three solid-pointed drills of different sizes were successively used in making the same hole.

"The hollow-pointed drill was also commonly used in pipe-making, especially when the material to be drilled was hard. The excavation made by this type of drill, with the addition of sand and water, was clean cut and usually of the same diameter throughout. The remains of a broken-off core are often found at the base of the bowl cavity.

"Another type of drill used by our Indians, was made of relatively soft wood, and used with the addition of sharp sand and water. In order to be able to seat this type of drill, a cavity had to be pecked where the hole was desired. Many of the cone-shaped and round-bottomed holes of aboriginal pipes can be accounted for by the wearing away of the stick drill, as the work progressed.

"There are also the bow drill, the strap drill and the pump drill each of which has been used to some extent by a few of our American tribes. These inventions merely increase the speed of the drill.

"In considering the various types of drills we must not lose sight also of the fact that in certain regions it is quite probable that slender tools were made of native copper. These would prove quite effective in drilling certain kinds of stone. . . .

"The firm holding of a pipe while being drilled was necessary. The Eskimo holds it between his feet. The Indian of the aboriginal pipe area, either split a portion of the limb of a tree or the stump of a sapling, wedged the split open, inserted the pipe, and removed the wedge." (West, Part I, pp. 387-388).

Similar drills were used in working stone, wood, shell, bone, antler, feathers, pottery, and copper. Another process for working these materials was by sawing them with the sharp edge of a stone flake; the serrated edge of a chipped tool; the thinly ground edge of a hard stone; a sharp animal tooth or shell; a sliver of cane; or a thong and damp sand.

STEPS IN THE MANUFACTURE OF CHIPPED TOOLS AND PROJECTILE POINTS

Plates 65 and 66

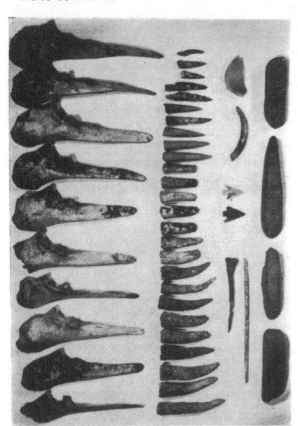

BELOW. Quarrying and chipping stone. Group in plaster illustrating percussion chipping at an aboriginal quarry workshop. Diorama, United States National Museum, Smithsonian Institution (After Holmes, 1897). The native on the left is using a stone pick to quarry the stone; the figure in the center holds a large boulder in prepartion for breaking a massive rock in front of him; the native on the right is chipping a core into a primary shape.

ABOVE. Flint-working kit from a Caddo burial. Against the teeth were two arrowpoints, against the nose, nine bone points; back of the head, sixteen pieces of antler, tines and drifts (the resilient antler, as a chisel, was placed against the edge of the flint, and smoothly transmitted to it the force of the hammerstone). In addition, there were ten knapping tools (left) of the various sizes made from deer leg bones and used in pressure flaking; two bone pins; a twisted bone; a beaver's tooth for fine chipping; a novaculite chip, and three jasper pebbles—same material as the points; a bottle; two bowls; and a stone celt. Arkansas (Courtesy, F. J. Soday).

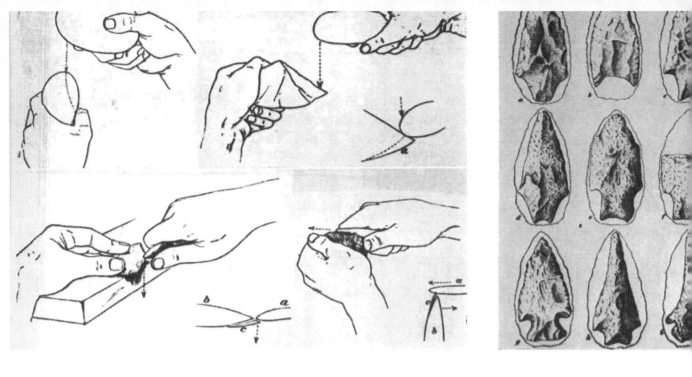

ABOVE. LEFT. UPPER. Two steps in percussion fracture. The boulder is struck with a hammerstone to shape one side at a time into a "turtle-back"—a primary form. a. the flake. LOWER. Two steps in pressure fracture or flaking. A bone or antler tool or an animal tooth was used to reduce the size of the blade, and bring it into desired shape. Pressure applied to one side of the flint blade released a chip from the other. The stone was sometimes rested on a support. a. the tool. b. the stone. c. the flake. RIGHT. Relation of the finished specialized "leaf-blade" implements—projectile points, reamers, and drill—to the original blades. A variety of chipped tools could be made from a primary "leaf-shaped" form.

BELOW. The original boulder and chipped stones illustrating two views—front and side—of the successive steps in flaking a boulder and making a projectile point. Left to right: boulder, partially chipped boulder, "turtle-backs," blades, and projectile points.

As a result of quarry-site explorations during the 1890's W. H. Holmes concluded that many flint implements were derived from biface "blanks," roughed out by percussion fracture at quarry sites and exported for specialization. He classified most quarry

debris as "rejects" or broken blanks. In recent years these views have been challenged by archeologists, who have found repeated evidence that some "rejects" show signs of rework and wear and were probably used as axes, choppers, wedges, scrapers, and knives. Recent explorations have shown that some quarry sites were not only places for a primary work and export, but also work-shops for the final manufacture of bone and wooden tools, the materials for which were brought to the quarry sites. Some of the biface blanks exported and cached (for hiding or to keep the stone "fresh") are believed to have been final forms of wedges, hoes, gouges, scrapers, and other tools. Investigations have shown that all chipped implements were not derived from carefully prepared blanks; many were doubtless made from flakes, some of which were struck from cores for the purpose. Kirk Bryan (1950) discusses Holmes theories and compares them with more recent investigations. He concludes that many arrowpoints were derived from easily available flakes, and many serviceable points were made in as few as one to ten minutes.

PARTS OF PROJECTILE POINTS

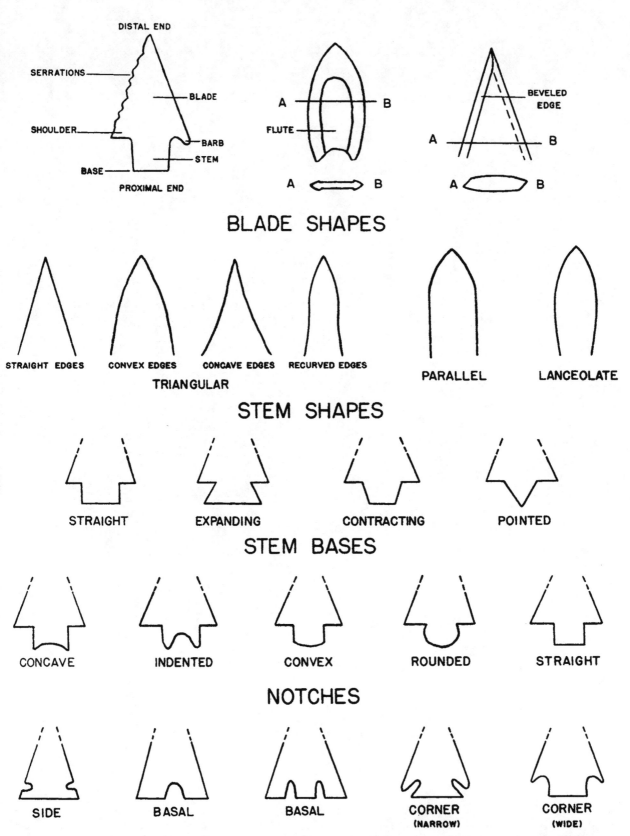

BLADE SHAPES

STEM SHAPES

STEM BASES

NOTCHES

Reproduced from Figure 7 in AN INTRODUCTORY HANDBOOK OF TEXAS ARCHEOLOGY, by Dee Ann Suhm, Alex D. Krieger, and Edward B. Jelks (Bulletin of the Texas Archeological Society, Volume 25); Austin, Texas, 1954. By permission of the Editor of the Texas Archeological Society, University of Texas, Austin. The publication contains many half-tones and line drawings illustrating projectile points, pottery types, and pottery decoration found on artifacts from Texas and near area.

RIGHT. UPPER. Two of six projectile points of similar shape and material found by O. G. Moore and Billy and Bobby Craig; longest, about 4 inches. Madison County, Alabama (Courtesy, Billy and Bobby Craig).

Since flint was scarce in some areas of the Southeast, as in Central Alabama, parts of Georgia, East Tennessee, and certain other sections, the Indians used quartz, quartzite, chalcedony, chert, novaculite (Arkansas area), and other similar stones for making chipped points and tools. In describing some of these, Lewis and Kneberg (1954, pp. 113-114) picture three points of "pure, rock crystal quartz," and describe other stones:

"The whiteness of milky quartz is due to cracks and bubbles which occurred at the time of crystallization. A third variety, known as smoky quartz, owes its cloudy brown color to the presence of organic matter. Still a fourth variety, rose quartz, gets its pale red color from a small quantity of titanium present in it.

"The commonest of all minerals is silica. The crystalline form is known as quartz, and the non-crystalline form as chalcedony. The wide distribution and hardness of this material, and the ease with which it lends itself to chipping, made it the most important of all stones in the development of mankind's tools.

"The numerous colored varieties of chalcedony are translucent. Flint is an impure chalcedony containing organic matter which makes it opaque. Chert is a still coarser, and more impure grade.

"Since quartz does not respond to the pressure of the bone flaking tool as readily as flint, it was probably used only when flint was not available." (Quoted by permission from Dr. T. M. N. Lewis, Editor, TENNESSEE ARCHAEOLOGIST).

RIGHT. CENTER. Five blue flint turkey-tail blades found in a burial in a shell mound; longest, about 8". Limestone County, Alabama (Courtesy, Harry Smith).

PROJECTILE POINTS

Plates 67 and 68

J. M. Kellberg (1955) discusses colors of stones:

"For most rocks and many minerals, color is not a diagnostic property. Limestones vary from black through all shades of gray to white and tan; shales may be black, gray, brown, red, or green; sandstones and quartzites are commonly white, gray, brown, red, or green; and slates are black, gray, brown or green. The so-called "greenstone" celts commonly found in this area were, in most instances, made from green slate. Such common minerals as quartz and calcite are found in many color phases. There are over 140 different varieties of quartz alone which are differentiated mainly on the basis of color and texture. As yet no one has been able to explain satisfactorily the reason for most of the color variations. In some rocks the red coloration probably is due to included iron in the ferric (Fe_2O_3) state, while a green color probably is due to included iron in the ferrous (FeO) state. Black color commonly is attributed to the presence of organic or carbonaceous material in the rock. In individual minerals, such as the many varieties of quartz, there is a great divergence of opinion among mineralogists as to the source of the different colors. Some attribute the color to minute traces of metallic elements, some to the exposure of the crystals to the effects of radiation, while others maintain that the color is purely an optical effect due to stresses set up inside the crystal." (Quoted by permission from The TENNESSEE ARCHAEOLOGIST).

BELOW. A variety of projectile points from Archaic and Woodland sites; longest, about 4". The one with the white background is beveled. This might have been a quick method of resharpening the point, or the point might have been used as a reamer or borer (Courtesy, Madison County Chapter, Alabama Archaeological Society.

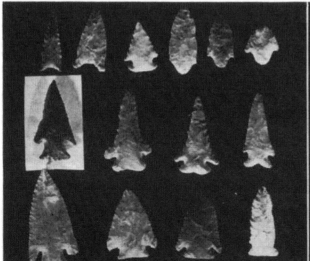

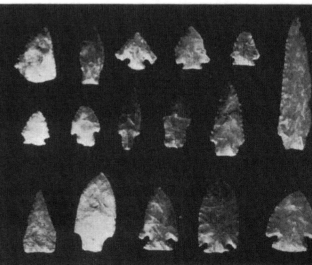

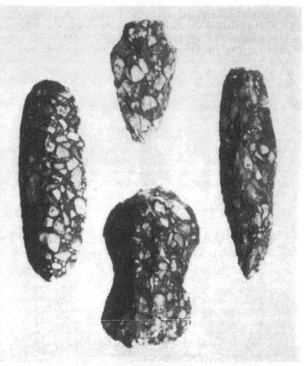

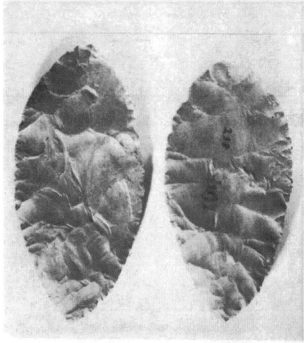

ABOVE. LEFT. Leaf-shaped blades; longest, approximately 6½". Alabama (Courtesy, E. S. Ginnane). RIGHT. LOWER. Archaic artifacts. Left to right. Top: straight based serrated knife, celt, notched knife, double-beveled (resharpened) knife, and clam opener. Center: grooved, chipped flint axe. Bottom: corner-notched spearpoint with serrated edges, flat-based knife, stemmed spearpoint (or dagger), celt, and large knife—7" long. Limestone County, Alabama (Courtesy, Dr. F. J. Soday). RIGHT. UPPER. Chipped stone implements made from "conglomerate"—a rock composed of gravel embedded in a finer material, as sand, which acts as a natural cement; it is found abundantly in the western part of Colbert County, Alabama, and this hard-to-chip material was often used by prehistoric man in that area. Left: celt, 4⅞"; right: flat-based knife, 5¼"; center: axe or maul, notched for hafting and a stemmed point. Colbert and Lauderdale Counties, Alabama (Courtesy, A. W. Beinlich). M. W. Hill (Lewis and Kneberg, 1954, p. 114) states:

"Frequently primitive man found it expedient to rework broken flint arrowheads and other tools, just as modern man sharpens steel tools or adapts broken tools to new usage. The basal portions of broken projectiles were often made into scrapers, or, if a small portion of the tip of a projectile were lost, the owner flaked a new tip with his bone flaking tool, probably without removing the flint from the shaft." (Quoted by permission from Dr. T. M. N. Lewis).

OPPOSITE PAGE. LEFT. Two projectile points—longest is about 9". Beautifully flaked. The small point is a "Clovis" type, possibly Paleo-Indian. Walker County, Alabama. The large point was an isolated surface find, relatively near a stone grave in which was discovered parts of a copper-plated ear spool and a long-neck bottle. Marion County, Alabama. It is similar in shape to some of the large points found at the Gahagan Mound (see Webb and Dobb, 1939, Plate 27-1). (Courtesy, Mr and Mrs. H. R. Steeves, Jr.; photographs on 69 and 70 by Ray).

RIGHT. Cache of ceremonial flint blades—two stemmed spearpoints, a flat-based knife—lower left, second item; and 8 double-pointed knives—longest 11". They are made from a concentric-banded, blue-gray flint nodule and the markings indicate that all of the artifacts probably were made from the same nodule; the flake was struck across the nodule. These are very thin and show secondary chipping; they were broken when found, and since some of the parts were missing they were probably ceremonially broken elsewhere and then deposited. Morgan County, Alabama (Courtesy, Dr. F. J. Soday).

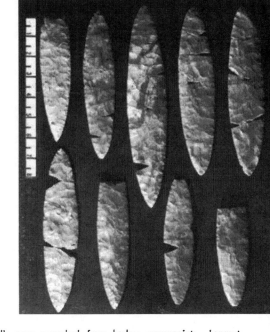

BELOW. UPPER. LEFT. Flint drills. These may have been used also as awls, perforators, or pins; longest about 2½" (Courtesy, R. E. Nelson). RIGHT. Assorted flint tools—knives, drills, perforator or awl, and scrapers. Some of these were hafted for easy use. Such tools were doubtless frequently reworked when broken or dulled. Some of the scrapers and drills were reworked from broken arrowpoints. Longest 3¼" Madison and Limestone Counties, Alabama. (Courtesy, Madison County Chapter, Alabama Archaeological Society). LOWER. LEFT. Flint celts; longest 7½". RIGHT. Five long flint blades; longest, 11"; Alabama (Courtesy, T. L. DeJarnette).

BELOW. Museum diorama showing an Indian family living in a cave or rock shelter. This is one of many interesting displays in the museum at Lookout Mountain, Tennessee (Courtesy Lookout Mountain Museum, Rock City Gardens, near Chattanooga, Tennessee).

The woman is sewing a garment, while her husband makes a spear. In front of him is a hafted knife, and at his right side is a hafted axe. The child is cracking nuts on a lapstone or perhaps cupped stone. At his right is a large grinding mill.

CAVES AND ROCK SHELTERS

Plate 71

ABOVE. The entrance to a large cave—Cathedral Caverns. The cave entrance is 128 feet long with a maximum height of 60 feet; one room is 150 feet x 1,000 feet and 40 feet high; another is 150 feet x 3,000 feet and 60 feet high. The dugout canoe was found in the mud of the Tennessee River near Triana, Alabama. It is part of the collection of Indian artifacts displayed at the Cathedral Caverns Museum; many Indian artifacts have been discovered in the cave (Courtesy, J. B. Gurley, Cathedral Caverns, Marshall County, near Grant, Alabama).

Many artifacts have been found on the surface or excavated at natural habitation sites, as caves and rock shelters. The interesting result of one such exploration is recorded in an article by Carl F. Miller, "Life 8,000 Years Ago Uncovered in an Alabama Cave," THE NATIONAL GEOGRAPHIC MAGAZINE, October 1956, pp. 542-558.

RIGHT. Entrance to a rock shelter which was once used by the Indians. It is one of several rock shelters in which Indian artifacts have been found in the Bama Scenic Rock Gardens. This shelter is 35 feet long, 20 feet deep, and 9 feet high at the opening. Outside one of the rock shelters near its entrance a large stationary rock has an artificial cup in its top surface which appears to have been used as the permanent base of a grinding mill (Courtesy, Bama Scenic Rock Gardens; located near U. S. Highway 11, between Birmingham and Tuscaloosa, near Vance, Alabama).

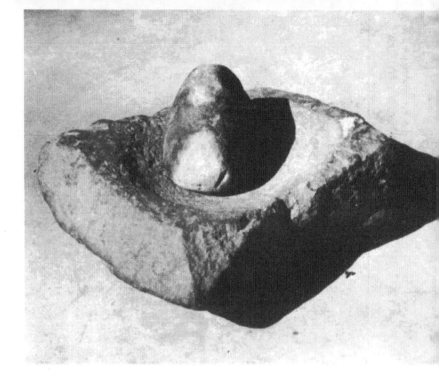

BELOW. Pitted or cupped stone, sometimes referred to as a nutting stone, about 10" diameter; these are particularly characteristic of Archaic culture sites. Since the cups are very similar in size, they may have been used in some way with drills, or they may have been only crushing and grinding stones for use with nuts, paint pigments, and other small objects. Often such stones were pitted on both sides—sometime with small pits on both sides; or with small pits on one side and a single wide deep concavity on the cther. Morgan County, Alabama (Courtesy, J. Ratliff. Photo by Ray).

"Waluvts: . . . they breake them with some stones and pound them in morters with water to make a milk which they vse to put into some sort of their spoonmeate . . . ." (Hariot, 1893, pp. 27-28). ". . . the Cherokee (before European contact) 'extracted their only saccharine from the pod of the honey locust, using the powdered pods to sweeten parched corn and to make a sweet drink . . . .' " (Henshaw, 1890, p. 349).

GRINDING STONES

Plate 72

ABOVE. Grinding mill—metate and mano found together. Metate or mortar, 7" x 9" x 3" Mano—grinding stone or hammerstone—4" x 3" x 2½". Such grinding mills are often pitted or cupped on both sides; frequently the cups are different diameters and depths, and were probably used for a variety of purposes. Often when they have a cup on one side only, they are found cup-downward; the Indians probably left them in that position to prevent weather damage and to disguise the stone when they left a camp or village site and could not carry it with them. Many of the base-stones of grinding mills weigh from 20 to 50 pounds. In rocky areas, large immovable stones with worked cups have been found near habitation sites; these served as stationary natural grinding stones. Though wooden mortars were used extensively by the natives of agricultural cultures, stone grinding mills were also used for crushing and grinding nuts, bark, acorns, roots, and corn. Clarke County, Alabama (Courtesy, M. E. Blake. Photograph by Abie Stratis).

RIGHT. Grinding mill—large forn pebbles—pictured in the position in which it was found. The faces of the stones are worn almost flat from use. They were found with typical Archaic points, drills, scrapers, and hammerstones. They are irregularly circular, about 4½" maximum diameter. Morgan County, Alabama (Courtesy, S. A. Mosley. Photograph by Ray).

"These kind of acorns they vse to drie upon hurdles made of reeds with fire vnderneath. . . . When they are to be vsed they first water them vntil they be soft . . . either to eate so simply, or els being also pounded, to make loaues or lumpes of bread. These be also kinds of which . . . the inhabitants vsed to make sweet oyle." (Hariot, 1893, p. 29). ". . . they dry the tongues of their venison; they make a caustic salt out of a kind of moss . . . ; this they dissolve in water and pound their dried venison till it looks like oakum and then eat it dipped in the above sauce . . . ." (Romans, 1775, pp. 93-94) (Swanton, 1946, p. 273, 285).

ABOVE. Five sandstone bowls inverted over a burial. These were found in a pre-pottery level of a shell mound; the level was referred to as "Archaic 3." All vessels show chisel marks, though some are smoother than others. In this same culture zone, was found steatite vessels; tubular stone pipes; limestone axes and hoes; "slate-shale objects with one or more grooves (whetstones) apparently used for polishing or pointing bone implements;" animal bones—worked and unworked; antler headdress; antler drifts; spearpoints; antler atlatl hooks; disk shell beads and shell pendants; stone gorgets; stone atlatl weights; and stone—barrel and cylindrical shaped—beads; fireplaces at this level "were distinguished by piles of river pebbles, generally cracked or broken and discolored by heat." Stone vessels, in graves, inverted over the head of "sitting burials" most frequently occurred in the graves of young children and infants. Some Archaic burials were accompanied by other artifacts, as bar gorgets, animal jaws, bone awls, flint points, and rarely, copper beads. Flint River—Tennessee River, Madison County, Alabama (Courtesy, Alabama Museum of Natural History. Illustration and description from Webb and DeJarnette, 1948, Museum Paper 23, Figure 11).

STONE BOWLS

Plates 73 and 74

BELOW. LEFT. Outlines of zoomorphic forms carved in relief on fragments of stone vessels. Poverty Point, Louisiana (After Webb, 1944, Pl. 35, Figs. 30 and 31; after Ford and Webb, 1956, Figs. 41 and 42). The eagle—12 cm. wide, 10 cm. high, has a design raised 2 mm. (Webb's exploration). The animal—9" x 3½"—was discovered in 1925 (Judge H. L. Lemley collection). RIGHT. Steatite vessel—27.9 cm. x 13.8 cm. Note, chevron decoration on lip, and chisel marks outside (Courtesy, D. C. Hulse; photograph by Jack D. Ray). Bushnell (1939, pp. 484-485) refers to decorations on two stone vessel fragments from South Carolina. One, a lug decoration (USNM 91843, Chester County) with seven and five crisscross lines; the other, a lip decoration (USNM 34905, Anderson County) of connecting X-marks forming a chain of diamonds. He refers to a similar specimen from Loudon County, Tennessee (Harrington, 1922, Fig. 16, p. 151).

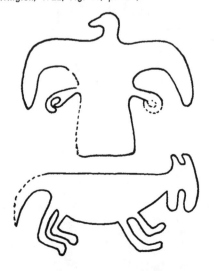

ABOVE. UPPER ROW. LEFT. Sandstone vessel, 18″ diameter, 7½″ high, and ¾″ thick with lug on left side. On the right is a fragment of a steatite rim sherd with decorative carving—chalked to show design. Limestone County, Alabama (Courtesy, J. W. Cambron). RIGHT. Sandstone vessel, 12″ diameter; it has been smoothed inside and outside by a native craftsman. Morgan County, Alabama (Courtesy, Lt. T. F. Moebes). CENTER ROW. LEFT. Steatite vessel, restored; rim diameter about 14″. Found at what appeared to be a workshop site, with scrapers, points and hammerstones. Morgan County, Alabama (Courtesy, S. A. Mosley). RIGHT. Steatite vessel. Maximum rim diameter, 41.5 cm. Maximum height 13.1 cm. Limestone County, Alabama (Courtesy, D. C. Hulse). LOWER ROW. LEFT. Steatite vessel; lug-type, about 8½″ diameter; covered in spots with redeposited lime from water leaching through a cave midden deposit. Limestone County, Alabama (Courtesy, J. Carr). RIGHT. Steatite vessel; lug-type. Morgan County, Alabama (Courtesy, Lt. T. F. Moebes).

C. H. WEBB (AMERICAN ANTIQUITY, 1944; Ford and Webb, 1956) describes features of the 2,724 fragments of stone bowls which he recovered from a cache at Poverty Point, Louisiana. Fifty-two had lip (most frequent) or rim decorations, including a single groove inside or outside the rim. Lip decorations included notches; one or two circular channels or grooves; transverse lines; chevrons—one with center punctate in each chevron; single and multiple zig-zag lines; cross hatching; and simple combinations of these. Lugs (or parts) were present on 105 fragments. A few lugs were decorated with transverse or diagonal lines, notches, and nodes; one had a groove and transverse lines. Many undecorated lips were rounded; some rims were smoothed; others, thinned by outer beveling; and a few, thickened. Twenty-nine fragments had drilled perforations for repair. Some 105 had portions of bases. There were no complete bowls (fragments formed one almost complete bowl). Vessel profiles varied from curved to slantingly straight; dimensions were: height, 7.5 to 18 cm.; rim width, 20 to 28 cm.; side-wall thickness, 8 to 25 cm.—average 14 to 15 cm. Most vessels had vertical gouge marks on the outer surface—a few, diagonal gouges. The inner surfaces frequently showed partial to total smoothing (occasional polishing) with horizontal grinding marks. The cache appeared to indicate purposeful placement; breaking before disposition; and the presence of fragments of some two to three hundred vessels represented in the broken sherds.

ABOVE. RIGHT. Cache of weights for throwing-stick or bannerstones. These were found in the ground in the position photographed. The top, or small stone, was broken and repaired after it was found by the owner. The large stone on the bottom was pecked into shape, but not drilled; the center stone was drilled and polished; the small stone was highly polished; they are made of greenstone or a green schist. North Alabama (Courtesy, C. W. McLemore). LEFT. Broken greenstone bannerstone showing a partially drilled hole with the core attached. The picture illustrates one method of drilling holes in stone. A reed or cane drill, with moist sand as the abrasive was often used by the natives. On the right is a typical core which resulted from such drilling; it is 1¼" long. It tapers in reverse to the taper inside the drilled hole, because the friction of the work cuts the outside of the cane, making it smaller, and the inside of the cane, making it larger, as the drilling progresses. The cane is fresh. The stone and core are from Franklin County, Alabama (Courtesy, H. K. Kleine).

WEIGHTS OR CHARMS FOR THROWING-STICKS

Plates 75 and 76

BELOW. UPPER. Bannertsone cache—three stones in different stages of manufacture. All are shuttle-shaped and made of greenstone. They illustrate various steps in the manufacture of such objects. Left. the stone has been pecked into shape and partially polished. Right. It has been completely shaped and further polished. Center. The stone is highly polished and drilled; it is 5¼" long. This represents a working cache; the depositor probably planned to return and finish the first and second pieces. Limestone County, Alabama (Courtesy, Dr. F. J. Soday). LOWER. Various shapes of bannerstones. Upper left. Incomplete—it has been shaped and highly polished, but the hole was not completed. Center stone is about 2" long. The two on the left and the one in the center are made of red-hematite; the one on the upper right, is rose-quartzite; on the lower right, hard slate. Autauga County, Alabama (Courtesy, T. L. DeJarnette).

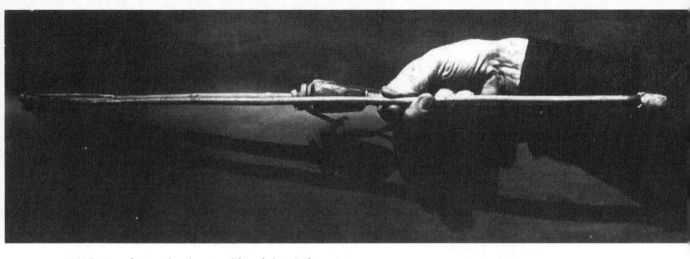

ABOVE. Reproduction of a throwing-stick and dart; it demonstrates the use of a stone weight or charm on the throwing-stick. The stick and dart are made of wood; the dart is feathered and has a flint point; the throwing-stick has finger loops of rawhide; this limits the fingers to a lesser degree than rigid rings. This reproduction of a throwing-stick was made by M. W. Hill, Alexandria, Virginia, with flint tools in less than three hours. He has experimented extensively in reproducing and using throwing-sticks.

There has been much debate about the purpose of these stones; they appeared during the Archaic Period and continued into the Woodland Period. They have frequently been referred to as bannerstones; however, a number have been found in association with atlatl or throwing-stick hooks and in positions indicating their likely association with throwing-sticks. The forms of these objects were more elaborately developed in the Ohio and Upper Mississippi areas than in the Southeast. The most complete book depicting the many and excellent forms of these objects is by Byron W. Knoblock, BANNERSTONES OF THE NORTH AMERICAN INDIANS, 1939. Discussions of throwing-sticks and throwing-stick weights or charms are found in Mason, 1885; Moore, 1916; Guernsey and Kidder, 1919, 1921, and 1931; Patterson, 1937; and Webb and DeJarnette, 1942.

RIGHT. Winged bannerstone, 5¼" from tip to tip, Morgan County, Alabama (Courtesy, Phillip Kyle).

BELOW. A variety of bannerstones or weights for throwing-sticks made of granite, pink quartz, steatite, diorite, red, green, and ferruginous slate, hematite, white and red quartz, and porphyry. Upper left. An undrilled stone; another is only partially drilled. These were found in Kentucky (Marshall, Graves, Hopkins, McCracken, Ohio, Crittenden, and Lyons Counties); Tennessee (Shelby, Obrion, and Hardin Counties); Mississippi (Alcorn and Tishominga Counties); and North Carolina (Polk and Clay Counties). They include the "pick," "bottle," "hour-glass," "wing," and other shapes (Courtesy, E. E. Curtiss).

ABOVE. LEFT. Three Archaic Period pipes. "Stone tubular pipes were made of sandstone, ground to conical form and reamed with a conical reamer at the distal end. The proximal end has a small cylindrical hole drilled into the conical bowl. With these pipes, there was found a pointed flint blade which may have served as a reamer, as shown in the illustration. One of these pipes was unfinished, and the others showed interior transverse grooves as if reamed, but by a reamer having a rough outline." (W. S. Webb and D. L. DeJarnette, 1948, pp. 49-50). In addition to the three pipes, other artifacts found with this burial were, "split bone awl, 4 flint points, turkey tarsometatarsus awl, shale abrader, 2 chert nodules, and an unworked long bone of a bird." (Ibid., p. 42). Madison County, Alabama (Courtesy, Alabama Museum of Natural History, Webb and DeJarnette, 1948, Museum Paper 23, Figure 20). RIGHT. Archaic burial. "With it were two flint points, a bone projectile point, and a large tubular pipe. This was a partially flexed burial of a girl about 13 years old. . . ." Lauderdale Co., Alabama (Webb and DeJarnette, 1942, p. 64, Pl. 75-2).

STONE TUBES—PIPES AND MEDICINE TUBES

Plates 77 and 78

Ford and Webb (1956, pp. 103-104 and Fig. 36) describe fragments of tubular pipes (none complete) found at Poverty Point, La. One was made of steatite—10 cm. long, and tapered from a diameter of 1.7 cm. to 3 cm. The small end was drilled with a hole 1 cm. in diameter, while the wider end had a large bore—probably the chamber for tobacco. Nine fragments of clay tubes—substitutes for stone and a very unusual occurrence for an Archaic site—were found. Ford and Webb (pp. 125-127 and Fig. 126) discuss sources of raw materials found there, and suggest that: steatite, chlorite and micaceous schists, hornblende, shale, slate, and fluorite probably came from the southern Appalachian region or (except steatite) from the Arkansas area; red ferruginous sandstone from northern Miss.; banded slate, gray-chert, flint, and copper from the Upper Mississippi-Great Lakes region; novaculite, gray-white chert, hematite, galena, magnetite, shale, and slate, from the Ozarks of northern Ark., and southern Mo.; red ochre from northwestern La.; catahoula sandstone from central La.; brown chert from eastern La., and southwestern Miss.; quartzite, flint, and quartz, including crystal, from the Hot Springs, Ark., area; and black argillite from eastern Okla. They refer to the apparently close connection between the sites of Poverty Point, La., Jaketown, Miss. (west-central), and Calion, Ark., (southwestern), and suggests that the latter were probably way stations for land and water trade routes. Many similar native trade goods were found at the three sites.

BELOW. LEFT. UPPER. Stone pipe from an Archaic burial; about 6" long; made of soft, reddish stone; found under the arm of a skeleton; at head of grave was a two-hole conch-shell gorget. Limestone County, Alabama (Courtesy, Dr. F. J. Soday). LOWER. Rough tubular stone pipe which appears to have been fashioned from a geode; about 4" long. Alabama (Courtesy, Alabama Department of Archives and History). RIGHT. Stone pipe about 4" long with carved decoration—chalked lines. Pipe has been restored along lower edge. Flint Creek, North Alabama (Courtesy, Lt. T. F. Moebes; photographs by Jack D. Ray).

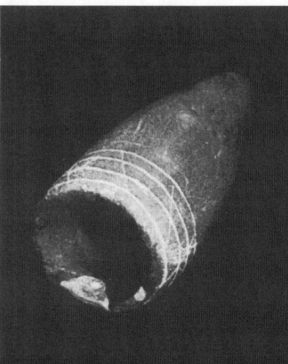

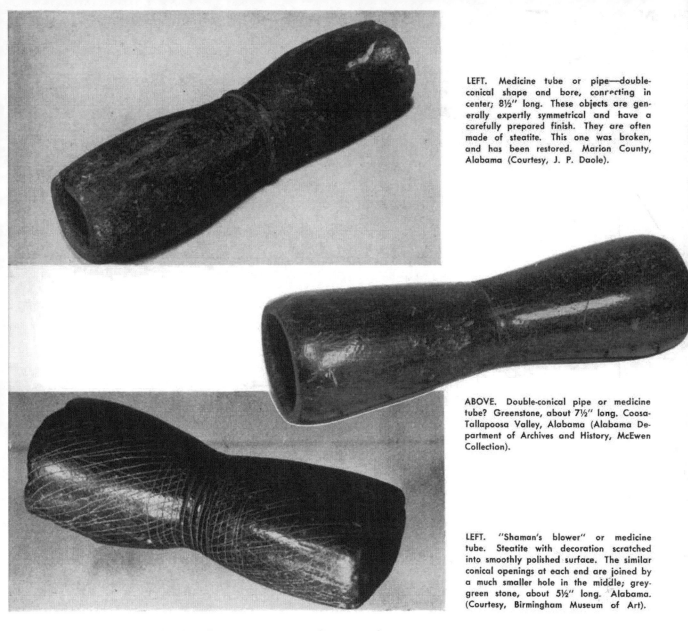

LEFT. Medicine tube or pipe—double-conical shape and bore, connecting in center; 8½" long. These objects are generally expertly symmetrical and have a carefully prepared finish. They are often made of steatite. This one was broken, and has been restored. Marion County, Alabama (Courtesy, J. P. Daole).

ABOVE. Double-conical pipe or medicine tube? Greenstone, about 7½" long. Coosa-Tallapoosa Valley, Alabama (Alabama Department of Archives and History, McEwen Collection).

LEFT. "Shaman's blower" or medicine tube. Steatite with decoration scratched into smoothly polished surface. The similar conical openings at each end are joined by a much smaller hole in the middle; grey-green stone, about 5½" long. Alabama. (Courtesy, Birmingham Museum of Art).

George A. West makes the following statements regarding stone tubes:

"The straight Tube is considered by our best authorities to be the most primitive form of smoking pipe. Its antiquity is indicated by its general distribution over the greater part of the United States and Canada. Its manufacture and use have prevailed up to quite a recent date, especially in the Pacific Coast region, where the more recent tubes are wholly or partly made of wood.

"Much has been written as to the probable use of these tubes, and the weight of evidence seems to warrant the conclusion that most of them were employed as smoking pipes, and others as medicine tubes. Very short elliptical ones were probably worn as beads, and another form, but a few mm. in length with bore of uniform diameter, may have been used in sizing and finishing arrow-shafts. (two paragraphs, p. 131).

"Authorities confirm the impression that many of the stone Tubes found, especially east of the Mississippi, were medical in their uses. The German Jesuit missionary, Jacob Baegert, in reference to the medical practices of the Indians of lower California, a century or more ago, says: 'There are many impostors among them pretending to possess the power of curing diseases, and the ignorant Indians have so much faith in their art that they send for one or more of these scoundrels whenever they are indisposed. In treating a sick person, these jugglers employ a small tube which they use for sucking or blowing the patient for a while, making also various grimaces, and muttering something which they do not understand themselves, until, finally, after such hard breathing and panting, they show the patient a flint, or some other object previously hidden about their person, pretending to have at last removed the real cause of the disorder.'" (Rau, Charles, 1865, p. 386; quoted by Jones, C. C., 1873, p. 363; and by West, 1934, p. 155).

"The observations of Baegert were confirmed by Venegas regarding the medicine men of the California Indian; 'One mode was very remarkable, and the good effect that it sometimes produced heightened the reputation of the physician. They applied to the suffering part of the patient's body the chacuaco, or a tube formed out of a very hard black stone; and through this they sometimes sucked, and other times blew, but both as hard as they were able, supposing that thus the disease was either exhaled or dispersed. Sometimes the tube was filled with cimarron or wild tobacco lighted, and here they either sucked in or blew down the smoke, according to the physician's direction; and this powerful caustick sometimes, without any other remedy, has been known entirely to remove the disorder.'" (Jones, C. C., 1873, pp. 363-364; quoting "Natural and Civil History of California, Vol. I, p. 97, London, 1759; West, 1934, p. 156). (G. A. West, 1934; quoted by permission from the Milwaukee Public Museum). The Southeastern natives probably used the tubes for similar purposes. Another type Southeastern tube has a more uniform diameter. Thruston (1890) mentioned several found in Tennessee. Ford and Webb (1956, pp. 102-103) describe three from Poverty Point, La.—one, 7.7 cm. long by 3 cm. diameter; another 5.5 cm. by 3 cm. Each had a uniform perforation—one, 7 mm. diameter—with rotary scars inside. The authors suggested that these were probably drilled with a cane and sand.

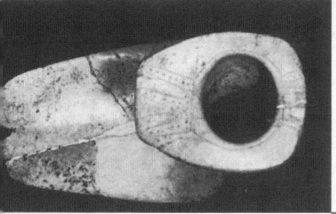

STONE PIPES—WOODLAND PERIOD

Plates 79 and 80

LEFT. Platform pipe, 4½" long with engraved decorations around bowl; from a cave in North Alabama (Courtesy, Lt. T. F. Moebes).

BELOW. Two modified platform or "monitor-type" pipes; 12" long. Stanly Co., North Carolina (Courtesy, H. M. Doerschuk).

George A. West describes platform or "monitor pipes" as flat-base, curved-base, and alate-stemmed. Regarding their manufacture he states:

"The Monitor Pipe was drilled and the bowl completed while the pipe was in the rough, and was worked down and polished after the drilling of the stem-hole. . . . in several Monitor pipes, noted in this paper, a portion of a stone drill was broken off and remained in the cavity . . . . Just what was used as a drill for producing these long, yet small, stem bores, is a matter not wholly solved. We know that the bore was started by the use of a very slender flint drill. This must have been followed up by an instrument that was strong and not flexible. There is good reason to believe it was made of copper. . . . It seems reasonable to conclude that the Monitor Pipe was coexistent with the 'copper age' of this country. . . . No pipe of the American Indian has a more striking appearance, better proportions, or finer finish than the Monitor. It is smoked without the addition of a separate stem. . . .

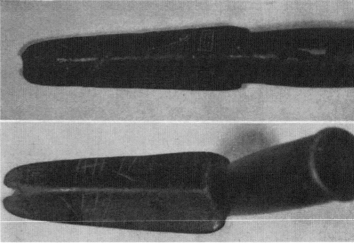

"The alate-stemmed Monitor Pipe has a high bowl placed at an obtuse angle to the stem. The base or stem is alate, and usually tapers toward the mouth-piece. Occasionally, these pipes have stem projections beyond the base of the bowl. The material of which they are made is usually chlorite, steatite or serpentine. They are found in the Ohio Valley area and in the adjoining states to the east of that area. . . . vary in length from 175 mm. to 455 mm. . . . bowl sometimes as much as 200 mm. high." He pictures variations from Virginia, Tenn., Ky., and the Carolinas. (G. A. West, 1934, pp. 157-163; quoted by permission from the Milwaukee Public Museum).

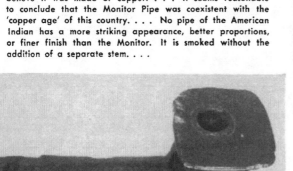

BELOW. LEFT. Black steatite platform or "keel-base" pipe, flat bottom; stem 8¾" long; bowl 3½" high. Tennessee (Courtesy, Frank, Frank, Jr., and Robert H. Morast collection). RIGHT. Two views of a curved-base steatite monitor pipe. Anderson County, Tennessee (Webb, 1939, NORRIS BASIN, BAE, Bull. 118, Pl. 90). Platform pipes from Southeastern Woodland sites are pictured by West (1934), and Setzler (1933, 1934). Ford and Willey (1940) write:

"A smoking complex is indicated for the Crooks site by the finding of five completed curved-base monitor pipes of clay, two doubtful stem fragments of clay, a fragment of a tubular pipe of clay, and a fragment of a monitor pipe of stone . . . . Most striking is the effigy pipe—9.5 cm. long; 4 cm. max. width, 1 cm. thick—. . . . Sitting on the flattened curved base is a small, well modeled animal figure—4 cm. high—facing the smoker . . . . The bowl opening is in the back. . . . it is made of clay-tempered paste, . . ." (Quoted by permission from the Louisiana Geological Survey).

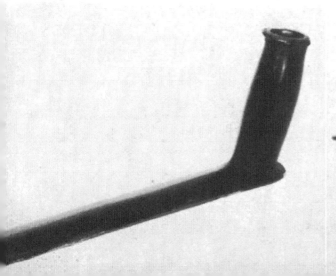

ABOVE. Three elbow pipe—types used in the Late Woodland and Mississippi Periods; largest, 6." Alabama (Courtesy, T. L. DeJarnette).

Many of the large pipes in the Southeast were used for ceremonial purposes. George A. West describes ceremonial pipes:

"The word 'Calumet' is said to be derived from the Norman word 'chalumeau,' a reed. As the Calumet, a synonym for the Pipe of Peace, was used in smoke offerings, it seems appropriate to treat this object at some length.

"The Calumet varied in form with the different tribes that made use of it. With the Indians south of the Great Lakes region, the pipe-head was often effigy in form. The Siouan Calumet was the type that predominated north and west of the Great Lakes. The pipe-head carried a high bowl rising at right-angles to the stem, in some instances carved and ornamented, and in others perfectly plain. The most prized material used in their manufacture was catlinite, although other varieties of stone were often employed. Its sanctity and deep—rooted veneration among the Indians are evidence of its existence and ceremonial use for a long time before the advent of the white man. Early explorers found it here and it is still made and used by many tribes. . . .

"No pipe was ever regarded by the American Indian with greater reverence and respect than the Calumet. To him it has a far-reaching significance. Its sanctity is seldom violated. It was used in the ratification of treaties and alliances; in the friendly reception of strangers; as a symbol in declaring war or peace, and it afforded its bearer safe transport among savage tribes. Its acceptance sacredly sealed the terms of peace, and its refusal was regarded as a rejection of the same. It was employed as a medium of appeal to the gods that their blessings might be secured or their anger appeased.

"The Calumet, with its highly organized emblematic development and symbolic adornments, was doubtless the greatest religious advancement of the American aborigines. To the tribes that made use of the Calumet, the pipe, although often used as an altar in the burning of tobacco as a sacrifice to their gods, was of far less significance to them than the shaft or stem. In fact, for certain uses, no pipe was attached to the stem and instead, the head of a duck, woodcock, or of some other bird was supplied. The colors and adornment of the stem varied with different tribes and the occasion of its use." (G. A. West, 1934, p. 231; quoted by permission from the Milwaukee Public Museum).

BELOW. "The effigy steatite pipe seems to represent a dog. Its greatest length is 16¼ inches and maximum height is 6⅛ inches. This pipe has lost a portion of one hind leg and a tip of one ear, and was beginning to disintegrate at the tip of the tail and at the nose. When removed from the mound it began to dry out and the surface began to scale off. A coating of ambroid prevented further deterioration . . . . Another steatite pipe—elbow—was taken from pit No. 7 . . . . was highly polished and beautifully worked. The bowl height was 4⅜ inches and the stem length was 3⅞ inches . . . . diameter of bowl outside was 2⅛ inches . . . .

"The total number of artifacts removed from the (Copena) mound was 49, distributed as follows: copper beads—strings 5; copper reel-shaped objects—5; copper spool—1; flint, small chip—1; galena balls—11; greenstone celts—11; greenstone spades—8; limestone spades—1; matting occurrence—2; pipes, steatite—2; (one is pictured below); slate spades—1; textile materials, occurrence —1." Lawrence Co., Alabama (Courtesy, Alabama Museum of Natural History; quotation by Webb, 1939, WHEELER BASIN, BAE, Bull. 122, Pl. 41 (b) and pp. 50-51—Site La° 37).

PEBBLES AND GEODES

Plates 81 and 82

Ornaments, fetishes, charm stones, effigies, polishing stones, paint pots, whetstones, toys, grinding stones, abraders, hammerstones, and drill sockets. Some show signs of much wear; others of having been worked, drilled, or slightly shaped. These were found in native burials or at Indian village or camp sites. Archeological excavations have produced many pebbles—some worked or decorated—singly or in caches. Ethnological publications—Colonial writers and historic investigations—have often referred to the medicine man's employment of pebbles. Hewitt (1939, p. 155) regarding Creeks:

". . . as soon as the disease was known the remedy was known and recourse was had to a medicine man. The person possessed a pouch, usually made of the whole skin of some animal, which was well filled with the remedies known to him or her. Some were compounded from roots, leaves, or herbs as well as pebbles, shells, or other strange objects, each of which had been acquired in accordance with certain esoteric formulae known only to . . . the medical fraternity . . . .

RIGHT. Water-worn stones. These pebbles were used as ornaments, toys and fetishes. Stones of unusual shape. color, and polish were doubtless sources of curiosity and charm to the Indians. Three stones show conical boes; others have natural holes; the heart-shape was worked. Longest 2⅞". Coosa-Tallapoosa Valley, Alabama (Courtesy, Alabama Department of Archives and History, McEwen Collection).

BELOW. UPPER ROW. LEFT AND CENTER. Quartz pebble with effigy design on each side; one head shows crest-type hair style; the other, a radiating headdress; 3" maximum diameter. Colbert County, Alabama (Courtesy, C. H. Worley). RIGHT. Fetish or charm stone; natural formation; 2" wide. St. Clair County, Alabama (Courtesy, W. H. McDonnald). LOWER ROW. LEFT. Human face effigy crudely carved; about 3½" long. Tuscaloosa County, Alabama (Courtesy, T. L. DeJarnette). CENTER. Animal effigy designed from a quartz pebble; unpolished—a few well-placed lines on a boulder; 4½" x 2½". Alabama (Courtesy, Birmingham Museum of Art). RIGHT. Fetish of highly polished, reddish-brown ferrous stone. There are circle and crescent-like impressions on one side and a crude footprint on the other. On the small end within the oval there are eight pricked dots; the pricking continues around the top and down both sides; 3¼" long. Madison County, Alabama (Courtesy, Elizabeth H. Chapman).

ABOVE. LEFT. Charm stones or fetishes worked into diamond, crescent, oval, and circular shapes; the top dark stone is greenstone—a schist; others are banded slate; longest, about 2". Madison County, Alabama (Courtesy, Madison County Chapter, Alabama Archeological Society). RIGHT. Polishing stones of quartz and quartzite. These were probably used for smoothing pottery. They show much wear. A good potter collected many varying sizes; by careful and long rubbing before firing, a pottery vessel could be given a finish which approached the appearance of glazing, though natives did not actually glaze their pottery. It has been said that potters treasured their polishing stones, and sometimes left them to their following generation. Longest, 2⅛". Coosa-Tallapoosa Valley, Alabama (Courtesy, Alabama Department of Archives and History, McEwen Collection). Le Petit describes medical practices: "They have a little basket in which they keep . . . their spirits; . . . small roots of different kinds, heads of owls, small parcels of the hair of fallow deer, some teeth of animals, some small stones or pebbles, and other triffles. It appears that to restore health to the sick, they invoke without ceasing that which they have in their basket." (Swanton, 1911, pp. 179-180).

BELOW. UPPER. Geode paint pot; 1¼" diameter. Central Alabama (Courtesy, Mrs. G. M. Nixon, McEwen Collection). CENTER. Geode paint pot; such formations found in native burials and village middens often contained the remains of red pigments; 1½" diameter. Alabama (Courtesy, Mrs. B. A. Douglass). LOWER. Geode bowl worked at the top, and slightly smoothed on the outer surface; excellent specimen. 4" diameter. Jefferson County, Alabama (Dr. and Mrs. C. M. Rudulph).

ABOVE. UPPER. Whetstones. These were used extensively for sharpening and shaping bone tools and ornaments. Similar stones with deep, straight trenches were also used for shaping arrow-shafts, as were stones with a hole in them. Whetstones were used in shaping wood, copper, and stone objects also. Longest pictured, 6¼". Morgan County, Alabama (Courtesy, J. B. Ratliff). LOWER. Hammerstones, grinding stones, mullers used with mortars, abraders, and drill sockets. Stones were used to pound or grind maize, acorns, nuts, and bark; to break the grain of hides; to smooth other stones or wood; to hammer copper; to strike chisels; to hold steady the top of a wooden drill—stones with a single pit. Many were used for multiple purposes. Longest, about, 3⅞". Talladega, Walker, Franklin, and Jefferson Counties, Alabama (Courtesy, H. K. Kleine).

"These savage doctors . . . take lettuce seed . . . and nuts with their shells on . . . and having placed all in a mortar, . . . they . . . pound them until they form a kind of opiate . . . their sick people take . . ." (Dumont, 1753, vol. 2, pp. 278-279).

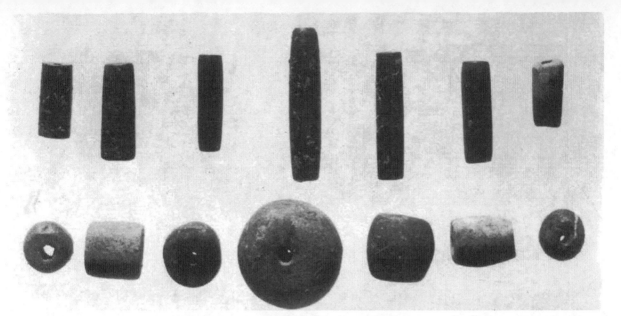

ABOVE. "Jasper beads. Twenty-six such beads were found in 8 burials in a shell mound at a 4 to 6 foot level. (Shell Mound Archaic site) They were carefully drilled and polished and strung, 1 or 2 in a necklace (in all but one case) with similarly shaped long cylinders of shell; the stone beads varied from ⅝" to 2¼" long and were ¼" to ½" diameter—one more than 1". A few were ground at the ends to produce a barrel shape; the large diameter beads were shorter, ½" to ¾" in diameter." (Courtesy, Alabama Museum of Natural History; BAE Bull. 129, Pl. 220 and Webb and DeJarnette, 1942, description p. 197). Such beads may have been traded from other areas, though jasper is found also in that section.

C. S. Brown (1926, p. 187) describes similar beads from Lawrence County, Mississippi:

"Mississippi has yielded fine examples of jasper and other handsome stone beads. The workmanship is often excellent and the perforations rather remarkable for length, delicacy, and accuracy. In some however, the perforation is incomplete. One from Lafayette County in the author's collection is 1¼" long and has a boring 1" deep in one end and a boring well begun in the other . . . .

"Charles Rau (1877, p. 291) describes and partially illustrates a remarkable find of jasper ornaments, mostly unfinished, in Lawrence County, Mississippi. Of the 449 pieces which came into the possession of the National Museum (there were 20 others) there were: 295 beads of cylindrical shape, ¼" to 1" in thickness, polished, but rarely perfectly cylindrical in form, ten showing the beginnings of holes; 101 round beads of a more compressed or discoidal shape, length ⅛" to ⅝", diameter ¼" to ¾", polished, five showing incipient holes; 2 small animal-shaped objects; 29 chipped or polished pieces; 22 jasper pebbles showing no work . . . . "

Brown described another collection from a site about 25 miles from the above, in which there were, "13 polished perforated beads of cylindrical form, 5 perforated beads of nearly spherical form, 1 carved deer, and several bird forms. On one of the long beads a separate ring of the same material was firmly fixed." (Quoted, by permission from the Mississippi Geological Survey)

Ford and Webb (1956, pp. 101-103, Figs. 37-38) describe 244 stone beads and small ornaments from the Late Archaic site, Poverty Point, Louisiana. These were made from: red jasper, translucent fluorite, green micaceous schist, hard black stone, quartz, dark gray slate, steatite, and gray, light, and dark chert. Several stages of manufacture were represented: most were finished and many, well-polished; a few shaped, with drilling unfinished; others with grinding incomplete. They include a variety of shapes: Tubular beads—99, ranging in length from 1-3.8 cm. and 4.9 mm. diameter; tapering drill from both ends; in incomplete bores, the hole-termination was rounded; one, was decorated with circular, parallel, grooves imitating a crinoid stem; (34 fragments of drilled fossil crinoid stems were found) another had circularly-placed, narrow, zigzag bands in bas-relief. Barrel-shaped beads—40, from 1-2.5 cm. long and 6-12 mm. in diameter. Flat beads—30, from 6-12 mm. diameter and 4-8 mm. long. Disc beads—4, from 2.4-4.3 cm. diameter and some 6 mm. thick. Bird effigy beads—19, modeled in the round, including seated owls and bird heads; also, profile bird heads; ½ to 3 cm. long; transverse hole through head, neck, or upper body for suspension. Other stone beads and ornaments—2 thick oval beads; one, 2 x 2 cm.; the other 4 x 3.5 cm.; one carefully made, drilled, effigy of a "butterfly" bannerstone, 1.8 x 2 cm.; small pendants—9 drilled with single and double perforations; shapes include, teardrop, plummet, circular, button-like, and rectangular; one, crudely incised, another with scalloped edge.

BELOW. LEFT. A variety of engraved pebbles, found near Badin, North Carolina. RIGHT. Front and back views of small drilled and simply engraved pebbles; longest, about 1½". North Carolina (Courtesy, H. M. Doerschuk). See Griffin, 1952, Fig. 163.

ABOVE. Problematical stones. Plummets and cones often found as burial associations in Woodland Period cultures. All the cones are 1" to 2" diameter; they are hematite except the one at the lower right, which is steatite and from North Carolina; sometimes such cones were made of other stones or galena. LEFT. Grooved plummets, both well-polished and crude examples. The above stones were collected from sites in Mississippi, Tennessee, Alabama, and Georgia (Courtesy, Frank, Frank, Jr., and Robert H. Morast collection).

STONE ORNAMENTS

Plates 83 and 84

RIGHT. THREE TOP ROWS. Six flat boat-shaped stones; the three slender shuttle-shaped stones and one conglomerate came from a Copena (Woodland) site in Limestone County, Alabama; the other conglomerate of flint and jasper and the steatite stone are from Archaic sites in Morgan and Limestone Counties, Alabama; longest in group about 3¼". Two of the Copena stones are grooved in the middle; one is engraved with a design. The purpose of these is not known; they might have been either atlatl weights or unfinished bar gorgets (Courtesy, Dr. F. J. Soday).

RIGHT. FOURTH ROW. Three expanding-center gorgets; these appear to be in various stages of manufacture from the most crudely roughed-out shape on the right to the decorated center object. Though none show drilling, the native craftsman might have planned these for two-hole gorgets; the larger is about 5" long; two others about 8" long are not shown in the group; green shale or schist. Alabama (Courtesy, Alabama Department of Archives and History, Beasley collection).

Ford and Willey (1940, pp. 106,114-116) describe stone artifacts from a Woodland Period, Marksville Complex, burial mound. These include: two unpolished "elongated pebbles smooth and water-worn . . . about 12 cm. long, 3 cm. wide, and 2 cm. thick."—one, with "a small crude rectangle scored near one end. At the top of the rectangle are five lines which radiate out in a sun-burst fashion. This pebble was associated with a flexed burial." Other stone ornaments include, plummets, boatstones, beads, pendants, gorgets, and a figurine. (Quoted by permission from the Louisiana Geological Survey).

RIGHT. LOWER ROW. LEFT. A concavo-convex steatite fragment from the side of a stone bowl was reworked into a diamond shaped ornament or charm about 4" long; it was engraved with a design imitating a bow and arrow. Alabama (Courtesy, Montgomery Museum of Fine Arts, A. R. Jones collection). RIGHT. Conical siltstone cup, associated with a Woodland Period burial; the object is finely ground and polished; 55 mm. high and 78 mm. diameter. Clarke County, Alabama (Courtesy, Alabama Museum of Natural History, Mus. Paper 19, p. 9).

BELOW. Two hold greenstone gorget, 7" x 2¼" x 1⅛" it was broken and repaired by the Indian owner. These two pieces were found at a site near Chattanooga, Tennessee, in 1949 — one piece, ten months later than the other. Note the holes drilled for repair; similar repair-holes are found on many types of broken artifacts, including stone bowls, pottery vessels, bannerstones, and bar gorgets. The natives often attempted to save or rework such items, which had doubtless taken them many days to produce. They lashed them together with vegetable fiber, a thong, or sinew. On stone and pottery vessels, they possibly used pitch, gum or asphalt in addition to the lashings (Courtesy, Frank, Frank, Jr., and R. H. Morast collection). Broken parts of reworked artifacts are frequently found.

ABOVE. Boat-shaped stones. Center stone has half-circles, or sun symbols incised on each side; McMinn County, Tennessee. Left. Upper to Lower. Steatite, Dawson County, Georgia; Fannin County, Georgia; ferruginous slate, Graves County, Kentucky. Right. Upper to Lower. All steatite; Pickett County, Tennessee; Cherokee County, North Carolina; Polk County, Tennessee; the last is unfinished and shows gouge-marks inside. Boat-stones are most frequently found with Woodland Period remains. (Courtesy, E. E. Curtiss). J. T. Patterson writes:

"The exact purpose for which the Indians made boat-shaped stones is entirely unknown . . . . Charles C. Abbott (1881) . . . .classified the boat-stones as varieties of gorgets . . . . there have been other suggested uses, such as paint cups, medicine stones, ornamental objects, and Wilson (1896) lists for the plainer kind such purposes as twine-twisters, handles for carrying parcels, or for the tightening of cords or lines . . . . The most frequently suggested purpose . . . . is that they were some sort of charm stones . . . . Some of the cup-like forms and a few of the boat-shaped pieces may have been used as containers . . . . but such use was probably incidental, and not the main purpose of the boat-shaped artifacts . . . . Their interment with the dead seems to have been very infrequent . . . . While the presence of such features as perforations, notches, or grooves would facilitate the attaching of the pieces to a shaft, yet specimens not having such features could also have been bound to a shaft by means of wrappings, as was done in the case of the atlatl stones of Arizona . . . . boat-shaped pieces could have been bound to the throwing-stick, either as a weight balancer or as a charm, or both." (Patterson, 1939, pp. 64-66; Quoted, permission The University of Texas Press).

RIGHT. Variety of highly polished stone gorgets typical of Archaic and Woodland cultures. The reel-shaped gorget as well as the more elaborate, expanding-center gorgets are usually found on Woodland rather than Archaic sites. Such gorgets are often made of greenstone, mica schist, steatite, hematite, and slate. North Alabama (Courtesy, R. E. Nelson).

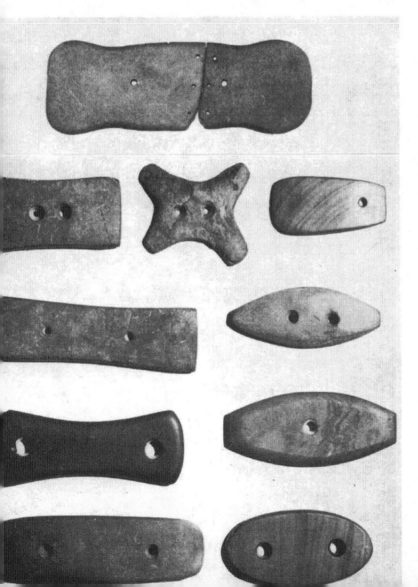

ABOVE. LEFT. Two carved stone pendants showing several cult designs—swastika inside concentric circles, hand and eye, bone, and steps. Longest is 4". Moundville, Alabama (Courtesy, Alabama Museum of Natural History; BAE Bull. 129, Pl. 58, No. 2). RIGHT. Five stone ear spools with carved designs including, swastika; cross; concentric circles; forked eye; chain; and square with corner loops—similar to design found on turkey or woodpecker gorgets from the Tennessee-North Alabama area, and pottery designs found in Arkansas area. The center spool is 3-¼" diameter. The spool with the chain design, lower left, shows traces of a thin copper coating; the other four do not show such traces, though many stone ear spools were copper-coated (Courtesy, Museum of the American Indian, Heye Foundation. Upper. l to r: 18/6521; 18/6433. Center. 20/684. Lower: 20/680; 20/682). Spiro, Oklahoma.

RIGHT. Four carved hematite plummets with animal designs in bas-relief—turtle, snake, and other animals; longest plummet is 3½" (Courtesy, Byron Knoblock collection). Spiro, Oklahoma.

RIGHT. NEAR. Ceremonial axe, 7⅝ inches long—spatulate shape. Hale County, Alabama (Courtesy, Museum of the American Indian, 17/1683). FAR. Ceremonial axe; it is worked to a chisel edge on broad end; 6⅜" long and 5/16" thick. A similar shape was found at the Moundville, Alabama, site, and is owned by the Alabama Museum of Natural History. Greenstone. Colbert County, Alabama (Courtesy, A. W. Beinlich).

The stone ornaments pictured on this page are typical of the best personal ornamental art forms of the Middle Mississippi Period cultures.

Webb and DeJarnette (1942, pp. 291-294) discuss the "Spatulate Form of Ax:"

"There can be no doubt that it was hafted, and that the hole sometimes found in such forms assisted in the attachment of the handle. They are often found showing stains on the stone of the decayed wooden handle. The general fact that they are never found chipped, or broken, but with perfect blades, although often made of soft and brittle stone such as limestone, schists, etc., has caused many writers to assume that this form was not an object of utility and could not have served as a cutting tool." They give 49 references (13 authors) as to Southeastern occurrence.

STONE ORNAMENTS

Plates 85 and 86

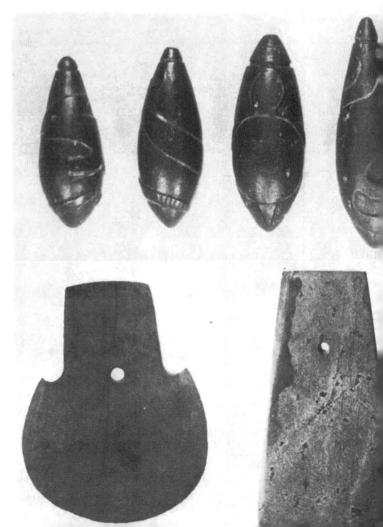

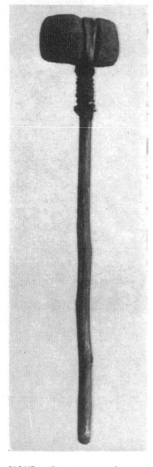

STONE TOOLS—PECKED, GROUND, AND POLISHED

Plates 87 and 88

Swanton quotes several early travelers who referred to the use of stone axes in the South-east: "Adair says that the stone axes of the Chickasaw 'in form commonly resembles a smith's chisel. Each weighted from one to two, or three pounds weight—They were made of a flinty kind of stone: I have seen several, which chanced to escape being buried with their owners, and were carefully preserved by the old people, as respectable remains of antiquity. They twisted two or three tough hiccory slips, of about two feet long, round the notched head of the axe; and by this simple and obvious invention, they deadened the trees by cutting through the bark, and burned them, when they either fell by decay or became thoroughly dry.' (Adair, 1775, p. 405).

"To make planks they merely indented the section of a tree at one end and then split it 'with a maul and hard wooden wedges.' |Ibid, p. 419). Beverley speaks of axes employed by the Virginia Indians as 'sharp Stones bound to the end of a Stick, and glued in the Turpentine' (Beverley, 1705, bk. 3, p. 60). In the Sound country of North Carolina Hariot (1893, p. 35) speaks of a gray stone used for hatchets and Smith also of 'a long stone sharpened at both ends' mounted in a wooden handle pickax-fashion and used as a battle-ax and a hatchet (Smith, John Tyler ed., 1907, p. 102). Catesby (1713-43, vol. 2, p. IX) also tells us that the warclubs set with celts ('stone ground to an edge') were used in hollowing out their canoes. The horn of a deer was mounted in the same way, and later the place of both was taken by iron." (Swanton, 1946, pp. 544-45).

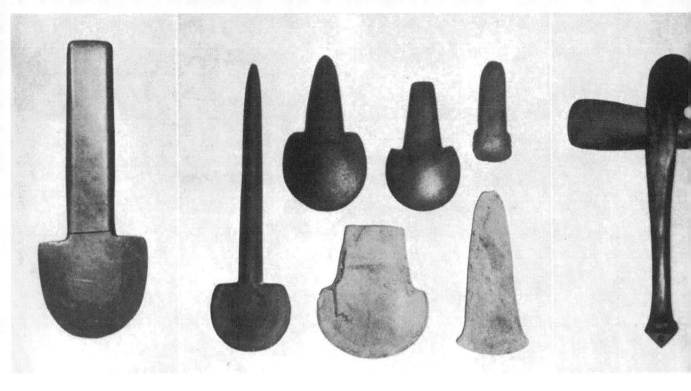

ABOVE. LEFT. Spatulate form of celt, probably ceremonial (Courtsey, Lookout Mountain Museum). CENTER. Spatulate forms; shortest, 4¾"; longest 12¾" from a rock shelter in Kentucky. Upper row. Left to Right. Reddish-brown, granite-like celt from eastern Arkansas, 6½" long. Second. Banded slate, dark green color, Middle Tennessee. Right. Greenstone celt, side notched. Lower row. Two tan flint spuds or celts from Western Tennessee (Courtesy, Frank, Frank, Jr., and Robert H. Morast collection). RIGHT. Celt with the reproduction of a probable ceremonial haft. Part of the Museum display of the Ocmulgee National Monument, Macon, Georgia (Courtesy, National Park Service).

BELOW. Stone celts from the Gahagan Mound, Red River Parish, Louisiana; longest is 14" of black slate (Photo, Courtesy, Louisiana State Exhibit Museum, collection of Dr. C. H. Webb, M.D., and M. E. Dodd, Jr.; permission from museum and collectors). Regarding polished stone artifacts from Gahagan, Webb and Dodd have the following observations:

"Celts constitute the majority of the polished stone artifacts, 19 occurring in the two pits. Some are rough tools, but many are undoubtedly ceremonial type, highly finished and unmarred by use. . . . Spatulate celts, such as the two of greenstone from Pit 2, (near left in picture below) do not appear in any collecions or in reports of any other excavations from this state (1939). . . . Moorehead illustrates several from Georgia, Kentucky, Alabama, and Florida, the latter taken from Moore's report of the St. John's River excavations. . . . He called attention to a band of discoloration around the handle of the celt, which he attributed to some detail of attachment. A similar band appears on all of the long Gahagan celts.

"Other polished stone artifacts include the discoidals. The boatstone found by Moore in Pit 1, (Webb and Dodd explored pits 2 and 3) increased the polished stone forms from this mound to three—the ceremonial celt, discoidal (chunky stone), and boatstone.

"This list of stone forms is completed by mention of the ear discs, pulley or spool type of which 9 occur. The largest pair, is identical with one of several pairs illustrated by Thoburn found in a Caddoan earth lodge ruin near Fort Coffee, Oklahoma." (Webb and Dobb, 1939, p. 107; quoted by permission from the Texas Archeological Society).

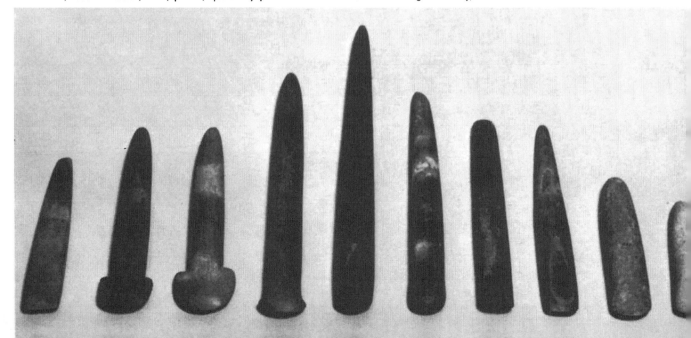

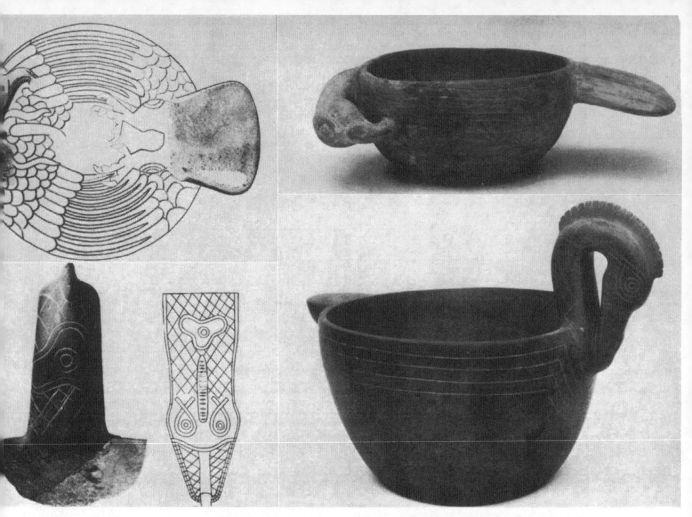

ABOVE. Two stone bowls from Moundville, Hale County, Alabama. UPPER. Limestone bowl representing an eagle or vulture in combined engraving and relief. Sides and bottom of the bowl are decorated with an engraved pattern depicting wings, feathers, legs, and feet. Bowl is 13¾" in outside diameter. LOWER. Diorite bowl representing a crested bird. This is a famous example of North American Indian art; it is beautifully carved, proportioned, and engraved. Its height to the top of the crest is 11¾" (Courtesy, Museum of American Indian, Heye Foundation, Cat. Nos. 17-20 and 16-5232. Drawings are also Courtesy, Museum of the American Indian, and from the original drawings by Moore, 1907, Figure 79, and 1905, Figures 170 and 171.

CEREMONIAL BOWLS AND MONOLITHIC AXES

Plates 89 and 90

Ceremonial stone bowls and monolithic stone axes are among the rarest objects of the Middle Mississippi ceremonial paraphernalia. Monolithic axes have a wider range of distribution, and have been symbolized frequently. Lewis and Kneberg (1946, p. 121) report a monolithic axe in the Dallas Component at Hiwassee Island, Tenn., and monolithic axe symbols in the Mouse Creek Focus, Tenn. They picture (Ibid., Fig. 27) a sketch of one of several stone pipes carved in this symbolic shape, and a photograph (Ibid., Pl. 72c) of a fragment of the stem of a claystone elbow pipe, on the underside of which is engraved the outline of a monolithic axe. Pendants imitating a monolithic axe have been reported from several Middle Mississippi sites. One such ornament about 2" long is owned by A. W. Beinlich. C. B. Moore (1899, Fig. 13, p. 305) pictures a vessel shred from the Alabama River area that has an incised design which appears to be a conventionalized representation of a monolithic axe.

BELOW. Two stone bowls from the Spiro Mound, Le Flore County, Oklahoma. LEFT. Dog effigy stone bowl with shell inlay eyes; gray shale, discolored brown from age; 5⅝" outside diameter (From the Byron W. Knoblock collection. Photo, courtesy H. W. Hamilton and the Missouri Archaeological Society, Hamilton, 1952, Pl. 30 B). RIGHT. Serpent effigy stone bowl, 7¼" outside diameter (Courtesy, H. M. Trowbridge collection. Photo, courtesy, H. W. Hamilton and the Missouri Archaeological Society. This stone bowl and another with a human effigy handle, the same size, also from Trowbridge collection are pictured, Hamilton, 1952, Pl. 31).

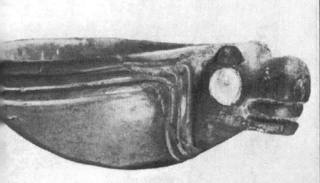 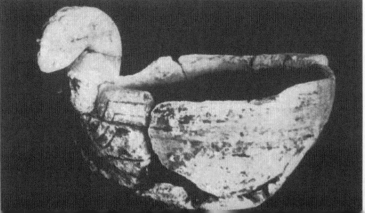

ABOVE. LEFT. Monolithic axe, 17" long. Etowah, Bartow County, Georgia (Courtesy, Georgia Historical Commission). Several monolithic axes have been found at this site; another is pictured in Moorehead, 1932, Fig. 52a. RIGHT. Monolithic axe, 11⅛" x 5⅜" x 1⅛" with weathered engraving on the side representing several cult designs—hand, bone, star, forked eye, and head with speech symbols. Found near Ballground, Georgia, along the Hightower or Etowah Rivers (Courtesy, Smithsonian Institution, United States National Museum, 317-614).

Monolithic axes found at the Spiro Mound, Le Flore County, Oklahoma (Hamilton, 1952, Pl. 56, and Burnett, 1945) are the most stylized of this type artifact. On several, the top of the stone haft (above the bit or blade) tapers to a slender end, in effigy of the sharp nose and head of a wolf or other pointed-nose animal; on each side of this taper, and around the end (top of haft) is carved—in bas-relief—the open mouth with prominent teeth interlocking; behind this, lower on the haft, is an incised circle or eye.

Monolithic axes were carved from a single piece of stone; they were pecked, ground, and polished. Monolithic axes often have a small semicircular extension at the base of the handle with a hole in it, which hole was probably used for suspension of the axe or for attachment of ceremonial paraphernalia. Webb and DeJarnette (1942, pp. 299-300) discuss these artifacts, and list twelve references to monolithic axes in the writings of nine authors. Among the sites at which these have been found, they list, "Mississippi County, Arkansas; Cumberland River near Nashville, Tennessee; Moundville, Alabama; Etowah, Georgia; York District, South Carolina; Hamilton County, Tennessee; Cuba; Hispaniola; Puerto Rico; Honduras; Nicarauga." Webb and DeJarnette further state, "From these references it is apparent that there is no area of concentration of this artifact, and that it is relatively rare . . . . (The above list) may suggest that it has been introduced into this country by way of the West Indies." These may have been used in ceremonials in the same way as a mace or baton, as a symbol of rank or office. They appear to have served a symbolic or ornamental rather than utilitarian function, because they do not show the wear which characterizes tools and weapons.

RIGHT. Monolithic axe, 11¼" long. Moundville, Hale County, Alabama (Courtesy, Museum of the American Indian, Heye Foundation, 17-891).

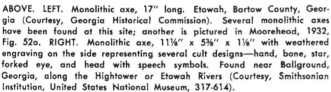

RIGHT. Four chipped flint ceremonial objects from the famous Duck
River cache. These bizarre shapes
were probably used only for special
purposes by the leaders or some
delegated group. They may have
been maces, batons, badges or symbols of rank for ceremonial display
or cutting? One appears to be an
effigy of an axe, another, an effigy
of an eagle's claw; longest, about
12''. Humphreys County, Tennessee
(Courtesy, University of Tennessee).

On Plate 110 are pictured three
copper ceremonial objects similar
in shape to the flint ceremonial
blades. The copper objects might
have served the same ceremonial
purpose as the flints or they might
have been symbolic representations
of the flint objects.

Small eccentric flint forms are
sometimes found; they occur more
frequently west of the Mississippi
River. Lewis and Kneberg (1954)
outline several flints from Oklahoma. Some eccentric flints appear
to be conventionalized arrowpoints,
eagles, snakes, and lizards.

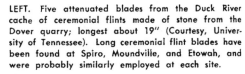

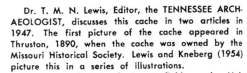

LEFT. Five attenuated blades from the Duck River
cache of ceremonial flints made of stone from the
Dover quarry; longest about 19'' (Courtesy, University of Tennessee). Long ceremonial flint blades have
been found at Spiro, Moundville, and Etowah, and
were probably similarly employed at each site.

Dr. T. M. N. Lewis, Editor, the TENNESSEE ARCH-
AEOLOGIST, discusses this cache in two articles in
1947. The first picture of the cache appeared in
Thruston, 1890, when the cache was owned by the
Missouri Historical Society. Lewis and Kneberg (1954)
picture this in a series of illustrations.

In 1894 a farmer plowing a field on the Link
Farm in Humphreys County, Tennessee, discovered a
cache of 46 ceremonial flints. These were beneath
limestone slabs which were probably the remains of a
stone grave. Two stone images were found at the
same place at a greater depth several months later.
In 1936 the University of Tennessee investigated the
site and among other objects, found a smaller cache
of similar specialized flints in the fill of a burial
mound and discovered others on the clay floors of
native house sites. (Lewis and Kneberg, 1954, p. 42).
A resident of the section discovered in Humphreys
County four other eccentric chipped forms; they are
about 6¾'' long, and shaped much like the top of
the axe pictured above; each appears to be an
effigy of a human head with a hair-knot or handle
protruding at the back of the head. (Ibid., pp. 60
and 65). (See Waring and Holder, Figure III for
the outline).

The flints of the Duck River Cache show exquisite
and highly skilled workmanship; the longest blade
in the cache measures 27½''; most of the objects are
specialized in form; among them are two turtle
effigies—7'' to 9'' long; and several chipped stone
disks. These ceremonial objects were made of flint
which the natives secured from the prehistoric quarry
at Dover, Tennessee; chips of flint, several feet in
thickness still remain at that site. (Ibid, pp. 37, 42,
and 45).

Until recent years, the Duck River Cache was
owned by the Missouri Historical Society; it has now
been purchased by the State of Tennessee and placed
into the custodianship of the University of Tennessee,
Knoxville. (Photographs published courtesy, University of Tennessee Department of Anthropology). See
J. B. Griffin, 1952, Fig. 108, for a depiction of characteristics of the Duck River Culture.

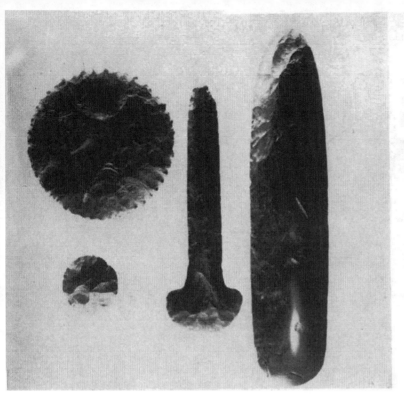

ABOVE. LEFT. Four unusual flint objects—two disks, a spatulate form, and well-made large spade, 13½" long. Alabama (Courtesy, T. L. DeJarnette). RIGHT. Chisel-celt of Dover flint, 6" long and double-barbed spear or mace of Dover flint, 7½" long. Tennessee (Courtesy, D. B. Long; photograph by Tom-Clare Studio).

CEREMONIAL FLINTS

Plates 91 and 92

RIGHT. Ceremonial flints from the Spiro Mound, Le Flore County, Oklahoma. Maces, 10⅞" and 11" long (Courtesy, H. M. Trowbridge Collection; photograph courtesy, H. W. Hamilton).

Several human figures in native designs pictured herein appear to be holding a flint blade (See Pls. 24, 44, 48). Hamilton (1952, Pls. 34-47) pictures many Spiro chipped maces and blades—from 6" to 22" long. Some have been partially ground and polished. Chipped maces were found in the Duck River cache. They are also reported by S. C. Dellinger in a cache of four such objects from northeastern Arkansas (In Lewis and Kneberg, 1954, p. 86); two had short handles and were possibly hafted for use. They might have been the reworked remains of broken, longer objects. This was a popular symbol; a design in this shape, 24¼" long was carved on a high bluff above Mound Bottom, Harpeth River, Cheatham County, Tenn. (Ibid., pp. 48 and 84).

RIGHT. Eccentric shapes of flints. Group on left and two turtles on right are after pictures found in Thruston, 1890 and Lewis and Kneberg, 1954. These unusual shapes often range from 6" to 12" long; the more attenuated blades are often longer; some of the maces are also longer. The slender, long blades in the center, right top, are drawn to a different scale, and are after pictures found in Moorehead, 1932; the longest is about 26¼"; they are from the Etowah, Georgia, site and show similar design, workmanship, and material to some of the Tennessee flints. The large flint at the right is drawn to a different scale and is actually smaller than the Etowah flints; it is about 8" long, and was found at Moundville, Alabama; it is pictured by Moore, 1905. These drawings are included to show the variety of shapes among the finely chipped bizarre flint forms of the Mississippi Culture Period. Other batons and maces from Tennessee and Spiro are outlined or pictured in Lewis, 1954; and Hamilton, 1952. See Plate 20.

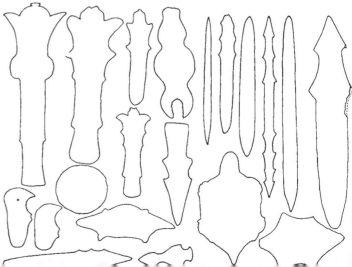

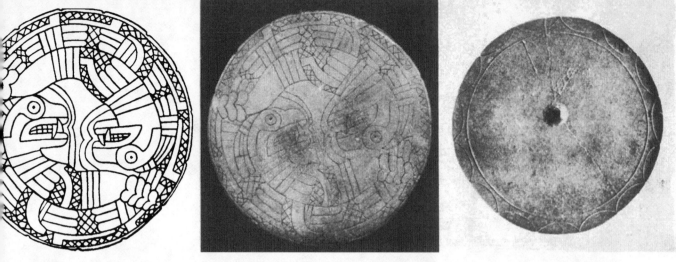

ABOVE. Stone disk with serpent design; 8½" diameter. LEFT. Line drawing after Hodge, 1912 (Photo, Courtesy, Peabody Museum, Harvard University, 14784). CENTER. The actual stone disk (Courtesy, Ohio State Museum). Right is the reverse side (Courtesy, Mississippi Geological Survey, Brown, 1926, Fig. 183). Issaquena County, Mississippi.

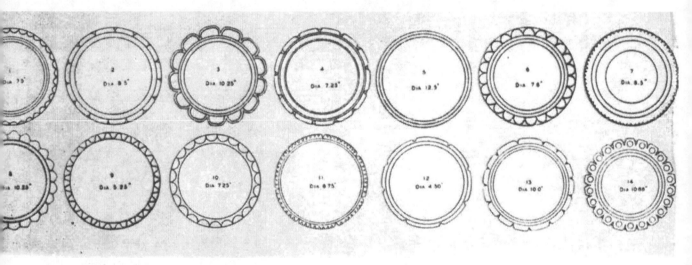

ABOVE. Line drawings showing variety of types of decorative designs applied to stone palettes (After Webb and DeJarnette, 1942, Figures 92 and 93). These are from a number of sites including: Arkansas Port, Arkansas; Lake Washington, Mississippi; Hardin County, Lick Creek, and the Nashville area, Tennessee; Lauderdale and Hale Counties, Alabama; and Etowah, Georgia; numbers 9-14 are from Hale County, Moundville, Alabama.

BELOW. Three stone disks. LEFT. Stone disk 12" diameter; sun-circle or scalloped design. Etowah Temple Mound, Georgia. Lewis H. Larson, Jr., Archaeologist-in-charge of excavations at Etowah states: "This object was most certainly used as a palette for mixing ceremonial paints. All of those which we have found in the mound have had various types of mineral pigments such as ochre and graphite associated with them." (Correspondence, Courtesy, Georgia Historical Commission). CENTER. Blue slate disk, 7¼" diameter; Yadkin River, Stanly County, North Carolina (Courtesy, Dera K Kirk). RIGHT. Sandstone disk, 10¼" diameter. Moundville, Alabama (Courtesy, Museum of the American Indian, Heye Foundation, 17-1475).

ABOVE. Two stone disks found at Moundville, Alabama. LEFT. Engraved disk showing hand and eye, skull and bi-lobed arrow design; 8.75" diameter (Courtesy, Peabody Museum, Harvard University, 48122). RIGHT. Ceremonial disk with rattlesnake and hand and eye design; 12.5" diameter (Courtesy, Alabama Museum of Natural History).

STONE PALETTES

Plates 93 and 94

Webb and DeJarnette (1942, pp. 287-291) discuss stone disks:

"These circular stone disks, made of many materials, such as sandstone, slates, fine grained gneiss, etc., vary in size from 12.5 inches to 4.5 inches in diameter. Nearly all are notched on the edges, and a few are elaborately engraved. Some are concave on one face as if used as palettes for grinding paint. Many have been found with lead or iron oxides smeared on them. Most of them have been found in graves. A few are drilled with a single hole for suspension. Many are decorated with one or more concentric incised circles. Such circles usually occur on the 'reverse' side, that is, opposite to the engraving, if any, or opposite the notches, where the notches are not duplicated on both sides. Many are found broken which may suggest intentional breaking in some cases. One case reported indicated fragments of a single disk were found in five different burials and the disk completely restored . . . . the vicinity of Moundville, Alabama, has yielded by far the greatest number of disks, as well as the largest, most carefully wrought, and most elaborately engraved ones . . . . they were not carried to the south and east (of Moundville), but . . . were confined to the interior drainage basin and to sites reached from the Mississippi River and the Gulf. None are known to have been reported from Florida and the Atlantic seaboard." (Quoted courtesy, Smithsonian Institution, Bureau of American Ethnology).

The designs engraved on paint palettes are characteristic symbols of the Southern Ceremonial Complex. Stoddard (1904, p. 153; Waring and Holder, 1945, Fig. III-t) reported a stone palette from the Menard Mound, Arkansas, on which there is a banded ogee or open eye symbol carved in bas-relief. Brannon (Arrowpoints, Vol. 17, 1923, p. 118) pictured a badly weathered Moundville disk, 11" diameter owned by the Alabama Museum of Natural History; it has on it one remaining element of the design which is near the outer margin and was described as "the winged sun pierced with an arrow" —a bi-lobed arrow design. The circle which may be a sun-symbol has a cross inside. The Alabama Department of Archives and History owns a disk about 6" in diameter from the Alabama River area.

BELOW. Two rectangular stone palettes; though a few have been found in this shape, the round ones predominate. The circular form may have been associated with sun-worship or may have been a natural design of formal symmetry, which is a basic element of the best of native art. LEFT. Slab, 13½" wide, Hale County, Alabama. RIGHT. Slab. 11" wide, Madison County, Alabama (Courtesy, Museum of the American Indian, Heye Foundation, 17-1493 and 10-2401).

GAMESTONES

Plates 95 and 96

RIGHT AND LEFT. Two views of a massive stone pipe depicting an Indian preparing to roll or throw a "chungke" stone; this appears to be a bi-concave stone of the type found at Gahagan Mound, Louisiana, and many other mound sites. He holds in the left hand what appears to be two sticks. The sticks may be the same objects as appear to be broken-sticks in the hands of several of the figures pictured on shell gorgets from the Middle Mississippi Valley. This pipe was found in Muskogee County, Oklahoma. It is 8½" high and of brownish-red pipestone. (The pipe is displayed at the City Art Museum of St. Louis (E-2759) and is from the Whelpley collection; permission to reproduce it here was granted by W. V. Hauser, Executor of the Estate; also permission from the Museum; the photographs were furnished, courtesy, Dr. Franklin Fenenga, University of Nebraska, Laboratory of Anthropology, Lincoln Nebraska).

James Adair (1775, p. 401) describes the game of "chungke":

"The warriors have another favorite game called chungke, which, with propriety of language, may be called 'running hard labor.' They have near their state-house a square piece of ground well cleaned, and fine sand is carefully strewed over it, when requisite, to promote a swifter motion to what they throw along the surface.

"Only one or two on a side play at this ancient game. They have a stone about two fingers broad at the edge, and two spans round; each party has a pole of about eight feet long, smooth and tapering at each end, the points flat. They set off abreast of each other at six yards from the end of the play-ground; then one of them hurls the stone on its edge, in as direct a line as he can, a considerable distance toward the middle of the other end of the square; when they have run a few yards, each darts his pole anointed with bear's oil, with a proper force, as near as he can guess in proportion to the motion of the stone, that the end may lie close to the stone; when this is the case, the person counts two of the game, and, in proportion to the nearness of the poles to the mark, one is counted, unless by measuring both are found to be at an equal distance from the stone. In this manner, the players will keep running most part of the day, at half speed, under the violent heat of the sun, staking their silver ornaments, their nose, finger, and ear rings; their breast, arm and wrist-plates; and even all their wearing apparel, except that which barely covers their middle. All the American Indians are much addicted to this game, which to us appears to be a task of stupid drudgery; it seems, however, to be of early origin, when their forefathers used diversions as simple as their manners. The hurling-stones they use at present were, time immemorial, rubbed smooth on the rocks, and with prodigious labour; they are kept with the strictest religious care, from one generation to another, and are exempted from being buried with the dead. They belong to the town where they are used, and are carefully preserved."

LEFT. Two stone discoidals, 5¼" and 5½" diameter (Courtesy, Lookout Mountain Museum).

RIGHT. UPPPER. Three "chungke" stones from Creek sites in the Coosa-Tallapoosa Valley, Alabama. Largest is about 5" diameter, and has a center perforation; all bi-concave. (Courtesy, Alabama Department of Archives and History, Mc-Ewen Collection). LOWER. Variety of discoidals-steatite, quartz, and red and gray sandstone—including several bi-concave stones; largest is the gray, granite-like stone, left, 5¼" (Alabama); Smallest on the right, is the semi-perforated, 1¼" diameter. One has an engraved cross. Georgia and Tennessee. (Courtesy, Frank, Frank, Jr., and Robert H. Morast).

ABOVE. LEFT. Engraved discoidal; green-stone, 1¾" diameter (Lookout Mountain Museum). RIGHT. "The youth at their exercises." From an engraving by De Bry after a drawing by Le Moyne, who visited Florida in 1564-65. Timucua tribe. The natives are throwing balls at a target —a frame of rushes, twigs or reeds on top of a post; others are shooting bows and arrows; and still others are racing (Courtesy, Smithsonian Institution, BAE, 1186-b-13).

RIGHT. NEAR. Four granite discoidals; largest 4⅛" diameter and 1-7/16" thick. Spiro Mound, Oklahoma (Courtesy, P. F. Molloy). FAR. UPPER. Two stone balls; larger, 3½" diameter—quartzite; smaller, 1-1/3" diameter—sandstone. Carson site, Coahoma County, Mississippi (Courtesy, Dabney Carson Pelegrin). LOWER. Two discoidals; large sandstone bi-concave discoidal is about 4" maximum diameter and about equal thickness. Small greenstone or banded schist discoidal with slightly convex sides is about 1¼" wide. The large stone appears to be a chunkey stone; the small was probably a counter used in a game (Courtesy, Jessie Eleanor Dilworth).

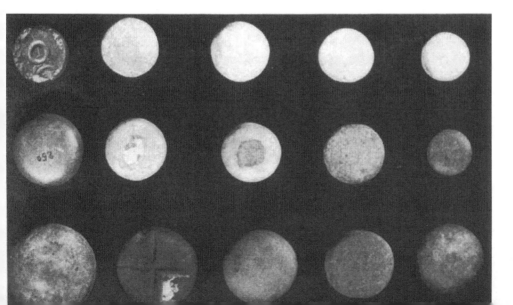

RIGHT. Assortment of game-stones; largest about 2" diameter (Courtesy, Alabama Department of Archives and History, Beasley collection; all photographs this source were made by Jack D. Ray).

"The Creeks also had another game distantly resembling chunkey. This was called 'rolling the stone,' or 'rolling the bullet,' and was played by rolling a large marble or bullet along a trench with the object of making it come to rest in certain hollows which counted differently depending on the difficulty of reaching them." (Swanton, 1946, p. 684). However, the most frequently described game resembled lacrosse. South-eastern Indians played with two ball-sticks.

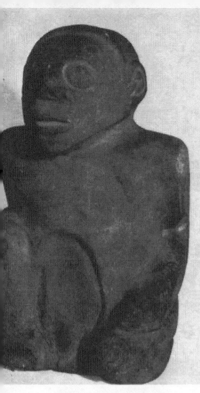  

ABOVE. LEFT AND CENTER. Stone images of a man and a woman, 13¼" and 13¾" high. Tennessee. Woman—Rhea County (Courtesy, Museum of the American Indian, 7277 and 21-965). RIGHT. Sandstone figure, 17½" high; depicts elderly man; excellent workmanship. Wilson County, Tennessee (Courtesy, University of Tennessee). There is a similar figure in the L. D. Yeaman collection, Carthage, Tennessee.

Le Petit mentions images of stone and clay in the Taensa temple. Describing the temple of Talomeco "Garcilaso's informants stated, there were 12 statues of giants made of wood arranged in pairs, . . . diminishing in size inward so as to create an apparent perspective. Around the four sides . . . were two rows of statues, one of men and one of women. . . . The coffins of the dead were placed below on a raised platform and above each was a wooden image of the deceased . . . . (Garcilaso, 1723, pp. 132-133)." (Swanton, 1946, p. 614).

BELOW. Three stone images from Bartow County, Georgia. LEFT AND CENTER. Male and female figures found at Etowah in a grave in Mound C; they are 22½" and 24" high, and made of marble native to North Georgia. The female wears a skirt and belt. Various facial features and what are probably articles of clothing, are represented in paint—ochre red, white, carbon black, and a greenish or blue black. The ears and lips are red; the eyeballs are white, and the pupils, black. A black streak extends horizontally across the face of each figure. Each has a carved headdress; the female has a pack-like object represented on her back. The male is seated with legs crossed while the female is kneeling with her feet drawn under her body (Courtesy, Georgia Historical Commission; description by Lewis H. Larson, Jr., Archaeologist, GHC). RIGHT. Side view of a stone image, 21½" high; the flat breast indicates that it may portray a male figure; legs are crossed; hands are on knees—one hand with palm turned outward; there is carved checker-work on the head and what may be a hair knot or ceremonial paraphernalia protruding from the back of the head. Raccoon Creek, Bartow County, Georgia (Courtesy, Cornell College Museum, Powers Collection).

LEFT. FAR. Stone image, 14" high; both arms were missing when discovered; hands are still on hips. Found near a mound; the neck was broken when struck by a plow (Courtesy, Judge H. L. Webster. Photo, courtesy, D o u g Underwood). NEAR. Brown sandstone figure, 7" high. It has a headdress similar to figure at its left. This may represent a hair style or a snake coiled on top. Kentucky Lake, Tennessee (Courtesy, D. B. Long. Photo by Tom-Clare Studio). Two wooden masks and an effigy pottery vessel pictured herein show coiled snakes.

BELOW. Two similar stone images; the raised line across the face of each make each appear to be wearing a helmet; the figures are 20½" x 6¼" x 3¾". Knox County, Tennessee (Courtesy, Smithsonian Institution, USNM, 6462).

STONE IMAGES

Plates 97 and 98

Webb and DeJarnette (1942, pp. 294-297) discuss the occurrence of stone images; they list 29 references by eight authors, giving the location of these discoveries; the sites include: Natchez, Mississippi; Catoosa Springs, Georgia; Etowah River, Georgia; Marion and Trigg Counties, Kentucky; Henderson, Kentucky; Massac County, Illinois; and many counties in Tennessee—Perry, Hardin, Henry, Smith, Humphreys, Trousdale, Sumner, Knox, Roane, and Wilson; the Cumberland River Valley, Tennessee and Kentucky and a site near Franklin, Tennessee. They state:

"It will be noted that their distribution seems to center about the State of Tennessee and in that State the general vicinity of the Cumberland River . . . . nothing seems to suggest connection with Moundville, although at Etowah, Georgia, seven or more of these images have been found. They are, as elsewhere, to be associated with the use of stone graves.

"That they may be attempts to represent specific individuals, rulers, or important personages and to preserve their image after death seems probable, in view of reports of early travelers. . . ."

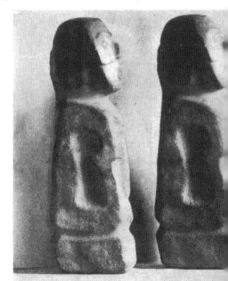

LEFT. Fluorite figure, 10" high; weighs 18 pounds; legs crossed and hands on knees; raised band over head; narrow band leads from two engraved circles in the center of the forehead to the ear as if the figure wears a decorated bandeau or tiara. Both arms were missing; one was found. From bottom land of the Ohio River, near Tolu, Kentucky (Courtesy, E. E. Curtiss. Photograph used by permission from COURIER-JOURNAL AND LOUISVILLE TIMES).

"Their principall temple . . . is . . . at Pamunky. Neere unto the towne, with in the woods, is a chief holie howse, proper to Powhatan . . . and it is accompanied with two other sixty feet in length, filled with images of their kings and devills, and tombes of the predicessors. This place they count so holie as that none but the priests and kings dare come therein." (Va.-N. C. area) (Strachey, 1849, p. 90; Swanton, 1946, p. 614).

RIGHT. Two views of a stone image, 17½" x 5⅛" x 3-3/16", from Lincoln County, Tennessee (Courtesy, Smithsonian Institution, USNM, 388049).

MASSIVE STONE PIPES—EFFIGIES

Plates 99 and 100

ABOVE. LEFT. Dark red sandstone pipe; 8½" high; it is naturalistically executed; pipe bowl in back; the figure appears to wear a helmet; Moundville, Alabama (Courtesy, Museum of the American Indian Heye Foundation, 17-2810). RIGHT. Dark red pipestone; about 8" high. The hair knot is the same as found on some stone images. Shiloh, Tennessee (Courtesy, National Park Service, Shiloh National Military Park).

Heavy flat-base platform pipes were c e r e m o n i a l accouterment, sometimes used in religious ritual and often used only by tribal leaders, as in historic times. "Captain John Smith (1607) says the 'Werowance' of 'Rappahanah . . . caused his mat to be spread on the ground, where he sat down with a great majesty, taking a pipe of tobacco, the rest of his company standing about him. . . .' " (Arber's edition, Smith's works, 1884; McGuire, 1899).

LEFT. Redstone pipe; 20.5 cm. Man leaning forward to smoke through a tube. Spiro. Craig Burial Mound. Le Flore County, Oklahoma (Courtesy, University of Oklahoma, Stovall Museum, B 99-2).

ABOVE. Two views of a red sandstone effigy pipe; 7" long and 4¾" high. Lookout Mountain, Tennessee (Courtesy, The Reading Public Museum and Art Gallery, 32-394-1; all photographs from this Museum were made by S. C. Gundy, Assistant Director). Pipes were made of steatite and other stones native to the region.

MASSIVE STONE PIPES—EFFIGIES

Plates 101 and 102

G. A. West (1934) describes pipe manufacture:

"In the fabrication of aboriginal stone pipes, the most desirable material obtainable was chosen. The selection of rock was determined by its heat-resisting qualities, its color, and its susceptibility of being easily worked into shape. In many instances, exceedingly hard rock was used, especially when it did not require an excessive amount of labor to give to it the desired shape. The type of stone used naturally varied with its accessibility.

"Many kinds of rock were employed by the aboriginal for pipe-making. Among the most common were: catlinite, steatite, sandstone, limestone, slate, granite, chlorite, diorite, and even fossil coral.

". . . Material for pipe-making, in its raw state, as well as after its manufacture into pipes, often became articles of commerce, and reached distant tribes. . . .

"The rock had to be quarried and selected. Only a small portion of the available material in any quarry is fit for pipe-making. Stone mauls and wedges, of harder rock, are necessary for this work. The pipe-maker, or artisan, for that is what he must have been, was probably not the one who did the quarrying. . . .

"To detect imperfections in the rock, and to avoid transporting unnecessary weight, the selected pieces were roughly pecked into shape . . . at the quarry.

ABOVE. Two views of a stone effigy pipe—figure of a woman; 6¼" high and 2⅛" wide. Lookout Mountain, Tennessee (Courtesy, The Reading Public Museum and Art Gallery, 32-390-1). The eye of this figure resembles the form of the "open eye" symbol. Many massive stone pipes carved by Mississippi Period craftsmen were in the round, effigy in form, and emphasized eyes, hands, legs and feet.

BELOW. LEFT. Steatite pipe with two stem openings—one on each end; bowl is in center; 3⅝" long; and 1¾" high. Graham County, North Carolina (Courtesy, The Reading Public Museum and Art Gallery, 32-702-1). RIGHT. Turtle peace pipe with two stem openings; diorite; 4" long; 2" high; and 2¼" wide; reddish brown. North Carolina (Courtesy, The Reading Public Museum and Art Gallery, 30-320-1). See Plate 130 for an example of a multiple stem pipe in pottery. These unusual pipes—with two to twelve stems—were mentioned by Colonial writers; some of them appear to have been made at an even earlier period.

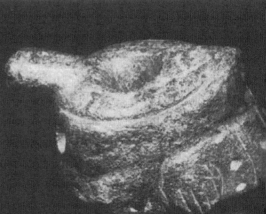

RIGHT. Two views of a stone pipe which appears to represent human sacrifice. The executioner has in his hand a claw shaped object, seemingly similar in shape to some of the ceremonial flints. Note, ear spools, clothing, board strapped to back and banded ornaments on arms and legs; 9¾" high (Courtesy, Museum of the American Indian, Heye Foundation, 21-4088).

BELOW. LEFT. Human effigy pipe of stone, painted in various colors; depicts person smoking a short-stem pipe; 22.4 cm. high; 22 cm. long; and 9.3 cm. wide. Spiro, Craig Burial Mound. RIGHT. Red pipestone human effigy pipe beautically carved; 23.4 cm. high. Spiro, Craig Burial Mound, Le Flore County, Oklahoma. (Both pipes are pictured Courtesy, University of Oklahoma, Stovall Museum).

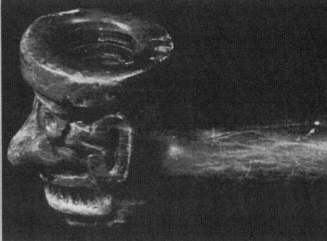

ABOVE. LEFT. Human effigy pipe, 5" long, 3½" high and 2" wide. Arkansas (Courtesy, The Reading Public Museum and Art Gallery, 32-395-1). RIGHT. Stone effigy pipe—human head; 5" long, 3" high. The impressions left by the reamer are plain inside the bowl. South Georgia (Courtesy, The Reading Public Museum and Art Gallery, 32-398-1).

"The careful worker sometime began his task by excavating both bowl and stem cavities. For this purpose drilling was necessary. . . . In order to enlarge the drill bores to any desired size, he resorted to the processes of reaming, scraping, or gouging. Specialized tools were employed for this purpose. . . .

"Many partly finished pipes are found which indicate that, in most instances, however, the pipe is brought nearly to the desired shape before the excavation of the bowl and stem cavities. . . .

"Saws made of stone were sometimes used to reduce the rock to the desired shape. The cord, with sand and water, was also employed for sawing stone.

"Abrasion was much used, which consisted in rubbing the specimen, where needed, with hard, gritty stone, or sand and water. Tools of chert, jasper, or other hard stone, fashioned into the form of scrapers and chisels, were skillfully employed in producing the carvings and other ornamentation, that so many ancient stone pipes possess. Incised lines and inlaid work required the employment of sharp-pointed instruments. . . . The tools employed for this fine work were not the frail, shattered splinters of rock, but carefully prepared narrow-bladed chisels and pointed awls, probably provided with short handles.

"Polishing of the pipe-bowl, when the material permitted a polish, was accomplished with sand, talc or other cutting material available. Buckskin or vegetable fabric was used in the final finish, and doubtless the rubbing of the human hand provided much of the gloss found in finer specimens." (G. A. West, TOBACCO PIPES. . . ., 1934, pp. 333-334; quoted by permission from the Milwaukee Public Museum).

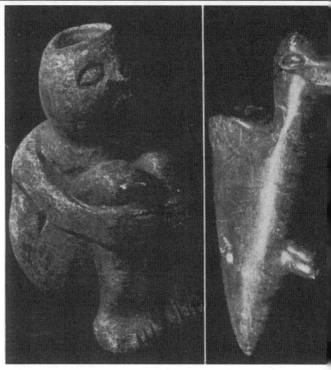

ABOVE. LEFT. Stone pipe in the form of a seated man; 6" high; 4¼" wide (back to front). Found in 1793. Bartow County, Georgia (Courtesy, The Reading Public Museum and Art Gallery, 32-391-1). RIGHT. Steatite bird pipe; 6½" long and 2¼" wide. Found in a grave in 1843. Bartow County, Georgia (Courtesy, The Reading Public Museum and Art Gallery, 32-396-1; photo by S. C. Gundy).

BELOW. LEFT. Frog effigy pipe of reddish-brown stone; 4⅛" long; 3¼" high; and 2¼" wide. Found in a grave in southern Tennessee in 1823 (Courtesy, The Reading Public Museum and Art Gallery, 32-392-1). RIGHT. Effigy pipe—cat, puma, tiger, or dog? 5¾" long. Moundville, Hale County, Alabama. A number of similar effigy pipes have been found at this site. Their facial markings are somewhat like those found on the so-called serpent effigy vessels from the Walls-Pecan point area, which are illustrated herein (Courtesy, Museum of the American Indian, Heye Foundation, 17-893). See Plates 54 and 124.

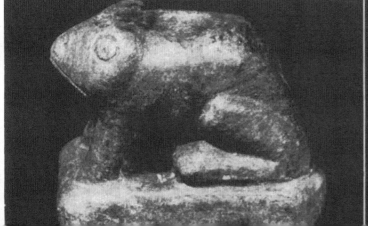

ABOVE. UPPER ROW. Two views of a frog effigy pipe made of red claystone; the spots are in the stone and are yellowish-white; it is 6½" high, 7⅛" long, and weighs 7½ pounds. It is from the Gahagan Mound, Red River Parish, Louisiana, and was removed from a burial pit during the excavations of Dr. Clarence H. Webb, M. D., and M. E. Dodd, Jr., in 1938 (Webb and Dodd, 1939) Dr. Webb describes the pipe:

"The figure is that of a large male frog, holding a female with the left paw or foreleg; the projection on the left side of the pipe is the head of the female frog; the male frog is expressing the eggs from the egg sac with the right paw. The egg sac is the round (cylindrical) object with a teat-like projection from the center. Naturalists have described this occurrence and undoubtedly the Indian artist was a good naturalist. The head of the female is almost inverted, as would be necessary for the lower abdomen and egg-sac to show in its position; the legs of the female would be more distinct, except that some weathering and scaling-off has occurred. They are beneath the right forepaw of the male. This pipe is an unusual naturalistic example of the fertility and reproductive theme which is indicated in several of the Spiro pipes, of approximately the same time period and culture, which is early Caddoan. The frog is undoubtedly a bull-frog, which is well represented in this state at the present time.

"This pipe is from the Gahagan mound; it was found in one of the two immense burial pits from which all of the other artifacts came. These pits were 19½ x 15 and 12 x 11 feet in diameters, and contained 6 and 3 burials, respectively. The site is located on the Red River, in Red River Parish, northwestern Louisiana." (quoted from correspondence). A human effigy stone pipe was also among the pit placements. Very few artifacts in these pits were "placed directly;" they were not arranged near the individual bodies of the deceased as were many "grave-goods" of the middle and late Mississippi Period burials. Most of the artifacts from these pits were found in groups on the floor along one side of each pit or in the mound fill. The artifacts found in these pits included excellent examples of prehistoric stone and copper objects, but there was little pottery; some of the pottery shreds showed red pigment in decoration; others had a black glossy surface engraved with fine lines in the form of concentric circles, scrolls, and triangles. Other burial pit placements included, fragments of baskets, a mass of marginella shells (ground holes in the shoulders), flint points—small and large; masses of galena, quartz crystal, celts, discoidals (chunkey stones), ear spools, shell beads, shell spoons, and many copper artifacts (described herein). For a further description of excavations at Gahagan, see Webb and Dodd, 1939— TEXAS ARCHEOLOGICAL AND PALEONTOLOGICAL SOCIETY, BU'LETIN, Vol. 11 (Courtesy, Dr. Clarence H. Webb, M. D., and M. E. Dodd, Jr., collection; displayed at the Louisiana State Exhibit Museum; photographs, Courtesy LSEM). See Plates 107-108.

The large, well-fashioned prehistoric pipes, as pictured above were doubtless ceremonial paraphernalia. De Batz in the Historic Period refers to "little idols" which might have been sacred pipes:

"There are at the door of the temple wooden figures of birds: there are in the temple a quantity of little idols, as well of wood as of stone, which represent dragons, serpents, and varities of frogs, which they keep inclosed in three coffers which are in the temple, and of which the great chief has the key." (Margry, 1875-86, vol. 5, pp. 467-469; Swanton, 1911, p. 282).

MASSIVE STONE PIPES — EFFIGIES

Plates 103 and 104

RIGHT. Four views of a large bird effigy pipe of dark reddish brown stone. This pipe was carefully carved on all sides; it appears to represent an owl. It was found near a river in a plowed field in Talladega County, Alabama, but probably was imported from the Tennessee-Kentucky-Carolina area where the large, carefully carved and polished bird pipes are more numerous. Mica filled the eyes when found, but disintegrated in cleaning. The workmanship is remarkable; it is about 6" long (Courtesy, John L. Ogletree, Jr.; photographs by the Bill Wilson Studio, Birmingham, Alabama).

OPPOSITE PAGE. LOWER ROW. LEFT. Large crayfish effigy pipe of reddish brown stone; it is a remarkably accurate depiction of an American crayfish, exemplifying the two large legs with pinchers in front; the four small legs on either side; and the five segments and bottom divisions of the tail. It represents the careful observation of the Indian artist. The bowl of the pipe is in the center of the top-back; the pipe is 6½" long, 4½" high, 3½" wide, and weighs 3½ pounds. It was found on Dauphin Island, Alabama in 1922 during an excavation for a house (Courtesy, Theodore R. Vaughan, Sr.; photograph by Harold Wigley). RIGHT. Large frog effigy platform pipe of weathered sandstone; 11.7" long; Claiborne County, Mississippi (Courtesy, Museum of the American Indian, 7294).

BELOW. Four large bird pipes of stone. UPPER ROW. LEFT. Unusual pipe with two effigy heads—a duck and an owl; 10" x 6". Scott County, Virginia (Courtesy, Smithsonian Institution, USNM, 211243). RIGHT. Large steatite bird pipe with hooked bill; 7¼" long. Coffee County, Tennessee (Courtesy, Museum of the American Indian, Heye Foundation, 7757). LOWER ROW. LEFT. Parrot pipe of mottled blackish stone, probably steatite; 29 cm. long, 10.5 cm. wide, and 11 cm. high. Tennessee (Courtesy, Brooklyn Museum, 41.235). RIGHT. Bird effigy pipe of steatite; it may represent a dove; 23 cm. long. Rowan County, North Carolina (Courtesy, H. M. Doerschuk). Bird pipes are most frequently found in the Tennessee-Carolina-Kentucky area. Their related culture complex has not been established, because they are often isolated finds. They appear to be of more recent origin than those shown on preceeding pages; however, they are more massive than typical Creek and Cherokee pipes of the Historic Period.

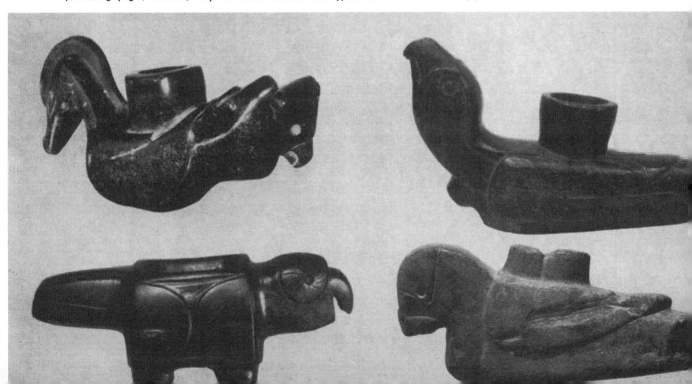

ABOVE. Animal and human effigy pipes, a tomahawk effigy pipe, and plain elbow pipes. Lower left. Note, metal inlay on stem, bowl, and bear. South and North Carolina (Courtesy, University Museum, University of Pennsylvania, 492, 2514, 2502, 2507, 2513, 2517, and others). James Adair (1775, p. 423) wrote the following regarding Cherokee pipes:

"They make beautiful stone pipes; and the Cherokee the best of any of the Indians: for their mountainous country contains many different sorts and colors of soils proper for such uses. They easily form them with their tomahawks, and afterward finish them in any desired form with their knives; the pipes being of a very soft quality till they are smoked with, and used to the fire, when they become quite hard. They are often a full span long, and the bowls are about half as large again as those of our English pipes. The forepart of each commonly runs out with a sharp peak, two or three fingers broad, and a quarter of an inch thick— on both sides of the bowl, lengthwise, they cut several pictures with a great deal of skill and labor, such as a buffalo and a panther on the opposite side of the bowl; a rabbit and fox; and, very often, a man and a woman puris natur alibus. Their sculpture cannot be much commended for its modesty. The savages work so slow, that one of their artists is two months at a pipe with his knife, before he finishes it. . . . The stems are commonly made of soft wood about two feet long, and an inch thick, cut into four squares, each scooped until they join very near the hollow of the stem."

STONE PIPES —
CHEROKEE AND CREEK

Plates 105 and 106

ABOVE. Animal effigy pipe with a small human on the stem facing the smoker; about 5½" long. Talladega County, Alabama (Courtesy, J. D. Wilkinson; photograph by Jack D. Ray).

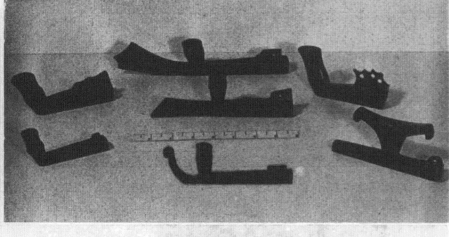
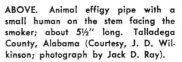

LEFT. Seven stone pipes; longest about 9"; steatite and catlinite (redstone). Coosa-Tallapoosa Valley area, Alabama. Several were found at the site of Sawogoni, which was reputedly a Shawnee town in the Creek Confederacy (Courtesy, Dr. R. P. Burke, M. D.; photograph by Arthur Reed). See Burke, 1937, AP 21:5-6:41-46.

LEFT. Five stone pipes, including boat, animal, and tomahawk effigy pipes; steatite and catlinite; longest about 7". Coosa-Tallapoosa Valley area, Alabama (Courtesy Alabama Department of Archives and History, McEwen Collection; photograph by Jack D. Ray).

RIGHT. Creek pipe of catlinite, about 6" long; effigy of a mother holding a child in front of her. The line on the side of the bowl of the pipe is an abrupt color change from dark red to reddish-pink stone, characteristic of some pieces of catlinite. It has the characteristic expanding base with a nob on top of the stem, and engraved parallel lines around the stem-opening. Talladega County, Alabama (Courtesy, F. George and N. Davis; photograph by Roy Howell). For pictures of other Creek pipes and references to their occurrence as burial associations see, Burke, 1937, and various copies of ARROWPOINTS. For pictures and a description of Cherokee pipes see, Witthoft, 1949. Colonial writers often mentioned the natives' tobacco pipes. Pipes are frequently found with Creek burials.

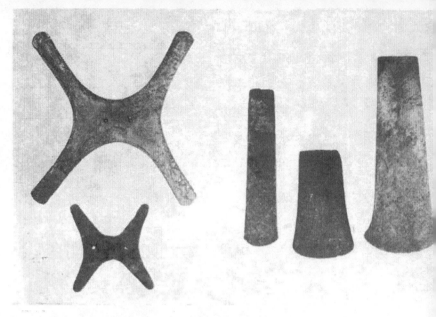

RIGHT. NEAR. Reel-shaped ornaments or tools of copper. Found at Woodland Period sites; typical of the Copena Culture; large reel, 6" longest measurement. Tennessee River area, Alabama (Courtesy, Museum of the American Indian). FAR. Three copper celts; longest is 7¾"; the one on the left has the print of the haft near the narrow end. Alabama (Courtesy, Museum of the American Indian, Heye Foundation).

BELOW. UPPER. Two copper earspools. LOWER. Outline d r a w i n g s showing methods of making copper ear spools. B is a galena and clay filled spool (Courtesy, Alabama Museum of Natural History). Ear spools are sometimes found with cordage wrapped around the central cylinder. It probably held the spools apart.

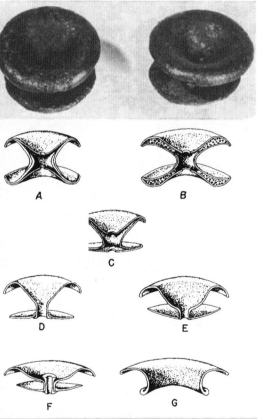

A   B

C

D   E

F   G

COPPER CEREMONIAL OBJECTS AND ORNAMENTS

Plates 107 and 108

BELOW. Copper artifacts from the Gahagan Mound, Red River Parish, Louisiana. LEFT. Two long nose copper masks; the head is 2¾" high and nose is 7½" long. The head of the mask is 2" wide. Williams and Goggin, 1956, give an interesting comparison of similar "Long Nosed God" masks and mention others found at the Grant Mound, St. Johns River, Florida, the Big Mound, St. Louis, and Aztalan, Wisconsin. Gahagan is the only site in which a pair has been found, and these are in a relatively good state of preservation. A pipe found at Spiro (Hamilton, 1952, Pl. 10; pipe is owned by the University of Arkansas) shows similar objects worn as ear ornaments, possibly attached to a wooden frame. RIGHT. Copper hands, 4½" long and 3¾" maximum width (All copper artifacts pictured here from the Gahagan Mound are from *the collection of Dr. C. E. Webb, M. D., and M. E. Dodd, Jr.,* and are exhibited at the Louisiana State Exhibit Museum; photographs by the museum; reproduced by permission from the museum and owners).

"Of greatest interest are the copper ceremonial objects, especially the human effigy masks or faces, each made from two sheets, one cut to form the oval face, the other to form a long grotesque nose which was inserted through a slit in the face and bradded with narrow copper strips. A groove across the forehead with lateral holes allowed for attachment of the mask."

Regarding shell ornaments, Webb described "seven shell ear ornaments, largest an unperforated disc form, 1½" in diameter. Four have copper bosses on one surface, covering the perforations and the knot for attaching the string (preserved by copper) . . . . The most remarkable shell group is the mass of over 300 beads made from marginella shells. Similar beads, prepared for stringing by grinding a hole in the shoulder, were described by Moore with Caddo pottery at the Douglas site, on the Arkansas River below Little Rock; also in the Spoon River focus in Illinois by Cole and Deuel." Webb refers to the "Florida sequences," Coles Creek pottery similarities. Hopewellian-type traits, and other comparisons (Webb and Dodd, 1939, pp. 107 and 108; quoted by permission from the Editor of the Texas Archeological Society, Austin).

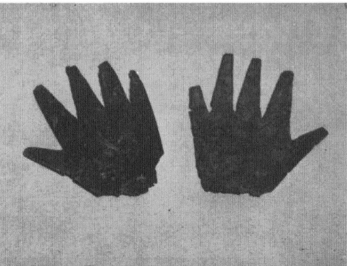

ABOVE. LEFT AND RIGHT. Two embossed copper hair ornaments; one bi-lobed with a feather type object on top which has been broken. They show evidence of riveting. The one on the right still has a fragment of a bone pin attached. Left—11⅝'' high; Nashville, Tennessee. Right—10'' high; Jackson County, Alabama. CENTER. UPPER. Pair of copper disc ear ornaments; 2¼'' wide; Montgomery County, Alabama. LOWER. Two copper gorgets; 4'' diameter. Alabama (Courtesy, Museum of the American Indian, Heye Foundation; hair ornaments—15-868 and 7960; ear ornaments—17-3077; and gorgets—17-3117 and 17-202).

RIGHT. Hafted ceremonial copper celts; the wooden handle is carved at the top to represent the head of a crested bird with mouth open (facing back of blade) and tongue out; shell inlay eye; longest blade, 8⅝''; longest handle, 17''. The Spiro Mound, Le Flore County, Oklahoma (Courtesy, Museum of the American Indian, Heye Foundation, 18-9077).

BELOW. Copper artifacts from the Gahagan Mound, Louisiana. LEFT. Parts of ear ornaments—copper over wood; the metal has almost worn off two specimens. Also, a copper bead and a copper over wood bead; longest bead, 2½''; largest square 3⅛''. CENTER AND RIGHT. Back and front views of stone disk ear spools, largest 2½'' diameter. These were covered on their outer surface with a thin layer of copper. There is also an imitation animal tooth of wood which is covered with copper (Courtesy, Louisiana State Exhibit Museum and Dr. C. E. Webb, M. D., and M. E. Dodd, Jr., collection; photograph by the museum).

"Of the 29 ear ornaments from Pits 2 and 3 at Gahagan, 15 are copper-coated and two are made of sheet copper alone. The latter two are large square plaques of sheet copper, with concentric circles or squares in repousse. Three elliptical beads of wood are each covered with a single sheet of copper. The five curved pendants of copper-covered wood, found in one group, are undoubtedly bear-claw effigies, similar to those of bone or stone found in some of the Ohio mounds." (Webb and Dodd, 1939, p. 104; quoted by permission from the Editor of the Texas Archeological Society, University of Texas, Austin).

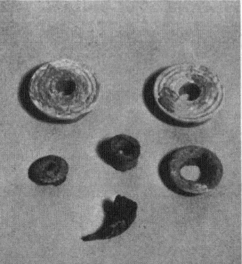

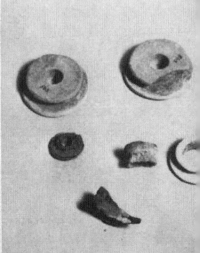

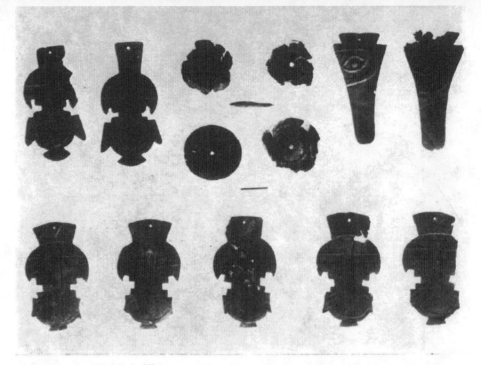

RIGHT. Copper pendants and ear ornaments found with the elaborate burial pictured in Chapter I, Plate 6. Lauderdale County, Alabama. (Courtesy, Alabama Museum of Natural History; BAE. Bull. 129, 1942, Pl. 253, figure 1). In that publication Webb and DeJarnette (pp. 227-229) describe these artifacts:

"There were 11 artifacts of copper with burial No. 23. . . . Two were copper ear ornaments made by covering circular disks of wood (cedar) with very thin sheet copper. These copper ornaments were embossed in circular form, each outer surface having two concentric circles. The wooden disks were well preserved by the copper salts and appear so truly of circular form as to suggest that they were turned on a lathe. In these wooden disks the outer surface, which was very smooth, was raised into a circular cone which fitted exactly into a similar cone pressed into the copper coating. This raised cone in the embossed copper coating was concentric with the two embossed concentric circles on the outer face. Each of these ornaments was associated with a bone pin about 1 inch long, which appears to have been set into the wooden disk perpendicular to its under face, and perhaps was a pin through the ear for attachment. One of these pins, copper stained, is also shown in the picture.

"A total of nine very thin copper pendants . . . were found in association near the pelvis of skeleton No. 23. These pendants are stamped or cut from very thin sheet copper. The edges are cut and smooth, the corners and points sharp and complete. There is no evidence of the use of shears, which would seem to suggest that they were made by being stamped and cut over a die. Seven of these pendants are embossed with a cross, placed symmetrically over the long dimension of the pendant. The over-all dimensions of these pendants are: length, 3.2 inches, and maximum breadth, 1.8 inches. Five of these pendants are nearly exact duplicates of each other, both in the pattern of the edge design and the embossed crosses. These five are shown in the lower row. Two others, duplicates of each other in form, but differing from the first five, have the same embossed cross. The remaining two, duplicates of a third form, have only the eye design embossed thereon. The exactness of the forms of these duplicates and the embossed patterns would seem to argue that they were cut and embossed, all of each kind, at the same time by the same process. At the upper end of these pendants, in a flared extension of the sheet, is embossed a triangle in the center of which is a small hole, made by punching a sharp needle through the sheet copper. The rim of the hole is rough on one side only, showing the direction from which the tool was thrust. Found with these pendants was a small copper pin which fits this hole and, seemingly, was used to hold them all together. One of the set of five pendants had been broken in two just below the expanded extension at the top by which it was suspended. It was repaired by overlapping the two broken edges and using a small strip of thin copper as a staple-shaped rivet. The ends of the thin sheet of copper were bent down on the reverse side. The effect of this repair was to shorten the pendant by about 0.25 inch and make it a little thicker at the junction.

"In general appearance, these nine pendants are quite similar to four lots of copper pendants reported by Moore. Two of these lots, one of seven and one of eight, were found at Thirty Acre Field (Moore, 1900, p. 334), Montgomery County, Ala. One lot of 11 pendants was found on the Charlotte Thompson place (Moore, 1900, p. 327), Montgomery County, Ala. The other lot of 13 was found with a burial in Mound H at Moundville (Moore, 1905). Of this last group, in speaking of burial No. 2, Moore says:

'Near the right elbow were thirteen pendants of sheet copper all similar but no two exactly alike, each in the form of an arrowhead, bearing a repousse eye. These lay with the bases together, the pointed ends spread in fan shaped fashion as if the bases had been strung together through a perforation in each, and the points had spread somewhat on the arm.'

"The suggestion that a number of pendants were attached together is quite in accord with the finding at this site. The 'repousse eye' seems to be common to some of the pendants in every group. In the excavation of Mound C (the temple mound) at Etowah, Moorehead (1932, p. 40, fig. 17) found 10 copper pendants made from thin sheet copper, and each embossed with a cross. These were very similar to a group of 14 copper pendants taken from the same mound during the excavation of Thomas (1894) for the Bureau of American Ethnology. These pendants all bear the embossed cross, but are thought by Willoughby (1932, p. 42) to be miniature representations of a ceremonial baton. Many other copper pendants were found by Thomas at Etowah. Some of these are very elaborate representations of dancing warriors. The human figures thus portrayed, . . . carried in the hand a 'baton' very similar in form to these small copper pendants." (Quoted courtesy, Smithsonian Institution, Bureau of American Ethnology, Bulletin 129).

LEFT. Copper gorget with embossed circles and cross design. Regarding recent explorations at the Etowah mound, Lewis H. Larson, Jr., states, "We have found copper sun symbols all of which are rather fragmentary. We have two fragmentary copper plates now in the process of restoration which bore human or anthropomorphized eagle designs, one sheet hair ornament with an eagle design, also fragmentary, and one large copper plate with the open-eye or ogee design." (Courtesy, Georgia Historical Commission).

LEFT. Oval objects of wood covered on one side with thin sheet copper, a narrow band of which has been turned under on the undecorated, smooth, reverse side of the wood. In shape these resemble chipped flint blades. Each has a symmetrically carved design, over which the copper was carefully worked. One design appears to imitate a leaf pattern; nature designs are very rare in primitive art. The other two objects have a series of carved circles down and on either side of a central axis. Off center, toward the blunter end is an uncarved band which was not covered with copper, but has fragments of red cordage still adhered to it. The lower object has four corner perforations (two with cordage in them) in the band. These are described by Burnett, 1945, p. 41 (Courtesy, Museum of the American Indian, Heye Foundation, 20-703, 20-704, 18-9333).

COPPER CEREMONIAL OBJECTS

Plates 109 and 110

BELOW. Copper pendants and a restored gorget; longest pendant is about 4¾". Alabama (Courtesy, Museum of the American Indian, Heye Foundation, 17-200, 17-201, 17-156, and 17-203).

At Moundville Clarence B. Moore found several copper pendants and gorgets which had a single pearl attached to the center top, where the suspension holes are located.

In regard to copper pendants, Webb and DeJarnette (1942, pp. 297-298) write:

"These artifacts are usually found in burial association. They are made from very thin sheet copper and usually occur in groups of 5 to 15 in a single cache. They are usually embossed, and the outline carefully cut to form. They are approximately 4 inches long and about 1.5 inches broad."

Webb and DeJarnette give 13 references regarding the finding of these ornaments and show on a map that similar ornaments have been found in Montgomery, Hale (Moundville), and Lauderdale Counties, Alabama, and at Etowah, Georgia. Lewis and Kneberg (1954, p. 33, Figure 2) show an example of such a pendant, 3½" long, found in a child burial in Cheatham County, Tennessee. Webb and DeJarnette conclude (1942, p. 297):

"From the number of occurrences in and about Moundville, it would appear that Moundville may well be regarded as the center of distribution of this type of artifacts." (Quoted, courtesy, Smithsonian Institution, Bureau of American Ethnology, Bulletin 129).

ABOVE. Fragments of a large embossed copper plate; 17" long and 9" wide. Etowah, Georgia (After Thomas, 1894, Plate XVII, p. 305). A line drawing of this is shown in Plate 20. Willoughby (1932, p. 45-47) states: "In cutting out such patterns as (the eagle) after the sheet was prepared the only tools necessary were a good supply of grinding stones and sharp flints, with perhaps a few simple implements of bone, plus an abundance of patience which most Indian workmen possess." (Quoted, permission of Yale University Press, and Phillips Academy). In addition they probably used wooden tools for embossing sheet copper plates. They hammered the copper sheets from copper nuggets believed to have been transported from the Lake Superior area. The large copper plates are made of several sheets of copper riveted together. Watson (1950) describes the riveting present on the Wulfing Plates (Missouri). Such work was similar on pieced copper plates.

Chapter 7

POTTERY

Quotation from John R. Swanton, THE INDIANS OF THE SOUTH-EASTERN UNITED STATES, Bureau of American Ethnology, Bulletin 137, 1946, pp. 549-555—excerpts. Quoted courtesy, Smithsonian Institution, Bureau of American Ethnology.

"In 1541, when the Chickasaw attacked De Soto's army, then in occupancy of their town, Biedma tells us that, after the manner of Gideon, they brought fire in little pots, presumably made of clay, with which to ignite the houses.[1] We are also told that large pots were used in making salt in the province of Tanico, probably in southern Arkansas.[2]

"Although Du Pratz's description of pottery making is thrown into a hypothetical form, it seems to represent the process as he had observed it among the Natchez. He says that the women

'go in search of heavy earth, examine it in the form of dust (i.e., before it had been wet), throwing out whatever grit they find, make a sufficiently firm mortar, and then establish their workshop on a flat board, on which they shape the pottery with their fingers, smoothing it by means of a stone which is preserved with great care for this work. As fast as the earth dries they put on more, assisting with the hand on the other side. After all these operations, it is baked by means of a great fire.

'These women also make pots of an extraordinary size, jugs with a medium-sized opening, bowls, two-pint bottles with long necks, pots or jugs for bear's oil, which hold as many as 40 pints, also dishes and plates like those of the French. I have had some made out of curiosity on the model of my earthenware. They were of a rather beautiful red color.'[3]

"Du Pratz says also:

'(Between the Tunica town opposite the mouth of Red River and the Natchez are) many bluffs which occur together; among them is the one called Ecore Blanc, because one finds there many veins of white earth, rich and very fine with which I have seen very beautiful pottery made. On the same bluff one sees veins of ocher which the Natchez get to daub on their pottery which was very pretty; when it was coated with ocher it became red on being baked.'[4]

'Quite close to Natchitoches are banks of cockle-shells like those of which is formed the Isle aux Coquilles. This neighboring nation says that their ancient word teaches them that the sea formerly came to this place; the women of this nation go there to collect them, they make of them a powder which they mix with the earth of which they make their pottery which is recognized to be of the best.'[5]

"Dumont[6] says that the women made 'all kinds of earthen vessels, dishes, plates, pots to put on the fire, with others large enough to contain 25 to 30 pots of oil.' Elsewhere he continues at length thus:

'Moreover, the industry of these Indian girls and women is admirable. I have already reported elsewhere with what skill, with their fingers alone and without a potter's wheel they make all sorts of pottery.

'After having gathered the earth suitable for this kind of work, and having well cleansed it, they take shells which they grind and reduce to a very fine powder; they mix this very fine dust with the earth which they have provided, and, moistening the whole with a little water, they knead it with the hands and feet, forming a dough of which they make rolls 6 or 7 feet long and of whatever thickness is desired. Should they wish to fashion a dish or a vessel, they take one of these rolls and, holding down one end with the thumb of the left hand they turn it around with admirable swiftness and dexterity, describing a spiral; from time to time they dip their fingers in water, which they are always careful to have near them, and with the right hand they smooth the inside and outside of the vessel they intend to form, which, without this care, would be undulated.

'In this manner they make all sorts of utensils of earth, dishes, plates, pans, pots, and pitchers, some of which contain 40 and 50 pints. The baking of this pottery does not cause them much trouble. After having dried it in the shade they build a great fire, and when they think they have enough coals they clear a place in the middle where they arrange the vessels and cover them with the coals. It is thus that they give them the baking which is necessary. After this they can be placed on the fire and have as much firmness as ours. Their strength can only be attributed to the mixture which the women make of the powdered shells with the clay.[7]

"The work of the neighboring Tunica also seems to have been good. Gravier says that they 'have no riches but earthenware pots, quite well made, especially little glazed[8] pitchers, as neat as you would see in France'[9] Pénicaut found the Pascagoula women making 'large earthen pots, almost like big kettles, which hold perhaps 40 pints, and in which they have hominy cooked enough for two or three families,' the cooks taking turns providing it. He adds that 'these pots are of clay and of a round shape almost like windmills.'[10]

---

[1] Bourne, 1904, vol. 2, p. 23. [2] Robertson, 1933, p. 193. [3] Le Page du Pratz, 1758, vol. 2, pp. 178-179; Swanton, 1911, p. 62.
[4] Le Page du Pratz, 1758, vol. 1, p. 124. [5] Le Page du Pratz, 1758, vol. 1, pp. 163-164. [6] Dumont, 1753, Vol. 1, p. 154.
[7] Dumont, 1753, vol. 2, pp. 271-273 (as translated in Holmes, 1903, p. 57). [8] Indian pottery was never glazed, but rather highly polished by careful rubbing. [9] Shea, 1861, p. 135; Swanton, 1911, p. 315. [10] Penicaut in Margry, 1875-86, vol. 5, pp. 388-389; Swanton, 1911, p. 303.

"Bartram[11] states that the clay out of which the Creeks made pottery, as well as that which they used as plaster for their buildings, was generally obtained in a large artificial pond 'just without the town,' where they also cultivated, or rather kept, angelico.

"Although this industry no longer exists among the Creeks, I obtained two descriptions given by old people from memory, and a third from a member of the incorporated Alabama tribe. Jackson Lewis, the Hitchiti informant, said that when a woman wanted to make a pot she hunted about until she found a clay that would not crack, and, if she could not discover such a clay, she mixed the clay she could get with the finest sand, thereby accomplishing the same result. In shaping the pot she first laid down a flat piece to form the base, and then made a ribbon of the remaining clay which she led round and round spirally, adding to her ribbon as required, until the pot was completed. Then she would take a mussel shell and smooth the pot with it both outside and inside. The inside surface, however, she made appear almost as if glazed by rubbing it with a small stone. . . . She sometimes ornamented the edges of the pot by pinching it between two fingers. The pot was fired by turning it upside down upon the ground, leaning various combustibles against it all about, and setting these on fire. As fast as the fagots gave way, she replaced them until the pot became red hot, when she allowed the fire to burn out and the pot to cool. During the baking, and while the pot was still very hot, she might take the feather of a turkey and trace designs on the outside with the quill end. As she did this, the quill would burn and color the parts of the pot over which it was passing. Sometimes they got some very red stones found here and there in the hills, and perhaps the same as those out of which they made their red paint, pounded them into powder, and put some on the end of a stick with which they then made designs in the same manner as with the quill. Designs might also be made by making incisions with a pointed stick before the pot had hardened. So far as Lewis knew, they never put netting over their pots during the process of manufacture, but they took a corncob and stroked the sides of very large pots to roughen their surfaces if they were to be used in cooking.

"My Upper Creek interpreter, Zach Cook, said that the potters of his acquaintance first laid down a flat piece of clay for a foundation and then coiled a thin strip round and round for the superstructure. They either used the clay, described as a blue pipe clay, plain, or else pounded up pieces of old pottery and mixed them with it. They claimed that this latter kind was the stronger. . . .

"According to my Alabama informant, Charlie Thompson, later chief of the Texas band, pots were made of fine white or dark blue clay mixed with a smaller quantity of burned bones and white sand to prevent them from cracking. . . .

"Adair's description is presumably particularly applicable to the Chickasaw, but might also have covered the Creeks and the Cherokee:

'They make earthen pots of very different sizes, so as to contain from two to ten gallons; large pitchers to carry water; bowls, dishes, platters, basons, and a prodigious number of other vessels of such antiquated forms, as would be tedious to describe, and impossible to name. Their method of glazing them, is, they place them over a large fire of smoky pitch pine, which makes them smooth, black, and firm. Their lands abound with proper clay, for that use; and even with porcelain, as has been proved by experiment.'[12]

"Speck says that the pots of Taskigi Creeks were made

'of clean red clay coiled upon a disk-like base. To fire these they were covered with dried grass and the mass was ignited. When the combustible covering had burned off the pot was black, and so hard that it could withstand the effects of daily contact with fire. Pipes of unbaked clay are still made in some of the remote parts of the Taskigi district.[13]

"Paint was made of red ocher, lampblack, black lead, cinnabar, and tobacco-pipe clay. The walls of houses, and often walls and roofs, were made of clay mixed with grass or Spanish moss."[14]

Pottery is considered a product of the Woodland and Mississippi Periods.[15] Woodland natives experimented with a variety of decorative techniques—incised lines; fingernail, brush, comb, and reed marks; cord and fabric marks; stamps—dentate, crenulate, roulette, checker, parallel, and complicated; and (rarely) paint. However, incised lines and paint did not flourish until the Mississippi Period. In addition to fiber-tempered pottery, Woodland people used a variety of granular tempering materials including, sand, clay, grit, crushed stone—limestone and others. Mississippian peoples added crushed shell to the list.

[11] Bartram, 1792, p. 325. Swanton states (p. 551), "In 1739 Governor Oglethorpe observed the Indians of Coweta town 'dress their Meat in Large pans made of Earth and not much unlike our Beehives in England' (Bushnell, 1908, p. 573) . . . Swan noted among the Upper Creek 'earthen pots . . . from one pint up to six gallons . . . they have no variety of fashion; these vessels are all without handles, and are drawn so nearly to a point at the bottom, that they will not stand alone.' (Swan, 1855, p. 692)." [12] Adair, 1775, p. 456. [13] Speck, 1907, p. 109. [14] Swanton, 1946, p. 243. [15] Found at Late Archaic site, Poverty Point, La., (Ford and Webb, 1956).

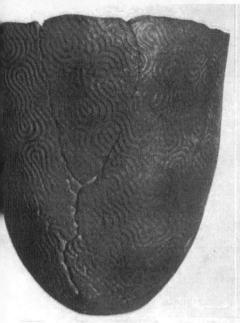
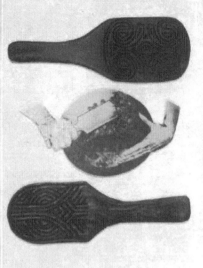
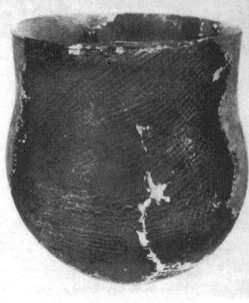

ABOVE. LEFT. Plaster cast of a vessel with Swift Creek complicated stamp; 9¾" high. Ocmulgee National Monument, Georgia (Courtesy, National Park Service). CENTER. Reproduction of two carved wooden paddles of a type probably used for impressing designs on pottery vessels. Ocmulgee, Macon, Georgia (Courtesy, National Park Service). RIGHT. Pottery vessel with a check-stamp design; it has been restored; about 9" high. Clark County, Alabama (Courtesy, Alabama Museum of Natural History).

WOODLAND PERIOD POTTERY

Plates 111 and 112

LEFT. Fabric-marked pottery vessel; 10½" high. Decoration was made by impressing a net or loosely woven fabric on the soft clay before firing. Cordmarking was also a Woodland method of decorating vessels. Yadkin County, North Carolina (Courtesy, Wachovia Museum, 41-P-19).

BELOW. LEFT. Zone-stamped pottery vessel with a "reverse swastika" design; 8" high; 5" diameter at top; and 3⅛" diameter at the bottom which is approximately square. Incised lines and rocker stamp. From a mound in Pocosin Hammock, Gulf of Mexico, near Horseshoe, Florida (Courtesy, Mrs. H. H. Simpson; photograph, courtesy, Florida State Museum). RIGHT. Sand tempered pottery vessel with incurving, notched rim; about 9" maximum diameter; 5½" rim diameter. It appears to be dentate stamping (Courtesy, A. W. Beinlich).

The vessels on this plate are zone-stamped pottery vessels from a Woodland Period site, Marksville, La. These vessels appeared in an article by Frank M. Setzler, 1933, "Pottery of the Hopewell Type from Louisiana." (see bibliography). The vessel on the right at the top of the page is an excellent example of zoned stamping; it has wide incised lines outlining the zoomorphic form— snake or bird effigy, and a type of dentate stamping enhances the design. Note, cross-hatching at the rim and fingernail prints or punctates beneath. (These pictures are reproduced, courtesy, Smithsonian Institution, United States National Museum). For further examples of Marksville and Marksville type pottery, see Setzler, 1933; Griffin, 1952, Figs. 140 and 141; and Ford and Willey, 1940. The artifacts pictured and described by Setzler were excavated by G. Fowke in the Red River Valley, Louisiana, in 1926.

RIGHT. Pottery vessel, 4⅜" high; 3¼" diameter (331688)—USNM number. In addition to this zone stamped ware, there were plain, undecorated vessels and incised pottery vessels at this site.

BELOW. Six Marksville vessels. The two vessels on the lower row decorated with hearts and zoomorphic forms are 4-13/16" high and 5⅛" maximum diameter (331689 and 113697). They have notched rims. The vessel, upper row center, has a decoration beneath the rim which characterizes a number of Marksville vessels—a series of alternate short parallel lines and punctates; it is 4" high and 6-23/32" diameter (331696). Vessel, upper left, is about 4" high (331686). Vessel, upper right, odd shaped (331700); vessel, lower center, shoe-shape (331694). See J. B. Griffin, 1952, Fig. 140 for a summary drawing picturing the Marksville complex.

". . . the Marksville works contained one vessel (upper right) that can be considered a typical Hopewell vessell. In addition, the other vessels from Mounds 4 and 8 embody one or more typical Hopewell characteristics. More than this, the variety of forms at Marksville not only shows designs characteristic of the typical Hopewell in the North, but these same vessels have certain features that are similar to other southeastern pottery decorations." (p. 21). "Independent invention of so complicated a technique of decoration where there is such striking similarity would seem improbable." (p. 6) Setzler describes the resemblances as "deeply incised grooves . . . cross-hatched incised lines and the encircling line of bisected cones (just below the rim) . . . parts of the vessel . . . roughened uniformly . . . by means of the roulette . . . (or) concentric grooves or bands . . . (or) by means of zigzag lines." (p. 5). He points out however, "the tempering used in the Marksville pottery (either pulverized potsherds or small particles of hard clay) differs radically from that common to the northern Mississippi (Hopewell) type (grit or shell)." (p. 6). The bases of the Marksville vessels he examined were flat, and there was only one 4-lobed vessel resulting from Fowke's excavation.

Some of the many references to Woodland pottery types are found in: Burke, 1933, 1934—Cent. Ala.; Caldwell and McCann, 1941—Ga.; Fairbanks, 1956—Ga.; Ford, 1935, 1936, 1951—La.; Ford and Willey, 1940—La.; Goggin, 1947 and others—Fla.; J. B. Griffin, 1939—Wheeler Basin, Ala.; 1950, 1952—Southeast; Haag, 1942—Pickwick Basin, Ala.-Miss.-Tenn.; Moore (intermittent through series); Phillips, Ford, and Griffin, 1951—Lower Miss. Valley; Sears, 1956—Ga.-Fla.; Suhm, 1954—Texas-La.; Webb, 1938—Norris Basin, Tenn.; Webb and Wilder, 1951—Guntersville Basin, Ala.; Willey, 1949—Fla.

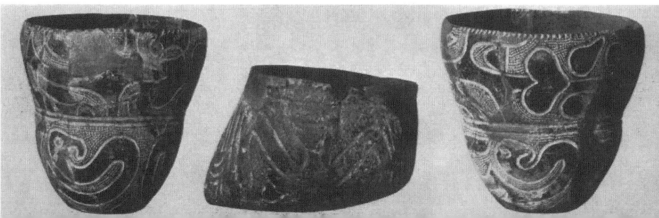

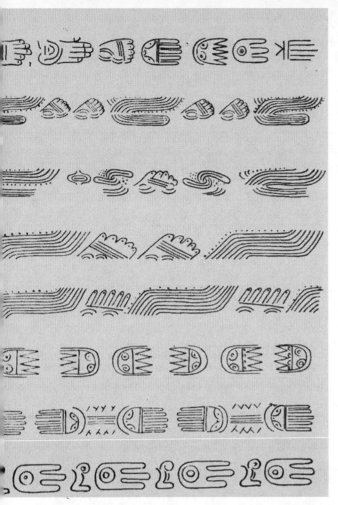

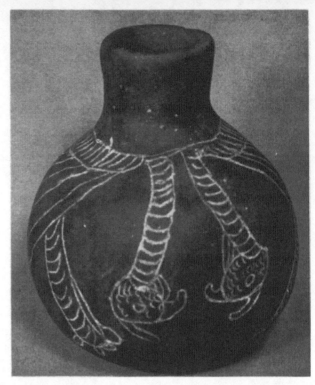

ABOVE. Shell-tempered vessel about 5½" high; the design covers the body of the vessel; it is chalked to show the detail of the turkey design—there are two inverted heads, two feet, two wings, and three tail feathers; the latter are opposite the head or on the back of the vessel. One foot projects near the base of each head. The lines are thin. Elmore County, Alabama (Courtesy, Wiley Hill, III; photograph by John Scott).

LEFT. Bands of designs which are incised above the shoulder of pottery vessels found in the Gulf coast area of Alabama and northwestern Florida. The hand was a prominent design element; other cult designs found in similar band-type decorations were the bone, step, circle, slanting eye, forked eye, and ogee (After Holmes, 1903, Pl. LXXXIII). See J. B. Griffin, 1952, Fig. 182 for other cult designs of the Gulf Coast-Fort Walton focus.

BELOW. UPPER ROW. Three well polished black-filmed vessels from Limestone and Lauderdale Counties, Alabama. The designs have been chalked for photographing. Left. Bowl with incurving rim; it appears to have been a bottle reworked around the rim; maximum diameter, 6½" (Courtesy, Dr. F. J. Soday). Center. Cup with slightly curving, wide, flat handle; unusual design repeated around outside; 3" x 4½" (Courtesy, P. Kyle). Right. Water bottle with two winged serpents with plumes, forked eye, and rattles; ogee with barred oval is repeated on the neck; 6¾" high; maximum diameter, 7⅜" (Courtesy, A. W. Beinlich).

LEFT. CENTER ROW. Three vessels from Moundville, Alabama. After Clarence B. Moore. Left. Cup with skull and hand and eye design repeated around vessel, 4.75" diameter; Moore, 1905, Fig. 62. Center. Unusual rectangular vessel with steps design, 2.6" high; Moore, 1907, Fig. 23. Right. Water bottle with hand and eye design, 5.7" diameter; Moore, 1905, Fig. 21. LOWER ROW. Three pottery vessels. Left. Vessel with decoration appliqued on sides—it is a repetition of hands; 5.4" high. Walls, Mississippi. Davies Collection. University of Mississippi (Courtesy Mississippi Geological Survey; after Brown, 1926). Center. Unusual pottery vessel from Moundville, Alabama; 6.2" high. After Moore, 1907, Fig. 22. Right. Bird design with two wings—one on either side —and a tail and two feet behind. The loop eye is like the eye on the ceremonial stone bird-bowl from Moundville, Alabama. Lauderdale County, Alabama (Courtesy, Alabama Museum of Natural History, BAE, Bull. 129, Pl. 119). Moundville led all sites in producing ceremonial vessels with engraved cult designs. See Plates 33-38. These were cut into black filmed vessels.

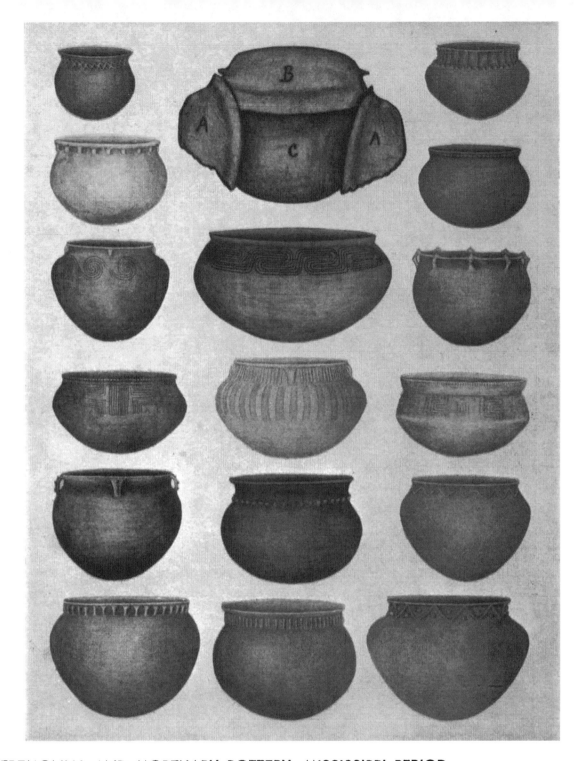

CEREMONIAL AND MORTUARY POTTERY—MISSISSIPPI PERIOD

Plates 113 and 114

ABOVE. Drawings of burial urns; these were drawn by Dr. R. P. Burke, M. D., Montgomery, Alabama; they depict a variety of burial urns from the Lower Tallapoosa-Upper Alabama River area. (Reproduced by permission from Dr. R. P. Burke, M. D.). Those pictured range from 4" to 14" diameter. The large covered vessel at the center top, represents an urn (C) or receptacle for bones; it is covered with a typical flare-rim vessel (B) which has a typical design engraved on the inside of its rim (not showing); it was an unusual urn burial because a third vessel, broken in half (A), was placed, half on each side of the urn, perhaps for a ceremonial purpose. These vessels are shell-tempered, and in Dr. Burke's field notes, each is carefully identified as to site, color, and size. Though these burial urns show a variety of decorations, the majority of the receptacle urn vessels from this area are undecorated except for strap or loop handles or appliqued nodes or strips around the neck. The most extensive burial urn site yet investigated was at Taskigi. Many of the urns contained the bones of a single person; some held multiple burials at Taskigi. Regarding urn burial at that site, P. A. Brannon states (1935, Vol. 20, pp. 40-41):

"In view of the fact that by far the larger number of urn-burials (at Taskigi) are babies and children, the majority of cases show only decayed bones and many cases show no bones. . . . It (the burial urn) is merely a domestic vessel which was used to bury the dead when this occasion arrived. . . . The cover, in most cases, is, artistically speaking, and even from quality of the ware, much superior to the urn." (Bones of adults were cleaned and disarticulated before being placed into urns).

"Burial urns from the lower Tallapoosa range in size from ten inches in diameter to as much as thirty inches. We have found several cases where there were the bones of what was assumed to have been a still born child, and the urn was hardly over four inches at the rim. This is rare." Globular vessels were usually receptacles for bones. See Plates 39 and 40 for urn covers.

PAINTED POTTERY

Plates 115 and 116

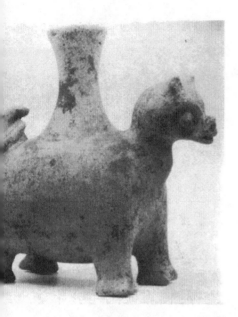

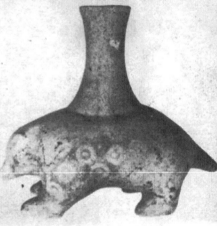

LEFT. Long-neck, shell-tempered pottery, animal effigy bottle; 8½" high and 8¾" long. From a stone grave; Cumberland River, Tennessee (Courtesy, Peabody Museum, Harvard University, 13994).

RIGHT. UPPER. Shell-tempered effigy bottle; with the faint remains in negative painting of sun-circles on the body and the neck; parallel lines around center neck and tail; 8" high (Courtesy, University of Tennessee). LOWER. Shell-tempered effigy bottle. Webb and DeJarnette (1942, p. 53) state:

"This water bottle, an effigy representing possibly a coon or bear, is 8 inches in height and has a maximum length (nose to tail) of 9 inches. The surface of this vessel, originally a cream-yellow colored clay, has been painted by the application of a light brown stain to produce the effect of circular spots. These spots—almost invisible to the eye because of the leaching effect of the earth in which the vessel was buried—are easily photographed on any film sensative to red. The paint was applied to produce a negative image, i. e., the background was painted out leaving the image to be formed in the natural color of the clay." North Alabama (Courtesy, Alabama Museum of Natural History; BAE Bull, 129, Pl. 63, Fig. 1).

The best painted designs were often applied to long-neck bottles. At some sites, as Moundville, Alabama, ceremonial symbols were frequently painted on bottles and unusual shapes, as rectangular vessels. In the Middle Mississippi Valley area, where geometric designs (and quantity) predominated, many ceremonial symbols were used on both bottles and bowls; C. B. Moore pictures a shallow bowl from that area with a pained human design—the rarest of all their painted designs. Symbols on vessels pictured here include the sun circle, cross, star, hand, skull, and step. See also Plates 8, 51, 52, and 118. Paints were made from mineral and vegetal substances including, ochre, galena, graphite, roots, barks, and berries; it was often applied before firing.

BELOW. Three effigy owls. LEFT. Water bottle about 12" high. Tennessee (Courtesy, University of Tennessee). CENTER. Bottle painted to imitate texture of feathers. Shell-tempered; 6⅜" high; traces of reddish-brown slip on head and shoulders. The surface was scaling-off, so it was varnished which gives it a more glazed appearance; it was well polished, but no native pottery was glazed. Davidson County, Tennessee (Courtesy, Vanderbilt University). RIGHT. Owl effigy with feather marks painted on back; found near skull of a burial; on each side of head were conch shells—one 18" long. Monroe County, Tennessee (After Thomas, 1894, pp. 386-87). The keenly observant native artists created excellent characterizations of humans, birds, and animals.

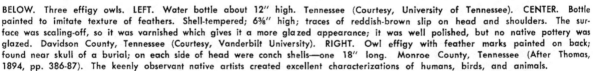

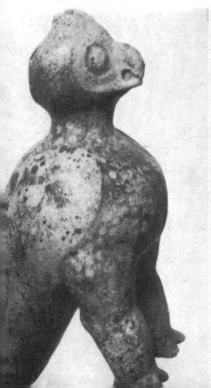

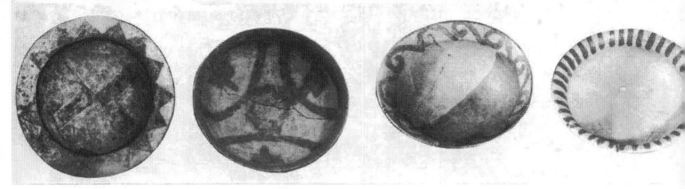

ABOVE. Four painted pottery vessels. LEFT. Creek vessel from Tallapoosa River area, Alabama; about 8" diameter (Courtesy, L. P. Goodwin). SECOND. Vessel about 7" diameter; red on buff. Yell County, Arkansas (Courtesy, Museum of Arts and Sciences, Rochester; AR 156). RIGHT. Third and fourth vessels are red on buff, from Tallapoosa-Coosa Valley area, Alabama; about 13" diameter (Courtesy, Alabama Department of Archives and History, Brame Collection). A red paint was applied directly to the vessel on the right which had a light cream to tan colored slip covering the basic darker paste, from which the vessel was modeled.

RIGHT. UPPER. Four painted shell-tempered bottles; highest 10⅜"; one has on it the faint remains of a star and hand design repeated four times. Three seem to be examples of direct painting of white and red on a tan paste background— the basic color (Courtesy, Frank, Frank, Jr., and Robert H. Morast). LOWER. Two painted "tea pot" shaped bottles; examples of direct painting of red and white on buff base; 7½" high and 10¼" high. Dog or other animal effigy in center has a red wash or paint over entire surface and teeth are painted white; maximum height, 7"; maximum length, 11" (Courtesy, Frank, Frank, Jr., and Robert H. Morast collection).

It has been said that negative painting resulted from drawing the design in grease or wax; then dipping the vessel into a slip; and firing it; the grease burned off, leaving the design in the original color of the vessel, and the slip on all the surfaces around it. Though painting generally characterized the Mississippi Period, there were some examples of painting among the native cultures of the Florida area in the Woodland Period, even of a negative-type painting in Crystal River area. (See: Willey, 1948, pp. 325-28). Another native method of decorating vessels with paint, was the rubbing or tracing of paint pigment, often red, into incised lines. A wash or slip applied to the entire surface was generally the most frequent type of application of color; however, at some sites direct painting was the only type used. Rarely, direct painting was applied to negative painted pottery, as at Sikeston, southeastern Missouri. Painted pottery was doubtless part of the ceremonial complex.

BELOW. Three long-neck water bottles. This shape pottery vessel seems to have been more frequently painted than was the bowl or plate. LEFT. Negative painted water bottle with circle-cross design; about 9" high. Dark chocolate paint was applied to a light cream-colored background. Design repeated three times around bottle. North Alabama (Courtesy, Alabama Museum of Natural History, BAE, Bull 122, Pl. 97, p. 87). CENTER. Bottle 7¼" high; with designs in red and black on a light buff background. Maximum diameter 7"; Yell County, Arkansas (Courtesy, Rochester Museum of Arts and Sciences, AR 220). RIGHT. Negative painted vessel. Moundville, Alabama (Courtesy, Alabama Museum of Natural History). Bottle necks were made separately and later attached.

POTTERY BOTTLES— VARIETY OF FORMS

Plates 117 and 118

ABOVE. LEFT. Caddo bottle—Fulton Aspect, Glendora Focus; see J. B. Griffin, 1952; Suhm and Krieger, 1954. RIGHT. Weeden Island vessels. Franklin Co., Fla. (Courtesy, Museum of the American Indian, Heye Foundation, 17-3715, 17-4534, and 17-4919).

BELOW. UPPER ROW. Four Caddo bottles. Second. Glendora-type compound vessel—four bottles in one—the smaller ones serve as legs. Center bottles were incised; others, engraved. The engraved lines on right bottle were filled with red pigment (hematite) to bring out the design. Arkansas (Courtesy, Dr. F. J. Soday). CENTER ROW. Left. Shell-tempered vessel with thumb-print design. North Alabama (BAE-B 129, Pl. 122). Center. North Alabama (Courtesy, C. H. Worley). Right. Vessel 7" diameter. South Alabama (Courtesy, Fairhope Public Library). LOWER ROW. Left. Bottle with 4 legs, decorated with stylized hand motif in applique. St. Francis River site, Ark. Center. Modified human effigy vessel. Southwestern Tenn. (Courtesy, K. L. Beaudoin collection). Right. Shell-tempered effigy vessel, 7½" high with three globular legs. North Alabama (BAE-B 122, Pl. 87(b); photo, Courtesy, Alabama Museum of Natural History). Symmetry in form resulted from the craftsman's technical skill.

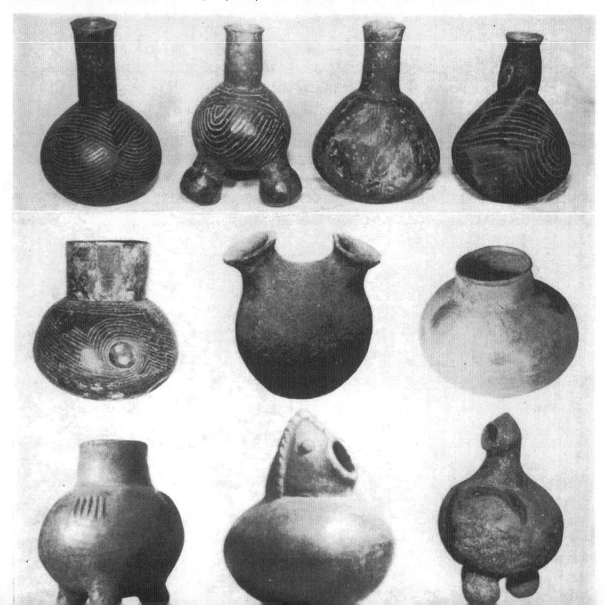

ABOVE. Pottery bottle found with a burial. Chapman and Anderson (1955, p. 21 and Figs. 20-21) describe it:

"A most unusual black, polished water bottle of Bell Plain paste was found adjacent to the right shoulder blade. It has a gadroon border around the upper shoulder area ½" from the juncture with the neck, below which are a series of 26 wide smooth vertical grooves dividing the vessel body into 26 raised sections. The base is an added ring 3¼" in diameter, and is ½" high making it quite distinct from the rest of the vessel. The height is 6⅞" and the body diameter is 7". The neck is 3⅛" in diameter expanding to 3⅝" at the orifice. The height of the rim is 2½". The inner rim is beveled toward the interior and the rim is thickened and rolled outward to form a smooth bead that projects outward and overhangs the rim exterior." (Photograph and quotation reproduced by permission from the editor of the MISSOURI ARCHAEOLOGIST, and the Missouri Archaeological Society). See Plate 125.

RIGHT. A variety of shell-tempered bottles. TOP TO BOTTOM. FIRST ROW. Five peaked or hooded effigy bottles, 4" to 6" high. Arkansas. SECOND ROW. Eight gourd-shaped bottles with effigy heads highest, 8½"; the owl-bottle at the front center, is from southern Kentucky—near the Tennessee border; it is 5" high. The other four bottles in the front row—with human heads—range in height from 4½" to 6". The three bottles in the back row, have animal-like human heads. Arkansas. THIRD ROW. Seven Nodena Red and White perpendicular-striped bottles ranging in height from 4⅛" (front center) to 9⅜" (left). Arkansas. FOURTH ROW. Five bottles ranging from 7¼" to 10⅞" high. The two end bottles are painted red. Note, the step design of legs—center and right. Four medallion heads are spaced around the body of the bottle at the left, front. The bottle on the right, front, originally had a long neck; it was repaired by the native owner. BOTTOM ROW. Nine stirrup-neck bottles. Note, triple stirrup at center rear. The two similarly shaped bottles at the front, 4⅜" and 5½" high, were found —one on top of the other—in a child's burial. Arkansas (Courtesy, Frank, Frank, Jr., and Robert H. Morast collection; photographs by Norman L. Morrow, Jr.).

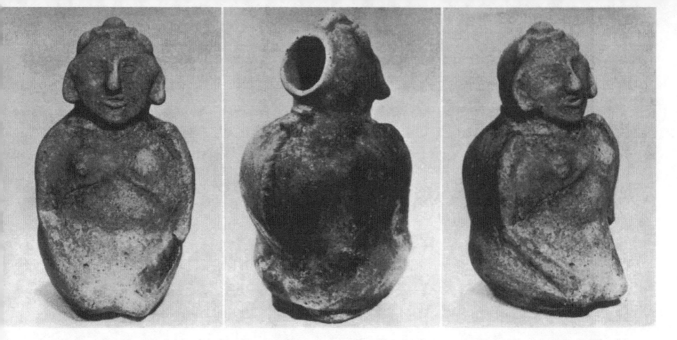

ABOVE. Three views of a shell-tempered bottle, 6½" high. It represents a kneeling hunch-back female with her hands placed on the knees. The liquid was poured into the hole in the back of the head; this is typical of the human effigy bottles. Lewis, 1954, p. 194, mentions a comparison between such figures and similar ones of the Southwest and Chihuahua, Mexico area; he also points to the frequency with which this type is found in the Memphis and southeastern Missouri area and the Cumberland River area (Courtesy, D. B. Long, Photograph by Tom-Clare Studio).

POTTERY BOTTLES — HUMAN EFFIGIES
Plates 119 and 120

BELOW. UPPER ROW. Four shell-tempered pottery bottles; highest, 6". Left to right. Poinsett County, Arkansas; New Madrid County, Missouri; Cross County, Arkansas; and Scott County, Missouri (Courtesy, B. W. Stephens collection). LOWER ROW. LEFT. Kneeling figure taken from a mound on the "Nodena Place," Mississippi County, Arkansas, by Capt. W. P. Hall, 1881; 10¾" high; 9" maximum width (Courtesy, Davenport Public Museum). CENTER. Shell-tempered hunch-back effigy bottle; 5¾" high Tennessee (Courtesy, Vanderbilt University, Thruston collection). RIGHT. Bottle, 6" high; New Madrid Co., Missouri (Courtesy, B. W. Stephens).

RIGHT. NEAR. Pottery water bottle with human faces modeled into the bowl; 6¾" high. Williamson County, Tennessee (Courtesy, Museum of Arts and Sciences, Rochester, AR 17670). FAR. Water bottle with three separate heads modeled into tripod legs, 7" x 5½"; Richmond County, Georgia (Courtesy, Smithsonian Institution, United States National Museum 135197).

RIGHT. NEAR. Pottery effigy; 10⅜" high, 3-15/16" wide and 2-7/16" thick; decorated with serpent designs. Rapids Parish, Louisiana (Courtesy Edward Neild Collection; Photo by Smithsonian Institution, USNM, 32653-C, Cat. 377973). FAR. Effigy water bottle, 10" x 6"; Richmond County, Georgia (Courtesy, Smithsonian Institution, USNM, 171849). A head of this style, with male chest and arm stubs, broken from a vessel or image is in the Ocumlgee Museum (Pope, 1956, p. 35). Unusual hair style—incised parallel lines radiating back from line delineating forehead. Similar hair treatment but different head structure is found on fragment from Louisiana (Ford and Willey, 1940).

BELOW. Three human effigy water bottles. LEFT. Effigy with arms folded in front of chest and left hand visible in picture. North Alabama (Courtesy, Chicago Natural History Museum, 50639). CENTER. Shell-tempered bottle, about 8" high. Lower Tallapoosa River, Alabama (Courtesy, Alabama Department of Archives and History; Paulin Collection). RIGHT. Reddish-brown shell-tempered vessel, 7" high. Tennessee (Courtesy, Vanderbilt University, Thruston Collection).

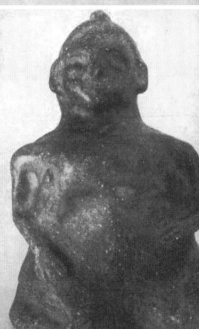

ABOVE. Group of shell-tempered pottery vessels, dark reddish brown in color; largest, 8½″ rim diameter and 6¼″ high. Sometime effigy heads of this type are hollow and intentionally filled with small stones or pellets of clay for rattles. Davidson County, Tennessee (Courtesy, Vanderbilt University, Thruston collection; all photographs from this source were made by Peggy Wrenne).

POTTERY BOWLS—HUMAN EFFIGIES

Plates 121 and 122

BELOW. UPPER ROW. LEFT AND CENTER. Two shell-tempered pottery vessels decorated with modeled human effigy heads. Shell-tempered vessels were typically found at sites of urn-burier cultures along the Alabama and lower Tallapoosa rivers; rim diameter of the vessel on the left is about 7½″ (Courtesy, Alabama Department of Archives and History, Paulin collection). RIGHT. The human effigy on this vessel has a snake coiled around the back of her head; the bowl is 3½″ deep with a rim diameter of 7⅞″ (Courtesy, Frank, Frank, Jr., and Robert H. Morast collection). LOWER ROW. LEFT. Bowl 6″ high and 8¼″ wide; from a mound near Jolly Bay, Choctawhatches Bay, Walton County, Florida. RIGHT. Bowl 4″ high and 8″ wide; from Marshall County, Alabama (Both of these bowls are pictured, Courtesy, Reading Public Museum and Art Gallery—15-49-18 and 38973; photo by S. C. Gundy).

ABOVE. Shell-tempered (polishing worked the shell away from the surface) pottery vessels with human effigy handles; note, hair styles. Height, about 14 cm. Walls, De Soto County, Mississippi (Courtesy, University of Mississippi, Davies collection).

BELOW. Shell-tempered effigies originally attached to vessels; some have pellets inside which rattle; highest, 4″. Gulf Coast, Alabama (Courtesy, Dr. and Mrs. C. M. Rudulph; Violet E. Nelson; Nell S. Jones; Dr. C. C. Cox; and the City of Mobile).

ABOVE. Three shell-tempered dark reddish-brown bowls with effigy handles. Left. Duck bowl, 4-1/16" high and 5⅝" rim diameter; the tail is broken. Center. Owl effigy 4-15/16" high; 7" rim diameter. Right. Bird effigy, 5½" high; 6" rim diameter. Davidson County, Tennessee (Courtesy, Vanderbilt University, Thruston collection; photograph by Peggy Wrenne).

POTTERY VESSELS—BIRD AND ANIMAL EFFIGIES

Plates 123 and 124

BELOW. Six shell-tempered effigy vessels. UPPER ROW. LEFT. Turtle effigy, 1⅝" high; 3⅛" rim diameter; dark reddish brown. Davidson County, Tennessee (Vanderbilt University, Thruston Collection). CENTER. Frog effigy, 2½" high; 4" wide. Coahoma County, Mississippi (Courtesy, Dabney Carson Pelegrin). RIGHT. Fish effigy, 2¾" high, 4½" rim diameter; dark reddish-brown. Tennessee (Courtesy, Vanderbilt University, Thruston collection). LOWER ROW. LEFT. Fish effigy about 7" long. Williamson County, Tennessee (Courtesy, Rochester Museum of Arts and Sciences, AR 17662). CENTER. Frog effigy, about 6½" maximum diameter; the bowl is highly polished and has a black film on outside similar to the blackware at Moundville. The front of the frog is shown; the back has similar small legs and a round "doughnut" type circle for the tail. The vessel is from a site of the urn-burier culture—Taskigi. Lower Tallapoosa River area. Alabama (Courtesy, Dr. R. P. Burke, M. D.). RIGHT. Turtle effigy vessel, 6¾" maximum width. Williamson County, Tennessee (Courtesy, Rochester Museum of Arts and Sciences, AR, 17664).

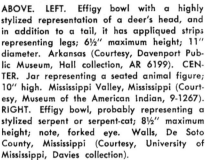

ABOVE. LEFT. Effigy bowl with a highly stylized representation of a deer's head, and in addition to a tail, it has appliqued strips representing legs; 6½" maximum height; 11" diameter. Arkansas (Courtesy, Davenport Public Museum, Hall collection, AR 6199). CENTER. Jar representing a seated animal figure; 10" high. Mississippi Valley, Mississippi (Courtesy, Museum of the American Indian, 9-1267). RIGHT. Effigy bowl, probably representing a stylized serpent or serpent-cat; 8½" maximum height; note, forked eye. Walls, De Soto County, Mississippi (Courtesy, University of Mississippi, Davies collection).

RIGHT. Two reddish-brown animal effigies. NEAR. This may represent a bat; 6" high; 8-7/16" rim diameter. Davidson County, Tennessee. The broken vessel is probably a beaver representation; he has a log in his mouth and shows the two large front teeth. Similar beaver effigies have been found at other sites where shell-tempered pottery was made. This is 3 1/16" high and 5" rim diameter (Courtesy, Vanderbilt University).

BELOW. Five shell-tempered pottery effigy vessels—three bottles or jars and two bowls. Upper row. Left to Right. Fish effigy, 6" high. Dunklin County, Missouri. Center. Frog effigy. Note, holes near rim of pot for suspension; 5" high. Mississippi County, Arkansas. Right. Bird effigy with wing representations on sides and underneath and feet and tail opposite head; 6" high. Poinsett County, Arkansas. Lower row. Left. Crested bird, with a tail-riding effigy of smaller bird; maximum height, 7¾". Poinsett County, Arkansas. Right. Bear or dog effigy, 6½" high; note, dimple in side. Many vessels with swirl designs from the site of Moundville, Alabama, have dimples; several dimple-vessels have cult designs—one an arrow. The dimple is also found on a few shell-tempered vessels from other southeastern sites, and especially in the Middle Mississippi Valley area. This vessel pictured was found in Dunklin County, Missouri (Courtesy, B. W. Stephens collection). See Plates 117 and 37 (Dimple designs, Moundville, Alabama).

ABOVE. Three views of a head effigy. This is a buff color decorated with incised lines and red paint; 5⅝" high; 5½" maximum width, back to front; flat base, 2¾" x 2⅛". The rim is narrow and is not thickened; it is beveled toward the interior. Red paint circles the eyes and crosses the bridge of the nose. The ears, the modeled hair at the back, and the rim of the vessel are covered with red paint. There are five perforations in each ear. At the front of the vessel below the rim is a projecting node through which there is a hole. A single incised line filled with red paint extends the length of the nose. In the back of the head, at the bottom is an appliqued strip which extends in a semi-circle around the hair-line. This appears as Figures 23 and 26 in Chapman and Anderson, 1955 (Reproduced by permission from THE MISSOURI ARCHAEOLOGIST).

THE CAMPBELL SITE—MISSOURI

Plate 125

BELOW. A variety of shell-tempered vessels from the Campbell Site, Pemiscot County, southeastern Missouri. These appear in Chapman and Anderson, 1955, Figures 23, 29, 36, 37, 38, 39. UPPER ROW. LEFT. Bottle, 7½" high by 8" maximum diameter. Rim is higher than other Campbell punctated vessels and punctations are in vertical rows rather than the usual horizontal lines. It has four stylized appliqued handles on upper rim surface. Second. Campbell punctated water bottle with an orifice 3" diameter, a slightly carinated body, and a notched disk base 2⅞" diameter. Third and fourth. Two effigy pottery vessels. These were found in the burial of a child; the bird effigy with another bird riding on the tail is typically found in the Middle Mississippi Valley area in shell-tempered pottery; 5⅛" diameter at orifice. The bowl has a decided flare about 1" from the top. Upper rim is decorated by horizontal notched rim fillet. CENTER. Two bowls. Left. Old Town Red bowl, 3¼" high, somewhat ovoid with orifice, 6⅝" by 6⅞"; originally covered with dark reddish brown slip; upper rim has been thickened and notched on outside. RIGHT. Bell Plain bowl with notched rim fillet; 2¾" high and 6¾" diameter at orifice. LOWER ROW. LEFT. Water bottle with annular ring base; another similar to this had four perforations in the base. At the bottom of the neck is a notched appliqued band; flaring neck; the rim, beveled toward the interior is thickened and modeled into a slightly overhanging bead on the exterior; 6½" high. CENTER. A horizontal compound vessel consisting of two short-neck, connecting water bottles, with an opening about ⅝" in diameter at the point the bodies join; a strap between the rims adds strength to the tie; total width, 8"; height, 3¼". RIGHT. Carson red on buff water bottle. Shows slight traces of a white slip; 8 red vertical stripes on the body and two horizontal stripes on neck; 6¾" high; 7¼" diameter; disk base, notched. Other vessels found at this site include a bottle with a pyramid-type head accentuated with notched appliqued bands (Reproduced by permission from THE MISSOURI ARCHAEOLOGIST). See also Plate 118.

CADDO POTTERY—SPIRO

Plate 126

ABOVE. Pottery vessels from the Spiro Mound. The drawings are reproduced from an article by Dr. Robert E. Bell, entitled, "Pottery Vessels from the Spiro Mound, Craig Burial Mound, Le Flore County, Oklahoma," OKLAHOMA ANTHROPOLOGICAL SOCIETY, BULLE-TIN, Vol. 1, March 1953, pp. 25-38 (Reproduced by permission from Dr. R. E. Bell—Dept. of Anthropology, University of Oklahoma—Editor of the OAS-B; vessels from collections of the Stovall Museum; Tulsa Museum; and Oklahoma Historical Society Museum). TOP ROW. Third, bottle 10½" x 7"; Fourth—drawn to a different scale—7¾" x 5". FOURTH ROW. Right, effigy bottle, 11" high; the bowl above it is 2⅜" x 5⅜". Dr. Bell states: "Most of the Spiro decorated pottery is engraved—probably after firing or at least after the clay was fairly hard. Effigy pieces at Spiro are rare; I know of only two human effigy specimens." (correspondence). Bur-nett (1945) mentions finely pulverized shell-tempering. Bell notes that the tempering generally appears to be other granular sub-stances. FOURTH ROW. Bowl with banded arrow or triangle decoration is 4" x 9½"; it was from a burial 177 which Dr. Bell de-scribes (p. 28) as ". . . a large multiple burial containing eight extended burials and five semi-flexed individuals." Six pottery vessels and "the following were found: . . . 1 effigy boat stone (crystal quartz), 1 stone mano, 23 stone beads, 2 mussel shell fragments, 1 stone celt, quartz pebbles (rattle?), 4 pieces of galena and some shell disc beads." In this article Dr. Bell lists burial associations from 36 burials which exemplify the wide range of Spiro artifacts. Regarding the Craig Burial Mound, which has been called the "Spiro Temple Mound," Dr. Bell writes: "The mound was only a burial mound as far as we know. No construction phases were evident in the cross-sections marking house floors or the like. There are other house or temple mounds at the Spiro site and most of them were excavated." (correspondence). Many whole or easily restored artifacts were found at the Spiro site.

BELOW. Typical Creek Indian pottery vessels displaying a variety of designs. These are drawings by Dr. R. P. Burke, M. D., Montgomery, Alabama. Dr. Burke collected thousands of Indian artifacts from the Coosa-Tallapoosa area of Alabama during the 1930's; in careful drawings he recorded the features of many of them. Some of the vessels below are in his collection displayed at the Montgomery Museum of Fine Arts. Many of his illustrations were reproduced in ARROWPOINTS edited by P. A. Brannon, 1920-1937. The vessels below were found at the Creek site of Tulsa. They appear to be sand tempered. The rim diameters of the vessels vary from 4½" to 10½"; they are drawn to different scales, therefore the variation is not apparent in the picture. Second Row. Center. A restoration drawing exemplifying a typical design. Right. A roughly three-sided vessel about 10½" maximum diameter; it is unusual because it is not symmetrical and because it is decorated with roughly parallel lines over its entire surface. Creek pottery characteristically has band designs, often 1" to 3" placed as shown below. These vessels vary in color from a dull pinkish tan to dark brown and do not have a wash or slip (Courtesy, Dr. R. P. Burke, M. D.).

OPPOSITE PAGE. LEFT. Large storage vessel with typical Creek Indian design incised around neck; 14" high; 17½" rim diameter. Coosa-Tallapoosa Valley area, Alabama (Courtesy, Huntingdon College, Houghton Memorial Library; photo by Scott Photographic Services). RIGHT. Creek water jug about 12" x 12" with typical Creek design below neck. Elmore County, Alabama (Courtesy, J. P. Daole; photo by Jack D. Ray). Large vessels are rare.

ABOVE. Two stamped vessels from the Peachtree Mound, North Carolina (Setzler and Jennings, 1941, Pl. 33A. Courtesy, Smithsonian Institution, USNM, 384967 and 384968). Stamping was a frequent method of decoration in the Appalachean area.

INCISED CREEK VESSELS AND SOUTH APPALACHIAN STAMPED POTTERY

Plates 127 and 128

BELOW. Variety of stamped designs and vessel shapes. UPPER ROW. LEFT. Stamped vessel. Hollywood Mound, Ga. (After Holmes, 1903). CENTER. Cherokee cooking pot, 10½" high and 12½" rim diameter; complicated stamp—four triangles forming a square with the opposite triangles similarly marked with punctates and other opposites with bars (Courtesy, North Carolina Department of Archives and History). RIGHT. Stamped vessel, 10" diameter. Cherokee (After Holmes, 1903). LOWER ROW. LEFT. Stamped burial urn, 6½" high. Bryan County, Georgia (Courtesy, Museum of the American Indian, Heye Foundation, 17-4486). CENTER. Large stamped pottery vessel, 24" high. A smooth cover pot was found with this; it is a storage vessel. Pee Dee River, Montgomery County, North Carolina (Courtesy, Wachovia Museum, H. M. Doerschuk Collection, Ri-15; Ed T. Simons, photographer). RIGHT. Vessel with stamped impression; 14" high (After Holmes, 1903).

    The well known Mississippi Period site at Etowah, Georgia, produced many vessels with stamped designs as well as others with incised-band designs similar to the incised designs found on some of the Creek vessels in the Coosa-Tallapoosa River area, Alabama. The use of the stamping technique at Etowah, doubtless reflects the wide-spread use of stamping methods which flourished in the Georgia area during the Woodland Period; famous examples of which were found in the Swift Creek culture—several stages of which are recorded. The later Savannah River complexes produced stamped designs somewhat similar to some of the Etowah patterns. The still later, Irene and Lamar cultures also produced stamped designs as well as incised decoration; and some of those later vessels combined incising and stamping in separate areas of decoration on the same vessel. (Moorehead, 1932; Caldwell, 1941).

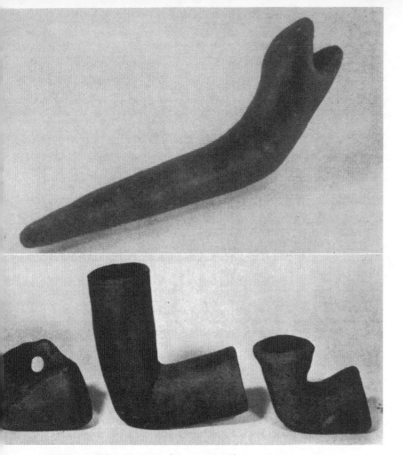

OTHER POTTERY ARTIFACTS

Plates 129 and 130

LEFT. UPPER. Reptile effigy pipe, 8⅜" long; shell-tempered; terra cotta color. Smith Co., Tennessee (Courtesy, Vanderbilt University, Thruston collection). LOWER. Three pottery pipes; one was restored; highest 4¼". Alabama (Courtesy, Museum of the American Indian, Heye Foundation, 17-991, 17-3632, and 17-2806).

OPPOSITE PAGE. UPPER. Pipe (see description under picture) decorated with two deer, outlined by punctates or dentate stamping; black-brown; polished. See J. B. Griffin, 1952, Fig. 23, for Woodland traits in the Virginia area.

Webb and Ford (1956) report two zoomorphic forms on stone bowls shreds found at the Late Archaic site, Poverty Point, La. (Plate 73). Woodland pipes were infrequently produced in animal forms. For a stone pipe in an animal shape, see Plate 80. On Plate 79 reference is made to a curved-base effigy pottery pipe found at the Crooks Mound, La. (Ford and Willey, 1940).

An unusual object found at the Woodland site—Crooks Mound, La.—was the fragment—top to chin—of a hollow human effigy head, 5 cm. Ford and Webb (1956, pp. 49-50, Fig. 16) picture 13 cruder modeled figurines—2 to 6 cm. high—from Poverty Point, La., a Late Archaic Site.

RIGHT. UPPER. Variety of pottery artifacts. Upper row. Left. Earspool with cupped ends, 3" long, from Arkansas. Center. Two pottery trowels 2½" high from Etowah mound area, near Cartersville, Georgia. Right. Pottery trowel, 3⅞" high from Arkansas. Center row. Left. Ear spool from Obion County, Tennessee. Center. Discoidal, 3" diameter, fully shaped before firing. Arkansas. Most pottery discoidals which are found have been shaped from pottery vessel sherds and some of them show fragments of the original decoration. Right. Castaway dab of fired clay, showing finger prints of aboriginal who worked it. Semicircular row of small items. Left. Three ear plugs from Middle Tennessee. Center. Three ear, nose, or lip plugs from Arkansas. Right. Three ear pins from Arkansas. Lower corners. "Button?" or spindle whorl? Tenn. and Ark. (Courtesy, Frank, Frank, Jr., and Robert H. Morast). In Late Archaic—Poverty Point, La., Jaketown, Miss.—and Woodland—Tchefuncte, Troyville, and Marksville—horizons in Louisiana, and near area, have been found many small—2 to 8 cm.—crudely modeled fired clay objects. Ford and Webb (1956, pp. 39-49, Figs. 15-16) term them, "artificial cooking stones," of which "tons" have been found, often massed in kitchen middens. They classify 11 types occurring at various stratigraphic levels at Poverty Point and Jaketown (See also, Ford, Phillips, and Haag, 1955, pp. 39-57, 110-112). Many are irregular wads of clay with careless finger marks. Others appear to be crude effigies of melons, buds, or marine animals, snakes, rattles or the penis—a design used as late as historic Creek pipes. Sometimes the objects are marked with deep grooves—parallel, converging, checker, opposing from four directions, and dented around the wide periphery of biconical shapes. See Czajkowski, 1934, Fig. 6; Ford, 1936, Fig. 40v; Ford and Willey, 1940, pp. 119-121, Fig. 53; Moore, 1913, pp. 15-16, 72-74, Fig. 2, Pl. 2; and Setzler, 1933, Pl. 6, Fig. B.

RIGHT. LOWER. Drawing by Eleanor F. Chapman, Art Director, THE MISSOURI ARCHAEOLOGIST. It is a reconstruction drawing of the type native house located at the Campbell site, a late Mississippi site in Pemiscot County, southeastern Missouri. It shows a native applying plastic clay to the thatched sides of a house; the hardened remains of wattle-and-daub construction of house walls has been found at many Mississippi Period sites in the Southeast. (Chapman and Anderson, 1955, Fig. 43). (Reproduced, courtesy, Eleanor F. Chapman and The Missouri Archaeological Society).

ABOVE. Pipe—5⅞" long; bowl, 1½" high; rim diameter, ¾"; opening, 3/16".
Richmond Co., Va. (Courtesy, B. C. McCary; photo by T. L. Williams).

RIGHT. Large shell-tempered pottery pipe with 7 stem holes; 4¾" high; 5½"
maximum width; bowl thickness, ½" to ⅝"; it is decorated with a dentate
stamp of fingernail design. Kingston, Tennessee. There is a bird pipe of
similar paste and decoration, also from Tennessee in this same collection
(Courtesy, St. Joseph Museum, Claude Mason collection).

BELOW. Creek Indian pottery pipes from the Coosa-Tallapoosa River area,
Alabama. These are drawings made by Dr. R. P. Burke, M. D., Montgomery,
Alabama. The pipes are carefully identified in Dr. Burke's field notes, and
each pipe is drawn to scale on an individual page. Pipes shown here were
found at Fusihatchie, Hoithlewalli, Koasiti, Tulsa, and several other Creek
town sites; most of them were burial associations. The canoe pipe, top left,
was found in a burial at Hoithlewalli, and is pale greyish terra cotta, 4" wide
at the top; a similar pipe from the same site is pictured, top right, and is 3½"
wide. Second row. The two human effigy pipes on the left were found
together in a grave at a site on the Tallapoosa River; they are 3¾" and
1⅞" high, respectively; the second has small holes from the nostrils, ears, and
mouth into the pipe bowl, and will emit smoke from those openings as well as
from the stem-hole at the back of the head; other "grave goods" found with
the pipes were, thirteen hundred small blue trade beads—size of buckshot—,
one pair of thick copper arm bands, another pipe, one iron tomahawk, a
large amount of red paint, and numerous iron bracelets. Creek burials often
included European trade goods (Courtesy, Dr. R. P. Burke, M.D.).

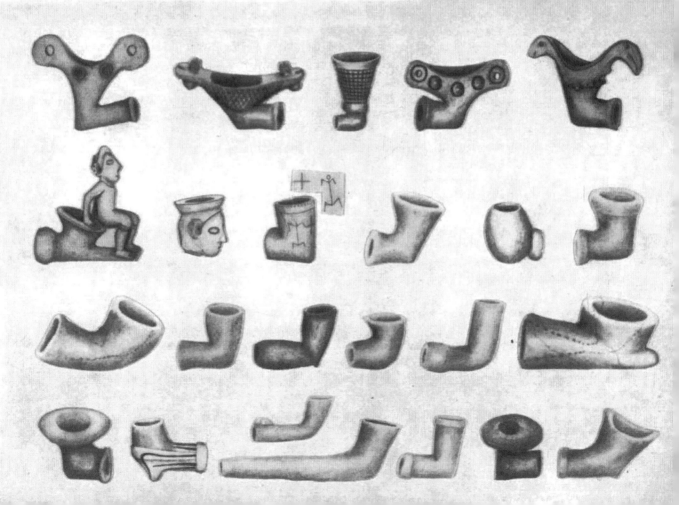

Chapter 8

WOOD

Quotation from John R. Swanton, THE INDIANS OF THE SOUTH-EASTERN UNITED STATES, Bureau of American Ethnology, Bulletin 137, 1946, pp. 244-248—excerpts. Quoted courtesy Smithsonian Institution, Bureau of American Ethnology.[1]

"Cane supplied one of the most important of all raw materials. Besides the use of its seeds (for food), it was employed in making baskets and mats; as building material; in making fishing crails and traps, spears, and arrows; as backing for wattle walls; in making beds in houses and in the construction of corncribs; as a substitute for the shuttle in weaving; as knives and torches; in the 'spiral fire' at Creek councils; in making boxes, cradles, sieves, fanners, hampers, blowguns, blowgun arrows, shields, stockades and fences, rafts, litters, flageolets, counters, drills, and tubes through which to blow into the medicines; as pipes to blow the fire in burning out mortars and in smoking; and sometimes a section was employed to hold braids of the hair.

"Hickory was used in house frames, in backing for walls, as arrow shafts, in making fishing crails and drags, and as firewood. From it was obtained some of the punk used in kindling fires, and the bark was employed in covering houses and making fires for burning pottery. Pestles were made out of 'red hickory,' and the Choctaw say they used white hickory or 'switch hickory,' which they cut in the fall, in the manufacture of bows. Walnuts supplied a dye widely used in basketry and an oil with which the hair was anointed.

"The inner bark of the mulberry was employed as thread and rope, in making textiles, nettings worn by girls, and netting for women's hair. This was one of the sources of tinder along the lower Mississippi; from the roots a yellow dye was obtained, and Lawson says that of the 'white mulberry' bows were sometimes made, perhaps after the introduction of the white mulberry through Mexico.

"From the sumac, according to one informant, a black dye was made; according to another, a yellow dye; and according to a third, yellow and red dyes. It is said that berries of the common sumac were rubbed in the hair, and, according to a Natchez informant, an infusion of leaves of the Rhus Truphydon was poured over pots to give them a bluish tint.

"Cypress was the favorite wood for the manufacture of canoes. Drums were made out of cypress knees. Split shingles and bark from this tree were used as house coverings. At a place where a limb came out, punk was obtained to be used as tinder.

"We find pine employed in making house frames, canoes, frames for skin boats or rafts, and bows. It was used for torches, especially in fire-fishing, and as tinder; and houses were covered with its bark, while pitch-pine soot was used in making tattoo marks.

"Bass bark was used in the manufacture of ropes and thread, sometimes including bowstrings.

"The wood of the black gum or tupelo gum was employed in making drums, and gum wood was worked into dishes and spoons.

"Oak trees supplied the favorite firewood, and the four logs forming the sacred fires of the Creeks were usually oak. Mortars were also made of it. White oak withes formed the backing of wattle walls, and they were employed in putting fish traps together, in the tops of beds, and in the frame of leather boats. Sticks of this wood were also used in kindling fires. White-oak was employed in covering houses, while red-oak bark was used as a dye, and skins undergoing tanning were soaked in an infusion of this bark. Garcilaso de la Vega is our sole authority for the employment of oak bows.

"Locust wood is said to have been used sometimes in frames for houses, and black locust was the favorite bowwood east of the Mississippi.

---

[1] Swanton states, "The following enumeration of such materials is drawn from the printed sources mainly and does not profess to be absolutely complete." In other places in the book he quotes colonial writings as sources of information used in Chapters 7, 8 and 9.

"Sassafras wood was used for house frames, fire sticks, and sometimes for bows, and from it was made a deep yellow dye. West of the Mississippi Osage-orange, the bois d'arc, was the great bowwood.

"House frames and bows were also made of cedar, while cedar bark was employed in covering houses.

"House frames in Florida were made of palmetto (Sabal palmetto), and in the southern sections generally, palmetto leaves were widely used as roof coverings. They were also employed in baskets and panniers and even for clothing, while arrow points were made from the harder sections. Whitford has identified the material of which a Cherokee basket was made as palmetto.

"The largest canoes were of poplar, and poplar was used in the manufacture of stools and the doors of houses; also fire sticks were sometimes of this wood.

"Ash splints sometimes formed the tops of beds, and in Virginia there is mention of ash leaves as an extemporized trowel. Prickly ash is said to have been a favorite material for canoe poles.

"Slippery-elm bark was one of the sources for cordage, and threads are said to have been obtained from it out of which textiles were woven. When beech trees were to be found, mortars were made from them.

"Maple bark is mentioned as another source of cordage, and there are at least two notices of a dye extracted from a variety of maple, apparently the red maple, but said to be a dark purple dye. Maple was not used in the manufacture of mortars, as it gave a bad taste to the flour.

"Firesticks were sometimes of willow, and the Alabama made a deer call out of the button willow.

"Some of the bark canoes used in the northern interior of this section were probably of birch. . . .

"From the box elder spoons were made. Wood of the tulip tree was employed for the same purpose. Another wood of which spoons were made was the sycamore.

"The seat of the litter in which the Great Sun of the Natchez was carried about was covered with leaves of the 'tulip laurel.' Elm wood was made into spoons and elm bark into canoes.

"The horse chestnut or buckeye was one of the main sources of fish poison. . . . Nuts of the red buckeye (Aesculus pavia) were used as eyes in the deer decoy.

"The wild peach was one source of red dye, and skins to be tanned were sometimes soaked in an infusion of the bark of this tree. Bows and arrow shafts in Virginia were of witch-hazel.

"Dogwood was an occasional source of material for baskets and bows, and 'red dogwood' was used for arrow shafts. Arrow shafts were also made of the black haw. Ironwood was sometimes employed for bows.

"Natchez bows, according to Du Pratz, were of 'acacia'—probably black locust.

"The hackberry was sometimes used in baskets. Chinquapin nuts were occasionally strung as beads.

"The material of which thread, fish nets, and fish lines were made is frequently referred to as 'silkgrass,' a name which probably covered several different plants, including, . . . Indian hemp (Apocynum cannabinum), stringless nettle (Boehmeria cylindrica), woods nettle (Laportea Canadensis), . . .

"From rushes and flags were made mats, house coverings, and bed coverings, particularly in the northeast. . . . Yucca fibre was used for cord in the western part of the area. . . .

"Spanish moss was used as clothing in the southern sections, particularly by women and girls, and the pillow employed along the Mississippi in flattening the heads of infants was often stuffed with it. It was also employed as tinder, especially in supplying the tinder for fire arrows. . . .

"Grass was used sometimes for clothing and, mixed with clay, was commonly used in constructing the walls and roofs of houses. In the west, bundles of grass formed the sole thatch of houses.

"Milkweed (a plant of European origin) . . . has been identified in textiles from the Southeast by A. C. Whitford, in places as wide apart as the Cherokee country, the Machapunga of eastern North Carolina, and Arkansas.[2] (Other wooden objects were clubs, swords, images, paddles, counters, arrow points, and pipe stems).

[2] "The devil's shoestring was employed as a fish poison. Another . . . the berries of the Cocculus Carolinus.
"The red root (Sanguinaria canadensis) was a principal source of red dyes . . . . and the yellow root (Hydrastis canadensis) . . . of a yellow dye . . . . The 'dog tail weed' is given as a source of a dark red dye. . . . A low shrub called the 'buchbush' was one source of blowgun arrow shafts.
" 'Barks' are mentioned vaguely as employed in making fish nets, fishlines, and headdresses for the inland Siouans of Virginia, for bowstrings, wrist-guards, shields, and trumpets.
"Cords from the pawpaw (Asimina triloba) have been identified by Whitford. Textiles from the button-snakeroot(Eryngium yuccaefolium) were found in two bags obtained from Arkansas. . . . Textile material from the moosewood (Dirca palustris) was identified by him in a mat from the same region.
" 'Creepers' are mentioned employed as cords. Grapevines were used sometimes as substitutes for cord.
" 'Leaves' sometimes provided a makeshift clothing. 'Seeds' were used in headdresses. An 'herb' . . . for stain used in tattooing. Thistledown was commonly used in feathering blowgun arrows."

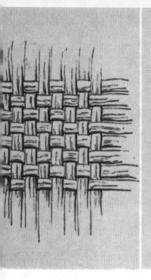   

ABOVE. Four steps in making a plain, checker-woven basket. Left to Right. Bottom of basket; method of building up the sides; sides finished but untrimmed, and preparing basket for rim (After O. T. Mason, 1884, Plates LI and LII, Figures 85-88). In producing plain or checker plait, the weft crosses the warp in regular, over-one-under-one movement. Both the warp and weft are flexible. When the warp is rigid and the weft is flexible the resulting weave is termed "wicker."

Basketry was the forerunner of cloth-making. The former of these textile arts was first developed by people of the Archaic cultures. Baskets, as wooden and stone containers preceded pottery and served as models to be copied by early potters. Natives, who had mastered the coil process of basketry transferred their skill into coiling pottery, and often decorated it with stamped, cord-marked, or woven designs reminiscent of the textured-appearance of baskets.

Baskets as well as mats and fabrics were made by both coiling and weaving processes. There are three basic types of weaving—plain plaited (example above), twilled, and twined (examples below). There are many variations of each.

Mason (O. T. Mason, 1904, pp. 188-189) states: "Basketry is the mother of all loom work and beadwork. . . . No wide gulf separates the different varieties of textiles, however, beginning with such coarse products as brush fences and fish weirs and ending with the finest lace and needlework.

"In form basketry varies through the following classes of objects: Flat mats or wallets, generally flexible; plaques or food plates . . . slightly concave . . . . (from) coarsest sieve to that of sacred meal tray; bowls . . . ; pots . . . ; jars and fanciful shapes . . . .

"In the manufacture of their baskets the Indians have ransacked the three kingdoms of nature—mineral, animal, and vegetal." (He points to their use of mineral dyes and paints for decoration and asphalt for waterproofing. Sinew thread, feathers, porcupine quills, hair, skin and other animal products have also been utilized). "The chief dependence, however, of the basket maker is upon the vegetal kingdom. Nearly all parts of plants have been used by one tribe or another for this purpose—roots, stems, bark, leaves, fruits, seeds, and gums. . . . The split outer portion of the stems of the cane was the favorite basket material of the Southern Indians. . . ."

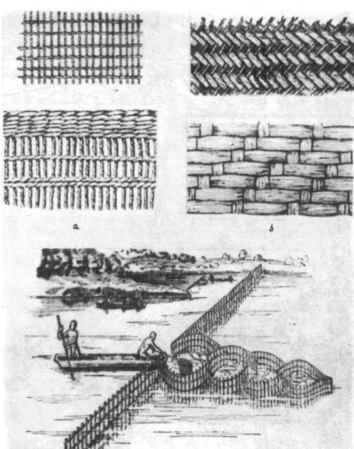

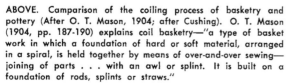

ABOVE. Comparison of the coiling process of basketry and pottery (After O. T. Mason, 1904; after Cushing). O. T. Mason (1904, pp. 187-190) explains coil basketry—"a type of basket work in which a foundation of hard or soft material, arranged in a spiral, is held together by means of over-and-over sewing—joining of parts . . . with an awl or splint. It is built on a foundation of rods, splints or straws."

RIGHT. a. example of "twined or wattled basketry: weft of two or more elements is bent around warp." b. examples of "diagonal or twilled basketry. Two or more weft strands over two or more warp strands." c. Twined fish trap (After Holmes, 1896 and O. T. Mason, 1904).

BASKETS —
COILING AND WEAVING

Plates 131 and 132

RIGHT. Laborers with their baskets and harvest. From an engraving by De Bry after a drawing by Le Moyne, who visited Florida in 1564-65. Timucua tribe. Some of the natives have a tump line around their forehead for holding the load.

BELOW. UPPER ROW. LEFT. Twilled splint baskets said to have been used in a game. Similar shallow baskets were frequently used as containers, and the very shallow baskets for winnowing grain. Cherokee. Qualla Reservation, North Carolina (Courtesy, University Museum, University of Pennsylvania, 46-695 a). RIGHT. "Burden basket made of split cane in twilled weave on a square bottom; the sides round with the growth of the basket; halfway, it begins to flare; top is finished with oversewing and turned down warp; no ornamentation. The squaw from whom it was bought refused to part with the much worn carrying strap; neither a new one nor money to buy several new ones tempted her—she always answered, 'You take your money and buy you a new one.' Diameter at bottom 9½"; at top 20"; height 16"; 16 warp to inch. Choctaw. Muskhogean family. Heidelberg, Mississippi." (Courtesy, Lauren Rogers Library and Museum of Art; photograph by Jack Lynch). LOWER ROW. Left. "Shallow basket made of cane, twilled, and on the usual square or rectangular bottom; on the sides, yellow and black canes are brought into the weave; 3½" high; sides, 12" x 12¾"; 7 warp to inch. Choctaw. Louisiana." Center. "Basket of very rare weave made of small, smooth willow splints and cane brake splints; bottom is square; warp splints are placed side by side in groups of four or five and held by single woof (weft) splints; at the sides all the warps are grouped in fours or fives and held flat by the woof strands of willow and cane dyed (vegetable dyes) red, green and yellow; border has an oversewing of cane, the warp being bent under the stitches. Diameter at top, 10¼"; at bottom, 6"; height, 5". Choctaw. Rankin County, Mississippi." Right. "Round basket made of cane splints, twilled weave, on a square base and rounding on the sides; a few yellow and brown (possibly black originally) splints form a crossing on each side. This is a very rare specimen since it is woven double and this tribe, nearly always, wove single elements. About 100 years old. Diameter, 12"; height, 6". 6 canes to inch. Jones County, Mississippi." (Courtesy, Lauren Rogers Library and Museum of Art; photograph by Jack Lynch). Cane appears to have been the favorite Southeastern basket material.

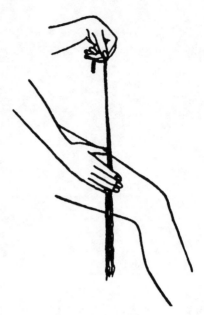

LEFT. UPPER. Reproduction of a weaving frame. Split canes substitute for shuttles and separate the fixed vertical warp strands. The weft or woof was woven across the warp with a needle or bodkin. Though hand weaving was slower than using a loom with a heddle and shuttle, it enabled the natives to produce a variety of woven materials (Courtesy, Columbus Museum of Arts and Crafts, Inc.; display in the Isabel Garrard Patterson Memorial, Chattahoochee Valley Prehistoric Indian Arts Section, which includes reproductions of perishable artifacts).

LEFT. LOWER. "Rabbit Hair garment, with fringed edges at top, bottom, and one side. The background color is dark red; half circles in dull yellow ornament the ends; on the right a portion is missing; open twill-twined weave. Warp about ten to the inch, double woof about three to the inch. Size 26½ x 39 inches. H. M. Trowbridge collection, No. 2743" (Willoughby, C. C., 1952, p. 118; quoted by permission from The Missouri Archaeological Society). Willoughby discusses Southeastern fabrics:

"The loom . . . was . . . unknown among (Southeastern) earthwork builders . . . but some form of frame was necessary for . . .

"The larger proportion of cordage prepared for loom weaving was spun with the aid of a spindle and whorl, but most of that used for frame weaving was spun by rolling between the palm of the hand and the bare thigh, which seems to have been a very effective way, as the size and regulation of the cord could be easily controlled by this method.

"In the cloth that I have examined from the Spiro Mound group of eastern Oklahoma, we find cordage of the following materials: vegetal fibers of different kinds, some of which are too badly disintegrated for identification; hair or wool from the buffalo and the hair of the rabbit, used either alone or in combination with vegetal fiber. Rabbit hair however, was a favorite material as it was easily procured, could be readily dyed, and, like the mountain goat wool of the northwest was spun into yarn by itself or in combination with vegetal fiber or used as a wrapping over a foundation of somewhat stronger vegetal material . . . feather garments from capes to long cloaks were in not uncommon use throughout the United States. . . .

"A fragment of another mantle from the Etowah Mound group in Northern Georgia showing a symmetrical arrangement of concentric circles enclosing a cross together with equal arm crosses, appears in my paper in Moorehead's report on the Etowah exploration. All of these decorative designs apparently are produced in the same general way termed by Holmes 'the lost color process.' This was followed in the decoration of certain pottery, calabash vessels, cloth, etc. in various sections of America.

"In the simpler forms of this process the designs were drawn in hot wax or a similar substance which when cold were impervious to the dye used in coloring the body of the cloth. . . . After the waxed (designs) were cool and hard the cloth was probably immersed in cold red dye, then washed in cold water, after which it (the cloth) was placed in hot water which removed the wax from the half circle; leaving the designs in the original color of the cloth." (Willoughby, 1952, pp. 107-116, excerpts; quoted by permission from the Missouri Archaeological Society).

LEFT. Line drawing showing the hand and leg used in the preparation of thread or cordage; the spindle and whorl was a later method. John Smith described spinning: "Betwixt their hands and thighes, their women vse to spin, the barkes of trees, Deere sinewes, or a kind of grasse they call Pemmenaw, of these they make a thred very even and readily. This thred serveth for many vses." Hist. Virginia. Richmond, 1819, pp. 132-133; Holmes, 1896, p. 23).

RIGHT. UPPER. Drawing by Eleanor F. Chapman, Art Director, MISSOURI ARCHAEOLOGIST. This is Figure 45 in Chapman and Anderson, 1955, THE CAMPBELL SITE. It is the reconstruction of a burial scene of the type indicated by the remains found at that site (Courtesy, Eleanor F. Chapman and the Missouri Archaeological Society).

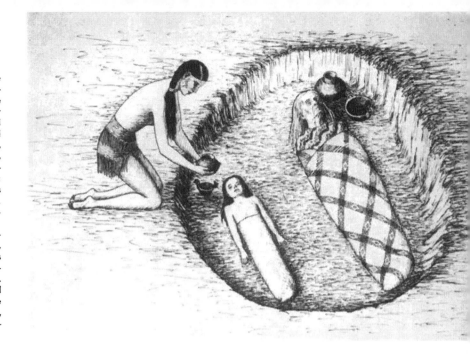

FABRICS
AND MATTING

Plates 133 and 134

RIGHT. LOWER. Large cane mat; 6 feet 3 inches by 7 feet. Chitemacha, Louisiana (Courtesy, Museum of the American Indian, Heye Foundation, 1-9515).

Holmes (1896, pp. 18-21) discusses matting:

"No class of articles of textile nature were more universally employed by the aborigines than mats of split cane, rushes, and reeds. . . . Mats are not so varied in form and character as are baskets, but their uses are greatly diversified; they served for carpeting, seats, hangings, coverings, and wrappings, and they were extensively employed in permanent house construction, and for temporary or movable shelters. . . .

"Mats were used not only in and about the dwellings of the aborigines, but it was a common practice to carry them from place to place to sleep on, or for use as seats or carpeting in meetings or councils of ceremonious nature. . . .

"Frequent mention is made of the use of mats in burial. . . .

"The sizes of mats were greatly varied; the smallest were sufficient for seating only a single person, but the largest were many yards in length, the width being restricted to a few feet by the conditions of construction. . . . It was a common practice to interweave strands of different size, shape, or color, thus producing borders and patterns."

VILLAGE CONSTRUCTION

Plates 135 and 136

RIGHT. A Timucua village with a palisade. Florida. From an engraving by De Bry after a drawing by Le Moyne, who visited Florida in 1564-65. There are two guard houses at the entrance—one at each end; a canal leads to the palisade entrance. Warriors with bows and arrows and spears protect the village (Photograph, courtesy, Smithsonian Institution, Bureau of American Ethnology). Le Moyne writes:

"The chief's dwelling stands in the middle of the town, and is partly underground in consequence of the sun's heat. Around this are the houses of the principal men, all lightly roofed with palm branches, as they are occupied only nine months in the year; the other three, as has been related, being spent in the woods." (1875, p. 12).

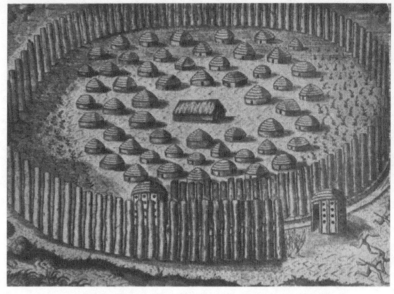

BELOW. UPPER. Diorama of a ceremony in the earthlodge at Ocmulgee National Monument, Macon, Georgia. This is thought to have been the winter council house of the Master Farmers, an early Mississippi Period culture, described as Macon Plateau (Fairbanks, 1956, p. 57). Excavations in the 1930's revealed the lower walls, floor features and fallen timbers lying on the floor; from a study of these, the earthlodge was reconstructed. From the outside it resembles a "frog-house" with an enclosed canopy-type tunnel leading in; this doubtless broke the direct force of cold air, which might have come through a flimsy door. The earth on top is held up by heavy bracing logs, and a network of smaller logs converging at a hole in the center. (details are shown in diorama). It is about 42 feet in diameter; at the foot of the outer wall a "low clay bench about 6 inches high encircles the room and is divided into 47 seats, separated by a low ramp of clay. Each seat has a shallow basin formed in its forward edge, and three such basins mark seats on the rear portion of a clay platform. . . ." (Pope, 1956, p. 31). The platform is on the west side, and opposite the entrance; it is shaped like the head and shoulders of an eagle, somewhat similar to that part of the copper plates found at Etowah; it is higher than the circular row of seats. The head, shown in the picture above, has on the head, the "forked eye." (Courtesy, National Park Service, Ocmulgee). LOWER. Model of a Lamar Village of the late prehistoric culture; this village has two mounds (one not shown here) with a square between. The mound is unusual because it has a spiral ramp leading to the summit where the temple or council house is located (Courtesy, National Park Service, Ocmulgee).

ABOVE. LEFT. Drawing reconstructing the interior of a structure. Feature 2, Site LU°21, Seven Mile Island, Alabama. Webb and DeJarnette (1942, pp. 47 and 48) state that the small posts around the side appear to have been driven into place, rather than trenched, which was a frequent method of placement. Post molds are evident. The four large corner posts are set inside, and into holes, which were vertical on the outside but dug with an inside slant, and packed from the inside. The large posts were about a foot in diameter. The structure was 20 x 23 feet. A banquette of puddled clay followed the inside line of the building; and close, around the outside was a channel or gutter. There was one doorway on the north side; and a fire basin 1.8 by 1 foot of puddled clay was slightly east of the center of the building (Courtesy, Alabama Museum of Natural History; BAE. Bull. 129, Pl. 69-2). RIGHT. Reconstruction of a "double curvilinear stockade," maximum diameter 76 feet; and a rectangular, almost square building, 17.5' x 18'. The posts for the enclosure averaged 0.6 foot diameter and 1.3 feet in depth. See: DeJarnette and Wimberly, 1941, pp. 55 and 56. This was a feature of a village area, east of the domiciliary mound. (Courtesy, Alabama Museum of Natural History, Museum Paper 17, Fig. 46).

Archeological publications are full of descriptions of the remains of primitive buildings. Webb, 1938, describes several types of houses used at sites in the Norris Basin, including thatched houses—cane and grass on poles—and houses covered with earth. Webb, 1939; Webb and DeJarnette, 1942; and Webb and Wilder, 1951 describe village construction of the Tennessee River area.

RIGHT. UPPER. Model of an Acolapissa village, Louisiana, 1732. Model in U. S. National Museum, after De Batz drawing. Muskhogean family (Courtesy, Smithsonian Institution, USNM, 31-249 A). LOWER. Miniature Group showing house, temple, mound, litter-carriers, dugout canoe, corn crib, and life activities of Natchez Indians (Courtesy, American Museum of Natural History, 318418).

"The inside of their houses is furnished with genteel couches to sit, and lie upon, raised on four forks of timber . . . they tie with fine white oak splinters, a sufficient quantity of middle-sized canes of proper dimensions, to three or four bars of the same sort, which they fasten above the frame; and they put their mattresses a-top which are made of long cane splinters. Their bedding consists of the skins of wild beasts, such as of buffalo, . . . bears, . . . and deer, which they dress with the hair on . . . ." (Adair, 1775, p. 419-420).

Hariot describes this: "First, they choose some longe, and thicke tree . . . and make a fyre on the grownd abowt the Roote thereof, kindlinge the same by little, and little with drie mosse of trees, and chipps of woode that the flame should not mounte opp to highe, and burne to muche of the lengthe of the tree . . . . vntill the tree fall of yts owne accord. . . . Then burninge of the topp, and bowghs of the tree . . . . they raise yt vppon poles laid ouer cross wise vppon forked posts, at suche a reasonable heighte as they may handsomlye worke vppon yt. Then take they of the barke with certayne shells. . . . On the other side they make a fyre accordinge to the lengthe of the bodye of the tree. . . . That which they thinke is sufficientlye burned they quenche and scrape away the shells, and makinge a new fyre they burne yt agayne. . . ." (Hariot, 1893, Pl. 12; Swanton, 1946, p. 591).

ABOVE. "The manner of makinge their boates." From an engraving by De Bry after a water color by John White, 1587; coastal area of present N. Carolina. Southern Algonquians (Courtesy, Smithsonian Institution, BAE, 44,479-C).

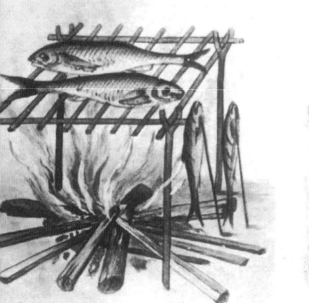

LEFT. FAR. "The broyling of their fish ouer the flame of fier." From a water color by John White, 1587, in the coastal region of present N. Carolina. Southern Algonquians (Courtesy, Smithsonian Insʻitution, BAE, 18,730). NEAR. Wooden mortar and pestle. Chitimacha tribe (Courtesy, Smithsonian Institution, BAE, 1182-c; BAE Bull. 43, Pl. 21).

BELOW. "Killing an alligator." Timucua. After De Bry; after Le Moyne (Courtesy, Smithsonian Institution, BAE, 44-534-A).

"They put up, near a river, a little hut full of cracks and holes, and in this they station a watchman, so that they can see the crocodiles (or alligators) and hear them a good way off; for, when driven by hunger, they come out of the rivers and crawl about on the islands after prey, and if they find none, they make . . . a frightful noise. . . . Then the watchman calls the rest of the watch . . . . and taking a portion, ten to twelve feet long, of the stem of a tree, they go out to find the monster, who is crawling along with his mouth wide open . . . . with great quickness they push the pole, small end first, as deep as possible down his throat, so that the roughness and irregularity of the bark may hold it from being got out again. Then they turn the crocodile over on his back, and with clubs and arrcws pound and pierce his belly, which is softer. . . . (Le Moyne, 1875, p. 10 (illus.); pl. 26. Swanton, 1922, p. 358. Swanton, 1946, p. 332).

LOGS, LIMBS, AND HAFTED TOOLS

Plates 137 and 138

BELOW. Reproductions of hafted tools. These were made by Malcolm W. Hill, Alexandria, Virginia (Courtesy, M. W. Hill). Immediately below is an excerpt from an article on hafting, written by Malcolm W. Hill; he wrote this for quotation in this publication; however, it contains many phrases which appear in an article Mr. Hill wrote for publication in the late Virgil Y. Russell's book, INDIAN ARTIFACTS, Revised Edition, 1957, Casper, Wyoming (Quoted by permission from Mrs. Virgil Y. Russell and Malcolm W. Hill).

"Among primitive civilizations, cutting was done with the sharpest edges which could be conveniently obtained. Tools were made of progressive hardness from wood, bone, shell, slate, etc., to the ultimate of flint. Natural formations were occasionally used, but more often the material had to be worked to fit it for the particular cutting job. Early man first held such tools in his hand, but there is evidence that at an early date he learned the desirability of hafting his tools.

"Natives doubtless found that by using the natural form of the materials they could save time. Hollow material, as bone, antler, horn, and plants like cane, bamboo, and other pithy growths, were sought. Those did not require drilled sockets, and were easy to prepare. The use of prongs and stubs of branches afforded good anchors for lashings. Tools mounted at an angle to the main axis of the haft were often lashed to a stub limb extending from the stick at the desired angle. The hoe, a very common tool, was usually mounted in this fashion. When heavy tools like the so-called spade (a post hole digger) were hafted, it was important that the stone be made to butt against a part of the haft (either the base of the prong or a stub on its side); the shocks from use, were thus borne by the haft and not by the lashings. Large thick tools, which were too big to mount in a prong without unduly weakening it, were hafted with the use of splints lashed to the handle; these extended over the sides of the stone tool and permitted a strong friction grip to hold the stone in place. This also avoided excessive weight in the handle.

"Rawhide, sinew and gut were the best lashing materials; rawhide and animal products put on when damp, would shrink tighter when dry. When those materials were inconvenient or not available, other less durable and stretchy materials were substituted. Vines (trumpet vine, wisteria, honeysuckle and grapevine), inside bark, and many grasses, which have tough fibers and are flexible, could be wound tight without breaking. Small thread-like fibers were necessary for very small hafting jobs. They were obtained from hair (animal and human), and the inner bark of trees, which can be divided into fine fibers when the bark is green. Yucca, when green or dry, produces strong fibers. Pitch or asphalt, gums, and glue were used to hold some of the haftings in place; those also helped in waterproofing the hafting. When lashings became loose, as was most frequent in the case of vegetable fibers, small removable or glued wedges were used as a quick way to tighten a set of loose lashings.

"There were many methods of lashing a tool to a handle, and the method chosen probably depended on a combination of factors including, the purpose of the tool, the skill of the craftsman, the type haft available, the urgency of production, and the type lashing at hand. Doubtless after much experience in lashing, the native learned that in every hafting, there must be a sensible relationship between the haft and the stone tool; any edged tool will suffer damage when the haft is too big, too long, or the lashing too tight or too loose.

"The natives took precaution, to protect the lashing, as well as the tool; many arrowpoints and tools were smoothed in the area where the lashing bound them, to prevent their cutting the lashings. When wooden hafts were used, sometime the knot of rawhide, gut or fiber, was countersunk into a hole drilled for the purpose, as modern screw heads are often sunk.

"Among the small hafted tools were, bit and hand drills, knives, chisels, rasps for leveling high spots, scrapers, awls, hammers, fish scalers, skinners, tomahawks, saws, gigs, scarifiers for bark removal, skin-slitters, groovers or notchers and gravers. Among the large hafted tools were, hoes, axes, post-diggers, choppers, scrapers and mauls.

"In all of the native craftsmanship, there was a continual need for a cutting edge, and it was usually best handled when hafted; a handle allowed more use of pressure, more accuracy, and more skill." Shown below are several hoes or spades, knives, and adzes. Malcolm W. Hill is a retired engineer and an amateur archaeologist; he has experimented with hafting for many years, and given such reproductions to several museum. He has also experimented with throwing-sticks and darts. See Plate 76.

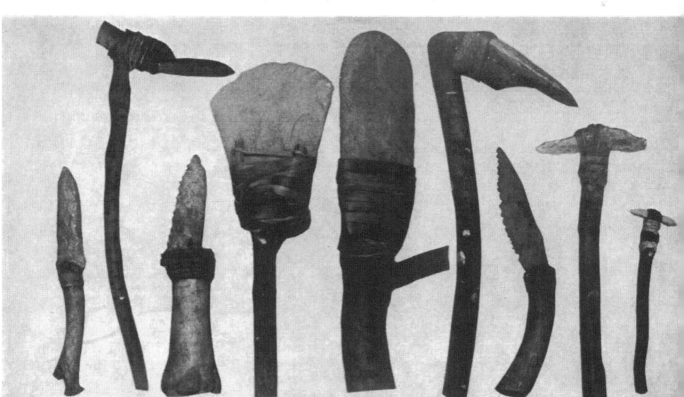

WOODEN MASKS

Plates 139 and 140

BELOW. "Their dances which they use at their high feasts." From a water color by John White, 1587, in the coastal region of present N. Carolina. Southern Algonquians. The male dancers have a crest of hair with feathers sticking into it; Indians from several villages often gathered for such feasts; a native's identity was sometime signified by marks on his back, as the arrows on the back of some of the dancers pictured; three maidens in the center interlock arms and continually circle. The outside dancers are replaced at intervals by others lined on the side, but not shown in the picture. This dance began at sunset. Fire was used to light night dances. They dance around posts on top of which are carved images; they carry boughs of trees, arrows, and gourd rattles (Courtesy, Smithsonian Institution, BAE, 18,724).

ABOVE. Two wooden masks worn by performers in the Feather and Eagle Dance. Eastern Cherokee Reservation. N. Carolina (Courtesy, Smithsonian Institution, USNM, 133,010 and 133,009).

"The Indians have Posts fix'd round their Quioccasan, which have Mens Faces carved upon them, and are painted. They are likewise set up round some of their other celebrated places, and make a Circle for them to dance about, on certain solemn occasions." Beverley, 1705, bk. 3, p. 46). "The place where they meet (from all about) is a broade playne, abowt the which are planted in the grownde certayne posts carued with heads like to the faces of Nonnes couered with theyr vayles." (Hariot, 1893, pl. 18). "Lawson (1860, pp. 285-286) says that the Indians of the Piedmont country set up 'idols' in their fields to encourage the young men in their work . . . ." Martyr mentions this. (Swanton, 1946, p. 615).

LEFT. Painted wooden masks from Key Marco, Florida, recovered in 1896 by F. H. Cushing (Courtesy, Smithsonian Institution, BAE, Florida 21). For a discussion of Key Marco masks, see Mason, 1950 and Cushing, 1897). The native craftsman probably sometimes carved the details of a mask on a large section of a log, in order to hold it secure; later he could detach the mask and finish the sides and back. It has been suggested that Indians sometimes carved a mask on the side of a standing tree, and later felled the tree to finish the mask. Masks recovered from Marco gave little indication of the probable size of the original block of wood. (For a discussion of Marco masks see Plates 58, 60; pp. 103-104). For other masks see Plates 141-142 and 147-148.

RIGHT. Four wooden masks with fur decorations. Faces are rough and tool marks are evident. These were used in the Eagle Dance. East Cherokee Reservation, N. Carolina (Courtesy, Smithsonian Institution, USNM, 272,971-272,974. Collected by James Mooney). Masks were used for a variety of purposes. They were worn in dances in imitation of persons and animals; sometimes the impersonations were intended to be ridiculous and at other times, serious. Masks were also used for decoys in hunting, and they were worn in hunting ceremonies in an effort to placate the spirits of animals, or to give the hunter good luck. Masks were sometimes worn by medicine men to add strength to their conjuring. Masks were worn in rituals as a means of symbolizing the characteristics of the animals or humans depicted. Cushing (1897, pp. 390-392) discusses the primitive philosophy and belief that by wearing masks and changing the expressions of face, the personality is likewise changed, at least, during the wearing. Cushing (pp. 390-391) states: ". . . they reason that expression controls, rather than that it is the result of, character or disposition—so far at least as these animals are concerned. It follows that they believe the changes in the expression of a man's face to be similarly effective. They observe that his face is far more mobile than is that of any animal, and hence believe that he is more capable of changing; that according as his mood changes, his face changes; and they reason that vice versa according as his face is changed his mood must necessarily change. Further, they believe . . . that his traits or his entire character may, for the time being be changed by wholly altering, with paint or other marking, with mask or other disguise, the entire expression of his countenance or aspect. . . . Thereby, it is believed that so far as he resembles in facial aspect or expression one kind of being or animal or another kind of being or animal, he will become that being or animal, or at least, be possessed by its spirit."

LEFT. FAR. Wooden mask. The snake coiled on the head has engraved lines imitating the texture of scales, and has paint imitating spots. Speck and Witthoff (Speck, 1950, p. 27) believed the mask was worn by a warrior to show his intention to fight. Also, the idea has been expressed that such masks were the property of medicine men, and had "a magicoreligious purpose in the exorcism of disease." Cherokee. N. Carolina (Courtesy, University Museum, University of Pennsylvania). NEAR. Wooden mask, 10" long; maximum width, 5" (Courtesy, North Carolina Department of Archives and History). Masks on this plate have been identified as masks used in dances and ceremonies of Cherokee Indians. Other Cherokee masks are pictured on Plates 147-148.

WOODEN MASKS AND IMAGES
Plates 141 and 142

RIGHT. Kewas, a wooden image 4 feet high guarding the bones of dead chiefs in the temple at Secota; it was black except for a flesh-colored face, white breast, and white spots on the thighs; it wore copper and shell beads, and had a hair-style like the Florida Indians; sometimes there were several such images in a temple. After an engraving by De Bry of a water color by John White (Rare Book Room, New York Public Library). "They thinke that all the gods are of human shape, . . . they represent them by images . . . Kewasowok . . . Them they place in . . . temples . . .; Where they woorship, praie, sing, and make . . . offerings vnto them. In some Machicomuck we have seene but one Kewas, in some two, and in other some three;" (Hariot, 1893, p. 38).

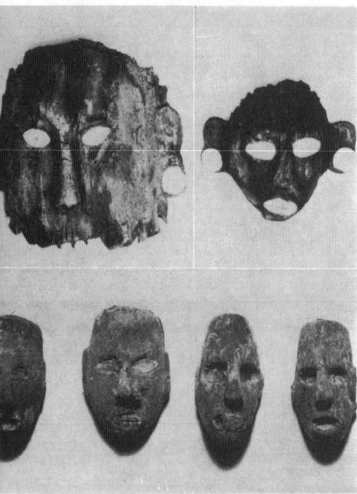

ABOVE. LEFT. UPPER. Two wooden masks of red cedar with shell inlay on eyes, ears and mouth. Spiro; Craig Burial Mound, Le Flore County, Oklahoma (Courtesy, University of Oklahoma). LOWER. Four small human effigy masks of red cedar; one on left is about 2⅜" long; eyes and mouth were originally filled with shell inlay; often such small masks from this site, are stained by copper, but do not show copper overlay; the back is hollow, as if they had been mounted. Spiro Mound (Courtesy, University of Arkansas collection. Photograph courtesy, H. W. Hamilton, 1952, Fig. 27).

ABOVE. RIGHT. Wooden statue, 7½" high. Lake Okeechobee, Florida (Courtesy, Smithsonian Institution, USNM, 316,254). There probably were many wooden images throughout the Southeast which have now decayed and left no evidence. Moorehead, 1910, Vol. 2, p. 27, pictures a wooden image from a cave in the upper Cumberland area. Swanton (1928, p. 707) writes of wooden images: "The eastern Siouan tribes were addicted to the use of wooden images in connection with certain of their festivals. In some Creek towns wooden images were brought out during the annual ceremonies, but their use was very limited. On the other hand we have references to the employment of such images in the Carolina area going back to the voyage of Ayllon's captain in 1521. Peter Martyr speaks of two idols in the courtyard of the sovereign Datha's palace which were exhibited during the sowing season and at the time of harvest. . . ." (Swanton gives other references to images in his publications of 1928 and 1946).

ABOVE. LEFT. Plaque of walnut bark with spider carved on it; about 5" long. Moundville, Alabama (Courtesy, Chicago Natural History Museum, 50639). RIGHT. Wooden rattle in form of a turtle, with fragments of sheet copper overlay. Front limbs resemble flippers; rear legs are missing; mouth and eyes are evident; 6⅞" long. Spiro Mound, Oklahoma (Courtesy, Museum of the American Indian, 18/9307).

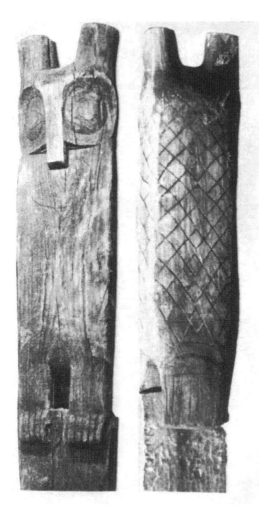

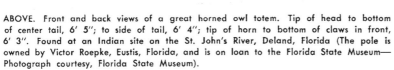

ABOVE. Front and back views of a great horned owl totem. Tip of head to bottom of center tail, 6' 5"; to side of tail, 6' 4"; tip of horn to bottom of claws in front, 6' 3". Found at an Indian site on the St. John's River, Deland, Florida (The pole is owned by Victor Roepke, Eustis, Florida, and is on loan to the Florida State Museum—Photograph courtesy, Florida State Museum).

RIGHT. UPPER. Mask of red cedar with shell inlays for eyes and mouth; effigy of deer-man with antlers; 11⅜" maximum height. The shallow sockets on the ears, representing ear spools were probably originally filled with shell inlay; the back of the mask has been hollowed to a depth of ¾"; surface is smooth and without tool marks; one side is badly weathered but intact. See Burnett, 1945 (Courtesy, Museum of the American Indian, Heye Foundation, 18/9306). LOWER. Two wooden bird-heads, a duck and a crane? Palm Beach, Florida (Courtesy, Smithsonian Institution, USNM).

MUSICAL INSTRUMENTS

Plates 143 and 144

ABOVE. Drum, 30" high; made by Ahojobe; Choctaw tribe. Tammany Parish, Louisiana (Courtesy, Smithsonian Institution, BAE, 1102-b-7; also Bushnell, 1909, BAE Bull. 48, Pl. 7-a). Bushnell (p. 22) describes this: "It is made of a section of a black gum tree; the cylinder wall is less than 2 inches in thickness. The head consists of a piece of untanned goat skin. The skin is stretched over the open end, while wet and pliable, and is passed around a loop made of hickory about half an inch thick. A similar hoop is placed above the first. To the second hoop is attached four narrow strips of rawhide, each of which is fastened to a peg passing diagonally through the wall of the drum. To tighten the head of the drum it is necessary merely to drive the peg farther in. In this respect, as well as in general form, the drum resembles a specimen from Virginia in the British Museum, as well as the drum even now used on the west coast of Africa. It is not possible to say whether this instrument is a purely American form or whether it shows the influence of the Negro." Adair (1775, p. 116) noted "two clay-pot drums covered on the top with thin wet deer-skins, drawn very tight . . ."

BELOW. Ceremonies after war; scalps, legs, and arms of the enemy hanging from poles in the square; the sorcerer curses the enemy and dances with an image in his hand; three musicians accompany—two with rattles and one beating on a stone. After an engraving by De Bry after a drawing by Le Moyne, who visited Florida in 1565. Timucua tribe (Rare book room, New York Public Library). One musician uses gourd rattles similar to those pictured (opposite page).

ABOVE. Choctaw flute or flageolet made of cane; wrapped with leather on top end. Small effigy face carved under top windhole; burned cross-hatching decoration on upper part (Courtesy, Smithsonian Institution, USNM. Densmore Collection, 365,174).

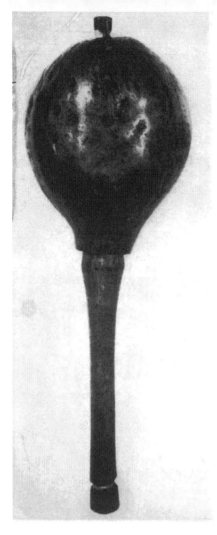

When discussing musical instruments of the Southeastern Indians, in addition to drums, Swanton (1946, pp. 620-629) speaks of rattles, flageolets, and rasps:

"Lawson observed among the Waxhaw a rattle consisting of a gourd with corn in it. . . . When he comes to discuss the culture of the Piedmont tribes in general, he speaks of 'a rattle, made of a gourd, with some beans in it' (Lawson, 1860, pp. 98, 286). Aaair, Bartram, Penicaut, and Du Pratz mention gourd rattles in use among the Chickasaw, Creeks, Pascagoula, and Chitimacha. . . . In a certain dance they stated that two sticks were struck together. . . .

"The terrapin shell rattles worn by Creek women about their ankles during the annual dances in the Square Grounds represent another type, but there is little mention of this outside of the Creek Nation. The following description by Romans may apply to a substitute or to an earlier form:

'I observed the women dressed their legs in a kind of leather stockings, hung full of the hoofs of the roe deer in form of bells, in so much as to make a sound exactly like that of the Castagnettes: I was very desirous of examining these stockings and had an opportunity of satfsying my curiosity on those of my landlady at her return home. I counted in one of her stockings four hundred and ninety-three of these claws; there were nine of the women at the dance with this kind of ornament, so that allowing each of them to have had the same number of hoofs, and eight hoofs to a deer, there must have been killed eleven hundred and ten deer to furnish this small assembly of ladies with their ornaments.' (Romans, 1775, p. 95).

"Over much of the Gulf area, when it was first visited by Europeans, it was customary to welcome strangers of quality coming in peace by sending men forward, usually including the chief himself, blowing upon flutes, or rather flageolets. This custom is first alluded to by Cabeza de Vaca in his account of the Narvaez expedition to Florida. . . . This was Timucua territory.

"The custom was again observed by the followers of De Soto among the same people. Flageolets are probably to be understood by the 'trumpets' in the hands of Indians near the Withlacoochee River, since conch-shell horns are mentioned separately (Garcilaso, 1723, p. 45).

"Bartram describes the flutes seen by him belonging to the Creek (or rather Seminole) and perhaps the Cherokee tribes, as

'. . . made of a joint of reed or the tibia of the deer's leg: on this instrument they perform badly, and at best it is rather a hideous melancholy discord, than harmony.' (Bartram, 1792, p. 503).

"A rasp is shown in Catlin's painting of the Choctaw eagle dance. The Chitimacha say that they formerly used a dried alligator skin for that purpose (Swanton, 1931, a, pl. 6, p. 222; 1911, p. 350). The Hasinai missionary Espinosa (1927, p. 165) saw the Indians make (noise by rubbing slitted polished sticks across a hollow skin)."

ABOVE. Gourd dance rattle, 12½" long. Eastern Cherokee Reservation, N. Carolina (Courtesy, Smithsonian Institution, USNM, 133,007. Collected by James Mooney). The dance rattles of the prehistoric Indians were probably elaborately decorated with carved or burned designs. Similar rattles were used with dances and songs.

RIGHT. "Their manner of praying with their rattles about the fire." From a water color by John White, 1587, in the coastal region of present N. Carolina Southern Algonquians (Courtesy, Smithsonian Instituion, BAE, 18,717). Hariot describes this:

'when they haue escaped any great danger by sea or lande, or be returned from the warr in token of loye they make a great fyre abowt which the men, and woemen sitt together, holdinge a certaine fruite in their hands like vnto a rawnde pompion or a gourde, which after they haue taken out the fruits, and the seedes, then fill with small stons or certayne bigg kernells to make the more noise, and fasten that vppon a sticke, and singinge after their manner, they make merrie: as my selfe observed and noted downe at my beinge amonge them.' (Hariot, 1893, pl. 17; Swanton, 1946, p. 626). Rattles were numerous.

Chapter 9

ANIMAL PRODUCTS

Quotation from John R. Swanton, THE INDIANS OF THE SOUTHEASTERN UNITED STATES, Bureau of American Ethnology, Bulletin 137, 1946, pp. 249-253—excerpts. Quoted courtesy, Smithsonian Institution, Bureau of American Ethnology.

"The most important food animal was the deer, and deerhide probably formed the most important single material entering into native dress. One of the bones from a deer's foot was used to remove the hair from skins. The head and neighboring parts were turned into a decoy for stalking . . . deer. . . . The ribs were made into bracelets, part of the horn mounted on a club, and tips of the horns formed one of the commonest types of arrow points. The heads of drums were usually made by stretching a deer skin over a pot, keg, or cypress knee. Balls used in the great southern ball game were covered with deer hide, and the rattles which women wore about their ankles in dances were sometimes made of the hoofs of deer. Flutes or flageolets were sometimes made of the deer's tibia. The sinews, skin, or entrails were employed as thread or string, and bowstrings, fish nets, and the cords to fasten ballsticks together were constructed by their means. According to Strachey, bows were scraped by the use of a twisted deer hide. Parts of the horns and bones were made into needles, and the brains were employed in tanning skins. Ornaments were made from the horn, deer bones were worn stuck through the hair in Florida, and toward the north stained deer's hair was metamorphosed into crests for warriors. Deer horn was also boiled to make glue, and glue was extracted from deerskins to dilute coloring matter. Indians living toward the north hunted elk for food, and used its hide for clothing, particularly moccasins.

"The bear was probably the next most useful animal. It was hunted for its flesh, but still more for its fat, which was preserved in skins. Heavy winter robes and bed coverings were made of the skins, and moccasins were also cut out of them. Thongs of twisted bear guts were utilized as bow strings, and bows were sometimes finished by dipping them in bear's oil. This oil was used constantly to anoint the hair and indeed the entire body. Bear claws were thrust through the ears as ornaments.

"In spite of the fact that bison disappeared from the Gulf region rather rapidly in colonial times, they were formerly much relied upon as raw material for many purposes. . . . The flesh . . . as food . . . the skins as clothing and robes to sit upon or throw over beds . . . (and for) shields. . . . The horns were used as ornaments on headdresses, and they were worked into dishes and spoons. The shoulder blade was used as a hoe and in dressing skins. Bison hair was woven into cords. . . .

"Quivers and body armor were made of hide. . . . Animal bones were . . . raw material for beads and arrow points, and powdered bone . . . employed . . . as tempering for pots."

"A fox skin was sometime metamorphosed into a pouch. . . . Weasel skins . . . ornaments to the headdress. . . ."

(Other animals used for food, clothing (skins), and textiles (woven hair) include the panther, opossum, rabbit, wildcat, and polecat. Skins of the fox and wolf were used in making wrist protectors).[1]

---

[1] "The beaver was eaten and its skin used in . . . clothing, particularly pouches. The beaver tooth, usually set in the end of a stick, was an important tool, and one writer seems to imply that textiles were made of the hair.

"The muskrat was eaten and its skin formed a much prized article of clothing. . . . The companions of De Soto once found the skin or skins of muskrat made into something which they thought was a flag.

"The manatee was eaten by the Florida tribes, and 'two large bones' taken from its head, evidently the tusks, were placed in a chief's grave.

"Squirrels were a favorite . . . food and their skins were sewed into . . . clothing. The claws were thrust through apertures in the ears as ornaments. A twisted skin frequently did duty as a bowstring.

"The raccoon was eaten and its skin used for clothing, including pouches. Thongs of raccoon hide were employed to form the cage of a ballstick. Raccoon claws were sometimes thrust through the ears by way of ornament. According to one writer, textiles were made of raccoon hair. . . .

"The otter was eaten and the skins used for clothing. . . . Pouches were, however, made of them, and since the otter was connected closely with shamanistic practices we are apt to find otter skins in the priestly costume. According to Adair, an otter-skin strap held the gorget of the Chickasaw high priest in place."

"There is one notice of work in porcupine quills (Natchez) and references to porcupine quills in use to tie up the hair (Natchez) or to ornament the headdress (Creeks). The quills, or objects ornamented with them, were evidently imported.

"Snake . . . fangs were employed by doctors in scarification . . . and Virginia doctors ornamented their heads with snake skins stuffed with moss, with the rattles of rattlesnakes, and even wore live green snakes. There is mention of the use of 'vipers' teeth' as arrow points.

"Turtles and terrapin were eaten and the shells of the latter were turned into rattles, which women wore at dances fastened round their calves.

"The fin bones of various fish were employed to point spears, arrows, and other weapons, and as needles. We are told several times that fish scales, particularly the scales of the great brown spotted gar . . . were used to point arrows; and that also fish teeth were used for such purposes. . . . fish were also used for glue. In Florida small fish bladders, colored red, were worn in the ears.

SHELLS. "Some of the clams and periwinkles have particular importance because beads were made from them which not only came to be widely used as ornaments, but attained the status of media of exchange. Larger beads were made from the conch shell; a few large ones were worn on the crown of the head, as ear pendants in the form of spikes, and as breast ornaments or gorgets. This shell was also used in serving the black drink, and it was mounted on a handle and used as a hoe. Beads were used all over the clothing as ornaments, on the headdress, to bind braids of hair, in ears and noses, wrapped around necks, and on other parts of the body. Pearls, obtained most often from fresh-water mussels, were also widely used as ornaments about neck, ears, etc., and were insignia of wealth. Marginella and olivella shells were transformed into beads almost entire, except that the inner ends of the whorls were rubbed off in order to let a cord through for stringing.

"The shells of bivalves were employed as knives, in such occupations as the hollowing out of a canoe or scraping a bow into shape. With two such shells, the Virginians shaved off, or rather grated off, the hair of one side of the head. In North Carolina there is mention of arrow points made of shell, in one instance said to be oyster shell . . . ashes of shells and hot water are mentioned as a depilatory.

FEATHERS. "The turkey seems anciently to have been the most utilized of all birds, though it was rarely tamed . . . its feathers were used in making feather mantles, in the headdress . . ., as fans, and in feathering arrows; and the turkey cock spurs were turned into arrow points. They adorned the moccasins of the Chickasaw high priest.

"Ducks were also used for food and clothing, particularly clothing of an ornamental character. We hear of blankets made of mallard heads, and the Caddo sprinkled reddened duck (and swan) down on their hair.

"Eagle feathers were employed as ornaments to the person and marks of accomplishments. Fans were made of them. . . . Eagle claws were sometimes used to adorn the breechclout.

"Hawk feathers were also used as ornaments, and a hawk skin was sometimes tied to the hair . . . . hawk claws were fastened to the breechclouts as an embellishment.

"Swan feathers were worked into mantles, worn as parts of the headdress by successful warriors, and on the headdress of the Chickasaw high priest. . . .

"Crane or heron feathers were worn by Creek Indians as part of their headdresses, particularly by those belonging to one set of clans.

"An owl skin was often carried by the Creek medicine man or priest as a symbol of his calling."

(He also mentions the use of buzzard skins as head ornaments and buzzard feathers as fetishes employed by medicine men; the feathers of the pheasant, flamingo, cardinal, and other birds were used as ornaments and woven into cloaks.)

"Besides the species of bird mentioned, many others were drawn upon to feather arrows, to make splints to bind arrowheads to the shaft, as wrist guards, on shields, as towels, and fans, though these last seem usually to have been made of turkey feathers. Down from bluebirds, herons, cardinals, and other birds was powdered over the body after it had been covered with oil. Feathers were worn comparatively little by women. Bird bills were sometimes utilized as arrow points, and with quills certain Indians traced designs on pottery. . . . Bird claws . . . were thrust through the ears by way of ornament."

ABOVE. "Order of March Observed by Outina on a Military Expedition." From an engraving by De Bry after a drawing by Le Moyne; Timucua Indians. Florida. Outina, in the center of the orderly ranks, is smeared with red paint. Natives often wore animal heads and tails to make them ferocious in battle; note, weapons, tattooing on bodies and breastplates. Le Moyne and Le Challeux narratives emphasize the widespread hostilities among native villages; they mention arrangements for war, conduct during war, brutality of war, and celebration after victory (BAE. Neg. 44075). All photographs on these two pages are (Courtesy, Smithsonian Institution, Bureau of American Ethnology).

Original existing paintings by Jacques Le Moyne and John White are in the British Museum, London. They are the earliest visual records of the Southeastern Indians. A Flemish engraver, Theodore De Bry, published engravings of the John White watercolors in 1590, and of the Le Moyne paintings in 1591. Le Moyne was a member of the French Huguenot expedition to the Florida coast in 1564-65; he produced the paintings after returning to Europe.

John White's water colors were painted in 1587 during his residence at Roanoke Island, North Carolina, as Governor of the Second Virginia Colony; the English made their initial attempt to colonize that area as a result of Raleigh's promotion of the first Virginia colony in 1584-85; Hariot, a friend of Raleigh, spent about a year in the new colony, and wrote an account of the natives and the country. It was published in 1588; it was reprinted by Hakluyt in 1589; and in 1590, T. De Bry reprinted it again, along with his engravings of John White's water colors. John White was in the new world for a few months; he returned to England for supplies; however, the conflict there between England and Spain prevented his prompt return; when help finally reached Roanoke Island, the struggling colony had disappeared. The Hariot narrative and the John White pictures, therefore, became rare and valuable documents of the surroundings of a "Lost Colony." A reprint of these early narratives, along with all the DeBry engravings and the remaining original paintings, is found in Stefan Lorant's, THE NEW WORLD, 1946.

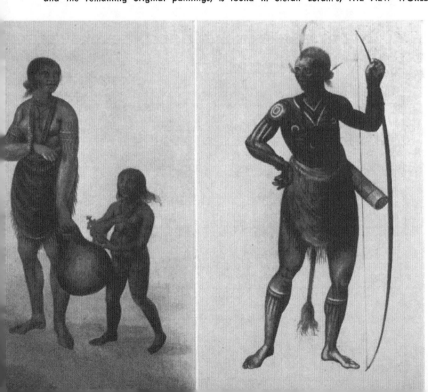

LEFT. FAR. "A Chiefe Herowans Wife of Pomeco and her daughter of the age of .8. or .10. yeares." The women and men wore similarly draped, fringed deerskins. The child wears a girdle of leather thongs and moss, and holds a doll of European origin; the woman is carrying a typical gourd container. NEAR. "The manner of their attaire and painting themselves when they goe to their general huntings or at theire Solemne feasts." Southern Algonquian. A weron or Lord of Virginia. They often wore a string of pearl beads in their ears (some of these probably were shell) and a necklace. Both men and women wore beads of pearls, bone, and copper. One account refers to a chief, who had a pair of silver ear ornaments, which bore traces of copper. The latter metal was frequently mentioned. It is known that in the Lake Superior area where copper is mined, it occasionally is found with a silver nugget, which may account for the above. Each picture is after a water color by John White, 1587, produced in the coastal region of the present N. Carolina (Courtesy, Smithsonian Institution; BAE. 18-725 and 18-723).

NATIVE COSTUMES—
SUMMER AND WINTER

Plates 145 and 146

"Most of the garments of these Indians were made of the skins of animals, though some were woven from threads of vegetable and animal origin, some were of feathers, and a few natural vegetable productions were used . . . . (Swanton, 1946, p. 439).

RIGHT. NEAR. "An Old Man in Winter Dress." The hair on top of his head is trimmed in the shape of the crest of a bird; the hair on the side of the head is gathered in the back and knotted at the neck; he wears a fringed leather garment with fur turned inward. His village has a palisade and is surrounded by orderly arranged corn fields. Southern Algonquian; North Carolina Coastal region. From an engraving by De Bry after a water color by John White, 1587 (Rare Book Room, New York Public Library). FAR. A man in lower Louisiana in winter dress. After a drawing by A. De Batz, 1732-35. Man wears skin robe with a simple design of red and black on the inside; animal hair is turned outward (BAE, Neg. 42-325 B; Smithsonian Miscellaneous Collections, Vol. 80, No. 5, Pl. 6; Swanton, BAE, Bull. 137, Pl. 70 2).

A. De Batz, made his drawings more than a century and a half after Le Moyne visited Florida; and almost two centuries after DeSoto's expedition through the Southeast, 1539-1541. Following De Luna's unsuccessful colony in 1559-1560, few Europeans penetrated the north Gulf Coast area, until the Frenchman, La Salle, reached the mouth of the Mississippi from the upper river in the 1680's; it was not until after the French colonization of Mobile in 1700 that travelers and traders became familiar with the region. During the eighteenth century, France, Spain, and England vied for control in the area and the story of their intrigue and trade is colorful. In addition to colonial records during this century, there are also the accounts by several travelers, a number of whom drew sketches of the country and natives.

The Southeastern Gulf coast was held by France and Spain until the French-Indian War of 1756-60, after which England took France's share. The Spanish, entrenched in New Orleans, grabbed England's claim to the Gulf Coast by force and treaty in 1880; by secret treaty Spain ceded Louisiana to France in 1800; and the United States purchased it in 1803. Spain held West Florida until the War of 1812; and held East Florida until the purchase by the United States in 1819. Though the Federal government had negotiated with the Indians for successive land cessions following the American Revolution, natives still held large tracts of land in the lower Southeast until Jackson became President, and sponsored the Indian Bill of the 1830's, which lead to their forceful removal to land west of the Mississippi.

BELOW. "Choctaw Savages painted as Warriors, carrying Scalps." After a drawing by A. De Batz, 1732-35. Man at extreme right seems to be wearing a European shirt. Bushnell thought the man was possibly a Natchez chief (BAE, Neg. 42-325) (SMC, Vol. 80, No. 5, Pl. 5 and Swanton, BAE, Bull. 137, Pl. 19).

LEFT. "The Indians have a way of hunting deer which we never saw before. They manage to put on the skins of the largest which have been taken, in such a manner, with the heads on their own heads, so that they can see out through the eyes as through a mask. Thus accoutered they can approach close to the deer without frightening them. They take advantage of the time when the animals come to drink at the river, and, having their bow and arrows all ready, easily shoot them, as they are very plentiful in those regions. (Le Moyne, 1875, p. 10 (illus.); Swanton, 1922, p. 357; Swanton, 1946, p. 313). "Deer stalking is described by our authorities as observed among the Powhatan Indians, the Siouan tribes, the Chickasaw and Choctaw, the Timucua, and the Natchez." (Swanton, 1946, pp. 312-321).

ABOVE. Indians hunting deer with decoys made of the skin and head of deer. From an engraving by De Bry after a drawing by Le Moyne, who visited Florida in 1564-65. Timucua tribe (Courtesy, Smithsonian Institution, BAE, 44-479).

MASKS AND DECOYS

Plates 147 and 148

RIGHT. Mask of fur with string for attaching; the strings were sometimes made of twisted milkweeds, other vegetable fibers or thongs; long ears were added to represent a wildcat. Such masks were used for decoys and magical purposes. Cherokee. North Carolina (Courtesy, University Museum, University of Pennsylvania, 46-6-3). Masks were most frequently made of leather or wood or a combination of these. "Copper Head Plates" also might have served as masks; a remarkable specimen (head with feather-type headdress) was found at Spiro— 10½" high by 6¾" (Ohio State Museum, 139/1-A).

BELOW. LEFT. Mask made of brown woodchuck skin. Used as decoy in stalking wild turkey and in the Booger Dance; clownish masks were worn by dancers or 'ghosts' impersonating the coming of the white man and the disease, distress, and loss which followed as they settled on Indian lands. This mask is 12½" wide and 9½" high. Cherokee (Courtesy, Denver Art Museum). RIGHT. Mask of skin with fur; ears added; nose, eyes, and mouth are cut through the leather; used for magical purposes to hunt turkeys and wildcats and to represent various animals in the Booger Dance. Cherokee, North Carolina (Courtesy, University Museum, University of Pennsylvania, 46-6-4).

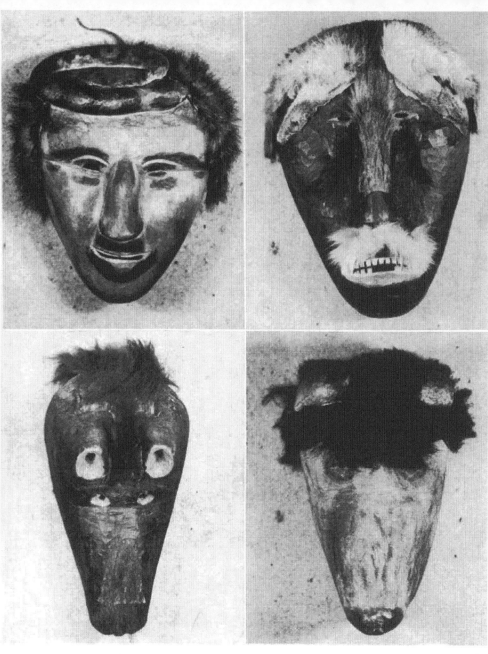

Five Cherokee masks of carved wood with leather added to give texture and realistic appearance; they also have been painted or touched with paint. Many of the Cherokee masks were made of buckeye; the red color used on them came from stain of red earth or from the liquid obtained by boiling sumac berries; boiled pokeweed berries or black walnut bark produced a black stain (Speck, 1950, p. 25) (The five masks on this page are pictured, courtesy, The Denver Art Museum).

LEFT. UPPER ROW. FAR. Mask worn by a warrior to show his intention to join a war party; worn during enlistment ceremony. It has a coiled snake on the head; small areas have black paint and raccoon fur; 10¾" long. NEAR. Mask representing a Negro; it was used in the Booger dance—a pantomime retelling the story of the coming of Europeans and slaves and the subsequent downfall of the Cherokee. Black and grey-white fur; 11½" long. LOWER ROW. FAR. Mask representing a bear; used in reciting hunting magic before the hunt; and in former times as a decoy; painted dark brown; 13½" long. NEAR. Mask representing a buffalo. Used in hunting magic and as a decoy. Made of poplar wood with bear-fur crown. 13".

BELOW. Mask representing a deer. Natural wood showing chisel marks; ornamented with brown animal hair, maximum height, 14½".

Dumont and du Pratz give accounts of the Natchez method of hunting deer:
"When a savage has succeeded in killing a deer he first cuts off its head as far down as the shoulders. Then he skins the neck without cutting the skin, and, having removed the bones and the flesh from it, he draws out all the brains from the head. After this operation he replaces the bones of the neck very neatly and fixes them in place with the aid of a wooden hoop and some little sticks. Then he re-covers them with their skin, and having dried this head partly in the shade and partly in the smoke, he thus has an entire deer's head, which is very light, and which with its skin preserves also its hair, its horns, and its ears. He carries it with him hung on to his belt when he goes hunting, and as soon as he perceives a bison or a deer he passes his right hand into the neck of this deer, with which he conceals his face, and begins to make the same kind of movements as the living animal would make. He looks ahead, then turns the head rapidly from one side to the other. He lowers it to browse on the grass and raises it immediately afterward. In fact, always concealing his face with his head, he deceives by means of his gestures the animal which he wishes to approach, and, if during this time it happens that the animal stops to gaze at him, the savage, though he has his leg in the air to move forward, stays it there, and has enough patience to remain in this posture until the living animal, taking him for another animal of his species, begins to approach him. Then the savage, seeing him within gunshot, lets the deer head fall to the earth, passes his ready gun from his left hand to his right with admirable skill and rapidly, shoots the animal, and kills it, for he rarely misses it." (Dumont, 1753, pp. 150-151; Swanton, 1911, pp. 69-70; Swanton, 1946, p. 315). Some of the human figures on engraved Spiro shells appear to have representations of deer heads hanging from their belts. "The hunter . . . provides himself . . . with the dried head of a deer . . . . (he makes) the same cry (as) these animals . . . he shows the head, which he holds in his hand, and causes it to make the movement of a deer . . . ." (du Pratz, 1758, vol. 2, pp. 69-72).

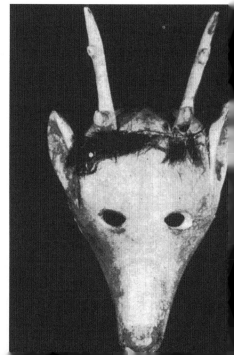

ANTLER ARTIFACTS

Plates 149 and 150

LEFT. Mounted head of a deer showing antlers (Courtesy, Dr. A. O. Haugen).

RIGHT. Webb and DeJarnette (1942, pp. 199-200) describes this plate:
". . . Blunt drifts, which might have been used in the indirect percussion frac-ture of flint; also antler chisels, and sections of antler, which were drilled transversely. These horn cylinders are about 4½ inches long, smoothly cut at the ends. Although no care was used to make the cut square, they were polished as if by use. A few were found which had partially decayed, and the horn had lost its surface. The transverse hole was near the center and was about one-half an inch in diameter. Its effect was to produce an object not unlike the head of a hammer. The use of such objects is conjectural. They might have been used to straighten the shaft of projectiles. Some of these were found in the general digging, but three seemed to have been in asso-ciation with burials (all were from the lowest levels of the Archaic shell mound) . . . . bone and horn were considerable in the early stages of the mound development, from the bottom to the 8-foot level; from the 7-foot to the 4-foot level the use of bone and horn increased to a maximum. Such use seems to have been abruptly reduced at the 3-foot level and to have increased slightly through the pottery zone." Antler was also used in hafting.
BELOW. Antler artifacts from a shell mound Archaic site. "Drifts, flakers, pendants, atlatl hooks, projectile points, carved antler section, and deer skull and antler 'head-dress'." The Flint River site, Madison County, Alabama. Courtesy, Alabama Museum of Natural History, Museum Paper 23, Webb and DeJarnette, 1948, Fig. 33). Webb and DeJarnette (pp. 63-65) state:
"Numerous antler tines, varying in length from whole tines to a short portion of the distal end, occurred (at this site). The tips of these tines were often quite blunt, suggesting their possible use as flaking tools, or possible punches. These tines would have served as excellent flakers. The proximal ends . . . were either fractured or cut. Cut distal portions of tines may be, in some instances . . . a by-product of the making of antler drifts or other implements. A number of the items . . . may be just unworked antler tine fragments.

"Antler drifts, made from sections of antler, are ground or worn on the ends and many show evidence of considerable grind-ing or abrasion through use over their entire surface. Seventy-six of the drifts were complete enough to permit measurements of length. Lengths ranged from 1¼ to 4⅜ inches with approximately nine-tenths of the drifts falling in the range of 1½ to 3½ inches. Two-thirds of the drifts were over 2¼ inches in length.

"About two-thirds of the whole drifts had a round transverse cross-section while the cross-section of the remaining third varied from elliptical to flattened-subrectangular forms. (Separate tabulations for round and elliptical drifts failed to show stratigraphic evi-dence for separate categories for these specimens). A few of the cylindrical drifts were made from sections of antler near the distal end of the tine and as a result had the shape of truncated cones.

"Socketed antler projectile points were made from the distal portion of antler tines. They are characterized by a conical socket for attachment to the projectile shaft. Generally the exterior surface is worked down to produce a sharp point and to remove the natural curve of the antler, making the projectile point asymmetrical.

"An antler headdress is shown. The sections of antler projecting from the skull are split longitudinally and the rear half of the antler is cut away in part. This may have been for the purpose of attaching an extension, or perhaps to reduce the weights of the extended antlers and thus make it easier to wear on the head. There are three holes in the skull, and a hole in each antler near its base. These perforations surely were used as aids in attaching the headdress to the head of the wearer. The edges of these perforations show smoothing as if strings or thongs had been passed through them.

"The finding of this antler headdress is re-garded as very signifi-cant. It came from the lower portion of Zone D and thus should be as-signed in time to the early portion of the Ar-chaic 3 period." They further state that such paraphernalia of shell mound people might have been the beginning of "a trait which later found expression in Adena (Webb and Haag, 1947) in copper antler head-dresses made of flat cop-per and later in Ohio Hopewell (Mills, 1932) in copper antler headdress-es made 'in the round,' by beating copper into thin sheets and rolling them on artifical antler forms."

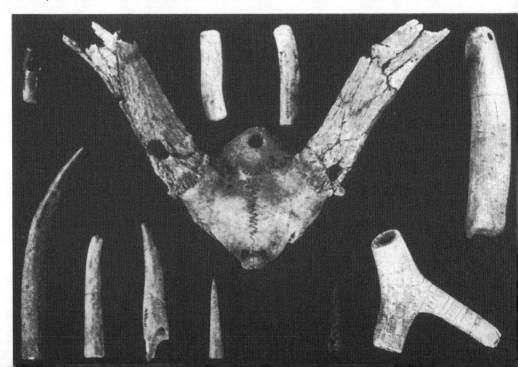

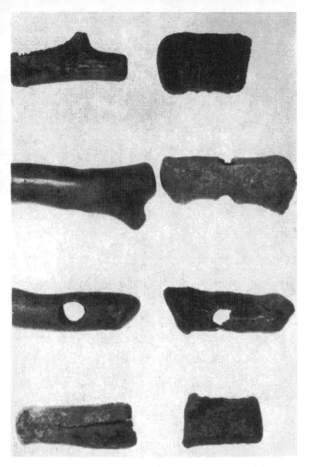

Webb and DeJarnette (1942, p. 280) discuss bone and antler atlatl hooks and atlatls:

". . . In the main, the throwing stick was made of a narrow, flat board varying from 15 to 23 inches in length. At one end there were handles, finger loops, finger grooves, finger holes, or pegs, as aids in holding it and in maintaining the placement of the projectile shaft upon it. At the other end, some form of hook, rising above the plane of the throwing stick, would engage the end of the projectile shaft and thus assist in propelling it forward by the quick 'throwing motion' of the hand and arm. This hook for engaging the projectile shaft is thus an indispensable part of the throwing stick, and its function is the essential element in the entire operation of casting the projectile . . . . in wooden throwing sticks the hook was carved out as an integral part of the weapon. . . . Such implements, if left in shell mounds, would soon decay. . . . As in Mexico and elsewhere, the 'throwing stick' under went gradual development; so in this region it is believed that modification of a complete wooden throwing stick led to the substitution of a bone or antler hook in place of the original wooden hook portion."

Webb and DeJarnette (1942, p. 280) state:

". . . While such a separate hook might take many forms, it would have to meet . . . two major requirements: 1, It would have to be made so that it could be easily and securely attached to the wooden portion of the throwing board; and 2, . . . be constructed as to engage efficiently the end of the projectile shaft in the act of throwing. . . . The number of atlatls thus made with such special hooks not integral parts of the weapon would probably be in small proportion to the total number in use, and one would, therefore, not expect to find bone and antler hooks extremely numerous."

Webb and DeJarnette (1942, p. 198-199) explain this plate:

"These hooklike objects were made of cut antler. They were from 3½ to 5 inches long and had been cut off smoothly at the basal end and drilled with a conical reamer. The hole was as large as the antler would permit at the basal end, and came to a point about half way up the shaft. The other end of the antler had been worked into a peculiarly shaped hook made by a knoblike projection cut obliquely to the shaft. The shaft had been cut and ground to a flat surface on one side under the hooklike projection.

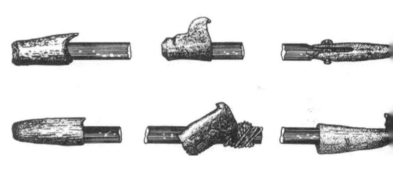

The hooklike form was accentuated by having a small round protuberance worked out on the lower edge of the knob, immediately adjacent to the flattened side of the shaft. These specimens were so much alike as to definitely suggest a similar use. It is believed these antler hooks were the ends of atlatls, which, when attached to wooden staves made efficient 'throwing sticks' for casting projectiles. It is suggested that the projectile shafts may have been made of cane, the hollow end of which, when thrown, would engage the protuberance on the atlatl hook.

"All of these atlatls (hooks) were found below the 3-foot level, and in or above the 6-foot level.

"Antler tips were often cut, sharpened, and conically drilled to produce projectile points . . . . Another artifact of importance at this site was a bone point . . . . made from the cannon bone of the deer. They were from 2¼ to 4½ inches in length. One end was sharpened to a blunt point; the other end tapered gradually to a rounded end. It is believed that these were points for projectile shafts and were used by simply inserting the slender end into a hollow cane, the blunt sharpened end being the effective point." Many bone and antler projectile points were used by the Historic Period natives also.

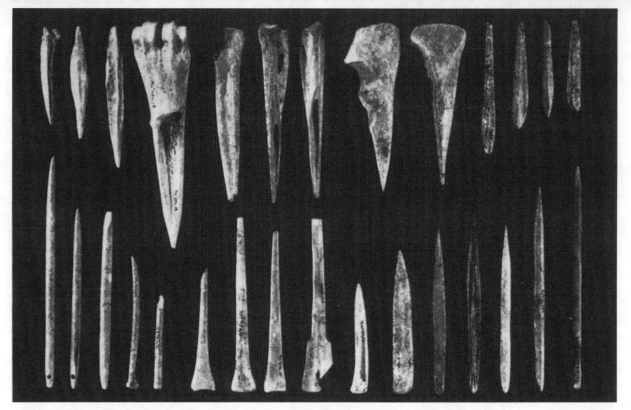

ABOVE. Bone artifacts from a shell-mound Archaic site in North Alabama. Awls, pins, needles, and projectile points (Courtesy, Alabama Museum of Natural History; from Webb and DeJarnette, Museum Paper 3, 1948, Fig. 30). Regarding various types of bone awls, Webb and DeJarnette (1948, pp. 57-60) give the following explanation:

BONE TOOLS—NEEDLES, AWLS, FISHHOOKS, PROJECTILE POINTS AND OTHERS

Plates 151 and 152

"Cylindrical awls were made from longitudinally split sections of long bones. They were ground down until they showed a circular cross-section. Some of these awls are tapered at both ends, while others have only one tapered end. In most instances (at this site) only one end of the double-tapered awls shows the wear and polishing which would result from use as a perforator. The tapering of the 'non-functional' end of the awl is usually less gradual and less finely executed. For these reasons it is believed that most double-tapered awls were neither intended nor used as perforators with two functional points.

"Split bone awls include awls from sections of bone which were obtained by cutting long bones lengthwise. Some of these awls show a portion of the epiphysis, while others are made solely from the body or shaft of the bone. Cross-sections of split bone awls vary considerably. Occasionally split bone awls are pointed at both ends.

"Cylindrical awls . . . became more numerous in the pottery horizon, while the converse was true of split bone awls.

"Splinter awls were made by pointing one end of a suitable bone fragment. The bone fragments used were not cut sections of bone, but were apparently produced by intentional or accidental rough fracturing of the bone. Splinter awls are crude and seldom show working other than at the point.

"Cannon bone awls include only those awls made from cannon bones which were not too modified by working to permit easy identification of the bone. Cannon bone awls were either split longitudinally and then pointed or the point was produced by an oblique cutting or grinding of the unsplit bone.

"Deer ulna awls were produced by grinding or cutting the distal portion of the bone into a point. In some instances a portion of the proximal end of the bone was removed or the proximal end was modified by grinding and polishing. above).

"Bird bone awls were made by cutting or grinding the bone at an oblique angle (or angles) thereby producing a point. Included in this category are three small mammal ulna awls.

"Pointed objects made from the tarsometatarus of large birds may have served either as awls or hairpins or both. Modification of the bone, produced in manufacturing the awl or pin, varies from oblique removal of one end to form a point, to splitting the bone longitudinally and pointing the end. Usually the proximal and less frequently the distal ends of the bone formed the head of the awl or pin. Awls or pins fashioned from the tibiotarsus occurred very infrequently, and were tabulated in one or the other of the preceding categories depending on method of working (i. e., either split awls, or obliquely cut). (see above).

"The implements termed bone pins resemble bone awls. They generally differ from awls in one or more of the following respects: better workmanship, an expansion of the head, greater degree of polishing, incised decorations on the head. Bone pins vary in cross-section from round and elliptical to flat. Cylindrical and elliptical pins frequently show a flattened, laterally expanded head. This flat area may be decorated with incised lines or the outline of the pin head may form a simple design or geometric figure.

"Fish spine awls are large spines which show no visible evidence of working or use, but which because of natural sharpness of point and hardness of bone, may have been employed as perforators.

"Bone 'bitten awls' resemble awls in size and general proportions. They vary from awls in having their functional end shaped like a bit instead of a point. Implements called 'bitted? awls' are smaller than 'fleshers' and probably served a different function.

"Implements termed 'fleshers' were made from deer long bones or other long bones of comparable size. The distinguishing feature of these implements is the functional end which is cut and ground to form a bit or cutting edge. (see above).

"Eyed bone needles were of the general shape as cylindrical awls, except they had an 'eye'? in the head and usually a smaller diameter. The majority of the needles were highly polished and round in cross-section, although elliptical cross sections occurred.

"Bone projectile points are shown at the lower left (of the picture above). It is surprising that so few were found at this site (Flint River shell mound, Madison County, Alabama), in view of their abundance in some shell middens. The explanation probably is that this site began Archaic 3 period (late)."

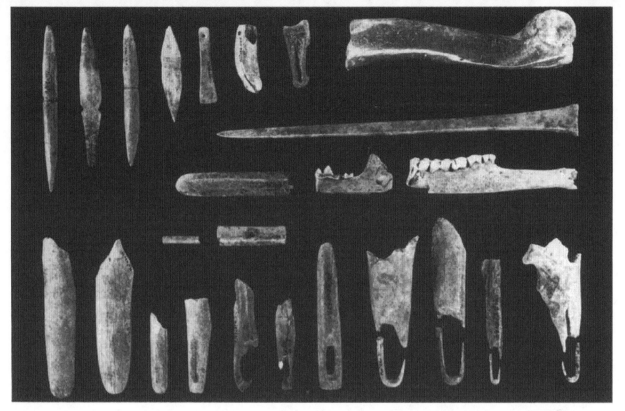

ABOVE. Bone artifacts from a shell-mound Archaic site. The Flint River, Madison County, Alabama (Courtesy, Alabama Museum of Natural History; from Webb and DeJarnette, 1948, Fig. 31). They give the following explanation (Museum Paper 23, 1948, pp. 60-61) of the picture:

"Long bone sections with double tapers and grooved in the center are shown (upper left). Some of these bone impletions show a similarity of bone points from Kentucky (Webb and Haag 1939, Fig. 13) shell middens. It is possible that these may be specialized projectile points, which were grooved for attachment to a line and used on a harpoon. The groove may have served for secure attachment to a shaft thrown by an atlatl. The point ranges in length from 2.75" to 4.75". Some of the shorter ones may have served as a toggle on a fish line in place of a fishhook.

"Bone fishhooks, bone spatulae splinters, deer ulnae spatulae, bone spatulae slotted, bone splinters bifurcated, and deer ulnae bifurcated, appear to be directly related to each other and to be involved in one stage or another of the manufacture of fishhooks. Spatulae made from bone splinters, split sections of bone, and deer ulnae quite probably represent the initial stage in the making of fishhooks. After the spatulae is worked into form a slot or eye is cut in it from the exterior side of the bone. Specimens with the slot cut through the bone and those showing partial cutting of the slot were all placed in the slotted category. Cutting of the sides of the slot would produce two pieces; one a fishhook, the other a bifurcated splinter or ulna, as shown above. It is significant that rarely are the two prongs of the bifurcated bones of the same length. The cutting of the bone on the side of the slot which forms the shank of the fishhook is generally so near the end of the slot that only the stub of a prong remains. For this reason the majority of the so-called 'bifurcated implements' actually have only one prong and the cut stump of a second.

"The fact that bifurcated objects are more numerous than specimens of the other related categories gives credance to the theory that they are a by-product of the making of fishhooks. The bulk of the fishhooks from this site show either a curvature resulting from the curve in long bones or a thickness which would preclude their having been manufactured from deer phalanges.

"The occurrence of two longitudinally split deer phalanges, which are believed to be fishhook blanks, would indicate that all of the fishhooks from this site were not made from long bones by the method outlined above."

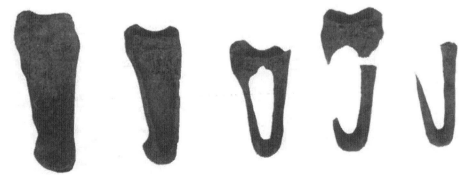

ABOVE. "Development of a fishhook from the toe bone of a deer." Lauderdale County, Alabama (Courtesy, Alabama Museum of Natural History; from Webb and DeJarnette, 1942, Pl. 221, Fig. 1) They explain the picture (p. 199):
"In the later stages of the (shell) mound, within the upper 3 feet, fishhooks were made from the toe bone of the deer. The bone was first split longitudinally, and the solid face ground off, leaving a bone loop of the characteristic cross section. From this near-triangular ring of bone a hook was made by cutting off the proximal end and leaving the distal end to be ground and polished into a hook. In all stages of manufacture hooks were found—many broken in the process. Bone pendants made from the leg bone of turtles were found as burial offerings. All were in the upper portion of the mound."

BONE TOOLS AND ORNAMENTS

Plate 153

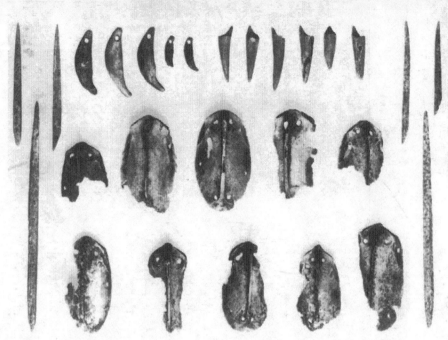

RIGHT. Bone and antler tools and ornaments. These were among the artifacts found in the elaborate burial pictured in Plate 6. Lauderdale County, Alabama (Courtesy, Alabama Museum of Natural History; BAE, Bull. 129, Pl. 253, Fig. 2). Webb and DeJarnette describe this plate (pp. 229-230):

"These long awls are made from a very heavy bone, and worked to cylindrical form so that the structure of the original bone is entirely obliterated. These awls are pointed at both ends and are about 6 inches long. With these, a number of bone pins occur. They are about 3.5 inches long, worked into small, well-made cylinders, pointed at one end, and on the other end, beveled into a chisel edge with the cut all on one side. This type of awl (long, cylindrical) was found duplicated scores of times, which suggests some specialized process for which this beveled end was specially adapted. The antler arrow points shown were also common to this site. These antler tips, from 1 to 1.5 inches long, are carefully scraped to a sharp point, drilled conically longitudinally at the base, and so cut obliquely at the base as to produce a very effective 'barb.' This type occurred frequently in burials at this site and was as often used as its companion, the small triangular flint point.

"A new type of bone pendant, first found with this burial, and later found elsewhere, seems to indicate a considerable use of the sterna of birds for the manufacture of pendants. Some of these are shown. The sternum was cut into a general oval at the back, about 1.6 inches by 3 inches. The edges were ground smooth and the dorsal surface of the bone brought to a flat surface. Usually six small holes were drilled at intervals, as shown . . . . These pendants seem to have been attached so that the keel extended outward. When found, they always occur in numbers from 8 to 12 or more, and never singly. They are always found in groups, at ankles and wrists of skeletons. This suggests some use requiring a number of them to be effective, as in bone rattles. The sternum of birds, while a relatively hard bone, is so thin that it readily decays. Thus, very few of these objects are found complete. They usually are broken and disintegrated."

BELOW. Outline drawings showing some of the carved and painted designs found on bone tools and ornaments from a variety of sites in the Southeast. Some of them are from Archaic sites, while others are Mississippi Period artifacts. Left to Right. FIRST ROW. Upper—after Thomas, 1894, p. 382, Big Toco Mound, Monroe County, Tennessee. Two lower. Collections in the United States National Museum, Sand mounds, Brevard County, Florida. SECOND ROW. After Moore, 1897, p. 122; from a mound on the Georgia coast; about 10" long; near the middle was a former fracture, repaired with bitumen by the native; split bone, 11.3". THIRD ROW. After

Thruston, 1890, p. 308. Tenn. FOURTH ROW. Bone gorget 4" long decorated as an animal face; after a drawing by Dr. R. P. Burke, M. D., ARROWPOINTS, 1933, Vol. 19, p. 40; in a burial at this site (Montgomery County, Alabama) were found 20 columella worked from conch shells; also shell beads made from the conch whorl, and celts and small stone points. It is now at the Montgomery Museum of Fine Arts, Graves collection. FOURTH ROW. Six lower fragments are carved and painted bone tools— after Claflin, 1931, Pl. 38, Stallings Island Mound, Columbia County, Georgia. FIFTH ROW. Two worked bones after Moore, 1895, Figures 18 and 35, Duval County, Florida. SIXTH ROW. Five fragments of bone showing carving; after the collection of Mrs. H. H. Simpson. Florida. SEVENTH ROW. Decorated dagger of deer bone, 8" long; after Bullen, 1952, Fig. 6. Cockroach Key, Tampa Bay, Florida, exploration by Florida Geological Survey. Below this is another fragment from the Simpson collection—part of an ivory tool or ornament. Bottom. After Moore, 1916, Green River, Kentucky; at this site he found asphalt used on several bone pins for sticking on them other decorations as carved shell. EIGHTH ROW. Two at top—after Thruston, 1890, Cumberland River, Tennessee; grooved needle about 3½" long. Two bottom. After Webb, 1938, Norris Basin, Tennessee. These bone objects might have been prickers for basket makers; pins for the hair or garments; awls; perforators; needles (grooved and eyelet); bodkins; pendants; or scarifying instruments. Simply decorated bone objects occur first with Archaic remains. Bone was also used for making fishhooks, fleshers, hafts, beads, and projectile points.

OPPOSITE PAGE. LOWER. Variety of shell tools. Left. Two views of a shell celt. Right. Shell spoons and a shell scraper. Center. Probable manner of hafting shell tools—hoe, adz, scoop, and scrapers. (After Holmes, 1883).

SHELL IMPLEMENTS

Plate 154

RIGHT. UPPER. Timucua council meeting. East coast of Florida. After an engraving by De Bry from a painting by Le Moyne, who visited Florida in 1564-65. According to Le Moyne the chief called together special men of the tribe for council during which they drank warm 'casina' from shell cups which a cupbearer passed around; he wrote that the natives took gourds full of 'casina' on journeys which were to last several days, because it gave them strength and assuaged their hunger. In the engraving, women making the drink strain it through a basket strainer to remove the parched leaves. A religious leader is envoking a blessing; Frenchmen watch (Rare Book collection, New York Public Library). LOWER. Two conch shell vessels found with burials. Limestone County, Alabama (Courtesy, Dr. F. J. Soday).

The "black drink" ceremony is mentioned by many colonial period writers. Lewis and Kneberg (1954, p. 68) summarize:

"The most famous beverage of the Southeastern Indians was a strong black tea which they called the 'white drink' but which British traders named the 'black drink.' The Creek Indians called it 'asi,' short for 'asi-luputski' which meant 'little leaves.'

"It was made from the leaves of a shrub belonging to the holly family that grows in the southern states near the coast. The leaves were roasted in a pot and then boiled in water. The almost black tea was poured . . . from one pot to another until a white froth formed . . . .

"It was supposed to purify the mind and enable the drinker to think more clearly. Although it was a purgative and stimulated the kidneys, its most important effect in the eyes of the Indians was to cause vomiting. It contained enough caffeine to give the same effect as an equal amount of strong black coffee.

"It was customary for all men to meet at least once a week (in some towns every morning) and drink this concoction before having any food. Women were never allowed to taste it.

"The ceremony of drinking took place in the town square where all men, according to their rank, had special seats around the edge. There was always a special black drink cook, and two or three young warriors were on hand to serve it. Many gallons had to be brewed because each man was expected to drink four or five quarts.

"In ancient times it was served in large conch shells. A young man would present one to a prominent warrior, thereafter backing up for a short distance and giving the black drink cry. As he began to sound the cry, the warrior would begin drinking and continue to do so as long as the cry lasted. A man's merits at this ceremony were judged by his capacity for imbibing the drink.

"Usually they took about a quart at a time and kept it down for half an hour or so. Then they hugged their arms across their stomachs and spouted as far as they could. . . .

"White traders learned to take the black drink. They found out that the Indians were more friendly and hospitable when they took part in the ceremony.

"Partly religious, the black drink ritual was important in creating bonds between participants. All joined in washing away their sins and in striving for greater wisdom in conducting the affairs of the town." (From TEN YEARS OF THE TENNESSEE ARCHAELOG-IST, Edited by Dr. T. M. N. Lewis and Madeline Kneberg; quoted by permission from Dr. T. M. N. Lewis).

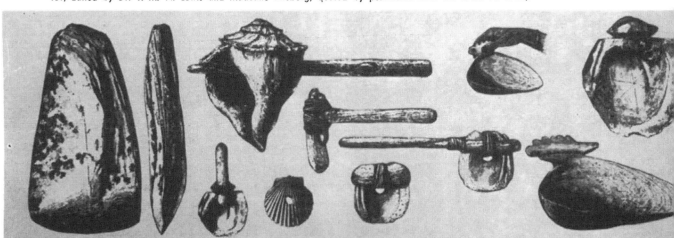

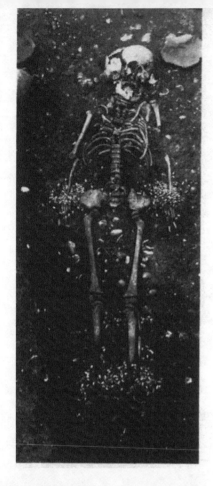

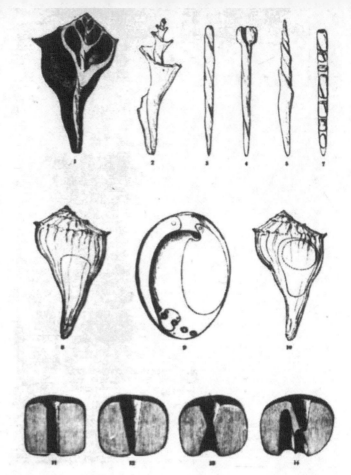

ABOVE. LEFT. An intrusive Mississippi Period burial in a shell mound. Note, shell beads at wrists, ankles, and beneath knees. A pottery bottle and vessels were also associations. Lauderdale County, Alabama (Courtesy, Alabama Museum of Natural History). RIGHT. Manufacture of shell artifacts. Upper row. Left to Right. 1. section of busycon perversum. 2. roughly trimmed columella. 3. and 4. shell pins made from columella. 5. columella. 6. Omitted. 7. manner of cutting beads. Center row. manner of cutting celts, pendants, and masks from the whorl of a conch and others. Bottom row. side-center view of shell beads showing perforations: countersunk cylindrical; conical; bi-conical; and imperfect attempt at bi-conical perforation. (Courtesy, Smithsonian Institution, BAE; after Holmes, 1883, Pl. XXIX).

SHELL ORNAMENTS

Plates 155 and 156

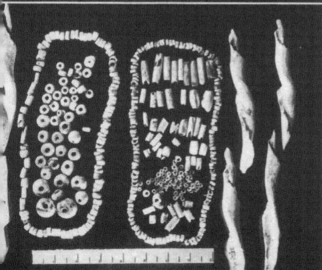

LEFT. UPPER. Cylindrical and disk-shaped shell beads. (Courtesy, Alabama Museum of Natural History; BAE Bull. 129, Pl. 223-2) Webb and DeJarnette (p. 198) describe this plate: "The large disks were made from sections of conchs (the whorl), and the large cylinders were made from the columella of large conchs. (Center, right) are shown a number of long beads nearly cylindrical but with the diameter tapering toward one end. This gave a slightly conical form and permitted the small end of one bead to fit into the hole in the large end of another. These beads were sections of dentalium, a marine gastropod, which produced its toothlike shell, as an elongated but slightly curved cone instead of a coiled spiral as do most gastropods. Dentalium beads may be identified by their conical shape and by the fine parallel longitudinal lines on their surface." On the left center are four anculosa shell beads. LOWER. Conch shell columella (longest 6½") and beads; several cylindrical bone beads are also in the picture. Occasionally similar columella are found in caches of a dozen or more. Morgan County, Alabama (Courtesy, James Ratliff).

RIGHT. UPPER. Pendants and gorgets made from conch shell. Fort Ancient Culture. Mason County, Kentucky (Courtesy, Russ Thompson). The pendant in the center is made from the columella of a conch with the end of the whorl still attached. It is the type worn by the human figures on several of the engraved shell gorgets.

RIGHT. CENTER. "Part of a string of 927 disc shell beads, 4 mm. to 15 mm. diameter; 10 cylindrical shell beads, 8 mm. to 27 mm. long; 5 cylindrical columella pendants perforated at one end, a fragment of a shell gorget and 3 fragments of a rim of a sandstone bowl, found in a Late Archaic burial in a shell midden." Also shown are 7 of 11 grooved or perforated pendants from a Woodland Period burial, from the same site. Madison County, Alabama (Courtesy, Alabama Museum of Natural History, Webb and DeJarnette, Museum Paper 24, Fig. 13, 1948).

BELOW. LEFT. A variety of forms of shell pendants and ornaments. Lauderdale County, Alabama (Courtesy, Alabama Museum of Natural History, BAE, Bull. 129, Pl. 222, No. 2). RIGHT. Shell pendants, gorgets, and a mask about 6" long (Courtesy, Alabama Department of Archives and History; Paulin collection).

The picture on the left includes objects found in the upper layers of an Archaic shell mound—small and plain pendants made from the conch whorl and others fashioned from the apex. Drilled shell beads—cylindrical and disk—were also found with Archaic remains. Long distance trade began during the Archaic Period.

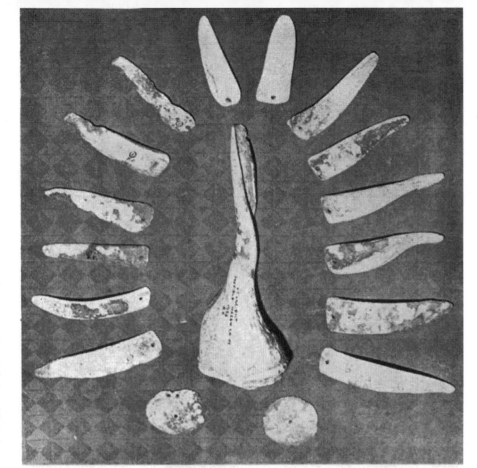

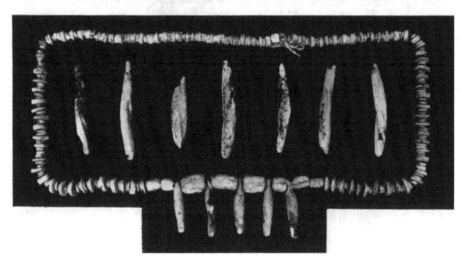

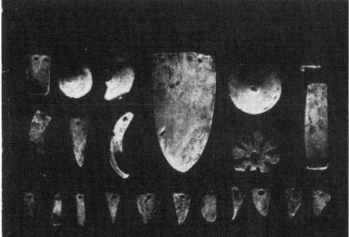

SHELL ORNAMENTS

Plates 157 and 158

LEFT. Reconstruction drawing by Eleanor F. Chapman, Art Director, the MISSOURI ARCHAEOLOGIST. It appears as Figure 46, THE CAMPBELL SITE (Chapman and Anderson, 1955), and is titled: "Campbell Site Man, Showing His Ornaments and Tattooed Facial Decoration." He wears a mask-type shell gorget (Courtesy, Eleanor F. Chapman and the Missouri Archaeological Society).

LEFT. LOWER. Drawing representing six shell gorgets or masks depicting a variety of facial markings. 1. and 2. McMahan Mound, Tennessee. 3. Brakebill Mound, Tennessee. 4. Lick Creek Mound, Tennessee. 5. Acquia Creek, Virginia. 6. Mound, Ely County, Virginia (After Holmes, 1883, Pl. LXIX). Several similar gorgets are in the artifact collection of the Alabama Department of Archives and History. Central Alabama.

BELOW. Figure carved in shell; 7 cm. long. The Craig Burial Mound—Spiro Mound, Le Flore County, Oklahoma (Courtesy, University of Oklahoma, Stovall Museum).

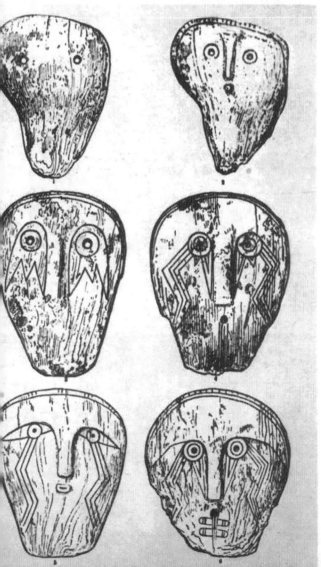

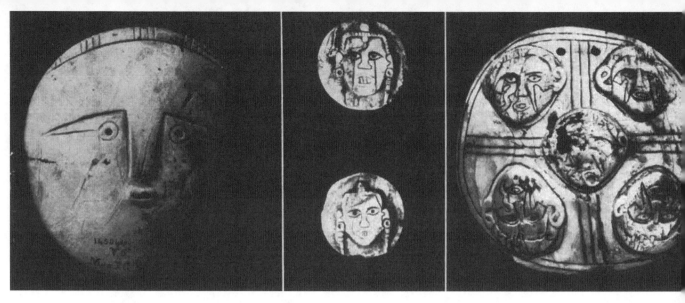

ABOVE. LEFT. Shell gorget; 10½ cm diameter; found in an ancient cemetery near the mouth of Potomac Creek, Stafford County, Virginia (Courtesy, Smithsonian Institution, United States National Muesum, 145-944). CENTER. Two shell cameos. Top. 1-11/16" diameter. Lower. 1-9/16" diameter. Spiro Mound, Oklahoma (Courtesy, H. M. Trowbridge; 2740 and 2741). RIGHT. Unusual shell gorget with cameo type carving in relief; 4¾" diameter. It is divided into four quarters by three parallel lines radiating from the center head. The design is completed on the outer margin by two circular lines. The eye, mouth, and ear designs are similar to many others found on engraved shell designs from Spiro. The Craig Burial Mound—Spiro Mound, Oklahoma (Courtesy, Museum of the American Indian, Heye Foundation, 18-9084). This Spiro gorget is one of the most outstanding gorgets recovered from the Southeast and near area. Others with human effigy motif also originated at Spiro. Another is found in the collection of the Museum of the American Indian, 18/7897.

BELOW. LEFT. Shell mask, 6¾" long. Stafford County, Virginia (Courtesy, John W. Melton; photograph by Thomas L. Williams, Williamsburg, Virginia). RIGHT. Shell mask found in a grave; 8⅜" long by 6⅛" wide. These objects have been called masks, because they occasionally have been found over the skull of a skeleton; also they clearly imitate faces with eyes, nose, and mouth carefully depicted in engraved line, excised circles, and bas-relief. Their purpose is unknown, but it was probably ceremonial, since they are relatively rare, often show little sign of wear, frequently have been carefully polished, and sometimes bear the cult design—the forked eye (Courtesy, Peabody Museum, Harvard University, 15374). Mask gorgets have been reported from sites throughout the Southeast. Lewis and Kneberg (1946, Pl. 83) picture shell mask gorgets from the Dallas Component at Hiwassee Island. One is similar to drawing No. 2 on the opposite page. In the collection of the Peabody Museum, Harvard University (No. 9636) there is a gorget from the Ely Mound, Lee Co., Virginia, similar to drawing No. 6 on the opposite page. Brannon (1935, pp. 33-35) has line drawings of four mask gorgets found in Central Alabama; three have bi-fork eyes. See Moore (1909) — Arkansas.

Marche du Calumet de Paix

ABOVE. LEFT. Two Cherokee Eagle Dance wands, made of eagle feathers in a wooden frame; 21" long. Upper left object in picture is a Creek turkey tail fan, white and tan feathers, red cloth at base; 15" long. From Koasati Creek. This fan was intended for everyday use (Courtesy, Denver Art Museum). RIGHT. Procession of the Peace Calumet. After Du Pratz (Courtesy, Smithsonian Institution, BAE, Bull 137, Pl. 84). In 1719 Du Pratz wrote:

"I had an opportunity during this trip to satisfy my curiosity on the subject of the calumet of peace, of which I had heard so much from the old French inhabitants. There having been war with the Tchitimachas, they asked for peace. A delegation arrived singing the calumet song, and with the calumet moving in rhythm they advanced, keeping time to the sound of the rattle.

"The calumet is the tube of a pipe at least one and one-half feet long, covered with a skin composed of the head and neck of a wood duck, of which the many-colored plumage is exceedingly attractive, and at the end of the tube there is a pipe. At the same end there is fixed a kind of wing of the white eagle, in shape of a quarter circle, and at the end of each feather it is encircled by a hoop dyed a bright red color, while the other end has none. . . . The speaker stood up while the assistant filled the pipe, and after smoking it, he dried it, and handed it to Mr. Bienville to do the same; then we all smoked it, after which the old man took the calumet and gave it to Mr. Bienville to keep. . . . They are dressed in their best, and never fail to hold in their hand a chichicois, which they also move in rhythm. The war calumet is a pipe of the same material and shape excepting the color of the feather, which are those of an aquatic bird, the flamingo. The head of the bird is skinned, the feathers being a whitish gray, which being dyed, only makes a light red, the hoop and tufts being black. The stem of the pipe is covered with the skin of a carancro, as black as a blackbird and as big as a turkey." (West, 1934, Pt. I, p. 239; McGuire, J. D., 1899, pp. 557-558; quoting from Du Pratz, Le Page, 1758, pp. 108, 105, 118).

BELOW. LEFT. "Characteristick Chicasan Head." Chickasaw Tribe. After Bernard Romans, 1775 (Courtesy, Smithsonian Institution, BAE, 1071-b). RIGHT. Eagle Dance, Choctaw. After Catlin, 1848 Catalog (Courtesy, Smithsonian Institution, 43459). In describing it, (Catlin, 1841, Plate 227, description, pp. 126-7, Vol. II) he wrote:

Characteristick Chicasaw head

"A very pretty scene, which is got up by their young men in honour of that bird, for which they seem to have a religious regard. This picturesque dance was given by twelve or sixteen men, whose bodies were chiefly naked and painted white, with white clay, and each one holding in his hand the tail of the eagle, while his head was also decorated with an eagle's quill. Spears were stuck in the ground, around which the dance was performed by four men at a time, who had simultaneously, at the beat of the drum, jumped up from the ground where they had all sat in rows of four, one row immediately behind the other, and ready to take the place of the first four when they left the ground fatigued, which they did by hopping or jumping around behind the rest, and taking their seats, ready to come up again in their turn, after each of the other sets had been through the same forms.

"In this dance, the steps or rather jumps, were different from anything I had ever witnessed before, as the dancers were squat down, with their bodies almost to the ground, in a severe and most difficult posture, as will have been seen in the drawing. The Choctaws were moved from Alabama and Mississippi to Oklahoma in the 1830's; this painting was made only a few years after that; in describing the tribe, he mentions the "ancient custom of head flattening" practiced by some of the tribe.

FEATHER ORNAMENTS

Plates 159 and 160

RIGHT. "The display with which a queen elect is brought to the king." Timucua tribe. From an engraving by De Bry, after a drawing by Le Moyne, who visited Florida in 1564-65 (Courtesy, Smithsonian Institution, BAE, 1186-b-14. Swanton, BAE, Bull. 137, Pl. 85). Her body is painted with a step-dot design, and she wears pearl or shell beads; the accompanying maidens and the queen-elect wear skirts made of Spanish moss. The bride-elect is seated on a beautifully decorated animal skin, and shaded by a canopy of boughs and two large feather fans carried by men at each side of the litter; they wear animal skins around their waist and tails dangling from the hair-knot; the knots may be similar in style to those depicted on the stone and pottery images found in other parts of the Southeast. The procession is lead by trumpeters and four guards line the rear. Each of the litter bearers carries a forked stick upon which to rest the litter poles when the procession stops.

"When the chief took a wife, Le Moyne tells us, she was brought in a litter preceded by men 'blowing upon trumpets made of bark, which are smaller above and larger at the farther end and having only the two orifices, one at each end. They are hung with small oval balls of gold, silver and brass, for the sake of a finer combination of sound.' (Le Moyne, 1875, p. 13; Swanton, 1922, p. 372; Swanton, 1946, p. 629).

"Le Moyne describes how the chief Saturiwa once came to visit him accompanied by a considerable military force, and 'next to himself were twenty pipers, who produced a wild noise without musical harmony or regularity, but only blowing away with all their might, each trying to be the loudest. Their instruments were nothing but a thick sort of reed or cane, with two openings, one at the top to blow into and the other end for the wind to come out of, like organ pipes or whistles.' " (Le Moyne, 1875, p. 3; Swanton, 1922, p. 375; Swanton, 1946, p. 628).

Swanton discussed featherwork among the Southeastern Indians (Swanton, 1946, pp. 454-456):

"From Virginia to Louisiana garments and blankets were made by fastening feathers upon a kind of netting. Feather mantles were perhaps worn for ornaments as much as for warmth. . . . Du Pratz thus describes the Natchez method of making these:
'The feather mantles are worked on a frame similar to that on which wig makers work hair. They lay out the feathers in the same manner and fasten them to old fish nets or old mulberry-bark mantles. They place them in the manner already outlined one over another and on both sides. For this purpose they make use of little turkey feathers. The women who can obtain feathers of the swan or Indian duck make mantles of them for the women of the Honored class.' (Le Page du Pratz, 1758, vol. 2, pp. 191-192; Swanton, 1911, p. 63). Of the Creeks Bartram (1792, p. 500) says:
'Some have a short cloak, just large enough to cover the shoulders and breast; this is most ingeniously constructed, of feathers woven or placed in a most natural imbricated manner, usually of the scarlet feathers of a flamingo . . . .'
"To this we may add the words of Dumont de Montigny:
'With the thread they obtain from the bark of the bass tree they make for themselves a kind of mantle which they cover with the finest swan feathers fastened on this cloth one by one, a long piece of work in truth, but they account their pains and time as nothing when they want to satisfy themselves.' (Dumont, 1753, vol. 1, p. 155; Swanton, 1911, p. 63). Lawson informs us, regarding the Siouan tribes, that:
'Their feather match coats are very pretty, especially some of them, which are made extraordinary charming, containing several pretty figures wrought in feathers, making them seem like a fine flower silk shag; and when new and fresh, they become a bed very well, instead of a quilt. . . . Others again are made of the green part of the skin of a mallard's head, which they sew perfectly well together, their thread being either the sinews of the deer divided very small, or silk grass. When they are finished they look very fine, though they must needs be very troublesome to make.' (Lawson, 1860, pp. 311-312).

"Le Moyne speaks of 'many pieces of a stuff made of feathers, and most skillfully ornamented with rushes of different colors' sent in from the western Timucua by a French officer (Le Moyne, 1875, p. 8; Swanton, 1922, p. 347).

"During dances some of the Creek Indian men and probably those of many other tribes carried turkey feather fans in their left hands as a sign of leadership and also to protect their eyes from the fire. Adair says that the Chickasaw women
'make turkey feather blankets with the long feathers of the neck and breast of that large fowl—they twist the inner end(s) of the feathers very fast into a strong double thread of hemp, or the inner bark of the mulberry tree, of the size and strength of coarse twine, as the fibres are sufficiently fine, and they work it in the manner of fine netting. As the feathers are long and glittering, this sort of blanket is not only very warm, but pleasing to the eye.' (Adair, 1775, p. 423)."

LEFT. "The Flyer" (White's caption) or "The Conjurer." From a water color by John White, 1587, in the coastal region of present N. Carolina. Southern Algonquians (Courtesy, Smithsonian Institution, BAE, 18,716). This doctor of enchantments has as his badge of office, a black bird attached to his head; his hair is shaved, except for a crest across the top of the head. He wears a breechclout of animal skin and has a pouch attached at the side. He is called on to give advice on many matters, including the war plans of the enemy. The sorcerer's grotesque movements, elusive manner, fetishes, and remedies made him an esteemed member of the tribe.

ACKNOWLEDGEMENTS

We thank the following for advice, co-operation, correspondence; for permission to reproduce pictures of their artifacts, their drawings, or their words; for permission to quote sources long recorded as authorities.

Plate numbers on which photographs appear are indicated.

MUSEUMS

And individuals with whom we talked or corresponded for permission, photographs and information.

ALABAMA DEPARTMENT OF ARCHIVES AND HISTORY, Montgomery, Ala., 39, 40, 43, 77, 78, 81, 82, 84, 96, 106, 120, 121, 156.
Photographs of artifacts from the following collections: Buckner Beasley; J. Y. Brame; Peter A. Brannon; John K. McEwen; and H. H. Paulin.

ALABAMA MUSEUM OF NATURAL HISTORY University and Moundville, Ala., 5, 6, 7, 10, 15, 35, 73, 77, 80, 84, 86, 92, 107, 109, 113, 116, 117, 136, 149, 150, 151, 152, 153, 155, 156.

AMERICAN MUSEUM OF NATURAL HISTORY New York, N. Y., 44, 49, 136.

BAMA SCENIC ROCK GARDENS, MUSEUM OF Vance, Ala., 71.

BIRMINGHAM MUSEUM OF ART Birmingham, Ala., 78, 81.

BROOKLYN MUSEUM Brooklyn, N. Y., 104.

CATHEDRAL CAVERNS, MUSEUM OF Grant, Ala., 71.

CHICAGO NATURAL HISTORY MUSEUM Chicago, Ill., 46, 120, 142.

CITY ART MUSEUM OF ST. LOUIS St. Louis, Mo., 95.

COLUMBUS MUSEUM OF ARTS AND CRAFTS, INC., Columbus, Ga., 133.
Display in the Isabel Garrard Patterson Memorial, Chattahoochee Valley Prehistoric Indian Arts Section.

CORNELL COLLEGE MUSEUM Mount Vernon, Iowa, 97.

DAVENPORT PUBLIC MUSEUM Davenport, Iowa, 119, 124.

DENVER ART MUSEUM Denver, Colo., 147, 148, 159.

FAIRHOPE PUBLIC LIBRARY MUSEUM Fairhope, Ala., 117.

FLORIDA STATE MUSEUM Gainesville, Fla., 111, 142.

GEORGIA HISTORICAL COMMISSION Atlanta, Ga., 90, 91, 97, 109.

HUNTINGDON COLLEGE MUSEUM, HOUGHTON MEMORIAL LIBRARY, Montgomery, Ala., 40, 127.

HUNTSVILLE PUBLIC LIBRARY MUSEUM Huntsville, Ala., 1.

INDIAN SPRINGS SCHOOL MUSEUM Helena, Ala., 5.

HELEN KELLER BIRTHPLACE MUSEUM Tuscumbia, Ala., 15.

LAUREN ROGERS LIBRARY AND MUSEUM OF ART, Laurel, Miss., 132.

LIGHTNER MUSEUM OF HOBBIES St. Augustine, Fla., 25.

LOOKOUT MOUNTAIN MUSEUM, ROCK CITY GARDENS, INC., Lookout Mountain, Tenn., 63, 71, 88, 95, 96.

LOUISIANA STATE EXHIBIT MUSEUM Shreveport, La., 88, 103, 107, 108.

MADISON COUNTY CHAPTER, ALABAMA ARCHAEOLOGICAL SOCIETY, Huntsville, Ala., 1, 4, 5, 16, 68, 82.

MILWAUKEE PUBLIC MUSEUM Milwaukee, Wis., 64.

MOBILE PUBLIC MUSEUM Mobile, Ala., 16, 122.

MOUND STATE MONUMENT Moundville, Ala., See Alabama Museum of Natural History.

MONTGOMERY MUSEUM OF FINE ARTS Montgomery, Ala., 40, 84.

MUSEO NACIONAL DE ANTROPOLOGIA Instituto Nacionalde Antropologia E. Historia, Mexico, D. F., 18.

MUSEUM OF THE AMERICAN INDIAN, HEYE FOUNDATION, New York, N. Y., 10, 24, 26, 35, 41, 43, 46, 47, 86, 89, 90, 91, 92, 97, 99, 100, 102, 104, 107, 108, 110, 117, 118, 124, 128, 129, 134, 142, 158.

NATIONAL PARK SERVICE, UNITED STATES DEPARTMENT OF INTERIOR, Washington, D. C.
NATCHEZ TRACE PARKWAY Natchez, Miss., 6.
OCMULGEE NATIONAL MONUMENT Macon, Ga., 3, 13, 87, 88, 111, 135.
SHILOH NATIONAL MILITARY PARK Pittsburg Landing, Tenn., 99.

NORTH CAROLINA DEPARTMENT OF ARCHIVES AND HISTORY, Raleigh, N. C., 128, 140.

OHIO STATE MUSEUM Columbus, Ohio, 91.

PEABODY MUSEUM OF ARCHAEOLOGY AND ETHNOLOGY, Harvard University, Cambridge, Mass., 13, 46, 91, 92, 115, 158.

READING PUBLIC MUSEUM AND ART GALLERY, Reading, Pa., 101, 102, 121.

ROCHESTER MUSEUM OF ARTS AND SCIENCES Rochester, N. Y., 46, 116, 120, 123.

SMITHSONIAN INSTITUTION Washington, D. C.
BUREAU OF AMERICAN ETHNOLOGY, 11, 16, 45, 47, 49, 50, 51, 58, 65, 79, 80, 91, 96, 110, 113, 115, 117, 128, 131, 135, 137, 139, 143, 144, 145, 146, 147, 149, 150, 154, 155, 156, 157, 159, 160.
UNITED STATES NATIONAL MUSEUM, 25, 32, 35, 47, 62, 90, 98, 104, 112, 120, 128, 136, 139, 140, 141, 142, 143, 144, 158.

SAINT JOSEPH MUSEUM St. Joseph, Mo., 130.

UNIVERSITY OF ARKANSAS MUSEUM Fayette, Ark., 26, 28, 53. p. 38.

UNIVERSITY MUSEUM, THE UNIVERSITY OF PENNSYLVANIA, Philadelphia, Pa., 58, 105, 132, 147.

UNIVERSITY OF OKLAHOMA, STOVALL MUSEUM, Norman, Okla., 23, 27, 99, 100, 141, 157.

UNIVERSITY OF MISSISSIPPI MUSEUM University, Miss., 55, 113, 122, 124.

UNIVERSITY OF TENNESSEE MUSEUM Knoxville, Tenn., 44, 45, 48, 93, 97, 115.

VANDERBILT UNIVERSITY MUSEUM Nashville, Tenn., 8, 115, 119, 120, 121, 123, 124, 129.

WACHOVIA MUSEUM, OLD SALEM, INC. Winston-Salem, N. C., 111, 128.
We appreciate the aid of the following—
ADAH:Peter A. Brannon, Jessie E. (Mrs. Leonard) Cobb, Alex L. Bush. AMNH: Walter B. Jones. AmMNH: Martha Demaras, Barbara A. Donat. BSRG: E. D. Herring. BMA: R. F. Howard. BM: Flora S. Kaplan. CC: J. B. Gurley. CNHM: C. C. Gregg. CAMSL: T. T. Hoopes. CMAC: Margaret S. (Mrs. J. W.) Bloomer. CCM: J. H. Ennis. DPM: A. L. Baily, DAM: R. G. Conn. FPL: Anna Braune, Mrs. James B. Gaston. FSM: Ripley P. Bullen GHC: Lewis H. Larson, Jr. HCM: Willa M. Boysworth. HPL: Dorothy Webb. ISS: H. E. Wheeler. HKBM: Lurline Cook, R. B. Martin. LRLMA: Nell Davis. LMM: E. Y. Chapin, III. LSEM: H. B. Wright. MPM: R. E. Ritzenthaler. MoPM: Caldwell DeLaney. MCCAAS: E. C. Mahan, T. C. Stogner, C. V. Brosemer, W. B. Edwards. MSM: David L. DeJarnette. MMFA: Frances G. Nix. MNA: Eusebio Davalos Hurtado, Roque J. Ceballos Novelo. MAIHF: E. K. Burnett. NPS-ONM: Louis R. Caywood. SNMP: C. E. Shedd, Jr. NCDAH: Christopher Crittenden, Joye E. Jordan, Dorothy R. Phillips. OSM: R. S. Baby. PMAE: Katherine B. Edsall. RPMAG: Earl J. Poole, Samuel C. Gundy. RMAS: Alfred K. Guthe. SI-BAE: M. W. Stirling, Margaret C. Blaker. USNM: F. M. Setzler, Waldo R. Wedel. SJM: R. E. Coy. UAM: S. C. Dellinger. UMUP: Carolyn G. Dosker, Frances Eyman. UOSM: Robert E. Bell. UMM: Robert L. Rands, Julien R. Tatum. UTM: T. M. N. Lewis. VUM: W. B. Jewell, C. W. Wilson, Peggy Wrenne. WMOS: F. P. Albright.

We also appreciate the aid of the following: British Museum, London, E. C. Murray. Choctaw Area Field Office, Philadelphia, Miss., Paul Vance. Fort Lashley Historical Monument, Talladega, Ala., R. F. Blackford. Frick Art Reference Library, New York. Kansas City Museum, J. H. Howard. Mississippi Department of Archives and History, Charlotte Capers. Mobile Chamber of Commerce, R. W. Gay, Marian Acker MacPherson, S. Blake McNeely. North Carolina Department of Conservation, Marian Rabb. Oklahoma Historical Society, E. L. Fraker, Mrs. C. E. Cook. United States Department of Interior, Indian Art and Crafts Board, J. Ed Davis. Washington and Lee University, Wheeler National Wildlife Refuge, T. A. Atkeson.

INDIVIDUAL OWNERS OF ARTIFACTS

Cities are in Alabama unless otherwise indicated.

BARNES, G. E., Memphis, Tenn., 55.
BEAUDOIN, K. L., Memphis, Tenn., 117.
BEINLICH, A. W., Sheffield, 69, 86, 111, 113.
BLAKE, M. E., Fairhope, 72.

BURKE, DR. R. P., Montgomery, 39, 40, 42, 106, 114, 123, 127, 130.
CAMBRON, J. W., Decatur, 1, 3, 4, 6, 74.
CARR, JERRY, Decatur, 4, 74.
CHAPMAN, ELIZABETH H., Birmingham, 81.
COX, DR. C. C., Mobile, 122.
CRAIG, BILLY AND BOBBY, Gurley, 68.
CURTISS, E. E., Benton, Ky., 76, 79, 85, 98.
DAOLE, J. P., Atlanta, Ga., 39, 78, 127.
DAVIS, NORMAN, Talladega, 106.
DeJARNETTE, T. L., Birmingham, 6, 16, 42, 70, 75, 81, 94.
DILWORTH, JESSIE ELEANOR, Huntsville, 96.
DODD, M. E., JR., Shreveport, La., 88, 103, 107, 108.
DOERSCHUK, HERBERT M., Los Altos, Calif., 79, 84, 104, 128.
DOUGLASS, NELIA (MRS. B. A.) Bessemer, 82.
DURANT, GRACE H. (MRS. W. L.) Mobile, 16.
GEORGE, FRANK, Munford, 106.
GINNANE, E. S., Birmingham, 69.
GOODWIN, LEWIS P., Montgomery, 14, 116.
HAY, MRS. JOHN B., SR., Bremen, 3.
HILL, WILEY C., III, Millbrook, 15, 113.
HULSE, DAVID C., Decatur, 4, 73, 74.
JONES, A. R., Eclectic, 84.
JONES, NELL S. (MRS. J. E.), Gulf Shores, 6, 122.
KIRK, DERA K., Badin, N. C., 91.
KLEINE, HAROLD K., Birmingham, 1, 75, 82.
KNOBLOCK, BYRON W., Quincy, Ill., 86, 89.
KYLE, PHILLIP, Decatur, 76, 113.
LONG, DONOVAN B., Humboldt, Tenn., 1, 94, 98, 119.
McCARY, BEN C., Williamsburg, Va., 130.
McDONNALD, W. H., Ragland, 81.
McLEMORE, CHARLES W., Decatur, 75.
MARTIN, R. B., Sheffield, 15.
MELTON, J. W., JR., Glen Allen, Va., 158.
MOEBES, LT. T. F., Decatur, 6 15, 16, 74, 77, 79.
MOLLOY, PAUL F., Lincoln, Ill., 96.
MORAST, FRANK, FRANK, JR., and ROBERT H., Chattanooga, Tenn., 52, 79, 84, 85, 87, 88, 95, 116, 118, 121, 129.
MOSLEY, S. A., Decatur, 72, 74.
NEILD, EDWARD, Shreveport, La., 120.
NELSON, ROBERT E., Sheffield, 70, 85.
NELSON, VIOLET E., Gasque, 122.
NIXON, MRS. G. M., John K. McEwen collection, Rockford, 82.
OGLETREE, JOHN L., JR., Sylacauga, 104.
PELEGRIN, DABNEY CARSON (MRS. J. P.), Clarksdale, Miss., 96, 123.
RATLIFF, JAMES B., Decatur, 4, 6, 43, 72, 82, 155.
RAY, JACK D., Decatur, 4.
RUDULPH, DR. AND MRS. C. M., Birmingham, 82, 122.
RUSKIN, GERTRUDE (MRS. S. H.), Decatur, Ga., 14.
SIMPSON, MRS. H. H., High Springs, Fla., 111.
SMITH, HARRY, Decatur, 68.
SODAY, DR. FRANK J., Decatur, 1, 3, 4, 5, 10, 43, 65, 69, 70, 75, 77, 84, 113, 117, 154.
STEEVES, MR. AND MRS. H. R., JR., Birmingham, 10, 70.
STEPHENS, B. W., Quincy, Ill., 49, 119, 124.
SUMMERS, MR. AND MRS. C. G., Birmingham, 4.
THOMPSON, RUSS, Lexington, Ky., 8, 156.
TROWBRIDGE, H. M., Kansas City, Kans., 25, 27, 89, 94, 133, 158.
VAUGHAN, T. R., SR., Irvington, 103.
WATERS, S. A., Moulton, 56.
WEBB, DR. CLARENCE H., Shreveport, La., 88, 103, 107, 108.
WEBSTER, JUDGE H. L., Columbia, Tenn., 2, 98.
WHEELER, H. E., Birmingham, 5.
WILKINSON, J. D., Birmingham, 106.
WORLEY, C. H., Tuscumbia, 81, 87, 117.
We thank also: Col. Lucien Beckner, Tatum Bedsole, Annie Burnum, Irby Byars, Mrs. Carl Cantrell, George D. Clem, Jr., Hennig Cohen, Alice DeLoach, Louise M. Duggins, J. K. Gilbert, W. H. Hauser, Casey Holland, Dan Josselyn, John P. Knudsen, J. E. Davis, Dr. Chapman J. Milling, John R. Mitchell, Richard D. Radford, W. R. Shinn, Clyde B. Sprinkle, J. E. Steere, Sr., E. Bruce Trickey, Spinks Willis, Steve B. Wimberly, T. A. Wilson, Jr., and L. D. Yeamen.

PUBLISHERS

BARNES & NOBLE, INC.
New York, N. Y., pp. 31-32.
UNIVERSITY OF CHICAGO PRESS
Chicago, Ill., 9, 12; p. 8, 33.
UNIVERSITY OF KENTUCKY PRESS
Lexington, Ky., 43.
UNIVERSITY OF TEXAS PRESS
Austin, Texas, 85, 86.
YALE UNIVERSITY PRESS
Cambridge, Mass., 29-32, 44, 49, 110.
JOHN WILEY & SONS, INC.
New York, N. Y., 9.

BULLETINS AND JOURNALS

AMERICAN ANTHROPOLOGIST
Menasha, Wis., 17-22, 49-50; pp. 38-55.
AMERICAN ANTIQUITY
Salt Lake City, Utah, 53-54.
FLORIDA HISTORICAL QUARTERLY
Gainesville, Fla., 61.
MISSOURI ARCHAEOLOGIST
Columbia, Mo., 25, 27, 28, 49, 117, 125, 129, 133, 134, 157.
OKLAHOMA ANTHROPOLOGICAL ASSOCIATION, BULLETIN, Norman, Okla., 126.
TENNESSEE ARCHAEOLOGIST
Knoxville, Tenn., See index, T. M. N. Lewis, Madeline Kneberg, M. W. Hill, Malcolm Parker, J. M. Kellberg, and Robert M. Tatum—quotations.
TEXAS ARCHEOLOGICAL SOCIETY, BULLETIN
Austin, Texas, 67.
We appreciate the aid of the following: AA: W. S. Godfrey, Jr. AnA: R. B. Woodbury. FHQ: T. W. Patrick. MA: R. O. Keslin, J. E. Wrench, Carl H. Chapman, Eleanor F. Chapman. OAA: R. E. Bell. TA: T. M. N. Lewis. TAS: E. M. Davis.

ASSOCIATIONS

ALABAMA ARCHAEOLOGICAL SOCIETY
Decatur, Ala.
AMERICAN PHILOSOPHICAL SOCIETY
Philadelphia, Pa., 56, 57-60; pp. 94-110.
BIRMINGHAM ANTHROPOLOGICAL SOCIETY
Birmingham, Ala.
FLORIDA GEOLOGICAL SURVEY
Tallahassee, Fla.
INSTITUTO INTERAMERICANO
Denton, Texas, 18.
LOUISIANA GEOLOGICAL SURVEY
Baton Rouge, La., 83.
MISSISSIPPI GEOLOGICAL SURVEY
University, Miss., 55, 83, 91, 113.
NATIONAL ARCHIVES AND RECORDS SERVICE
Washington, D. C., 7.
ROBERT S. PEABODY FOUNDATION FOR ARCHAEOLOGY, PHILLIPS ACADEMY, Andover, Mass., 29-32, 44, 49, 110.
WASHINGTON ACADEMY OF SCIENCES
Washington, D. C., 56.
We appreciate the aid of the following: AAS: F. J. Soday, J. W. Cambron, E. H. Mahan. APS: Gertrude D. Hess. BAS: Brittain Thompson. II: Carl B. Compton. LGS: L. W. Hough. MGS: W. C. Morse. RSPFAPA: Douglas S. Byers. WAS: F. M. Setzler.

OTHER INDIVIDUALS

CHAPMAN, ELEANOR F., Columbia, Mo., 129, 134, 157.
FENENGA, DR. FRANKLIN, University of Nebraska, Lincoln, Nebr., 95.
GRIFFIN, JAMES B., University of Michigan, Ann Arbor, 9, 12; p. 34.
GRIFFIN, JOHN W., St. Augustine Historical Society, St. Augustine, Fla., 61.
HAMILTON, HENRY W., Marshall, Mo., 25, 27, 28.
HAUGEN, ARNOLD O., Auburn, Ala., 149.
HILL, MALCOLM W., Alexandria, Va., 76, 138.
HOLDER, PRESTON, Washington University, St. Louis, Mo., 17-22; pp. 38-55.
RANDS, ROBERT L., University of Mississippi, University, Miss., 53-54.
RUSSELL, MRS. V. Y., Casper Wyoming, 138.
WARING, A. J., Savannah, Ga., 17-22; pp. 38-55.
SWANTON, JOHN R., pp. 33-35, 112-113, 164-165, 186-187, 202-203.

LIBRARIES

We appreciate the aid of the following: Air UniversityLibrary, Maxwell Air Force Base, Ala., J. K. Cameron; Alabama Department of Archives and History Library, Mrs. Jessie E. Cobb and Mary R. Mullen; Alabama Department of Education Library, Martha Blackshear; Alabama Public Library Service, Mrs. Fletcher Roberts; Birmingham Public Library; Chicago Public Library; Florida State University Library; Free Public Library of Philadelphia; Library of Congress; Montgomery Public Library, Dixie L. Fisher, and the late Juliette Morgan; New York Public Library; University of Alabama Library; University of Mississippi Library; University of North Carolina Library; University of Oklahoma Library; University of Pennsylvania Library. Also Alabama Libraries which aided us in finding collections.

PHOTOGRAPHERS AND PHOTOGRAPHIC SHOPS

Jack D. Ray, Decatur, Ala., photographed all private collections listed for Alabama owners except those of: Blake, Davis, George, Goodwin, Hill, Ogletree, and Vaughan. He also photographed the artifacts from the Alabama Department of Archives and History, and part of the Frank Morast collection, Chattooga, Tennessee.
Alex L. Bush, Montgomery, Ala., microfilmed research material.
We thank the many photographers, including those at museums, whose names we do not know. We appreciate the aid of the following: Helen Burke Studio, Atlanta, Ga.; Cameraland, Montgomery, Ala.; Guadagno Carmelo (MAIHF); The Courier-Journal and Louisville Times, Louisville, Ky.; D. Coghlan, Philadelphia, Miss.; Peter S. Gilchrist, Charlotte, N. C.; S. C. Gundy (RPMAG); Hiatt Photo Service, Jackson, Miss.; Roy Howell's Studio, Talladega, Ala.; Ledger Enquirer, Columbus, Ga.; Jack Lynch, Laurel, Miss.; Norman L. Morrow, Jr., Chattanooga, Tenn.; Arthur Reed, Montgomery, Ala.; Hugh M. Roberts, Mt. Vernon, Iowa; Satterwhite, Decatur, Ga.; Ed T. Simons, Winston-Salem, N. C.; Scott Photographic Services, Montgomery, Ala.; Thompsons Commercial Photographers, Knoxville, Tenn.; Times-Democrat, Cullman, Ala.; Tom-Clare Studio, Humboldt, Tenn.; Doug Underwood, Columbia, Tenn.; Thomas L. Williams, Williamsburg, Va.; Harold Wigley, Mobile, Ala.; Bill Wilson Studio, Birmingham, Ala., and Peggy Wrenne (VUM).

ENGRAVER

ALABAMA ENGRAVING COMPANY
Birmingham, Ala.

PRINTER

PARAGON PRESS, Montgomery, Ala.

PROOF READER

HELEN DOUGLASS BRADLEY.

SUBSCRIBERS

We thank the many libraries, individuals, and associations, who subscribed to this book before publication.

OTHERS

The individuals who encouraged and aided us in various way are too numerous to list. However, we do wish to express special thanks to the following: W. N. Barnett, Johnnie Baxter, J. R. Cain, Remelle Davis, August Dietz, Annie L. Douglass, B. A. Douglass, R. B. Douglass, Robert B. Faerber, T. G. Flinn, Dr. Max M. Foreman, Albert D. Fundaburk, John Gardner, Mary Ruth Graham, Katherine P. (Mrs. Ralph) Howard, J. E. Perry, Dr. Lorraine Pierson, Ethel "Polly" Pollard, Mrs. H. H. Pollitt, Norman T. Spann, Dr. Frank J. Soday, Cathryn Wright (Mrs. Frank) Tennille—WSFA-TV, Evelyn Turner, Harry Price, and Lila Wall.

BIBLIOGRAPHY

ABBREVIATIONS

AA
American Anthropologist. Publication of the American Anthropological Association. Menasha and Beloit.

AAn
American Antiquity. Publication of the Society for American Archaeology. Salt Lake City.

AAOJ
American Antiquarian and Oriental Journal. Chicago.

AmA
American Archaeologist. Columbus.

AmMNH-AP
American Museum of Natural History, Anthropological Papers. New York.

AMNH-MP
Alabama Museum of Natural History, Museum Papers. University and Moundville.

ANSP-J
Academy of Natural Sciences of Philadelphia, Journal of. Philadelphia.

AP
Arrowpoints. Alabama Anthropological Society. Montgomery.

APS-P
American Philosophical Society, Proceedings. Philadelphia.

BAE
Bureau of American Ethnology, Smithsonian Institution. Washington. AP—Anthropological Papers. AR—Annual Report. B—Bulletin.

FA
Florida Anthropologist. Publication of the Florida Anthropological Soc. Gainesville.

GHS-C
Georgia Historical Society, Collections. Savannah.

ICA-P
International Congress of Americanists, Proceedings. Washington.

LGS-AS
Louisiana Geological Survey, Department of Conservation, Anthropological Study. New Orleans and Baton Rouge.

MA
Missouri Archaeologist. Publication of the Missouri Archaeological Society. Columbia.

MAIHF
Museum of the American Indian, Heye Foundation. New York. C—Contributions. INM—Indian Notes and Monographs. MS—Miscellaneous Series.

MH-J
Mississippi History, Journal of. Publication of the Mississippi Historical Society and the Mississippi Department of Archives and History. Jackson.

MPM-B
Milwaukee Public Museum, Bulletin. Milwaukee.

NPS
National Park Service. Washington. ARS—Archeological Research Series. HH—Historical Handbook.

OAS-B
Oklahoma Anthropological Society. Bulletin. Norman.

OP
Oklahoma Prehistorian. Publication of the Oklahoma State Archaeological Society. Tulsa.

PMAE
Peabody Museum of Archaeology and Ethnology. Harvard University, Cambridge. P—Papers. AR—Annual Report.

SI
Smithsonian Institution. Washington. AR—Annual Report. CK—Contributions to Knowledge. MC—Miscellaneous Collections.

TA
Tennessee Archaeologist. Publication of the Tennessee Archaeological Society. Knoxville.

TAPS-B
Texas Archeological and Paleontological Society, Bulletin. Abilene and Austin.

UK-RA
University of Kentucky, Reports in Anthropology. Lexington.

UP
University of Pennsylvania. Philadelphia. FMSA-B—Free Museum of Science and Art, Bulletin. UM—University Museum. AP—Anthropological Papers. B—Bulletin.

USNM
United States National Museum, Smithsonian Institution. Washington. AR— Annual Report. B—Bulletin. P—Proceedings.

UTe
University of Texas. Austin. AP—Anthropological Papers. P—Publications.

WAS-J
Washington Academy of Sciences, Journal of. Washington.

BOOKS, BULLETINS, ARTICLES, AND OTHER PUBLICATIONS

Many of the books mentioned below have excellent bibliographies. Among them are: Dockstader, 1957; J. B. Griffin, 1952; Lewis and Kneberg, 1946; Martin, Quimby, and Collier, 1947; Phillips, Ford, and Griffin, 1951; Suhm, Krieger, and Jelks, 1954; Swanton, 1946 and 1953; Webb and DeJarnette, 1942; Willey, 1949; and all the various publications of the Bureau of American Ethnology.

ABELL, WALTER
1946. Stone Disks as Treaty 'Suns.' AAn 12:1:1-9.

ADAIR, JAMES
1775. History of the American Indians. London. Also, S. C. Williams, ed., 1930.

ALABAMA MUSEUM OF NATURAL HISTORY
1942. Mound State Monument. AMNH-MP 20.

ALLEN, GLENN T., JR.
1953. A Stratigraphic Investigation of the Hall Site, Wakulla County, Florida. Notes in Anthropology 1:2: Florida State University, Tallahassee.

ALVORD, CLARENCE W., and LEE BIDGOOD
1912. The First Explorations of the Trans-Allegheny Region by the Virginians, 1650-1674. Cleveland.

APPLETON, LEROY H.
1950. Indian Art of the Americas. Charles Scribner's Sons, New York.

ARROWPOINTS
1920-1937. Edited by Peter A. Brannon. Monthly bulletin Ala. Anthrop. Soc. Montgomery.

ASHLEY, MARGARET E.
1932. A Study of the Ceramic Art of the Etowans. In Moorehead, 1932:107-132.

BARRETT, S. A.
1933. Ancient Aztalan. MPM-B 13.

BASSETT, JOHN SPENCER
1901. The Writings of "Colonel William Byrd of Westover in Virginia, Esq." New York.

BARTRAM, WILLIAM
1791. Travels Through North and South Carolina, Georgia, East and West Florida . . . . New York. 1792, London. 1940, New York.
1909. Observations on the Creek and Cherokee Indians. With notes by E. G. Squier. Trans. Amer. Ethnol. Soc. 3:1:1-81: Reprint, 1853 edition.
1943. Travels in Georgia and Florida, 1773-74. A Report to Dr. John Fothergill. Annotated by Francis Harper. APS-Trans. n.s. 33:2.

BEALS, R. L.
1932. The Comparative Ethnology of Northern Mexico Before 1750. University of California Press, Berkeley.

BAERREIS, DAVID A.
1939. Two New Cultures in Delaware County, Oklahoma. OP 2:1:2-5.
1951. Preceramic Horizons of Northeastern Oklahoma. Anthropological Paper 6, Museum of Anthropology, University of Michigan, Ann Arbor.

BEADLE, B. V.
1942. A Recent Find of Carved Shell Effigies. The Minnesota Archaeologist 8:4:169.

BEAUDOIN, KENNETH L., EDITOR
1953. The T. O. Fuller Report. Memphis.

BELL, ROBERT E.
1947. Trade Materials at Spiro Mound as Indicated by Artifacts. AAn 12:3:181-184.
1952. Dendrochronology in the Mississippi Valley. In J. B. Griffin, 1952:345-351.
1953. Pottery Vessels from the Spiro Mound, Cr. 1, Le Flore Co., Oklahoma. OAS-B 1:March:25-38.
1956. A Copper Plummet from Poverty Point, Louisiana. AAn 22:1:80.

BELL, ROBERT E., and DAVID A. BAERREIS
1951. A Survey of Oklahoma Archaeology. TAPS-B 22:7-100.

BELL, ROBERT E., and ROLAND SCOTT HALL
1953. Selected Projectile Point Types of the United States. OAS-B 1:1-16.

BEVERLEY, ROBERT
1705. The History and Present State of Virginia . . . . London.

BEYER, HERMANN
1933. Shell Ornament Sets from Huasteca, Mexico. Tulane University, Middle American Research Series 5:4, New Orleans.

BIEDMA, LUIS HERNANDEZ DE. See Bourne, E. G., ed.

BLACK, GLENN A.
1944. Angel Site, Vanderburgh County, Indiana. Indiana Historical Society, Prehistoric Research Series 2:5:451-521.

BOAZ, FRANZ
1951. Primitive Art. Capitol Publishing Company, New York.

BOSSU, M.
1771. Travels Through that Part of North America Formerly Called Louisiana. 2 v, London. Paris, 1768.
BOURNE, EDWARD GAYLORD, EDITOR
1904. Narratives of the Career of Hernando De Soto. 2 v, Trail Makers, New York. Reprint: American Explorers, Allerton Book Co., New York, 1922.
BRANNON, PETER A.
1909. Aboriginal Remains in the Middle Chattahoochee Valley of Alabama and Georgia. AA n. s. 11:186-198.
1935. Shell Work at the Mouth of the Tallapoosa. AP 20:5-6:33-35B.
1935a. Taskigi Town, A History of the Site. AP 20:5-6:31-32.
1935b. Urn-Burial at Taskigi. AP 20:5-6:40-42.
1937. Bird Concept, Tallapoosa River. AP 22:1-2:18-30.
BRINTON, DANIEL G.
1859. Notes on the Floridian Peninsula, its Literary History, Indian Tribes and Antiquities. Philadelphia.
BROWN, CALVIN S.
1926. Archeology of Mississippi. Mississippi Geological Survey, University, Mississippi.
BRYAN, KIRK
1950. Flint Quarries . . . . PMAE-P 17:3.
BULLEN, RIPLEY P.
1950. An Archaeological Survey in the Chattahoochee River Valley in Florida. WAS-J 11:4.
1952. Eleven Archaeological Sites in Hillsborough County, Florida. Florida Geological Survey, Report of Investigations 8.
1955. Carved Owl Totem, Deland, Florida. FA 8:3:61-73.
BURKE, R. P.
1933. Orange-Red Pottery People. AP 19:32-42.
1934. Orange-Red Paint Culture. AP 20:1 & 2:2-12.
1936. Origin of Certain Pottery Designs. AP 21:5-6:4-20.
1937. Sawogoni Pipes. AP 21:5-6:41-46.
BURNETT, E. K.
1945. The Spiro Mound Collection in the Museum. MAIHF-C 14.
BUSHNELL, DAVID I., JR.
1904. Cahokia and Surrounding Mound Groups. PMAE-P 3:1.
1907. Virginia from Early Records. AA 9:8:45-57.
1908. The account of Lamhatty AA n.s. 10:568-574.
1909. The Choctaw of Bayou Lacomb . . . . BAE-B 48.
1919. Native Villages and Village Sites East of the Mississippi. BAE-B 69.
1920. Native Cemeteries and Forms of Burial East of the Mississippi. BAE-B 71.
1922. Archeological Reconnaissance of the Cahokia and Related Mound Groups. SI-MC 72:15:92-105.
1922a. Villages of the Algonquian, Siouan, and Caddoan Tribes West of the Mississippi. BAE-B 77.
1926. Ancient Soapstone Quarry in Albemarle County, Virginia. WAS-J 16:19:525-528.
1927. Drawings of A. DeBatz in Louisiana, 1732-1735. SI-MC 80:5.
1930. The Five Monacan towns in Virginia, 1607. SI-MC 82:12.
1934. Tribal Migrations East of the Mississippi. SI-MC 89:12.
1935. The Manahoac tribes in Virginia, 1608. SI-MC 94:8.
1937. Indian Sites Below the Falls of the Rappahannock, Virginia. SI-MC 96:4.
1939. Steatite. SI-AR 1939 (3555):471-490.
BYERS, DOUGLAS S.
1940. Two sites on Martha's Vineyard. Robert S. Peabody Foundation for Archaeology, Papers 1:1, Phillips Academy, Andover, Mass.
1943. The First Archaeological Conference on the Woodland Pattern. AAn 8:4:392-400.
BYRD, WILLIAM
1866. History of the Dividing Line and Other Tracts. 2v, Richmond, Reprint: William K. Boyd, ed., 1929, Raleigh. Also John S. Bassett, The Writings of

Colonel William Byrd . . . . 1901, New York.
CABEZA, DE VACA, ALVAR NUNEZ
1905. The Journey of Alvar Nunez Cabeza de Vaca . . . . translated by Fanny Bandelier. Trail Makers. New York. Also edited by F. W. Hodge in Spanish Explorers . . .
CALDWELL, JOSEPH R.
1952. Archeology of Eastern Georgia and South Carolina. In J. B. Griffin 1952: 312-321.
CALDWELL, JOSEPH, and CATHERINE McCANN
1941. Irene Mound Site, Chatham County, Georgia. University of Georgia Press, Athens.
CARR, LUCIEN
1881. Report on the Exploration of a Mound in Lee County, Virginia . . . . PMAE-AR 10.
CATESBY, MARK
1731-1743. The Natural History of Carolina, Florida, and Bahama Islands. 2v, London.
CATLIN, GEORGE
1841. Letters, and Notes on the Manners, Customs, and Conditions of the North American Indians, etc. 2v, New York.
CAYWOOD, LOUIS R.
1955. Excavations at Green Spring Plantation. NPS, Yorktown, Virginia.
CHAPMAN, CARL H.
1952. Culture Sequence in the Lower Missouri Valley. In J. B. Griffin 1952: 139-151.
CHAPMAN, CARL H. and LEO O. ANDERSON
1955. The Campbell Site. A Late Mississippi Town Site and Cemetery in Southeastern Missouri. MA 17:2-3.
CHARLEVOIX, PIERRE F. X. DE
1761. Journal of a Voyage to North America. 2v, London. Also in B. F. French, Historical Collections . . . 1851. 1866-1872. History and general Description of New France. Translated by John G. Shea, 6v, New York. Paris, 1744. London, 1761.
CLAFLIN, W. H.
1931. The Stalling's Island Mound, Columbia County, Georgia. PMAE-P 14:1.
COE, JOFFRE L.
1937. Archaeology of North Carolina. Bulletin of the Archaeological Society of North Carolina IV:May 1937:5-6.
1952. The Cultural Sequence of the Carolina Piedmont. In J. B. Griffin 1952:301-311.
COLE, FAY-COOPER, and THORNE DEUEL
1937. Rediscovering Illinois. Archaeological Explorations in and around Fulton County. Chicago.
COLE, FAY-COOPER, AND OTHERS
1951. Kincaid, A Prehistoric Illinois Metropolis. University of Chicago Press, Chicago.
COLLINS, HENRY B., JR.
1932. Excavations at a Prehistoric Indian Village Site in Mississippi. USNM-P 79:32:1-22.
COOVER, A. B.
1898. Letter to the Editor. AmA 2:5.
COTE, R. E.
1930. Moundbuilder Designs. Bruce Publishing Company, Milwaukee.
COTTER, JOHN, and J. M. CORBETT
1951. Archaeology of the Bynum Mounds, Mississippi. NPS-ARS 1.
COVARRUBIAS, MIGUEL
1954. The Eagle, The Jaguar, and the Serpent. Indian Art of the Americas, North America: Alaska, Canada, the United States. Alfred A. Knopf, New York.
COX, ISAAC JOSLIN, EDITOR
1905. The Journeys of Rene Robert Cavelier, Sieur de La Salle. 2v, Trail Makers (Series), New York.
COXE, DANIEL
1928. The Southern Frontiers, 1670-1732. Duke University Press, Durham. London, 1741. Also in B. F. French, Historical Collections . . . .
CULIN, STEWART
1900. The Dickeson Collection of American Antiquities. UP-FMSA-B 2:3.
1907. Games of the North American Indians. BAE-AR 24:1902-1903.

CUSHING, FRANK H.
1879. Soapstone Quarry, Amelia County, Virginia. SI-AR 1878:44-45.
1897. Exploration of Ancient Key Dwellers' Remains on the Gulf Coast of Florida. APS-P 35:153:329-432.
1897a. A Moundbuilder Village. The Antiquarian 1:1:7-10.
CZAJKOWSKI, J. R.
1934. Preliminary Report of Archaeological Excavations in Orleans Parish. Louisiana Conservation Review: 4:3: New Orleans.
DeJARNETTE, DAVID L.
1941. The Bessemer Site. AMNH-MP 17.
1952. Alabama Archeology, A Summary. In J. B. Griffin 1952:272-284.
DELLINGER, SAMUEL C., and S. D. DICKINSON
1940. Possible Antecedents of the Middle Mississippian Ceramic Complex in Northeastern Arkansas. AAn 6:133-147.
1942. Pottery from the Ozark Bluffs Shelters. AAn 7:3:276-289.
DEUEL, THORNE, EDITOR
1952. Hopewellian Communities in Illinois. Sci. Papers, Ill. State Mus. 5.
DICKINSON, S. D.
1941. Certain Vessels from the Clements Place, an Historic Caddo Site. TASP-B 13:117-132.
DICKINSON, SAMUEL D., and S. C. DELLINGER
1940. A Survey of Historic Earthenware of the Lower Arkansas Valley. TAPS-B 12:76-96.
DICKINSON, SAMUEL D., and H. J. LEMLEY, JR.
1936. The Ceramic Relationships of the Pre-Caddo Pottery from the Crenshaw Site. TAPS-B 8.
1939. Evidences of the Marksville and Coles Creek Complexes at the Kirkham Place, Clark County, Arkansas. TAPS-B 11.
DOCKSTADER, FREDERICK J.
1957. The American Indian in Graduate Studies. A bibliography of These and Dissertations. MAIHF-C 15.
DOUGLAS, FREDERICK H., and RENE D'HARNONCOURT
1941. Indian Art of the United States. The Museum of Modern Art, distributed by Simon and Schuster, New York.
DOUGLASS, A. E.
1882. A Find of Ceremonial Axes in a Florida Mound. AAOJ 4:2:100-109.
1885. Earth and Shell Mounds on the Atlantic Coast of Florida. AAOJ 7:3:140-147.
1890. Description of a Gold Ornament from Florida. AAOJ 12:1.
1919. Climatic Cycles and Tree Growth. Carnegie Institution Publication 289, Washington.
1942. Tree Rings and Chronology, University of Arizona, Bulletin.
DRUCKER, PHILIP
1943. Ceramic Stratigraphy at Cerro de las Mesas, Veracruz, Mexico, BAE-B 141.
1947. Some Implications of the Ceramic Complex of La Venta. SI-MC 107:8.
1952. La Venta, Tabasco, A Study of Olmec Ceramics and Art. BAE-B 153.
1955. The Cerro de las Mesas Offering of Jade and Other Materials. BAE-AP 44: BAE-B 157:25-68:PL. 27-54.
DUMONT DE MONTIGNY
1753. Memoires Historiques sur la Louisiane. Edited by Le Mascrier. 2 v, Paris.
DU PRATZ, ANTOINE S. LE PAGE. See LE PAGE . . . .
DYER, J. O.
1917. The Lake Charles Atakapas, 1817-1820. Galveston.
EGGAN, FRED R.
1952. The Ethnological Cultures and Their Archeological Backgrounds. In J. B. Griffin 1952:35-45.
ELLIS, H. H.
1940. Flint-Working Techniques of the American Indian. An Experimental Study. Ohio State Museum, Dept. of Archaeology, Columbus.
ESPINOSA, FRAY ISIDRO FELIS DE
1927. Descriotions of the Tejas or Asinai Indians, 1691-1722. Translated from the Spanish by Mattie Austin Hatcher. Southwestern Hist. Quart. 31:150-180. Spanish text in BAE-B 132:273-300.

EXPOSITION OF INDIAN TRIBAL ARTS, INC.
1931. Introduction to American Indian Art. Pt. I—Text by John Sloan and Oliver La Farge; Part II—Text by H. J. Spinden and others. New York.
FAIRBANKS, CHARLES H.
1946. The Macon Earth Lodge. AAn 12:2:94-108.
1952. Creek and Pre-Creek. In J. B. Griffin 1952:285-300.
1956. Archeology of the Funeral Mound, Ocmulgee National Monument, Georgia. NPS-ARS 3. Waring and Holder, 1945, bibliography refers to the manuscript—Mound C.
FEWKES, J. W.
1924. Preliminary Archeological Explorations at Weeden Island, Florida. SI-MC 76:13:1-26.
1928. Aboriginal Wooden Objects from Southern Florida. SI-MC 80:9.
FEWKES, VLADIMIR J.
1944. Catawba Pottery-making, with notes on Pamunkey Pottery-making, Cherokee Pottery-making and coiling. APS-P 88:2:69-124.
FONTANEDA, HERNANDO DE ESCALANTE
1854. Memoria de las Cosas y Costa y Indios de la Florida. In Buckingham Smith's Letter of Hernando de Soto, ... Washington.
FORD, JAMES A.
1935. Ceramic Decoration Sequence at an Old Indian Village Site Near Sicily Island, Louisiana. LGS-AS 1.
1935a. Outline of Louisiana and Mississippi Pottery Horizons. Louisiana Conservation Review, April: 33-38.
1936. Analysis of Indian Village Site Collections from Louisiana and Mississippi. LGS-AS 2.
1951. Greenhouse: A Troyville-Coles Creek Period Site in Avoyelles Parish, Louisiana. AmMNH-AP 44:1.
1952. Measurements of Some Prehistoric Design Developments in Southeastern States. AmMNH-AP 44:3.
FORD, JAMES A., PHILIP PHILLIPS, AND WILLIAM G. HAAG
1955. The Jaketown Site in West-central Mississippi. AmMNH-AP 45:1.
FORD, JAMES A., and GEORGE I. QUIMBY, JR.
1945. The Tchefuncte Culture, An Early Occupation of the Lower Mississippi Valley. Society for American Archaeology, Memoir 2:supplement to AA 10:3:2.
FORD, JAMES A., and CLARENCE H. WEBB
1956. Poverty Point, A Late Archaic Site in Louisiana. AmMNH-AP:46:1.
FORD, JAMES A., and GORDON R. WILLEY
1940. Crooks Site. A Marksville Period Burial Mound in La Salle Parish, Louisiana. LGS-AS 3.
1941. An Interpretation of the Prehistory of the Eastern United States. AA n. s. 43:3:325-363.
FOREMAN, GRANT
1932. Indian Removal. The Emigration of the Five Civilized Tribes of Indians. University of Oklahoma Press, Norman.
1933. Advancing the Frontier, 1830-1860. University of Oklahoma Press, Norman.
1934. The Five Civilized Tribes. University of Oklahoma Press, Norman.
FOWKE, GERARD
1894. Archaeological Investigations in James and Potomac Valleys. BAE-B 23.
1896. Stone Art. BAE-AR 13:1891-1892: 47-178.
1910. Antiquities of Central and Southeastern Missouri. BAE-B 37.
1922. Archeological Investigations. BAE-B 76.
1927. Archeological Work in Louisiana. SI-MC 78:7:254-259.
1928. Explorations in the Red River Valley in Louisiana. BAE-AR 44:1926-1927: 405-540.
FRENCH, B. F.
1846-1853. Historical Collections of Louisiana . . . . 5 pts. New York. Others numbers, 1869 and 1875, New York.
FUNKHOUSER, WILLIAM D., and WILLIAM S. WEBB
1928. Ancient Life in Kentucky. Kentucky Geological Survey 6:4, Frankfort.
GARCILASO, DE LA VEGA (EL INCA)
1723. La Florida del Inca. 2ed. Madrid. Also 1722, Madrid.

GATSCHET, ALBERT S.
1884, 1888. Migration Legend of the Creek Indians. Brinton's Library of Aboriginal American Literature, 1884, Philadelphia. Trans. Acad. Sci. St. Louis, vol. 5:1-2, 1888.
GILBERT, WILBUR H., JR.
1943. The Eastern Cherokees. BAE-AP 23:BAE-B 133:169-413.
GOGGIN, JOHN M.
1947. A Preliminary Definition of Archaeological Areas and Periods in Florida. AAn 13:2:114-127.
1947a. Manifestations of a South Florida Cult in Northwestern Florida. AAn 12:4:273-276.
1949. Cultural Occupation at Goodland Point, Florida. FA 2:3-4:65-91.
1949a. Cultural Traditions in Florida Prehistory. In John W. Griffin, 1949: 13-44.
GRIFFIN, JAMES B.
1938. The Ceramic Remains, Norris Basin. In Webb 1938:253-258.
1939. Report on Ceramics of Wheeler Basin. In Webb 1939:127-165.
1943. The Fort Ancient Aspect. University of Michigan Press, Ann Arbor.
1943a. Archeological Horizons in the Southeast and their Connections with the Mexican Area. En El Norte de Mexico y el Sur de Los Estados Unidos, Sociedad Mexicana de Antropologia 3:283-286, Mexico.
1944. The DeLuna Expedition and the "Buzzard Cult" in the Southeast. WAS-J 34:9:299-303.
1945. An Interpretation of Siouan Archeology in the Piedmont of North Carolina and Virginia. AAn 10:4:321-330.
1945a. The Significance of Fiber-tempered Pottery of the St. Johns Area in 1950. Prehistoric Pottery of the Eastern Florida. WAS-J 35:7:218-223.
United States. Loose-leaf notes from the Ceramic Repository, Museum of Anthropology, University of Michigan, Ann Arbor.
1952. Archeology of Eastern United States. Edited by James B. Griffin. University of Chicago Press, Chicago. Includes articles by various archeologists specializing in areas.
1952a. An Interpretation of the Place of Spiro in Southeastern Archaeology. In Hamilton 1952:89-106.
1952b. Culture Periods in Eastern United States Archeology. In J. B. Griffin 1952: 352-364.
1952c. Radiocarbon Dates for the Eastern United States. In J. B. Griffin 1952:365-370.
GRIFFIN, JOHN WALLACE
1946. Historic Artifacts and the "Buzzard Cult" in Florida. Florida Historical Quarterly 14:4:295-301.
1949. The Florida Indian and His Neighbors. Rollins College, Winter Park.
1952. Prehistoric Florida. A Review. In J. B. Griffin 1952:322-334.
GRIFFIN, JOHN WALLACE, and HALE G. SMITH
1948. The Goodnow Mounds, Highland County, Florida. Florida Park Service, Contributions 1, Tallahassee.
GUERNSEY, S. J. and A. V. KIDDER
1921. Basketmaker Caves in Northeastern Arizona. PMAE-P 8:2.
GUTHE, CARL E.
1950. Moundville, An Historic Document. AMNS-MP 29.
1952. Twenty-five Years of Archeology in the Eastern United States. In J. B. Griffin 1952:1-12.
HAAG, WILLIAM G.
1942. A Description and Analysis of the Pickwick Pottery. In Webb 1942:509-526.
1955. A Prehistory of Mississippi. MH-J 17:2:81-109.
HAAG, WILLIAM G., and CLARENCE H. WEBB
1953. Microblades at Poverty Point Sites. AAn 18:3:245-248.
HAKLUYT, RICHARD
1907. The Principal Navigations, Voyages, Traffiques and Discoveries of the English Nation. Dutton, Everyman's Library. London, 1589-1600.
HALE, J. P.
1897. An Ancient Woodcarving. A 1:5.
HAMILTON, HENRY W.
1952. The Spiro Mound. MA 14.

HARIOT, THOMAS
1893. A Brief and True Report of the New Found Land of Virginia. Reprint, London. Earlier editions 1588 and 1590. See S. Lorant, 1946; and Hakluyt, 1907.
HARRINGTON, M. R.
1920. Certain Caddo Sites in Arkansas. MAIHF-MS 10.
1922. Cherokee and Earlier Remains on Upper Tennessee River. MAIHF-INM 24.
HAWKINS, BENJAMIN
1848. A Sketch of Creek Country, in 1798 and 1799. GHS-C 3.
1916. Letters of Benjamin Hawkins, 1796-1806. GHS-C 9.
HAWLEY, FLORENCE M.
1938. Tree Ring Dating for Southeastern Mounds. In Webb 1938.
HAY, C. L., and OTHERS
1940. The Maya and Their Neighbors. Appleton-Century Co., New York.
HAYWOOD, JOHN
1823. Natural and Aboriginal History of Tennessee. Civil and Political History. Nashville. Reprint 1891 and 1915.
HENNEPIN, LOUIS
1698. A New Discovery of a Vast Country in America . . . . London.
HEWITT, J. N. B.
1939. Notes on the Creek Indians. Edited by John R. Swanton. BAE-AR 10: BAE-B 123:119-159.
HEYE, GEORGE G., F. W. HODGE, and GEORGE H. PEPPER
1918. The Nacoochee Mound in Georgia. MAIHF-C 4:3.
HIBBEN, F. C.
1937. Association of Man with Pleistocene Mammals in the Sandia Mountains, New Mexico. AAn 4:260-263.
HODGE, FREDERICK W., EDITOR
1912. Handbook of American Indians North of Mexico. BAE-B 30:2v:1907-1910.
HODGE, FREDERICK W., and THEODORE H. LEWIS, EDITORS
1907. Spanish Explorers in the Southern United States, 1528-1543. Narrative of Alvar Nunez Cabeca de Vaca, edited by F. W. Hodge. Narrative of Hernando De Soto by Gentlemen of Elvas, edited by T. H. Lewis. Original copyright by Charles Scribner's Sons; transferred — Original Narratives Series—to Barnes and Noble, New York.
HOLDER, PRESTON, and WARING, A. J., JR.
1945. The Deptford Complex (ms). (From Waring and Holder, 1945).
HOLMES, WILLIAM H.
1883. Art in Shell of the Ancient Americans. BAE-AR 2:1880-1881:179-305.
1884. Illustrated Catalogue of a Portion of the Collections Made by the Bureau of American Ethnology during the Field Season of 1881. BAE-AR 3:1881-1882:427-510.
1884a. Prehistoric Textile Fabrics of the United States Derived from Impressions on Pottery. BAE-AR 3:1881-1882:393-425.
1886. Ancient Pottery of the Mississippi Valley. BAE-AR 4:1882-1883:361-436.
1888. A Study of Textile Art in its Relation to the Development of Form and Ornament. BAE-AR 6:1884-1885:188-252.
1890. Excavations in an Ancient Soapstone Quarry in the District of Columbia. AA o.s. 3:321-330.
1894. Caribbean Influence in the Prehistoric Art of the Southern States. AA o.s. 7:1:71-79.
1896. Prehistoric Textile Art of the Eastern United States. BAE-AR 13:1891-1892: 3-46.
1897. Stone Implements of the Potomac-Chesapeake Tidewater Province. BAE-AR 15:1893-1894:1-152.
1901. Aboriginal Copper Mines of Isle Royale, Lake Superior. AA n. s. 3:684-696.
1903. Aboriginal Pottery of the Eastern United States. BAE-AR 20:1898-1899:1-237.
1903a. Shell Ornaments from Kentucky to Mexico. SI-MC 45:97-99.
1906. Certain Notched or Scalloped Stone Tablets of the Moundbuilders. AA n. s. 8:101-108.
1914. Areas of American Culture Characterization Tentatively Outlined as an Aid in the Study of Antiquities. AA n. s. 16:3:413-446.

1919. Handbook of Aboriginal American Antiquities. Part 1: Introductory. The Lithic Industries. BAE-B 60.

INVERARITY, ROBERT BRUCE
1950. Art of the Northwest Coast Indians. University of California Press, Berkeley.

JACKSON, A. T.
1935. Ornaments of East Texas Indians. TAPS-B 7:11-28.
1938. Picture Writing of the Texas Indians. UTe-P 3809:AP 2.

JAMES, GEORGE W.
1902. Indian Basketry. New York.

JENNINGS, JESSE D.
1941. Chickasaw and Earlier Indian Cultures of Northeast Mississippi. MH-J 3:3:155-226.
1946. Hopewell-Copena Sites near Nashville. AAn 12:2:126.
1952. Prehistory of the Lower Mississippi Valley. In J. B. Griffin, 1952:256-271.

JOHNSON, J. STODDARD
1898. First Explorations of Kentucky. Filson Club Publication 13. Louisville.

JONES, CHARLES C., JR.
1873. Antiquities of the Southern Indians. D. Appleton & Co., New York.

JONES, JOSEPH
1876. Explorations of the Aboriginal Remains of Tennessee. SI-CK 259.
1880. Explorations of the Aboriginal Remains of Tennessee. SI-CK 22:1-171.

JONES, WALTER B.
1939. Geology of the Tennessee Valley Region of Alabama, with Notes on the Topographic Features of the area, and the Effect of Geology and Topography upon Aboriginal Occupation. In W. S. Webb, 1939:9-20.
1942. Geology of the Pickwick Basin in Adjacent Parts of Tennessee, Mississippi, and Alabama. In W. S. Webb and DeJarnette, 1942:327-335.

JONES, WALTER B., and DAVID L. DeJARNETTE
1936. Moundville Culture and Burial. AMNH-MP 13.

KELEMEN, PAL
1943. Medieval American Art. New York.

KELLBERG, J. M.
1955. Identification of Materials from which Artifacts are Made. TA 11:1:9-13.

KELLY, A. R.
1938. A Preliminary Report on Archaeological Explorations at Macon, Georgia. BAE-AP 1:BAE-B 119:1-197.
1939. The Macon Trading Post, an Historical Foundling. AAn 4:4:328-333.
1939a. The Bull Creek Cemetery, Columbus, Ga. (ms) (From Waring and Holder, 1945).

KLEINE, H. K.
1953. A Remarkable Paleo-Indian Site in Alabama. TA 9:2:31-37. In Lewis and Kneberg, 1954:241-247.

KNEBERG, MADELINE
1952. The Tennessee Area. In J. B. Griffin, 1952:190-198.

KNOBLOCK, BYRON W.
1939. Bannerstones of the North American Indians. LaGrange, Illinois.

KRIEGER, ALEX D.
1945. An Inquiry into Supposed Mexican Influences on a Prehistoric 'Cult' in the Southeastern United States. AA 47:4: 483-515.
1946. Culture Complexes and Chronology in Northern Texas. UTe-P 4640.
1947. The First Symposium on the Caddoan Archaeological Area. AAn 12:3: 198-207.

LADDO, R. B.
1925. Non-Metallic Minerals. New York.

LARSON, LEWIS H., JR.
1955. Unusual Figurine from the Georgia Coast. FA 8:3:75-82.

LAUDONNIERE, RENE GOULAINE DE
1853. L'histoire notable de la Floride situee es Indes Occidentales . . . . Paris. Reprint of the 1586 edition, Paris.

LAWSON, JOHN
1860. History of North Carolina . . . . Raleigh, N. C. Other editions: 1714, London; and 1937, Richmond.

LEDERER, JOHN
1912. The Discoveries of John Lederer in three several Marches from Virginia . . . .

translated by Sir William Talbot. In Alvord, C. W. and Lee Bidgood. Other editions, London 1672; and Rochester, 1902.

LEMLEY, HARRY J.
1936. Discoveries Indicating a Pre-Caddo Culture on Red River in Arkansas. TAPS-B 8:25-55.

LEMLEY, HARRY J., and S. D. DICKINSON
1937. Archaeological Excavations on Bayou Macon in Arkansas. TAPS-B 9:11-47.

LE MOYNE, JACQUES
1875. Narrative of Le Moyne, an artist who accompanied Laudonniere's French expedition to Florida in 1564. Boston. Translation from De Bry, 1591.

LE PAGE DU PRATZ, ANTOINE S.
1758. Histoire de la Louisiane. 3 v, Paris. 1763, 2 v, London.

LEWIS, THOMAS M. N.
1947. Famous Duck River Cache Returns to Tennessee. TA 3:3:38-41.
1947a. The Duck River Cache. TA 3:4: 54-57.
1953. The Paleo-Indian Problem in Tennessee. TA 9:2:38-40.

LEWIS, THOMAS M. N., and MADELINE KNEBERG
1941. The Prehistory of the Chickamauga Basin. University of Tennessee, Anthropological Papers 1.
1946. Hiwassee Island. An archaeological Account of Four Tennessee Indian Peoples. University of Tennessee Press, Knoxville.
1947. The Archaic Horizon in Western Tennessee. University of Tenn., Record Extension Series 23:4.
1954. Ten Years of the Tennessee Archaeologist. Published by J. B. Graham, P. O. Box 12, Chattanooga, Tennessee.

LIBBY, WILLARD F.
1955. Radiocarbon dating. Second edition. University of Chicago Press, Chicago.

LILLY, ELI
1937. Prehistoric Antiquities of Indiana. Indiana Historical Society, Indianapolis.

LOCKETT, SAMUEL H.
1873. Mounds in Louisiana. SI-AR 1872: 429-430.

LORANT, STEFAN, EDITOR
1946. The New World: The First Pictures of America Made by John White and Jacques Le Moyne. Duell, Sloane, and Pearce, New York.

LOWERY, WOODBURY
1901. The Spanish Settlements Within the Present Limits of the United States, 1513-1561. New York and London.
1905. Spanish Settlements Within the Present Limits of the United States and Florida, 1564-1574. New York and London.
? Mss., Library of Congress.

MacCAULEY, CLAY
1887. The Seminole Indians of Florida. BAE-AR 5:1883-1884:469-531.

MacCURDY, GEORGE GRANT
1913. Shell Gorgets from Missouri. AA n. s. 15:3:395-414.
1917. Some Mounds in Eastern Tennessee. ICA-P 19:59-74.
1917a. The Wesleyan University Collection of Antiquities from Tennessee. ICA-P 19:75-95.

MacNEISH, RICHARD S.
1952. Archeology of the Northeastern United States. In J. B. Griffin 1952: 59-70.

McCARY, B. C.
1951. A Workshop of Early Man in Dinwiddie County, Virginia. AAn 17:9-17.

McGUIRE, J. D.
1896. A Study of the Primitive Methods of Drilling. USNM-AR 1894:625-756.
1899. Pipes and Smoking Customs of the American Aborigines, based on Material in the United States National Museum. USNM-AR 1896-1897:1:361-645.

McKENNEY, THOMAS L., and JAMES HALL
1854. History of the Indian Tribes of North America. 3 v, Philadelphia.

MAHAN, EDWARD C.
1954-1955. A Survey of Paleo-Indian and other Early Flint Artifacts from Sites in Northern, Western, and Central Alabama. TA 10-11.

MALLERY, GARRICK
1893. Picture Writing of the American Indians. BAE-AR 10:1888-1889:1-777.

MALONE, HENRY THOMPSON
1956. Cherokee of the Old South. A People in Transition. University of Georgia Press, Athens.

MARGRY, PIERRE
1875-1886. Decouvertes et establissements des Francais dans l'Ouest et dans le Sud de l'Amerique septentrionale (1614-1754). Memoires et documents originaux recueillis et publies par Pierre Margry. 6 v, Paris.

MARTIN, PAUL S., GEORGE I. QUIMBY, and DONALD COLLIER
1947. Indians Before Columbus. University of Chicago Press, Chicago.

MASON, J. A.
1935. The Place of Texas in Pre-Columbian Relationships Between the United States and Mexico. TAPS-B 7:29-46.
1937. Further Remarks on the Pre-Columbian Relationship between the United States and Mexico. TAPS-B 9:120-129.
1950. Primitive Wooden Masks from Key Marco, Florida Archeology. UP-UM 4:1.

MASON, O. T.
1884. Basket-Work of the North American Aborigines. USNM-AR 1884:291-307.
1885. Throwing-sticks in the National Museum. USNM-AR 1884:279-304.
1887. Cradles of American Aborigines. USNM-AR 1887:161-212.
1904. Aboriginal American Basketry. Studies in a textile Art Without Machinery. USNM-AR 1902:171-548. No. 128. 248 Plates.

MERENESS, NEWTON D., EDITOR
1916. Travels in the American Colonies. New York.

MICHEL, FRANCIS LOUIS
1916. Report of the Journey of Francis Louis Michel from Berne, Switzerland, to Virginia, October 2, 1701—December 1, 1702. Va. Mag. Hist. and Biog. Va. Hist. Soc. 24:1-43:113-141:275-303. Translated and edited by Prof. Wm. J. Hinke, Ph. D.

MILFORT, LE CLERC
1802. Memoire au coup-d'oeil rapide sur mes differens voyages et mon sejour dan la nation Creck. Paris.

MILLER, CARL F.
1956. Life 8,000 Years Ago Uncovered in an Alabama Cave. The National Geographic Magazine CX:4:542-558.

MILLING, CHAPMAN J.
1940. Red Carolinians. University of North Carolina Press, Chapel Hill.

MINER, HORACE
1936. The Importance of Textiles in the Archaeology of Eastern United States. AAn 1:3.

MONTGOMERY, H.
1910. 'Calf-Mountain' Mound in Manitoba. AA n. s. 12:49-57.

MOONEY, JAMES
1891. The Sacred Formulas of the Cherokees. BAE-AR 7:1885-1886:301-397.
1895. The Siouan Tribes of the East. BAE-B 22.
1900. Myths of the Cherokee. BAE-AR 19:1897-1898:1:3-576.
1928. The Aboriginal Population of America North of Mexico. SI-MC 80:7.

MOONEY, J., and F. M. OLBRECHTS
1932. The Swimmer Manuscript, Cherokee Sacred Formulas and Medicinal Practices. BAE-B 99.

MOORE, CLARENCE B.
1892. Certain Shell Heaps of the St. John's River, Florida, Hitherto Unexplored. Pt. 1, American Naturalist 26:912-922, Philadelphia.
1894. Certain Sand Mounds of the St. Johns River, Florida. ANSP-J 10:1:5-103.
1894a. Certain Sand Mounds of the St. Johns River, Florida. ANSP-J 10:2:129-246.
1894b. Certain Shell Heaps of the St. John's River, Florida, Hitherto Unexplored. Pt. 5 American Naturalist 28:15-26, Philadelphia.
1896. Certain River Mounds of Duval County, Florida. ANSP-J 10:4:448-502.
1896a. Two Mounds on Murphy Island, Florida. ANSP-J 10:4:503-516.
1896b. Certain Sand Mounds of the

Ocklawaha River, Florida. ANSP-J 10:4:517-543.
1897. Certain Aboriginal Mounds of the Georgia Coast. ANSP-J 11:1:4-138.
1898. Certain Aboriginal Mounds of the Coast of South Carolina. ANSP-J 11:2: 146-166.
1898. Certain Aboriginal Mounds of the Savannah River. ANSP-J 11:2:167-172.
1899. Certain Aboriginal Remains of the Alabama River. ANSP-J 11:3:289-347.
1900. Certain Antiquities of the Florida West Coast. ANSP-J 11:3:350-394.
1901. Certain Aboriginal Remains of the Northwest Florida Coast. Pt. 1. ANSP-J 11:4:419-497.
1902. Certain Aboriginal Remains of the Northwest Florida Coast. Pt. 2. ANSP-J 12:2:125-335.
1903. Certain Aboriginal Remains of the Florida Central West Coast. ANSP-J 12:3:361-438.
1903a. Certain Aboriginal Remains of the Apalachicola River. ANSP-J 12:3:440-492.
1904. Aboriginal Urn Burial in the United States. AA 6:5:660-669.
1905. A Form of Urn Burial on Mobile Bay. AA Jan-March.
1905a. Certain Aboriginal Remains of the Black Warrior River. Certain Aboriginal Remains on the Lower Tombigbee, Mobile Bay and Mississippi South and Florida. ANSP-J 13:2:125-325.
1907. Moundville Revisited: Crystal River Revisited: Mounds of the Lower Chattahoochee and Lower Flint Rivers: Notes on the Ten Thousand Islands, Florida. ANSP-J 13:2:125-325.
1908. Certain Mounds of Arkansas and Mississippi. ANSP-J 13:4:481-600.
1909. Antiquities of the Ouachita Valley. ANSP-J 14:1:6-170.
1910. Antiquities of the St. Francis, White, and Black Rivers, Arkansas. ANSP-J 14:2:254-362.
1911. Some Aboriginal Sites on the Mississippi River. ANSP-J 14:3:366-476.
1912. Some Aboriginal Sites on Red River. ANSP-J 14:4:482-640.
1913. Some Aboriginal Sites in Louisiana and Arkansas. ANSP-J 16:1.
1915. Aboriginal Sites on Tennessee River. ANSP-J 16:3:431-487.
1916. Additional Investigations on Green River, Kentucky: Additional Investigations on Mississippi River. ANSP-J 16:3:431-508.
1918. The Northwestern Florida Coast Revisited. ANSP-J 16:4:514-577.
1922. Additional Mounds of Duval and Clay Counties, Florida. MAIHF-INM.
MOOREHEAD, WARREN K.
1900. Prehistoric Implements. The Robert Clark Co., Cincinnati.
1905. Prehistoric Relics. Andover Press, Andover.
1910. The Stone Age in North America. 2 v, Houghton Mifflin Co., New York.
1917. Stone Ornaments of the American Indians. Andover.
1928. The Cahokia Mounds. University of Illinois Bulletin 26:4.
1931. Archaeology of the Arkansas River Valley. Yale University Press, New Haven.
1932. Etowah Papers I: Exploration of the Etowah Site in Georgia. Department of Archaeology, Phillips Academy, Andover, Massachusetts, and Yale University Press, New Haven, Connecticut.
MORGAN, RICHARD G.
1952. Outline of Cultures in the Ohio Region. In J. B. Griffin 1952:83-98.
MUIR, J. M.
1926. Data on the Structure of Pre-Columbian Huastec Mounds in the Tampico Region. Journal of the Royal Anthropological Institute of Great Britain and Ireland LVI.
MUSEUM OF MODERN ART
1940. Twenty Centuries of Mexican Art. Produced in cooperation with the Mexican Government. Prepared and printed in Mexico, Instituto de Antropologia e Historia de Mexico.
MYER, WILLIAM E.
1917. The Remains of Primitive Man in in Cumberland Valley, Tennessee. ICA-P 19:96-102.

1928. Indian Trails of the Southeast. BAE-AR 42:1924-1925:735-854.
NEUMANN, GEORG K.
1952. Archeology and Race in the American Indian. In J. B. Griffin 1952:13-34.
NUTTALL, ZELIA
1891. The Atlatl or Spear-thrower of the Ancient Mexicans. PMAE-P 1:173-205.
1932. Some Comparisons Between Etowah, Mexican, and Mayan Designs. In Moorehead 1932:137-144.
ORR, KENNETH G.
1939. Field Report on Excavation of Indian Villages in the Vicinity of Spiro Mound. OP 2:2:8-15.
1941. The Eufaula Mound. Contributions to the Spiro Focus. OP 4:1:2-15.
1946. The Archaeological Situation at Spiro, Oklahoma; a Preliminary Report. AAn 11:4:228-256.
1952. Survey of Caddoan Area Archeology. In J. B. Griffin 1952:239-255.
PATTERSON, J. T.
1937. Boat-Shaped Artifacts of the Gulf Southwest States. UTe-AP 1:2. Soc. Sci. Study 24; Bull. 3732.
PEABODY, CHARLES
1904. Exploration of Mounds, Coahoma County, Mississippi. PMAE-P 3:2.
PHILLIPS, PHILIP
1940. Middle American Influences on the Archaeology of the Southeastern United States. In Hay 1940:349-367.
PHILLIPS, PHILIP, JAMES A. FORD, and JAMES B. GRIFFIN
1951. Archaeological Survey in the Lower Mississippi Alluvial Valley 1940-1947. PMAE-P 25.
POPE, G. D., JR.
1956. Ocmulgee, National Monument, Georgia. NPS-HH 24.
POTTER, W. B.
1880. Archaeological Remains in Southeastern Missouri. Contributions to the Archaeology of Missouri, Archaeological Section of the St. Louis Academy of Science, Pt. 1:5-19.
POWERS, A. J.
1898. Another Georgia Image. AmA 2:1:12-14.
QUIMBY, GEORGE I., JR.
1942. The Natchezan Culture Type. AAn 7:3:255-275:311-318.
1951. The Medina Site, West Baton Rouge Parish, Louisiana. Field Museum of Natural History, Anthropological Series 24:2:81-135, Chicago.
1952. Archeology of the Upper Great Lakes Area. In J. B. Griffin 1952:99-107.
RANDS, ROBERT L.
1956. Southern Cult Motifs on Walls-Pecan Point Pottery. AAn 22:2:1:Oct: 183-186.
1957. Notes on the Hand-Eye and Related Motifs. AAn 22:3:Jan.
RAU, CHARLES
1872. Drilling in Stone without Metal. SI-AR 1868:392-400.
1877. The Stock in Trade of an Aboriginal Lapidary (Mississippi). SI-AR 291.
REYNOLDS, ELMER R.
1880. Aboriginal Soapstone Quarries in the District of Columbia. PMAE-AR 11:3:526-535.
RIGHTS, DOUGLAS L.
1947. The American Indian in North Carolina. Duke University Press, Durham.
RITZENTHALER, ROBERT E.
1950. Indian Masks. Reprint from Lore 1:4:Lore Leaves 2, Milwaukee Public Museum.
ROBBINS, WILFRED WILLIAM and OTHERS
1916. Ethnobotany of the Tewa Indians. BAE-B 55.
ROBERTSON, JAMES ALEXANDER, EDITOR and TRANSLATOR
1933. True Relation of the Hardships Suffered by Governor Fernando de Soto . . . by a Gentlemen of Elvas. 2 v, Florida Hist. Soc. Quart. 16:3:174-178.
ROMANS, CAPTAIN BERNARD
1775. A Concise Natural History of East and West Florida. New York.
ROWE, CHANDLER W.
1952. Woodland Cultures of Eastern Tennessee. In J. B. Griffin 1952:199-206.
ROYCE, CHARLES C.
1887. The Cherokee Nation of Indians;

A Narrative of their Official Relations with the Colonial and Federal Government. BAE-AR 5:1883-1884:121-378.
1899. Indian Land Cessions in the United States, BAE-AR 18:1896-1897:2:527-977.
RUSSELL, VIRGIL Y.
1957. Indian Artifacts. Revised, Enlarged Edition, Casper, Wyoming; first ed. 1951.
SCHOOLCRAFT, HENRY T.
1851-1857. Historical and Statistical Information Respecting . . . Indian Tribes of the United States. Bureau of Indian Affairs, 6 v, Philadelphia.
SCIENCE NEWS LETTER
1938. Oct. 15 (From Waring and Holder, 1945).
SEARS, WILLIAM H.
1951-1956. Excavations at Kolomoki: Season I and II (Mound E):1951. Seasons III and IV (Mound D):1953. Final Report:1956. University of Georgia Press, Athens.
SEEVER, W. J.
1897. A Cache of Idols and Chipped Flint Instruments in Tennessee. Antiquarian 1:6:142-143.
SELLARDS, E. H.
1941. Stone Images from Henderson County, Texas. AAn 7:1:29-38.
1944. Ancient Carvings. In Views in Texas Memorial Museum, Museum Notes 6:23-29.
1952. Early Man in North America. University of Texas Press, Austin.
SELLARDS, E. H., G. L. EVANS, and G. E. MEADE
1947. Fossil Bison and Associated Artifacts from Plainview, Texas. Bull. Geological Soc. Am. 58:927-954.
SETZLER, FRANK M.
1934. Pottery of the Hopewell Type from Louisiana. USNM-P 82:22(2963):1-21.
1940. Archeological Perspectives in the Northern Mississippi Valley. SI-MC 100.
SETZLER, FRANK M., and JESSE D. JENNINGS
1941. Peachtree Mound and Village Site, Cherokee County, North Carolina. BAE-B 131.
SHETRONE, H. C.
1930. The Mound Builders. D. Appleton & Co., New York.
SHETRONE, H. C., and E. F. GREENMAN
1931. Explorations of the Seip Group of Prehistoric Earthworks. Ohio Archaeological and Historical Quarterly 40:3: 343-509.
SHIPP, BERNARD
1881. The History of Hernando De Soto and Florida. Or Record of Events of Fifty-Six Years from 1512-1568. Narrative of Garcilaso de La Vega. Philadelphia.
SMITH, HALE G.
1948. Two Historical Archaeological Periods in Florida. AAn 13:4:313-319.
SMITH, JOHN
1884. The History of Virginia, 1608-1631. Edited by Edward Arber, English Scholar's Library: 16, Birmingham. 1907. Narratives of Early Virginia 1606-1625. Edited by Lyon Gardiner Tyler, New York.
SODAY, FRANK J.
1953. Indian Cultures of North Alabama. Mimeographed Bulletin.
1954. The Quad Site, A Palæo-Indian Village in Northern Alabama. TA 10:1:1-20.
SPECK, FRANK G.
1907. The Creek Indians of Taskigi Town. Mem. Am. Anthrop. Assoc. 2:2.
1909. Ethnology of the Yuchi Indians. UP-AP 1:1, Philadelphia.
1950. Concerning Iconology and the Masking Complex in Eastern North America. UP-B 15:1.
SPECK, F. C., and L. BROOM
1950. Cherokee Dances and Drama.
SPINDEN, HERBERT J.
1940. Sun Worship. SI-AR 1939(3555): 447-469.
SQUIRE, E. G., and E. H. DAVIS
1848. Ancient Monuments of the Mississippi Valley. SI-CK 1.
STARKEY, MARION
1946. The Cherokee Nation. Alfred A. Knopf, New York.
STARR, EMMETT
1921. History of the Cherokee Indians and Their Legends and Folklore. Warden Co., Oklahoma City.

STARR, F.
1897. A Shell Gorget from Mexico. The Antiquarian 1:3:57-62.

STAUB, W.
1921. Pre-hispanic Mortuary Pottery, Sherd Deposits and Other Antiquities of the Huastec. El Mexico Antiguo, Tomo I, Mexico.

STIRLING, M. W.
1934. Smithsonian Archaeological Projects Conducted under the Federal Emergency Relief Administration. 1933-34. SI-AR 1934:371-400.
1943. Stone Monuments of Southern Mexico. BAE-B 138.

STODDARD, H. L.
1904. The Abstruse Significance of 36 and 12. The American Antiquarian 26.

STRONG, W. D.
1935. An Introduction to Nebraska Archaeology. SI-MC 93:10.

STEWARD, JULIAN H.
1936. Petroglyphs of the United States. SI-AR 405-426.

STRACHEY, WILLIAM
1849. The Historie of Travaile into Virginia Britannia, expressing the cosmographic and commodities of the country, together with the Manners and Customs of the People. Hakluyt Soc. Publ. Vol. 6. London.

SUHM, DEE ANN, ALEX D. KRIEGER, and EDWARD B. JELKS
1954. An Introductory Handbook of Texas Archeology. Texas Archeological Society, Bulletin 25.

SWAN, CALEB
1855. Position and State Manner and Art in the Creek, or Muscogee Nation in 1791. In Schoolcraft, Indian Tribes 5:251-283.

SWANTON, JOHN R.
1911. Indian Tribes of the Lower Mississippi Valley and Adjacent Coast of the Gulf of Mexico. BAE-B 43.
1922. Early History of the Creek Indians and Their Neighbors. BAE-B 73.
1928. Social Organization and Social Usages of the Indians of the Creek Confederacy. BAE-AR 42:1924-1925:23-475.
1928a. Religious Beliefs and Medical Practices of the Creek Indians. BAE-AR 42:1924-1925:473-672.
1928b. Aboriginal Culture of the Southeast. BAE-AR 42:1924-1925:673-726.
1929. Myths and Tales of the Southeastern Indians. BAE-B 88.
1931. Source Material for the Social and Ceremonial Life of the Choctaw Indians. BAE-B 103.
1932. The Ethnological Value of the De Soto Narratives. AA n. s. 34:4:570-590.
1942. Source Material on the History and Ethnology of the Caddo Indians. BAE-B 132.
1946. The Indians of the Southeastern United States. BAE-B 137.
1953. The Indian Tribes of North America. BAE-B 145.

SWANTON, JOHN R., EDITOR
1939. Final Report of the United States De Soto Expedition Commission. House Document 71, 76th Congress, 1st Session.

TITTERINGTON, PAUL F.
1938. The Cahokia Mound Group and its Village Site Materials. St. Louis.

THOMAS, CYRUS
1887. Burial Mounds of the Northern Sections of the United States, including the Appalachian District. BAE-AR 5:1883-1884:3-119.
1891. Catalogue of Prehistoric Works East of the Rocky Mountains. BAE-B 12.
1894. Report on Mound Explorations of the Bureau of American Ethnology. BAE-AR 12:1890-1891:3-730.
1896. Stone Images from Mounds and Ancient Graves. AA 9:404-408.
1898. Introduction to the Study of North American Archaeology. Cincinnati.

THRUSTON, GATES P.
1890. The Antiquities of Tennessee and of Adjacent Areas. Robert Clark and Company, Cincinnati.

1892. New Discoveries in Tennessee. AAOJ 14.
1898. Ancient Stone Images in Tennessee. The American Archaeologist 2:9:225-227.

THWAITES, REUBEN GOLD, EDITOR
1896-1901. Jesuit Relations and Allied Documents, 1610-1791. 73 v, Cleveland.

TIMBERLAKE, LIEUT. HENRY
1765. Memoirs of Lieut. Henry Timberlake (accompanied Cherokee Indians to England in 1762) London. See reprints edited by Samuel C. Williams 1927 and 1928.

TOUMEY, MICHAEL
1858. Geology of Alabama. Alabama Geological Survey:2.

TYLER, LYON GARDINER, EDITOR
1907. Narratives of Early Virginia, 1606-1625. Scribner. New York.

VAILLANT, GEORGE C.
1932. Some Resemblances in Ceramics of Central and North America. Medallion Paper 12, Gila Pueblo, Globe, Arizona.
1939. Indian Art in North America. Harper & Brothers Publishers, New York.
1953. Aztecs of Mexico: Origin, Rise, and Fall of the Aztec Nation. Doubleday & Co., Garden City, New York.

WALKER, S. T.
1880. Preliminary Exploration Among Indian Mounds in Southern Florida. SI-AR 1879:392-413.

WALKER, WINSLOW L.
1935. A Caddo Burial Site at Natchitoches, Louisiana. SI-MC 94:14.

WARING, ANTONIO J., JR.
1945. Hopewellian Elements in Northern Georgia. AAn 11:2:119-120.

WARING, ANTONIO J., JR., and PRESTON HOLDER
1945. A Prehistoric Ceremonial Complex in the Southeastern United States. AA n. s. 47:1:1-34.

WATSON, VIRGINIA D.
1950. The Wulfing Plates. Products of Prehistoric Americans. Washington University Studies, New Series, Social and Philosophical Sciences 8, St. Louis.

WEBB, CLARENCE H.
1940. House Types Among the Caddo Indians. TAPS-B 12:49-75.
1944. Stone Vessels from a northeast Louisiana Site. AAn 9:4:386-394.
1945. A Second Historic Caddo Site at Natchitoches, Louisiana. TAPS-B 16:52-83.
1946. Two Unusual Types of Chipped Stone Artifacts from Northwest Louisiana. TAPS-B 17:9-17.
1948. Caddoan Prehistory: The Bossier Focus. TAPS-B 19:100-147.
1948. Evidence of Pre-Pottery Cultures in Louisiana. AAn 13:3:227-231.

WEBB, CLARENCE H., and MONROE E. DODD, JR.
1939. Further Excavations at the Gahagan Mound; Connections with a Florida Culture. TAPS-B 11:92-128.
1941. Pottery Types from the Belcher Mound Site. TAPS-B 13:88-116.

WEBB, WILLIAM S.
1938. An Archaeological Survey of the Norris Basin in Eastern Tennessee. BAE-B 118.
1939. An Archaeological Survey of Wheeler Basin on the Tennessee River in Northern Alabama. BAE-B 122.
1940. The Wright Mounds, Sites 6 and 7, Montgomery County, Kentucky. UK-RA 5:1.
1951. The Parrish Village Site. UK-RA 7:6:403-451.

WEBB, WILLIAM S., and DAVID L. DeJARNETTE
1942. An Archaeological Survey of Pickwick Basin in the Adjacent Portions of the States of Alabama, Mississippi and Tennessee. BAE-B 129.
1948. The Flint River Site. AMNH-MP 23.
1948a. Little Bear Creek Site. AMNH-MP 26.
1948b. The Perry Site. AMNH-MP 25.

1948c. The Whitesburg Bridge Site. AMNH-MP 24.

WEBB, WILLIAM S., and W. G. HAAG
1939. The Chiggerville Site 1, Ohio County, Kentucky. UK-RA 4:1.

WEBB, WILLIAM S., and CHARLES G. WILDER
1951. An Archaeological Survey of Guntersville Basin on the Tennessee River in Northern Alabama. University of Kentucky Press, Lexington.

WEDEL, WALDO R.
1943. Archeological Investigations in Platte and Clay Counties, Missouri. USNM-B 183.

WEST, GEORGE A.
1934. Tobacco Pipes and Smoking Customs of the American Indians. MPM-B XVII:I(Text)-II(Plates).

WHITEFORD, ANDREW H.
1952. A Framework Reference for Archeology of Eastern Tennessee. In J. B. Griffin 1952:207-225.

WILLEY, GORDON R.
1942. The Weeden Island Culture: A Preliminary Definition. AAn 10:225-254.
1948. The Cultural Content of the Crystal River Negative-Painted Style. AAn 13:4:325-328.
1948. A Prototype for the Southern Cult. AAn 13:4:328-330.
1949. Archeology of the Florida Gulf Coast. SI-MC 113.

WILLEY, GORDON R., and PHILIP PHILLIPS
1944. Negative-painted Pottery from Crystal River, Florida. AAn 10:1:173-185.

WILLEY, GORDON R., and R. B. WOODBURY
1942. A Chronological Outline for the Northwest Florida Coast. AAn 7:232-254.
? Ceramic Sequence on the Northwest Florida Coast (ms) (From Waring and Holder, 1945).

WILLIAMS, SAMUEL COLE, EDITOR
1927. Lieut. Timberlake's Memoirs, 1656-1765. Watauga Press, Johnson City, Tenn.
1928. Early Travels in the Tennessee Country. Watauga Press, Johnson City.
1930. Adair's History of the American Indians. Watauga Press, Johnson City.

WILLIAMS, STEPHEN
1957. James Kelly Hampson—1877-1956. AAn 22:4:398-400.

WILLIAMS, STEPHEN, and JOHN M. GOGGIN
1956. The Long Nosed God Mask in Eastern United States. MA 18:3.

WILLOUGHBY, CHARLES C.
1897. An Analysis of the Decorations Upon Pottery from the Mississippi Valley. Journal of American Folk-Lore 10:36:9-20.
1919. The Serpent Mound of Adams County, Ohio. AA n. s. 21:153-163.
1922. The Turner Group of Earthworks, Hamilton County, Ohio. PMAE-P 8:3.
1932. Notes on the History and Symbolism of the Muskhogeans and the People of Etowah. In Moorehead 1932:7-66.
1952. Textile Fabrics from the Spiro Mound. In Hamilton 1952:107-118.

WIMBERLY, STEVE B., and HARRY A. TOURTELOT
1941. The McQuorquodale Mound: A Manifestation of the Hopewellian Phase in South Alabama. AMNH-MP 19.

WINTEMBERG, W. J.
1923. Certain Eye Designs on the Archaeological Artifacts from North America. Transactions of the Royal Society of Canada. XVII:3.

WITTHOFT, JOHN
1949. Stone Pipes of the Historic Cherokees. Southern Indian Studies 1:2:43-62. University of North Carolina, Chapel Hill.
1952. A Paleo-Indian Site in Eastern Pennsylvania. APS-P 96:4:464-495.

WORMINGTON, H. M.
1939. Ancient Man in North America. Denver Museum of Natural History. Popular Series, No. 4.

YACOVLEFF, EUGENIO
1932. Las Falconidas en el arte y en las Creencias de los Antiguos Peruanos. Revista del Museo Nacional de Lima 1.

INDEX